My respect for Linda Sommer as an author and woman of God has knit our hearts together. We have a common interest—knowing Jesus and making Him known. I encourage you to take this daily journey with Linda through God's Word and be challenged to apply God's Word to your daily life.

—Babbie Mason
President
Babbie Mason Ministries

A life-giving and joyful prescription for success is a daily dose of God's Word. As Linda Sommer proves, the best part is that no matter where you are on the journey, you can take it with you and grow in praise and wisdom.

—Dr. Mark Rutland
President
Southeastern College

Linda Sommer, in all three of her devotional books, *Around the Word in 365 Days, You Can Take It With You,* and *Sunrise, Sunset,* has crafted three practical hands-on tools that will greatly enrich your reading of the Bible. Her daily devotionals provide clarity, encouragement, and real-life applications of key passages throughout the Scriptures.

—Dr. Kenneth Boa
President
Reflections Ministries

D1456846

SUNRISE

Morning and Evening Inspiration

SUNSET

SUNRISE

Morning and Evening Inspiration

SUNSET

Blessings,

LINDA SOMMER

Linda Sommer

Web Site & Blog Site - 404-277-0766
WWW.voiceofthesword.com
WWW.voiceofthesword.blogspot.com

CREATION HOUSE
A STRANG COMPANY

SUNRISE, SUNSET by Linda Sommer
Published by Creation House
A Strang Company
600 Rinehart Road
Lake Mary, Florida 32746
www.creationhouse.com

Unless otherwise noted, all Scripture quotations are from the New King James Version of the Bible. Copyright © 1979, 1980, 1982 by Thomas Nelson, Inc., publishers. Used by permission.

Scripture quotations marked KJV are from the King James Version of the Bible.

Cover design by Terry Clifton

Library of Congress Control Number: 2007924905
International Standard Book Number-13: 978-1-59979-201-9

First Edition

07 08 09 10 11 — 987654321
Printed in the United States of America

DEDICATION

This book is dedicated to my nephew, Staff Sergeant Christopher Van Der Horn, who is now a citizen of heaven. Chris was the first soldier killed in Iraq in 2006. He left his wife, Teresa, and two small children, Max and Liam. Chris re-enlisted in the army in 2004. He desired to be a servant leader to help train both our soldiers and the policemen of Iraq. His supreme sacrifice for our country earned him the Bronze Star and the Purple Heart. "Greater love has no one than this, than to lay down one's life for his friends" (John 15:13). Chris knew and loved the Lord Jesus Christ, and he had the opportunity to share His love for the Lord with his friends, his family, and the soldiers he trained.

Chris was both in the U.S. Army and in the Lord's army. He served well in both armies. The day after Chris was killed, I wrote the following:

I Am a Soldier

My boot camp was in heaven where I was trained for My mission.

My mission was to serve My country and obey the orders of My Commander in Chief.

My country was Earth and I was prepared to fight to take it back from the enemy.

My rank in heaven was a five-star general but I gave up that glory.

My glory was stripped when I reported for duty on earth as a babe.

My encounters with the enemy were many and even began in heaven.

My enemy's mission was to take my life when I was a small child.

My enemy did not know that My main mission was to lay My life down for others.

My battle was with principalities, powers, rulers of darkness and wickedness in heavenly places.

My uniform was an earth suit made of flesh, bone and blood.

My first rank on earth was a private, but I experienced every rank.

My commissioning service took place at the Jordan River where I was baptized.

My enemy uncovered his strategy when he tempted Me in the wilderness.

My mode of operation was to declare My Commander and Chief's words on earth.

My victory in the wilderness was won with the trusted Sword of the Spirit.

My enemy thought he had defeated Me when I died on the cross.

My flesh was torn and the weight of the sins of the world crushed My heart.

My burial was not accompanied with a military salute. It was at dusk.

My enemy was defeated when I rose from the tomb and ascended to heaven.

My original rank as general was restored but I will return as Captain of the Heavenly Hosts.

My duty in heaven and in hearts now is to train an army that is willing to die.

—LINDA SOMMER
JANUARY 2, 2006

This book is designed to strengthen all who fight in the Lord's army. May you become closer to the captain of the heavenly hosts, Jesus Christ, through reading *Sunrise, Sunset.*

ACKNOWLEDGMENTS

My loving appreciation to:

- The Three in One—My loving heavenly Father, who sent His Son, Jesus, to die for my sins; Jesus Christ, who is my Bridegroom and Best Friend; and the Holy Spirit, who taught, encouraged, and empowered me as I wrote this book.

- My husband and business manager, who supplied the financial support, encouragement, and prayers to help me complete the assignment given me by the Holy Spirit to write a trilogy of devotional books that are companion books to the *One Year Bible*.

- My twin sister, Lavilla, and Gail Deel, who helped proof the rough draft of the book.

- Allen Quain, manager of Creation House, and Virginia Maxwell, plus all the staff at Strang Communications who made this project possible.

- Tyndale House, who published the *One Year Bible* that has blessed me over the years.

- All those who have invested their finances and prayers in this project.

CONTENTS

FOREWORD

For some reason, I have always had kind of a "thing" for devotional materials. Ever since I became a believer in Jesus, I have picked them up wherever I could find them. Over the years, I have amassed quite a collection. They can be found in almost every room of my house, and I love when I have the time to read the daily portions in each of them. When I travel (as I often do for my work as a Jewish gospel singer), my pocketsize devotionals are a constant companion. (Because of them, I don't even mind flight delays!)

Every so often, someone sends me a book they think I might enjoy. One such item was a signed copy of *Around the World in 365 Days*, mailed to me by Linda Sommer, along with a nice personal greeting. I placed it on a shelf with some of my other devotional literature, but a long time passed before I read it. When finally I did, what I found was a surprise and a delight!

This was no "read a passage, consider a thought, recite a prayer" kind of publication (though those are great and I enjoy them). No, this was an in-depth commentary on the entire Bible, from Genesis to Revelation! Using the One Year Bible (and the Holy Spirit) as her guide, Linda invites you to travel with her on a journey through Scripture. Along the way she shares deep insights drawn not only from her diligent study of God's Word but also from her rich experience as His child. As you follow her day by day on this "stroll through the scroll" of divine revelation, you learn so many valuable lessons gleaned from the text she is referencing and from the life she is living. Still, even as you become acquainted with her as the writer of this excellent book, she never distracts you from her true objective—that you would come to know the author of *the Book*, the Bible.

In addition, Linda offers something very rare in this genre. As she takes you from January to December, she also teaches you about the Biblical calendar with its many feasts and holy days, still observed by Jewish people all over the world and celebrated by many other whose faith is rooted in the G-d of Abraham, Isaac, and Jacob. All who desire to be like Yeshua (the Hebrew name for Jesus) can't help but benefit from her sharing on the appointed seasons that were so much a part of our Lord's earthly existence. As a man living in Israel, His calendar was the Jewish calendar and, as our Messiah, He used it to reveal who He was—and still is!

In light of all this, there is no one better suited to lead us through Psalms and Proverbs than Linda Sommer. Her new book, *Sunrise, Sunset*, is sure to become a must-read devotional for all who love these ancient writings, still speaking so profoundly to us today. Psalms make up the hymnbook of the Jewish people and are beloved by all who worship the God of Israel. They were a major part of the synagogue liturgy with which I grew up and, to this day, provide the text for many of the songs I sing and have written. Proverbs are examples of Hebraic wisdom unparalleled in history and relevant for all people for all time. How blessed we are to have a friend such as Linda to help us more fully take pleasure in such scriptural treasure!

Incidentally, on page 77 of *Around the World in 365 Days* I happened upon a passage making reference to a Jewish music festival in St. Petersburg, Russia, and to a musician singing a song entitled, "He Is My Defense." To say I was thrilled would be an understatement for, you see, I was that person! However, that is not my motivation for singing the praises of Linda Sommer and her work. Her asking me to write this was in response to a message I left for her as part of a New Year's resolution to better communicate with people who had been a blessing to me. Feeling a pang of guilt as I commenced my yearly reading cycle in Linda's devotional, I decided to call her and though she wasn't home at the time, I left a message, belatedly expressing my gratitude for the gift she had sent me such a long while before. Eventually we spoke, and the result of our communication (in addition to my receiving more of her wonderful books) was her asking me to write this foreword.

In truth, I was reluctant to do so, simply because I had never written one before! However, I considered it a great privilege to have the opportunity to commend to you this gifted and gracious woman of God. And so, I'm pleased to recommend to you all of Linda Sommer's work and to join with you in the enjoyment of *Sunrise, Sunset*.

"From the rising of the sun until its setting, the name of the LORD is to be praised" Psalm 113:3.

May He be your praise as you read!

—Marty Goetz
A modern day psalmist whose music has been shared
worldwide through performances and recordings
www.MartyGoetz.com

INTRODUCTION

The devotionals in *Sunrise, Sunset* are designed for busy people who often rush to work without taking time to eat breakfast or receive the proper spiritual nutrition to support them throughout the day.

When my three boys were young, there were days I felt so helpless. My to-do list was overwhelming, and I knew I could not face such days in my own strength. The days I skipped my quiet times with the Lord were exhausting, and I soon discovered just a few minutes in God's Word every morning strengthened me for the day. If you are like me, you need wisdom at the beginning of every day. Each day begins with a reading from Proverbs, taken from *The One Year Bible*, followed by the Morning Wisdom section, which offers a practical application of the reading for each day.

My husband likes to read in bed before he falls asleep. Many people choose to read the Bible just before they retire in the evening. I can't think of a better way to fall asleep than reading God's Word, because those evening meditations most likely will lead to sweet dreams. The second half of each page in *Sunrise, Sunset* is titled "Evening Watch." This section includes readings from Psalms.

Sunrise, Sunset is the last book in a trilogy of devotional books. All three devotional books are companion books to *The One Year Bible*, published by Tyndale House. Each day's reading in *The One Year Bible* includes a passage from the Old Testament, New Testament, Proverbs, and Psalms. This arrangement in *The One Year Bible* gives freshness and diversity to each day's reading. The reader of these companion books can use his or her favorite translation of the Bible to read through the Bible in a year and can enjoy reading the passages that I chose to highlight for the day.

My first book, *Around the Word in 365 Days*, has traveled around the world. *Around the Word* is even available in Australia. My second book, *You Can Take It With You*, includes many passages in the Bible that I did not highlight in my first book. In addition, a summary of the day's reading, called "Daily Deposit," presents an investment you can make into your heavenly bank account.

One of my favorite musicals is *Fiddler on the Roof*, which is about a Jewish family who experienced both the triumph and tragedies of life. The song "Sunrise, Sunset" from this musical describes how fast the years pass during a lifetime. This book is dedicated to Sergeant Christopher Van Der Horn, my nephew who was killed in Iraq on the first day of the year 2006. He was only thirty-seven years old. His life ended earlier than he planned. The years do pass swiftly. However, they will have much more meaning if we daily apply God's Word to our lives. David the psalmist wrote:

> I rise before the dawning of the morning, And cry for help; I hope in Your word. My eyes are awake through the night watches, That I may meditate on Your word.
>
> —PSALM 119:147–148

David knew the most effective way to begin and end each day was reading God's Word. Join me as I begin each day this year with wisdom from God's Word and end each day by meditating on God's Word.

Morning Wisdom: Read Proverbs 1:1–6. When our boys were young, we challenged them to memorize Proverbs. We even paid them one dollar for every chapter they learned.

Proverbs is an excellent book for young men to memorize, because Solomon wrote Proverbs to impart wisdom to his sons. Solomon employed a ghostwriter to help him write Proverbs, and this ghostwriter charged nothing for His services. Solomon's "ghostwriter" was the Holy Spirit, who skillfully teaches us the truths found in God's Word.

One can read the words of wisdom in Proverbs and even memorize them, but unless these words of wisdom are received with understanding and obeyed, the reader will not gain the prudence and discretion intended by the Holy Spirit.

I challenge you to daily apply the wise counsel of the Great Counselor, the Holy Spirit, found in the pages of Proverbs. If you fulfill this challenge, you will live a fruitful life filled with the joy of the Lord.

> *Lord, help me today to apply the knowledge You give me through Your Word. I know wisdom is applied knowledge.*

Evening Watch: Read Psalm 1:1–6. Recently I sent some thoughts from God's Word to the assistant director of the Atlanta Symphony. She spoke at the Atlanta Pen Women's luncheon. Her talk led me to search the Bible for verses that applied to her talk. I shared these verses with her via e-mail. During the question and answer period of the luncheon, she was asked, "When do you know you are going to have a great concert?" She shared, "I know I am going to have a great concert when energy surges upward from my feet as I step on the platform. That energy bypasses my mind and flows straight from my heart to the orchestra and the audience."

In my e-mail to her I identified the feeling she had as God's powerful anointing described in Isaiah 11:1–2 and Acts 2. She read the e-mail and said that she would enjoy marinating on the words I wrote.

We learn in today's psalm reading that a man is blessed when he delights in God's Word. A hunger and thirst for God can only come to those who receive the tasty morsels of God's spiritual food, His Word. When we allow the Holy Spirit to interpret and teach us through God's Word, those tasty morsels can marinate in our minds all day long.

The spiritual food God has for you each day in this new year can nourish your soul. The meals God has prepared for you will be both delightful and delicious.

Jesus promises that if we daily listen to God's Word with our hearts, not just our ears, He and the Father will dine with us. However, we must first come to the table. God invites you to come dine with Him as you read the Bible through this year.

> *Lord, help me to be faithful in my daily Bible readings.*

JANUARY 2

Morning Wisdom: Read Proverbs 1:7–9. "Listen up!" is an expression parents often use when they are instructing their children. Solomon is telling his sons in today's passage to listen to both their mother and father. He exhorted his sons to listen to the instruction of their father and not to forsake the law of their mother.

Throughout the Bible God tells us to listen up. He gave a great promise to those who will listen and obey His Word. He promised that if His children would hearken (listen) and obey His Word, He would bless them throughout their days on Earth. In Deuteronomy 28:1–2 God told the children of Israel:

> Now it shall come to pass, if you diligently obey the voice of the LORD your God, to observe carefully all His commandments which I command you today, that the LORD your God will set you high above all nations of the earth. And all these blessings shall come upon you and overtake you, because you obey the voice of the LORD your God.

"The fear of the LORD is the beginning of knowledge" (Prov. 1:7). The fear of the Lord is also the beginning of wisdom, and wisdom is applied knowledge. When we fear the Lord, we will honor His Word with an obedient heart. Jesus told us the commandment we are to observe daily. Listen to His words: "This is My commandment, that you love one another as I have loved you" (John 15:12).

Lord, help me to love others today the same way You love me.

Evening Watch: Read Psalm 2:1–12. Many people today ask the same question that was asked in this psalm. The question is, Why is there evil in this world? The psalmist asked, "Why do the nations rage?" (Ps. 2:1). We live in a day when nations are raging. Scenes of war and terrorism flash before our eyes as we watch the nightly news. Jesus told us that in the last days there would be wars and rumors of wars. (See Matthew 24:6.)

Reread this morning's devotional and you will discover the answer to the question, Why is there evil in this world? Evil and wars exist, because many in this world do not hear and obey God's Word. The provision to overcome evil in this world is mentioned in this psalm. That provision is Jesus Christ, the King who God has set on His holy hill. The psalm ends with these words: "Blessed are all those who put their trust in Him" (v. 12). We have learned in both our readings today that trust and obedience to the Lord Jesus Christ pave the highway of blessings in our lives.

Father, thank You for sending Your Son to die for my sins and to pave the way for me to live a blessed life.

Morning Wisdom: Read Proverbs 1:10–19. All three of our sons are now serving the Lord and are teaching their children to fear the Lord. Two sons, however, veered off the right path for a season. They both were enticed to participate in ungodly activities by the wrong kind of friends. Our middle son, Ron, however, stayed true to the Lord his whole life, because he surrounded himself with Christian friends. He was friends with a neighborhood family whose father read one chapter of Proverbs daily to his family.

Our reading in Proverbs today warns against being enticed by evil, greedy people. Paul gave a similar warning to Timothy when he wrote:

> Now the Spirit expressly says that in latter times some will depart from the faith, giving heed to deceiving spirits and doctrines of demons, speaking lies in hypocrisy, having their own conscience seared with a hot iron.
> —1 TIMOTHY 4:1–2

The King James Version uses the term *seducing spirits* instead of *deceiving spirits.* Seducing spirits are on the rampage in these last days, and they want to lure believers away from the path of the Lord Jesus Christ. The Word of God is the weapon of warfare against the enemy that will keep us from deception and seduction. The psalmist David wrote that he hid God's Word in his heart so that he would not sin against God. (See Psalm 119:11.) Daily sowing God's Word into our own hearts and the hearts of our children will help keep our families on God's righteous path.

Lord, help me to hide Your Word in my heart today.

Evening Watch: Read Psalm 3:1–8. No one has the power to win over Satan and his hoards of demons. In this psalm David was battling with accusing spirits. He wrote: "Many are they who rise up against me. Many are they who say of me, 'There is no help for him in God'" (vv. 1–2). These accusing spirits scoffed at his belief in God. Satan is the accuser of the brethren, and he uses even those closest to us to speak his accusations against us.

David overcame these wicked spirits (seducing and accusing spirits) by declaring out loud the truth about God. He skillfully used the sword of the Spirit, the Word of God, when he cried out, "But You, O LORD, are a shield for me, My glory and the One who lifts my head" (v. 3). To overcome Satan we need to both hide God's Word in our hearts and declare God's Word with our mouths. David also made his own declaration of faith when he cried out, "I will not be afraid of ten thousands of people Who have set themselves against me all around" (v. 6). David shouted, "Salvation belongs to the LORD" (v. 8). He knew only the Lord could save him from the onslaught of his enemies.

Thank You, Lord, that the battle is Yours and the victory is ours.

Genesis 8:1–10:32; Matthew 4:12–25; Psalm 4:1–8; Proverbs 1:20–23

Morning Wisdom: Read Proverbs 1:20–23. On our first trip to India I was overwhelmed with the noises around me as we walked the streets of Madras. I heard clucking chickens, mooing cows, roaring motorcycles, honking cars, shouting people, and shrieking elephants as they walked on the other side of the street. I wanted to shout, "Peace, be still!" The sounds were drowning out that still, quiet voice within me that gave me directions and instructions. For a moment I was swept up in the confusion all around me. I prayed, *Lord, help me to hear Your voice.*

During the concourse of our daily lives we may not hear this menagerie of sounds, but not a day goes by that we don't hear at least four voices speaking to us. We hear the voice of our own souls (mind, will, and emotions) saying, "I think…I want…I feel." We usually hear the voices of Satan's seducing spirits saying phrases like, "God won't care if you…" "A little won't hurt," or "No one will see." We hear the loving and sometimes not-so-loving voices of people conveying their opinions and desires.

In the midst of all of these voices, we need to still ourselves in order to hear the voice of God's wisdom calling loudly to us in the chief concourses of our lives. We can hear that voice speak to the gates of our souls (our five senses: sight, sound, taste, touch, and smell). God's wisdom shouts, "Don't watch that program on TV! Don't hear that music! Don't eat that second piece of pie! Don't view pornographic pictures on the computer! Don't smell that perfume or aftershave that stimulates lustful thoughts!"

The voice of God's wisdom shouts above the other sounds we encounter daily and cries out, "Don't do something or say something foolish!" We can either obey the exhortations and warnings of God's wisdom or ignore them. Which will you do today?

> *Lord, help me to stay tuned to Your voice today, and give me the strength to obey Your voice.*

Evening Watch: Read Psalm 4:1–8. The voices we hear during the daytime often invade our souls just before we go to bed. Worried thoughts whirl through our minds, and sometimes fearful thoughts about tomorrow rob us of our sleep. David knew how to silence the voices that seek to keep us awake all night. He told us to do three things: meditate within your heart on your bed, offer the sacrifices of righteousness, and put your trust in the Lord. (See vv. 4–5.) We need to meditate on God's Word, offering the sacrifice of praise and worship to Him before we go to bed. We need to lay our earthly burdens down and reach heavenward as we trust the Lord to perfect everything that concerns us. (See Psalm 138:8.) We can silence the voices when we pray this prayer:

> *Lord, I cast the cares of the day upon You, and I thank You for giving me a peaceful sleep in Your safe arms.*

January 5

Morning Wisdom: Read Proverbs 1:24–28. Our family is blessed with nine young grandchildren. Our sons are wise fathers who are teaching their children to obey when they give instructions to them. Their goal is to establish instant obedience in their children. That is a worthy goal, but it takes diligence in discipline to accomplish that goal.

We have a wise heavenly Father who wants to establish instant obedience in His children. However, His children often do not listen or obey His voice. As a senior citizen, I can look back over the times in my life when I did not heed God's gentle warnings and promptings. I even ignored His gentle discipline and had to take many make-up tests before I finally learned my lesson. So often I waited until I was in the middle of a mess before I prayed and cried out to God.

God takes no pleasure in seeing His children walk in disobedience to His Word. The scripture for today sounds almost cruel when it speaks of God laughing at calamities (the messes we bring upon ourselves through our disobedience). We know, however, that God is long-suffering and kind.

We can reach a point in our lives when we refuse to regard God's rebukes and defiantly disobey His voice. At those times, God withholds His voice of wisdom from us and allows us to only hear the voice of our own selfish souls crying out, "We think…we feel…we want." David wrote, "If I regard iniquity in my heart, The Lord will not hear" (Ps. 66:18). We regard iniquity in our hearts when we refuse to confess our sins and instead continue in them. God, however, always hears the repentant heart that cries, *I have sinned. Forgive me and help me Lord Jesus!*

> *Lord, I want to cooperate with You as You seek to establish instant obedience in my life.*

Evening Watch: Read Psalm 5:1–12. As you tune to God's voice daily, He is also tuned to hear your voice. He looks forward to hearing your voice as you speak to Him during your morning quiet times. David wrote in this psalm, "My voice You shall hear in the morning, O Lord; In the morning I will direct it to You, And I will look up" (v. 3).

God also loves to hear your voice in the evening just before you retire for a good night's sleep. David's heart rejoiced when he thought about God's faithfulness to defend him and His favor that shielded him throughout the day. When we end our day rejoicing in the Lord, we can look forward to spending the night in His presence. "In Your presence is fullness of joy; At Your right hand are pleasures forevermore" (Ps. 16:11). Jesus is our Caretaker, and He wants to hear you release every care to Him in prayer before you fall asleep tonight. When you do this you can rejoice and shout for joy as David did, because you can trust your night and the next day into His loving hands.

> *Lord, I release the cares of this day into Your hands. I trust You to work out the problems I faced during the day.*

Morning Wisdom: Read Proverbs 1:29–33. After 9/11 happened, many in our country were overcome with fear. Fear has a devastating effect on people. It paralyzes them and keeps them from being fruitful. Solomon gave the secret to overcoming fear in this passage. He wrote: "Whoever listens to me will dwell safely, And will be secure, without fear of evil" (v. 33). What a promise!

We now have a whole new branch of the government called Homeland Security. That branch's assignment is to keep this country safe from terrorism. God has His own security system called "Abiding in Jesus Christ." As we face the dark days ahead that will occur in these last days, we must remain in our Rock of safety. That Rock of safety is Jesus Christ.

In 1990 the Lord woke me up with the sound of an alarm that I heard with my spiritual ears. We live near the Chattahoochee River, and the sound I heard in my spirit reminded me of the alarm that goes off when the floodgates of this river are opened. They sound an alarm to warn people to get to the safe shores of the river before the rushing water is released. I knew God woke me with this sound for a reason, and I got out of bed to hear what He was trying to tell me. This is what I heard:

> I have opened the floodgates of good and of evil. Only those who cling to Me will survive this flood of evil. Those who look for security in material things or in the government system will not find it there. Only those who hide themselves in Me will find safety and security. Hide yourself daily in Me. I am your Rock of safety.

Lord, help me to remain in You this day.

Evening Watch: Read Psalm 6:1–10. Have you ever had a restless night? I have had my share of those nights that David described in this psalm. He wrote: "I am weary with my groaning; All night I make my bed swim; I drench my couch with my tears" (v. 6). David's enemies came against him, and his enemies were not all physical enemies. He daily faced a hoard of demonic spirits (workers of iniquity) who wanted to destroy him.

David shared how he got through those nights when he wrote, "Depart from me, all you workers of iniquity; For the LORD has heard the voice of my weeping" (v. 8). David knew the secret to overcoming Satan, who loves to attack his victims in the night. David supplicated. The translation of the Hebrew word *supplicate* means "to transfer a burden." When we have those horrific nights when Satan attacks, we need to supplicate—cry out to God with strong weeping and transfer our burdens to Him. This works!

Lord, I give every burden to You. Thank You for the victory!

Genesis 16:1–18:19; Matthew 6:1–24; Psalm 7:1–17; Proverbs 2:1–5

Morning Wisdom: Read Proverbs 2:1–5. We have been talking about how to have the victory during these last few days. Yesterday we learned that we need to remain in the Rock of safety, Jesus Christ. We also learned that we could overcome Satan in the night when we supplicate (transfer our burdens to the Lord).

We can only overcome these fearful times when we learn to fear the Lord. Our church has a proclamation that is printed on our bulletin every Sunday. We read that proclamation over our church on many Sundays. Part of the proclamation states, "Our church will grow daily in the fear of the Lord." Another minister commented to our pastor that people would not understand what that proclamation meant, so our pastor preached several Sundays on the subject of the fear of the Lord. Today's scripture helps us understand just what it means to fear the Lord. Solomon gave four steps to growing in the fear of the Lord:

1. Receive God's words.
2. Incline your ear to wisdom. Listen and obey God's Word.
3. Apply your heart to understanding. Ask the Holy Spirit to help you understand God's Word.
4. Cry out for discernment. Ask the Holy Spirit to teach you the ways of God.

The fear of the Lord is taught, not caught. We fear the Lord when we humble ourselves daily before Him with a reverent heart that seeks to do His will, not our own will.

Lord, I want to grow in the fear of the Lord. Help me, Holy Spirit.

Evening Watch: Read Psalm 7:1–17. How many of us could make this statement to God: "Judge me, O LORD, according to my righteousness, And according to my integrity within me" (v. 8). David made this statement, but He knew something that many Christians today do not know and understand. God looks at our hearts and He hears our hearts before He hears the words we speak.

God had a heart-to-heart relationship with King David. David was a man after God's own heart. David, however, sinned greatly against God when he committed adultery with Bathsheba and then had her husband murdered. God saw that David had a repentant heart, and He forgave David for this great sin.

David said, "My defense is of God, Who saves the upright in heart" (v. 10). That statement makes me want to jump for joy, because truly God defends us when the accuser, Satan, and his forces come against us. God is a just judge who no longer condemns me. He accepts me, because His very own Son lives within me and His Son is righteous.

Lord, thank You for giving me Your righteousness.

JANUARY 8

Morning Wisdom: Read Proverbs 2:6–17. We talked earlier this month about security and safety. When we hide ourselves daily in Jesus, we will be safe and secure in Him no matter what our circumstances are.

Our neighborhood has a neighborhood watch program designed to discourage thieves. Signs are posted all over the neighborhood that say, "Beware— Neighborhood Watch."

Jesus described Satan as a thief who comes in to steal, kill, and destroy. (See John 10:10.) This passage reveals a special security system against Satan we all can employ. This security system includes these five things we must seek after every day:

- wisdom
- knowledge
- understanding
- discretion
- prudence

We set the alarm to this system when we daily gain wisdom and knowledge from God's Word and ask the Holy Spirit to give us understanding, discretion, and prudence.

Have you set your security alarm today?

Lord, thank You for providing this state of the art security system.

Evening Watch: Read Psalm 8:1–9. We recently purchased a cat. The last time I had a cat was when I was a child. I forgot how to manage cats, but I was very surprised when I discovered how obedient this cat was. With the clap of my hands and a firm voice, Smokey obeys instantly.

This psalm explains how God has given mankind dominion over all of His creation. What a responsibility God has given to us! We are the caretakers of the whole world. David wrote:

> You have made him to have dominion over the works of Your hands; You have put all things under his feet.
>
> —PSALM 8:6

Every creature is under our feet. The good news is that Satan is a created being. Because of the excellent name of Jesus, we have dominion over Satan and his hoards of demons. I remember a bumper sticker that read, "Have you tormented the devil today?" Tomorrow when you awake, use the authority you have been given over Satan.

Lord, thank You for giving me all dominion in Your name over all the power of the enemy.

Morning Wisdom: Read Proverbs 2:18–22. I had a strange dream that portrayed the very description of the immoral woman in this Proverbs passage. I saw a young man going near a house of prostitution. He knocked on the door and entered. The moment he was on the other side of the door, a trap door opened and he fell into a deep pit. As I looked into the pit, I saw demons shaded by an eerie red glow. They were clapping their hands as they received this young man into their dwelling place.

Solomon warned his sons not to go near the dwelling place of the strange woman who flatters with her words. God has offered a safe and beautiful dwelling place for those who walk uprightly. David penned these words:

> Surely goodness and mercy shall follow me All the days of my life; And
> I will dwell in the house of the LORD Forever.
>
> —PSALM 23:6

Today if you will abide in the presence of the Lord, you will be able to overcome the traps Satan sets for you.

Lord, thank You for Your presence with me all day long.

Evening Watch: Read Psalm 9:1–12. As my car crested a hill in my neighborhood, I saw something red flash across my windshield. I thought it was a red ball, but then I looked on the side of the road. To my horror, I saw a small boy's lifeless body entangled in a mangled bicycle lying near the curb. This accident happened many years ago. The diligent prayers of my friends, family, and church were answered, and the life of this eight-year-old boy was spared. Later I was able to lead him to the Lord.

His parents, however, sued me for three hundred thousand dollars. The Lord spoke to my heart when the sheriff knocked on my door to hand me this lawsuit. The Holy Spirit instructed me not to be bitter against the boy's parents, because their lawyer had talked them into this.

I received a call from my insurance company advising me to get my own lawyer to fight this lawsuit. I told the insurance representative that I already had a lawyer. I hung up the phone and sang, "Joy is the banner flown from my heart because the King lives within me." Jesus is not only our King, but He is also the best lawyer we can employ. He is our Advocate. (See 1 John 2:1.)

David wrote, "You have maintained my right and my cause" (v. 4). I knew the Lord would maintain my cause also. The lawsuit was settled a year later out of court for one thousand dollars.

Lord, thank You for always maintaining my cause.

Genesis 23:1–24:51; Matthew 8:1–7; Psalm 9:13–20; Proverbs 3:1–6

Morning Wisdom: Read Proverbs 3:1–6. My constant prayer is that my beautician, doctor, dentist, and maids will outlive me. This may seem trivial, but I feel like I cannot live without their expert services. They are all special to me, and I am forever grateful for the excellent services they perform for me. Even more precious to me is my loving husband and three sons and their families. I want them to live forever, but I know we all have our appointment with death.

Just recently our church lost one of its most valuable members. She died of cancer at the age of sixty, which is very young to me. We all longed for her to be healed so she could continue her excellent work in God's kingdom here on Earth. She also had a strong will to live, because she wanted to teach and write more books about Jesus.

Why she died when she did is a mystery to me, but I have to trust that Jesus knew what was best for her. She certainly followed the prescription for long life presented in this passage of Scripture. That prescription is:

- Take God's Word daily with the water of the Holy Spirit.
- Obey God's Word.
- Trust in the Lord and acknowledge Him.

Lord, I desire to live out the days that You have appointed to me. Keep me fruitful in Your kingdom until that day.

Evening Watch: Read Psalm 9:13–20. We learned this morning that we all have our appointed time to die. David had the desire, as we all do, to be lifted from the gates of death. However, he did not want to live just to fulfill his own will. He wanted to live to tell of the Lord's praise and to rejoice in His salvation. David also wanted to live to see God's justice accomplished. He wanted to live to see the time when evil men and evil nations would no longer prevail on Earth.

There will be a day when evil nations and evil men will no longer accomplish their sinister desires, and every person's life on Earth will be judged by a just God. Those who know Jesus will be spared God's wrath, and they will escape punishment. We can take comfort in knowing that Jesus on the cross became sin for us so that we are now the righteousness of God in Him. (See 2 Corinthians 5:21.) If you believe that Jesus died for your sins, was buried, rose from the dead, and now lives to make intercession for you, join me as I thank God for the gift of His Son Jesus who died to give me eternal life. Before you retire to your bed tonight, pray this prayer with me:

Lord, fulfill Your will through me tomorrow and fill me with Your Holy Spirit. Help me to declare Your praise and the joy of Your salvation all day long. Amen.

Genesis 24:52–26:16; Matthew 8:18–34; Psalm 10:1–15; Proverbs 3:7–8

Morning Wisdom: Read Proverbs 3:7–8. We talked yesterday about how to live a long life. We live in a world today, however, that has been invaded by all kinds of health hazards. The pollution of the air and water threaten not only fish and fowl but also human beings. Just yesterday my sister e-mailed me about the dangers of microwaving food in plastic because toxins are released into our bodies from the plastic. The e-mail also warned against freezing water bottles. My response to this e-mail was, "Thanks a lot! Now you tell me!" Every day the medical field discovers medications and environmental practices that are carcinogenic. Now we face the threat of terrorists poisoning our food supply.

Satan would love to paralyze us with the fear of death or ill health, but we cannot allow him to do this. God has given us many instructions in His Word about taking care of our bodies and souls. Today's scripture gives us these instructions.

Do not be proud or wise in your own eyes. Fear the Lord by doing His Word and honoring Him. Depart from evil and call upon Jesus to help you overcome temptation. Following these instructions will help us stay in health. We cannot avoid completely all the environmental hazards to our health, but at least we can follow the instructions given in this scripture.

Lord, I humble myself before You this morning. Help me to live in the fear of the Lord all day long, and lead me not into temptation.

Evening Watch: Read Psalm 10:1–15. I usually watch the news just before I retire. My husband fades out way before the news comes on TV. We do not watch much television, but we do like to stay up-to-date on what's happening in the world. Last night I made the quality decision not to watch anymore late-night news. There was one evil report after another, and I went to bed with those reports still rolling around in my mind. I made the commitment to read a portion of God's Word just before I go to bed.

David wrote about the schemes of the wicked in this psalm. As I read this psalm I pictured wicked people like snakes sneakily slivering themselves into position to strike at their next unsuspecting victim. Their mouths filled with the venom of cursing, deceit, and oppression open wide to press their poisonous fangs into their victim's flesh. David also pictured wicked people as lions crouching to pounce on their prey. David asked the question, "Why do the wicked renounce God?" He gave the answer when he wrote, "He has said in his heart, 'You [God] will not require an account'" (v. 13). There will be an accounting, however, and the wicked will receive their just dues. We can rest tonight knowing that our just God will take care of the helpless and break the arm of wicked and evil men.

Lord, thank You for keeping me from the evil one.

Genesis 26:17–27:46; Matthew 9:1–17; Psalm 10:16–18; Proverbs 3:9–10

Morning Wisdom: Read Proverbs 3:9–10. In the introduction of my book, *You Can Take It With You,* I share an experience I had when I viewed the layers of civilization uncovered at Megiddo in Israel. Each layer of civilization was reduced to less than a foot of ash. As I looked at this amazing phenomenon, the Lord spoke this to my heart: "Why do you spend so much time taking care of ashes?"

Everything we possess will one day burn. Peter spoke about that day when he wrote:

> But the day of the Lord will come as a thief in the night, in which the heavens will pass away with a great noise, and the elements will melt with fervent heat; both the earth and the works that are in it will be burned up.
>
> —2 Peter 3:10

Proverbs 3:9 says, "Honor the LORD with your possessions, And with the firstfruits of all your increase." The truth is that we have no possessions, because the earth and everything in it belongs to the Lord. God has made us stewards of all the earth. However, we regain ownership when we receive Jesus Christ as our Lord, because then we become joint heirs with Christ, which means we possess all Christ possesses.

We honor the Lord with our possessions when we recognize that all we have is a gift from God. We become firstfruit givers when we give top priority to Jesus Christ, God's greatest gift to us.

Father, thank You for making me a joint heir with Your Son, Jesus Christ. Help me to be a firstfruit giver.

Evening Watch: Read Psalm 10:16–18. I have a friend who faithfully prays that God will change his heart and make him more like Jesus. God always honors prayers like these, because God hears the prayers of the humble in heart. As this psalm declares, "LORD, You have heard the desire of the humble" (v. 17). God hears our hearts before He hears the words we pray. God humbles Himself to look into the hearts of men. (See Psalm 113:6.)

If you want to get God's ear, then pray this prayer tonight before you turn your light out to go to bed:

Lord, I humble myself before You by casting my every care upon You, because I know You care for me.

Genesis 28:1–29:35; Matthew 9:18–38; Psalm 11:1–7; Proverbs 3:11–12

Morning Wisdom: Read Proverbs 3:11–12. My daddy loved his three girls, but he had to discipline us from time to time. He hung the razor strap he used to spank us on the wall in the kitchen. Every morning as we ate at the breakfast table, we were reminded to be obedient throughout the day or we would face the sting of the razor strap on our backsides. If ever we began to misbehave at the table, Daddy just pointed to the razor strap and we knew to straighten up and fly right.

God is a much better disciplinarian than any earthly father. However, He does not use a razor strap to correct us. Instead, He uses the rod of correction. That rod of correction is His holy Word. (See 2 Timothy 3:16–17.)

If we will read and meditate upon God's Word at the beginning of every day, we will be more likely to honor and obey God throughout the day. God corrects those He loves. I would rather be corrected by His rod of correction than by the circumstances He may allow in my life to discipline me.

Lord, help me to be faithful to read Your Word every morning and to heed Your Word throughout every day.

Evening Watch: Read Psalm 11:1–7. I have a friend who is bound to a wheelchair because of a back operation that inhibited her ability to walk. She can walk with a walker. She is now in her eighties and still lives alone. Her handicap and age has not stopped her from fulfilling her call. The Lord called her to be an intercessor for nations. Her charge is to pray for the righteous foundations of nations to be restored, and she has traveled the world to fulfill this charge. This psalm is the basis for her call and her charge. Listen carefully to this verse: "If the foundations are destroyed, What can the righteous do?" (v. 3).

Just recently my friend asked my husband and me to accompany her to Washington and Philadelphia to pray for the righteous foundations of our own nation to be restored. This was not the first time she has prayed for our nation, and it will not be the last time. We sat near the Liberty Bell in Philadelphia and prayed in a chapel in Washington while we listened as our friend declared foundational scriptures over our nation.

The foundations of our families that form our churches and nation are being severely attacked by Satan. Our schools need to teach the true history of our nation, which was founded by men and women who believed and declared God's Word. The Declaration of Independence was based upon God's Word, and our entire law system is based upon the Ten Commandments. Before you go to bed, pray for our nation.

Father, in Jesus' name I pray our nation will return to the righteous principles our founding fathers followed as they were obedient to Your Word. Forgive us for straying so far from You and Your Word.

Morning Wisdom: Read Proverbs 3:13–15. Over twenty years ago I urged my husband to get out of the stock market. Since that time, the market has had some crucial plummets in value. So many people look at the stock market as an indicator of the times, but in reality we already have a clear picture of what we are experiencing at this time in history. Jesus, the apostles, and many of the major and minor prophets wrote about our times in Scripture.

Through the pages of the Bible are great hidden treasures of wisdom and the Holy Spirit, our great Teacher, can help us understand what we read. Proverbs 3:13–14 says "Happy is the man who finds wisdom, And the man who gains understanding; For her proceeds are better than the profits of silver, And her gain than fine gold." We find wisdom and understanding in the Word of God. The investment we make as we spend time in God's Word will pay great dividends.

When we read and heed the instructions given in Scripture, we will live prosperous lives that are not dependent upon this world's monetary system. The proceeds we will gain are eternal, not temporal. One of these proceeds is the daily presence of the Lord, which gives us both joy and peace no matter what our circumstances may be. We also will see the fruit of investing the love of Christ and His Word into the lives of those we encounter day-by-day. Pay attention to the investment opportunities the Lord may give you today.

Lord, help me to invest in eternal things today.

Evening Watch: Read Psalm 12:1–8. *Purity* is a term that is rarely used today. Value-based teaching in public schools is a thing of the past. When I was in grammar school, we had to memorize scriptures. One of the psalms I memorized was Psalm 19. I recited, "The law of the Lord is perfect, converting the soul; The testimony of the Lord is sure, making wise the simple; The statutes of the Lord are right, rejoicing the heart; The commandment of the Lord is pure, enlightening the eyes" (Ps. 19:7–8). Many Christians today cannot even quote the Ten Commandments.

Psalm 12:6 says, "The words of the Lord are pure words, Like silver tried in a furnace of earth, Purified seven times." The Word of God has the power to purify our minds, hearts, and bodies. When silver is tried seven times and poured into a vat, a person is able to see his own reflection as he looks into the vat. When we allow the Word of God to purify and sanctify us, people will see the reflection of Jesus in our faces.

The Holy Spirit desires to change us into the image of Jesus Christ. We will cooperate with His purification and perfection assignment if we daily pour the tried Word of God into our hearts. Only the great Teacher, the Holy Spirit, can give us both understanding and application of God's Word. Allow the Holy Spirit to teach and train you to walk in purity. He will not be able to do this if you refuse to open the manual He uses in the classroom of life—the Word of God.

Lord, purify my heart with Your Word.

January 15

Morning Wisdom: Read Proverbs 3:16–18. When we were in India, we visited a school. Above the door of the school was a plaque that read: "WISDOM IS VIRTUE." I thought to myself, *Not all wisdom is virtue.* James spoke about two kinds of wisdom: the wisdom from above and the wisdom from below. (See James 3:13–18.) The wisdom from below is worldly wisdom, and it includes bitter envy, self-seeking, confusion, and every evil work. The wisdom from above is pure, peaceable, gentle, willing to yield, full of mercy and good fruits, without partiality, and without hypocrisy.

As we read today's Proverbs passage, we see what is promised to those who walk in the wisdom from above. We are promised length of days, riches and honor, pleasantness, peace, and happiness. Most people greatly desire what the wisdom from above promises. The pronoun *her* is used throughout this chapter when wisdom is described. However, wisdom is not a woman. Wisdom is a Man, and His name is Jesus. Jesus is made unto us all wisdom, and all the treasures of wisdom are found in Him. (See 1 Corinthians 1:30; Colossians 2:3.)

Wisdom from above is achievable only to those who believe in Jesus Christ and receive Him as their Lord and Savior. He is the Prince of Peace. His presence brings us peace and joy. (See Psalm 16:11.) Today tap in to the wisdom from above by spending time in the presence of our Lord and Savior Jesus Christ. Your day will be blessed.

Lord, help me to remain in Your presence throughout this day.

Evening Watch: Read Psalm 13:1–6. Was your day blessed today as you remained in the presence of the Lord? Often the enemies of worry, doubt, and depression seek to invade our souls and rob us of our joy and peace. David must have had a day when he battled thoughts of defeat, death, and fear.

When we begin to be submerged in a sea of negativity, we need to refocus on Jesus. This is exactly what David did in this psalm. He was about to drown in all the negative thoughts Satan was sending him when he declared, "But I have trusted in Your mercy; My heart shall rejoice in Your salvation. I will sing to the LORD, Because He has dealt bountifully with me" (vv. 5–6). David's declaration of God's mercy and his gratefulness for God's salvation caused him to begin to sing to the Lord. We can daily focus on Jesus immediately when we are having one of those down days.

Before you turn your light off, begin to thank God for Jesus Christ, who always causes us to triumph over our enemies. (See 2 Corinthians 2:14.)

Thank You, Lord, for the victory that is ours through Jesus Christ.

Genesis 32:13–34; Matthew 11:7–30; Psalm 14:1–7; Proverbs 3:19–20

Morning Wisdom: Read Proverbs 3:19–20. We talked yesterday about Jesus being the wisdom from above. Today's reading declares that the Lord founded the earth by wisdom. John told us that Jesus was with God in the beginning when he wrote:

> In the beginning was the Word, and the Word was with God, and the Word was God. He was in the beginning with God. All things were made through Him, and without Him nothing was made that was made.
> —JOHN 1:1–3

Our passage from Proverbs today tells us exactly how the earth was founded. God founded the earth by wisdom, Jesus Christ. Then God established the heavens through understanding, and by His knowledge the depths were broken up and the clouds dropped down the dew. The way God formed the earth is exactly the way God forms and establishes a godly home. Proverbs 24:3 reads:

> Through wisdom a house is built, And by understanding it is established;
> By knowledge the rooms are filled With all precious and pleasant riches.

David wrote in Psalm 127:1, "Unless the LORD builds the house, They labor in vain who build it." Families all over the world are falling apart, because husbands and wives are not walking in the fear of the Lord. Proverbs 9:10 says, "The fear of the LORD is the beginning of wisdom, And the knowledge of the Holy One is understanding."

As we seek Jesus—the Holy One—the wisdom, knowledge, and understanding we need to establish godly homes will be available to us.

Lord, help me to know You better today.

Evening Watch: Read Psalm 14:1–7. Do you think that God has "down days"? I can't help but think that when God looks down from heaven and sees the distressful things occurring on Earth, He must be saddened by what He sees. God sees so many people going their own way and worshiping false gods. How He must long to gather all the oppressed to Himself!

God certainly made it possible for the whole world to be relieved from sorrow, despair, depression, and oppression when He sent His Son, Jesus Christ, to die for the whole world. We know that Scripture tells us that Jesus was a Man of sorrows, and He was acquainted with grief. (See Isaiah 53:3–4.) Jesus bore our grief and carried our sorrows away when He died on the cross. Jesus can deliver us from oppression and depression today. Release your sorrows and cares to the Lord tonight. He is your refuge.

Lord, thank You for taking my sorrow, grief, and pain.

Morning Wisdom: Read Proverbs 3:21–26. Fear is one of the major strongholds in the lives of many Christians. Fear is Satan's anesthesia. He uses it to paralyze his victims before he does his diabolical surgery on them. There are many demonic forces that will come against us daily, but Satan uses the spirit of fear to lead his army of demons. Fear stands at the door of our souls and usually waits until we are asleep at night to attack.

Today's passage from Proverbs reveals God's anecdote to fear. We are exhorted not to allow the Word of God to depart from our eyes and to keep sound wisdom and discretion (v. 21). When we heed this exhortation, we will not only have sweet sleep, but we will walk in safety.

Wisdom and discretion are our bodyguards, and they can only be employed to keep us from fear if we are diligent in reading and hiding God's Word in our hearts daily. In these latter days we need our senses exercised to discern good from evil. (See Hebrews 5:14.) Sadly the seduction of worldly lusts has dulled the senses of many. The only way to sharpen our senses is through the daily discipline of reading the Word and spending time in prayer.

Trust is the opposite of fear. When we put all of our confidence in the Lord and none in ourselves, we enter a safe place. Trust is the place of strength that helps us overcome whatever Satan sends us throughout the day. "In quietness and confidence shall be your strength" (Isa. 30:15).

Lord, help me to trust in You and not be afraid no matter what I face today.

Evening Watch: Read Psalm 15:1–5. We learned this morning that trust is the opposite of fear. Love is also the opposite of fear. This psalm tells us that those who walk uprightly will abide in God's tabernacle. The person who walks uprightly will walk in righteousness, truth, love, kindness, and wisdom.

Jesus exhorted us to abide in His Word, abide in His love, and abide in Him. When we do these three things daily, we will abide in God's tabernacle of safety and assurance. We will also desire to share the love of Jesus Christ with others so that they too can experience the assurance and stability of His love. Sharing the love of Christ with others will become one of our top priorities.

Tomorrow when you awaken, know that Jesus never turns His back on you. Just as a loving father kneels down to coax his one-year-old to take his first steps, Jesus kneels down to coax you to keep on His path of righteousness. His face is ever towards you and His arms are outstretched to catch you if you begin to fall off the path.

Lord, thank You for loving me and leading me on Your path.

JANUARY 18

Morning Wisdom: Read Proverbs 3:27–32. Yesterday we talked about making the love of Jesus Christ known to others as a number one priority in this life. The love of Christ is clearly defined in 1 Corinthians 13, the love chapter. When one reads the love chapter, the reader has to realize that the love described is the love that only the Holy Spirit can achieve in and through us as we surrender our hearts daily to God. No man could achieve such heights of love without the help of the Holy Spirit.

These few verses in Proverbs 3 give us some things to set as our daily goals as we seek to demonstrate the love of Jesus Christ to others. Meditate on these "love goals" throughout your busy day and ask the Holy Spirit to help you display the love of Jesus in the following ways:

- Do good things for others as much as possible.
- Do not procrastinate when someone comes to you with a need. If at all possible, meet that need.
- Do not think evil thoughts about others or devise ways you can retaliate if others have done you harm.
- Do not strive with others without a cause. Avoid strife.
- Do not envy those who come against you.

What great counsel is found in these few verses! I believe the Holy Spirit, the great Counselor, inspired Solomon to write these words. Ask the Holy Spirit to help you obey His counsel today.

Lord, thank You for the Holy Spirit, who will help me follow His wise counsel.

Evening Watch: Read Psalm 16:1–11. After 9/11 and the dramatic destruction and loss of life experienced in the tsunami in January 2005, we all would like to find a safe place to hide from the storms of life. In this psalm David spoke of the safest place to be throughout our days and nights on Earth. That safe place is in the presence of the Lord, who both preserves us and maintains us through whatever circumstances we might face daily.

David felt the safe arms of the Lord, even at night. He declared that he experienced God's counsel in the day and God's instructions in the night seasons. He set the Lord ever before him, and this is why David was able to overcome both his physical enemies and spiritual enemies. David rejoiced in God's presence, and the joy of the Lord was his strength in troubled times. David wrote, "In Your presence is fullness of joy; At Your right hand are pleasures forevermore" (v. 11).

Lord, help me to remain in Your presence day and night.

JANUARY 19

Morning Wisdom: Read Proverbs 3:33–35. Over the years it has been our privilege to pray a blessing over many homes. When we bless homes, we pray over every room and declare that Satan and his demons have no right to invade that home. By faith we anoint the windows and doors of the home and place the blood of Jesus over the home as a protection. Often the Lord will give us special words to declare over each room in the home.

Tom and I know the importance of house blessings because of what we experienced when we first purchased the home where we live now. We purchased the home in 1972, but we were unable to occupy it for six months. We did some renovation of the house before we moved the furniture into the rooms. We noticed that every time we went into our new home, Tom and I would have a lot of strife between us. Finally we realized that we had not prayed over the home. The former owners had zodiac posters in every room, and their bookshelves were filled with a lot of occult material. After we cleansed the house and prayed over it, the strife ceased.

Today's scripture says that the "curse of the LORD is on the house of the wicked, But He blesses the home of the just" (v. 33). This verse confirms the importance of cleansing and praying prayers of blessing over places we occupy, even temporarily. Lately I have made it a practice to pray over the motel and hotel rooms we stay in when we travel. If you haven't prayed over the places you work and live, today might be a good day to bless those places. You can pray a prayer like this:

> *Father, in Jesus' name, I command any spirit that cannot confess that Jesus Christ of Nazareth is God in the flesh to leave this place, and I speak God's blessing over my workplace and my home.*

Evening Watch: Read Psalm 17:1–15. Have you ever put your foot in your mouth? I know I have on more occasions than I am willing to admit. Whenever I have put my foot in my mouth, I have given the devil a toehold on my tongue. The foot in my mouth belongs to Satan, and his demonic troops want to use my tongue as a catapult to shoot his fiery darts to wound others.

David was well aware of how Satan can use our tongues for destruction. He wrote, "I have purposed that my mouth shall not transgress" (v. 3). He added that it was by the words of God's lips that he was able to keep out of the path of the destroyer, the devil (v. 4).

Before you go to bed tonight, join David in his commitment not to transgress with his tongue. I will join you as we make this commitment by praying this prayer:

> *Lord, let the law of kindness be upon my lips always.*

Genesis 41:17–42:17; Matthew 13:24–46; Psalm 18:1–15; Proverbs 4:1–6

Morning Wisdom: Read Proverbs 4:1–6. Just recently my husband and I have been discussing the links between wisdom, understanding, and knowledge. One of my favorite verses in Proverbs is chapter 24, verse 3. It says that a house is built by wisdom, and it is established through understanding. We are in the building business on Earth. We are building a spiritual house for God to dwell in. We are the temples of the living God. Our spiritual houses need to have great understanding in these last days to establish God's will and His way in our individual lives.

In this chapter Solomon exhorted his sons to "know understanding" (v. 1). Understanding is the link between wisdom and knowledge. Wisdom is applied knowledge, and without understanding we will not be able to apply God's Word to our daily lives.

Solomon urged his sons to get wisdom and understanding and to let their hearts retain his words (v. 5). Solomon's words were filled with wisdom, but later in his life he failed to obey those words of wisdom. His heart did not retain the very commands he gave to his sons, because his understanding became clouded by his own lusts.

Only the Holy Spirit can give us understanding of God's Word. When we allow the Holy Spirit to take the things of Jesus Christ and reveal those things to us as we read God's Word, we will tap into the wisdom from above that will cause us to live peaceable, fruitful lives, and our spiritual houses will be established.

Lord, help me to depend upon the Holy Spirit to teach me how to apply God's Word to my everyday life.

Evening Watch: Read Psalm 18:1–15. *Lord, give me strength!* If I kept a record of the many times I have prayed that prayer, I know the number would be astronomical. We all need strength to live out our days, and David knew the secret of how to live an overcoming life. He was surrounded by distressful circumstances and destructive enemies, but he did not allow these things to overwhelm him. Yes, he would often momentarily "lose it," as we all do, but he knew exactly where to find what he had lost. Whenever he felt weak, he called upon the Lord to strengthen him. He had sure confidence that the Lord was present even in his darkest hours. He wrote that God "made darkness His secret place" (v. 11).

David was confident that as he depended upon the strength of the Lord he would always be able to overcome every dark season in his life. Tonight as you turn off your reading light, know with confidence that God is in the room with you, and He will strengthen you to face whatever comes your way tomorrow.

Lord, thank You for being present with me always.

Genesis 42:18–43:34; Matthew 13:47–14:13; Psalm 18:16–34; Proverbs 4:7–10

Morning Wisdom: Read Proverbs 4:7–10. Yesterday we talked about how vital wisdom and understanding are to us as we seek to build God's kingdom here on Earth. Solomon continued his exhortation to his sons to get wisdom and understanding. James gave us instructions on how to get wisdom. He said, "If any of you lacks wisdom, let him ask of God, who gives to all liberally and without reproach, and it will be given to him" (James 1:5). Wisdom and understanding are tailor-made gifts from God. They are designed to fit whatever situation or problem we might encounter throughout each day.

God is waiting patiently to grant us these gifts. All we have to do is ask, but so often we forget to ask. We try to work things out ourselves without going to God in prayer. These four things are promised to us if we will ask and receive wisdom from God: promotion, honor, grace, and God's glory.

After reading this passage I have made a commitment to ask God for His wisdom every morning. You might join me as I pray:

> *Father, thank You for Your anointing of wisdom and understanding, might and counsel, knowledge and the fear of the Lord and the Holy Spirit. I ask You now to pour out this powerful anointing upon me so that I can accomplish Your will in my life and glorify You today.*

Evening Watch: Read Psalm 18:16–34. Security and safety are two of the greatest needs of every human being. After 9/11 I would venture to say that these two needs are also top on the list of our nation and every nation. We live in troubled times, but there is a bridge over troubled waters. During recent floods in the Midwest and California, huge bridges were washed away along with homes and cars. Those bridges gave way because there was not enough support to withstand the mighty river waters as they roared under them.

Wouldn't you love to know that you could be safe and secure in every traumatic event in your life? We can have the same peace of mind David did when he wrote this psalm. Even though enemies confronted David continually, he trusted the Lord to deliver him and knew the Lord was his support. (See v. 18.) God is strong enough to draw us out of the floods of trauma, trial, and tragedy in our lives.

What about all those who perished in 9/11? Many probably prayed that very day for God to watch over them. The truth is that God was watching over them, and His strong arms were around those who trusted the day into His hands. Those who trusted in the Lord and perished in 9/11 fell into the arms of Jesus, who lifted them right into the presence of His holy Father. The Lord has the power to enlighten our darkest days. He also has a bountiful measure of grace to help us face those dark times in our lives with His strength, support, and grace. Sleep well tonight. You are safe in the arms of Jesus.

Lord, thank You for Your strength, grace, and support.

January 22

Morning Wisdom: Read Proverbs 4:11–13. Since my husband had his six-bypass surgery, we try to walk at least thirty minutes a day. We walk the same path every day, because this path is almost void of traffic and barking dogs. However, we do have to watch out for pinecones and rocks that could easily throw us off balance and cause us to fall. I hold my husband's hand tightly when we go down hills, because one time I did trip on a pinecone and fell.

Solomon exhorted his sons in this passage to follow the path of wisdom. He promised that if they did follow this path, their steps would not be hindered. They had to hold tightly to instruction in order to ensure that they could run on the path of wisdom without stumbling.

The Bible is our instruction manual for life, but few take the time to read it daily. If we are to walk the path of wisdom without any fear of stumbling, we need to daily have a firm grip on the instructions set forth in the Bible.

Whenever I encounter a problem that could throw me off the path of wisdom, I try to find a promise in God's Word that gives instructions about that problem. I have several promise books that list promises given in Scripture on various topics, such as financial and physical needs. When I find the promise that applies to my problem, I meditate on that promise and also declare it out loud. This little exercise has kept me on the path of wisdom on a multitude of occasions throughout my life. Today find promises in God's Word that are tailor-made for whatever problems you may face during the day.

Lord, help me to stand firmly on Your promises today.

Evening Watch: Read Psalm 18:35–50. I shared this morning how I hold my husband's hand as we take our walks together. His hand gives the security and support I need to keep me from stumbling over the objects that would cause me to fall. This passage from Psalms gives me such comfort, because it declares that God upholds us with His right hand. Not only that, but God also enlarges our path and clears the way so our feet do not slip. We can face the battles we may face tomorrow and every day with the assurance that God's right hand will not only supply support, but also will strengthen us and cause us to be victorious.

When we truly believe that God is upholding us with His right hand, we can shout the same declaration David shouted in this psalm. He cried out, "The LORD lives! Blessed be my Rock! Let the God of my salvation be exalted" (v. 46). Jesus truly is our Rock of safety who lifts us above the enemies of our souls. Know with assurance that He is holding your hand through every trial and every battle you may face this week and the rest of your life.

Lord, thank You for holding my hand and for giving me victory.

Genesis 46:1–47:31; Matthew 15:1–28; Psalm 19:1–14; Proverbs 4:14–19

Morning Wisdom: Read Proverbs 4:14–19. We once visited the Shrine of the Book in Jerusalem. The Shrine of the Book was built to house the Dead Sea scrolls discovered in Qumran over fifty years ago.

As we left the building, we were startled by a tall wall. One side of the wall was black marble and the other side was white marble. We asked our guide what this wall symbolized, and he quickly responded, "The black marble represents the sons of darkness, and the white marble symbolizes the sons of light." He said that the scribes who recorded the scrolls found by the Dead Sea belonged to a group called the Sons of Light.

The results of walking in darkness and walking in the light are compared in this passage. Those who walk in darkness are sleepless and violent. Those who walk in the light will grow brighter and brighter until that perfect day. I believe that perfect day will be the day when Jesus returns to rule and reign in Jerusalem. As we commit ourselves to walk in the light and rely on the Holy Spirit to help us stay on the just path, we can look forward to growing brighter and brighter every day we live on this earth.

When our son taught English in China, many of his students asked him, "What makes your face shine?" The glory light of Jesus was shining through him. Second Corinthians 4:6 speaks about this light:

> For it is the God who commanded light to shine out of darkness, who has shone in our hearts to give the light of the knowledge of the glory of God in the face of Jesus Christ.

Lord, may Your light shine brightly through me today.

Evening Watch: Read Psalm 19:1–14. This morning we talked about our lights growing brighter and brighter until that perfect day when Jesus returns. David revealed what will help us keep on the just path when he wrote, "The law of the LORD is perfect, converting the soul" (v. 7).

When we first begin to walk the just path, our souls often are still bound by oppressive strongholds that have affected our way of thinking, our emotional response to situations, and our willful actions. The soul (mind, emotions, and will) is being perfected throughout the lifetime of the believer. We all need soul surgery, and our skillful Surgeon, Jesus Christ, uses the two-edged sword, the Word of God, to delicately remove the dark areas of our souls.

As the various roots in our hearts, such as the root of rejection and the root of bitterness, are removed, the Holy Spirit is then able to shed abroad the love of Jesus Christ in our hearts. The law, testimony, statutes, and the commandments found in God's Word shed light on every dark area in our souls. God's Word is a lamp for our path.

Lord, shine Your light on my path.

Genesis 48:1–49:33; Matthew 15:29–16:12; Psalm 20:1–9; Proverbs 4:20–27

Morning Wisdom: Read Proverbs 4:20–27. Because of the deluge of TV, videos, movies, and computers, we have become a watching society instead of a listening society. The art of listening is being buried in a heap of taped messages, answering machines, and communications by e-mail.

Our passage today tells us exactly how we are to listen. Solomon urged his sons to give attention to his words by listening to what he said with their ears and their hearts. He also exhorted his sons not to let his words depart from their eyes.

He promised that if they listened and obeyed the words of wisdom he gave them, those very words would become life and health to them. Solomon's words of wisdom were inspired by God and translated into the book of Proverbs by the Holy Spirit. As we read Proverbs through this year, we need to ask the Holy Spirit to help us apply what we read to our everyday life. Solomon told his sons how to diligently guard their hearts daily. We need to follow his instructions to:

1. speak without deceit or perversion;

2. look straight ahead and ponder the path of our feet;

3. remove our feet from evil and let our ways be established.

We guard our hearts when we hear no evil, see no evil, and speak no evil. We walk in the Spirit when we listen carefully to the Holy Spirit as He narrates and interprets God's Word to us. If we obey the instructions given us through God's Word and through the still, small voice of the Holy Spirit, we will live blessed and fruitful lives.

Lord, help me to have listening ears and an obedient heart today.

Evening Watch: Read Psalm 20:1–9. This passage provides a great prayer that we can pray daily for our loved ones, friends, and leaders. The prayer based on this psalm is as follows:

May the Lord answer you in troubled times and may He defend you. May the Lord grant your heart's desire and fulfill His purpose in your life. May the Lord answer all of your requests. May Jesus Christ, the King of Glory, answer you when you call upon Him. May you always trust in the Lord and remember His name.

I plan to pray this prayer daily for the president of our nation and his staff, my pastor and his staff, my family members, and the members of my church.

Lord, thank You for the mighty prayers in Your Word.

Morning Wisdom: Read Proverbs 5:1–6. Almost every day we encounter open mouths that spill out words containing the wisdom of this world, which is the wisdom from below. (See James 3:13–17.) The old saying, "Sticks and stones may break my bones, but words will never hurt me," simply is not true. Words are the fiery darts that Satan shoots into our minds and hearts to wound us, and he uses people to be his hit men.

The mouth is a mighty weapon that can be used for evil or for good. The mouth is like the open barrel of a gun. The trigger of that gun is the tongue. The bullets in that gun are words Satan inspires us to say in a moment of frustration or strife.

Solomon warned his sons not to receive the words that came from the mouth of an immoral woman. He said, "The lips of an immoral woman drip honey, And her mouth is smoother than oil; But in the end she is bitter as wormwood, Sharp as a two-edged sword" (v. 3–4).

Solomon's description of the immoral woman's mouth can also be applied to Satan's mouth. Satan is the master of seduction. First he butters us up with sweet words that convince us that what he offers will not hurt us. We hear in our minds phrases like, "Just this one time won't hurt" or "No one will see." Then he oils the words he speaks to our minds with phrases like, "You deserve this; pamper yourself."

When we know Satan's strategies, we will have discretion and will be able to recognize immediately what Satan is up to.

Lord, I refuse to listen to Satan's seducing words today.

Evening Watch: Read Psalm 21:1–13. This morning I received a call from a friend who was about to go into a depression. She has battled depression before. I exhorted her to read some of the psalms out loud. This psalm would be a good one to read out loud to battle depression.

David must have written this psalm on an "up day," but I imagine he used these very words to speak to his soul on "down days." When you have a down day, tell your soul to do the following: rejoice in God's strength and salvation, thank the Lord for answered prayer, thank the Lord for His blessings and His presence with you, thank the Lord for His mercy and His might in defending you against your enemies, and exalt the Lord and sing praises to His power. If you will command your soul to speak words of thanksgiving and praise on your down days, I know your mind, will, and emotions will be lifted up and stabilized.

Lord, help me to remember to thank You even on my down days.

JANUARY 26

Morning Wisdom: Read Proverbs 5:7–14. "Children, remember to obey!" We hear this exhortation constantly when we visit our middle son, who has five young children. They even have a little song they sing about obeying their parents.

In this passage we can hear Solomon saying, "Children, obey!" He told his sons that if they got involved with an immoral woman, they would wish later that they had obeyed the voice of their teachers and inclined their ears to those who instructed them. We learn in these few verses the consequences of being involved with an immoral woman. Involvement with an immoral woman will cause a man to lose honor, wealth, length of blessed years, fruitful labor, and health.

This would be a good portion of Scripture for parents to read to their adolescent sons before their hormones begin to rage. I recently learned that the brain of a teenager is not fully developed. The area of the brain that has to do with risk taking and discernment is not formed completely until the age of twenty-one or older. The consequences, however, of promiscuous sex should be a no-brainer. We need to warn our children early on about the risks they will take. This passage would be an excellent passage for young men to memorize.

> *Lord, I pray today for great wisdom to rest upon the parents of teenagers.*

Evening Watch: Read Psalm 22:1–18. A person who feels abandoned is attacked by doubt, fear, loneliness, failure, rejection, grief, sorrow, and unworthiness. Satan is a bully, and he attacks us in those moments of weakness when we say to ourselves, "No one cares about me. If I died, people would not even miss me." Children who experience a divorce often feel abandoned by one parent or even both. Latchkey children who come home to an empty house may feel abandoned by their parents. Orphans and even grown-up orphans may still have that lingering feeling of abandonment. Jesus experienced abandonment on the cross to purchase acceptance for us by our heavenly Father.

On the cross Jesus quoted this psalm, "My God, My God, why have You forsaken Me?" (v. 1). The Father had no other choice than to abandon His Son for a moment in time. God has purer eyes than to behold evil, and when the sins of the whole world were laid upon Jesus, God had to turn His back on His only begotten Son. On that fateful day when Jesus experienced true abandonment from His heavenly Father, the way was provided for every emotionally or physically abandoned person to have his or her heart healed.

Tonight before you go to bed ask the Holy Spirit to reveal if you still suffer from either true or perceived abandonment in the past. Give Jesus those moments when you feel that sinking feeling in the pit of your stomach and that time when you cannot see the light. Jesus will heal the pain in your heart that you experience in those moments.

> *Lord, thank You for healing my heart.*

Exodus 4:1–5:21; Matthew 18:1–22; Psalm 22:19–31; Proverbs 5:15–21

Morning Wisdom: Read Proverbs 5:15–21. This passage contains one of my husband's favorite verses. He loves it when we come to these few verses in Proverbs that give the prescription for a happy marriage. Listen to Solomon's words:

> And rejoice with the wife of your youth. As a loving deer and a graceful doe, Let her breasts satisfy you at all times; And always be enraptured with her love.
>
> —PROVERBS 5:18–19

Even though my husband and I have been married for nearly fifty years, we still see one another as newlyweds. God has helped us keep the romance in our marriage alive. Believe it or not, the Holy Spirit can inspire marriage partners with creative ways to rejoice in their intimate times with one another. Remember, intimacy does not just include our sexual relationship. Intimacy with one another includes conversing and praying with one another and enjoying the simple pleasures of life together.

I have a friend who saves one night a week as a date night with her husband. She begins thinking and praying at the first of the week about how to make that time special. One time in the middle of winter she threw a blanket on the floor, fixed a picnic basket, and she and her husband enjoyed a picnic together after the children were in bed.

My friend credits the Holy Spirit for her creativity, and I have gained a lot of ideas for our intimate times from her. The prescription for a happy marriage is to consistently have creative times alone with your mate. Unfaithfulness would be rare if husbands and wives would commit themselves to give each other plenty of time to grow in the art of intimacy.

Lord, thank You for being interested in every aspect of my life.

Evening Watch: Read Psalm 22:19–31. When you hear the phrase, "Let's have church," what comes to your mind? Many probably envision a pulpit and pews filled with people who are dressed in their Sunday clothes. However, David's view of church was quite different. He shared in this psalm exactly what should happen in every church meeting. Here is the order of service: Declare God's name in the assembly; give praises to God by thanking Him for what He has done for you; worship God by focusing on who God is and the aspects of His character; feed and satisfy those who are poor in spirit with the spiritual food found in the Bible; and give testimonies about what the Lord has done for you. Whenever we are assembled in the name of the Lord, we are to do these things. When we do, we will be "having church," and lives and hearts will be changed.

Lord, thank You for the assembly of the saints.

Exodus 5:22–7:25; Matthew 18:23–19:12; Psalm 23:1–6; Proverbs 5:22–23

Morning Wisdom: Read Proverbs 5:22–23. Why do the wicked prosper, and how long will they seem to triumph? These were two questions David asked when he wrote many of the psalms. Solomon answered David's questions when he wrote that the wicked would be entrapped by their iniquities and bound in the chords of their own sins.

When we look at the world today, we do see that the wicked temporarily may prosper and often seem to triumph, but the truth is that the end of the wicked will be both physical and spiritual death. They will experience the death of their souls. In recent years I experienced seasons of fasting when I prayed for people who were bound by sin and entrapped in their own iniquities. I was inspired to do this when I read about God's chosen fast in Isaiah 58. Listen to Isaiah's words:

> Is this not the fast that I have chosen: To loose the bonds of wickedness…?
>
> —Isaiah 58:6

We will have a different view of the wicked when we see them as people who are victims of their own crimes. Sin is a crime. I often pray the following prayer for those I know who are bound in sin. You may want to join me this morning as I pray:

> *In the name of Jesus, I confess the sins of [name the people]. I remit their sins and ask You to give them a spirit of repentance and enable them to have godly sorrow over their sins. I pray these people will come to know You as Savior and confess their own sins before You so that they can be set free.*

Evening Watch: Read Psalm 23:1–6. I presently am teaching Psalm 23 to a group of elderly ladies who live in a retirement home. My challenge is to make this psalm so exciting that none of them will fall asleep as I teach.

No matter how hard I try, there always are a few ladies who dose off and drop their handouts on the floor. I am using a book called *A Shepherd Looks at Psalm 23* by W. Phillip Keller. One of his points in the book is that sheep under the management of a good shepherd will be well fed, well watered, clean, and free from lice. When we are under the management of Jesus, our Good Shepherd, we will be well fed by the Word of God, well watered by the Holy Spirit, and cleansed from sin by the blood of Jesus.

Thank You, Lord, for being my Good Shepherd.

Exodus 8:1–9:35; Matthew 19:13–30; Psalm 24:1–10; Proverbs 6:1–5

Morning Wisdom: Read Proverbs 6:1–5. We learn from this passage in Proverbs the dangers of cosigning on a loan. Whenever we cosign, even with a family member, we run the risk of not only losing money, but also losing our relationship with that family member or friend. If we have cosigned on a loan, we are exhorted in these verses to go to the cosigner and ask him to release us from our pledge. Sleepless nights are guaranteed to those who make a financial commitment to pay another person's loan.

Over the years we have helped our sons with down payments on their homes, but we never have cosigned on their mortgage loans. We are too aware of the dangers of this practice. I pray you will have the courage to say no when someone asks you to cosign on a loan.

Lord, thank You for the practical advice found in Proverbs.

Evening Watch: Read Psalm 24:1–10. We learned this morning how important it is for us to guard against making wrong financial decisions such as cosigning. Throughout our lives there are so many things we need to guard against. We need to guard our minds against deception and doubt. We need to guard our emotions against despair and depression. We need to guard our bodies against disease and destruction. To sum it up, we need to guard every part of our beings against the devil. We also need to guard against the two other enemies that seek to rob us of fruitful, meaningful lives. Those two enemies are our own flesh and the world in which we live. Our flesh so often demands its own way, and the world distracts us from our true purpose in life, which is to glorify God and enjoy Him forever.

This psalm reveals the secret to guarding ourselves against the devil, the flesh, and the world. We are exhorted in this psalm to "Lift up your heads, O you gates! And be lifted up, you everlasting doors!" (v. 7). There are three gates to our minds that we need to lift up daily to the Lord. All of those gates are located in the head part of the body. Our minds are influenced the most by what we see, what we hear, and what we speak. When we are careful not to allow the world to distract us from keeping our eyes upon Jesus, we guard the eye gate to our minds. When we refuse to listen to music, teachings, or even conversations that do not edify our inner man, we guard the ear gate to our minds. When we are careful to think and speak only those things that are true, honest, pure, beautiful, and of a good report, we guard the mouth gate to our minds.

When we are careful to guard the gates of our minds, we then will be able to lift up the everlasting doors. God created our souls (minds, emotions, and wills) to experience continual fellowship with Him. He created us to magnify, worship, enjoy, and glorify Him. When we focus our eyes on the Lord, submit our senses to enjoy Him, and set our wills to glorify Him, our hearts and souls will be guarded against all three of our enemies. Before you retire in your bed, submit your eye, ear, and mouth gates to the Lord.

Lord, sanctify my eye, ear, and mouth gates to my mind.

Exodus 10:1–12:13; Matthew 20:1–28; Psalm 25:1–11; Proverbs 6:6–11

Morning Wisdom: Read Proverbs 6:6–11. When I took science in high school, all the students were required to submit a science project to be judged at the local science fair. The project I submitted was a written report on the progress of ants in an ant farm (ants enclosed between two panes of glass). During a six-month period, I observed ants crawling in military procession to accomplish several tasks. I was amazed at how organized they were. They created tunnels through the sand that enabled them to go quickly from one end of the farm to the other. When I dropped tiny crumbs between the glass panels, the ants instantly mobilized into an army whose main goal was to either store the food or distribute the food to the other ants.

The passage of Scripture today warns against laziness. The exhortation was given, "Go to the ant, you sluggard! Consider her ways" (v. 6). When I observed these ants, I noticed they were always on the move. I have heard of busy bees, but I never knew ants could be so busy. They were tireless and worked as a team to get things done.

After my observations, I realized how lazy I am at times. One of my favorite things to do is to take a nap. In fact, one of the first things I plan when I wake up in the morning is when I will take my nap that day. I also love to fold my hands over my chest when I sleep. I guess I needed these verses in Proverbs this morning to remind me that I am a colaborer with Jesus Christ, and there is work in His kingdom today that He wants me to accomplish.

Lord, help me!

Evening Watch: Read Psalm 25:1–11. We learned this morning that ants are continually on the move to store food. We become as industrious and wise as ants when we store up spiritual food for future use. We store up our spiritual food for the future by memorizing and meditating on Scripture. When we memorize scriptures and hide God's Word in our hearts, we will remember the appropriate promise from God's Word that we need to declare.

We talked yesterday about lifting up the gates of our minds and allowing God to invade the everlasting doors of our souls. This psalm exhorts us to lift up our souls to the Lord. When we daily release our souls to the Lord and saturate our minds with the Word of God, we will be able to be victorious over our three enemies—the devil, the flesh, and the world. We lift the mind part of our souls to the Lord when we daily renew our minds by reading, memorizing, and meditating on God's Word. We lift up the emotional part of our souls when we anchor our emotions in hope (the calm expectation of good). The hope that will anchor our emotions from sinking when the waves of adversity seek to drown us is not wishful thinking. Stabilizing hope is grounded in Jesus Christ. He is our hope. We lift up the will part of our souls when we willingly submit ourselves to do God's thing and not our own. Tonight you can prepare for whatever faces you tomorrow by praying:

Lord, I lift my soul up to You. Purify my soul.

Exodus 12:14–13:16; Matthew 20:29–21:22; Psalm 25:12–22; Proverbs 6:12–15

Morning Wisdom: Read Proverbs 6:12–15. Wow! I didn't know winking was a sign of wickedness. I must admit that I have winked at times. I guess wicked people often wink when they try to seduce others by flirting with them. I have not seen wicked people shuffle their feet, but I have seen many saints point their fingers at others in the body of Christ. Part of God's chosen fast presented in Isaiah 58 is to fast from pointing our fingers at others. (See Isaiah 58:9.) Whenever we point our fingers at others in judgment and criticism or accusation, we have cooperated with Satan.

When I criticize and judge those in the body of Christ, I sow discord among the brethren, and this is an abomination to the Lord. Later in this chapter the Lord lists six things He hates, and one of these things is the person who sows discord among the brethren. Today I choose to fast from pointing my finger at anyone.

> *Lord, help me to shut my mouth if I am about to say critical, unkind words to others.*

Evening Watch: Read Psalm 25:12–22. We learned this morning the dangers of criticizing and judging others. Satan is the accuser of the brethren, and we become hit men for him whenever we use our tongues to criticize and judge others. Jesus said that the same judgment we place on others will come upon us. We learned earlier that the mouth is like a gun. The double barrel of the gun represents our lips. Our tongues represent the trigger of a gun. The words we speak are the bullets that Satan uses to wound others.

The only hope we have to speak what God wants us to speak is to walk in the fear of the Lord. We walk in the fear of the Lord when we have an awesome respect for God's Word and a heart that desires to do God's Word.

This psalm lists the blessings that come to a person who walks in the fear of the Lord. Prosperity, descendents who inherit the earth, revelation knowledge, and deliverance are all promised to those who walk in the fear of the Lord. When we walk in the fear of the Lord, integrity and uprightness will preserve us. We also will be willing to trust in the Lord and wait patiently for the answers to our prayers. When we walk in the fear of the Lord, the double barrel of our lips will shoot bullets against the devil, not against people. Our tongues also will extol the Lord instead of criticizing people.

David asked the Lord to keep his soul and deliver him. That would be a great prayer for you to pray before you fall asleep.

> *Lord, keep my soul from troubles tomorrow and deliver me from being ensnared by the fear of man and the words I speak. Keep me in the fear of the Lord all day long.*

FEBRUARY 1

Exodus 13:17–15:19; Matthew 21:23–46; Psalm 26:1–12; Proverbs 6:16–19

Morning Wisdom: Read Proverbs 6:16–19. "I hate it when you do that!" I have used that phrase many times to tell my husband to stop doing something I know is not good for him to do. For example, when he gets upset about something, I say, "I hate it when you do that! You're going to raise your blood pressure and that is not good for you!" The frustration I feel at those moments must be similar to the frustration God experiences when He sees His children disobey Him. He knows that if they disobey Him, things will not go well with them.

In these verses Solomon gave a list of seven things that the Lord hates. They are as follows:

1. A proud look
2. A lying tongue
3. Hands that shed innocent blood
4. A heart that devises wicked plans
5. Feet that are swift in running to evil
6. A false witness who speaks lies
7. One who sows discord among brethren

How Solomon came up with this list is a mystery to me, but when we look at Scripture we will discover the many times God warns against doing these seven things.

God knows how much harm those seven actions will cause, not only to us but also to those around us. We have to remember that God is love, and any hatred He experiences is rooted in His hatred of evil and in His loving desire to protect us from evil.

Lord, thank You for protecting me from evil.

Evening Watch: Read Psalm 26:1–12. We learned this morning that God's anger is rooted in His great love for us. You have probably heard this statement, "God hates the sin, but He loves the sinner." David was communicating in this psalm the loving-kindness God showed him in his lifetime. He saw God's acts of mercy and love towards him, and this is why David was able to trust God with all of his heart. It is easy for us to trust those who we know want our best in life. God has proven that He only wants the best for us.

A person who is forgiven much can love much. David had been forgiven of the sins of adultery and murder. David sought to walk in integrity and openness with God after Nathan confronted him with his own sins. David was so grateful for God's forgiveness that he loved to dwell in the presence of God. He wrote, "I have loved the habitation of Your house" (v. 8). In modern terms, David was saying, "I love to hang out with You, God." After David confessed his sins and repented, he was not afraid for God to examine his heart.

Lord, examine my heart and help me to walk in integrity.

February 2

Morning Wisdom: Read Proverbs 6:20–26. This passage from Proverbs says that the commandments are a lamp and the law is a light to keep us from going astray. The major laws of today are based on the Ten Commandments, but recent laws in the United States forbid the Ten Commandments from being displayed in courthouses and schools. I am afraid most Christians could not remember all the Ten Commandments if they were asked to recite them. This is why more and more darkness seems to be invading our schools and communities. I am convicted to pray for our nation this morning. Will you join me?

> *Lord, forgive our nation for putting aside Your Ten Commandments. Help every Christian parent to teach the Ten Commandments to their children. Even though we may not be able to display the Ten Commandments publicly, we can hide them in our hearts and receive the light we need to love mercy and walk justly and humbly with our God.*

Evening Watch: Read Psalm 27:1–7. This morning I shared how darkness has invaded our schools and communities and the lamp of God's law seems to no longer be shining brightly. However, the truth is that light has the power to invade the darkness. Darkness does not have the power to invade light. The Lord Jesus Christ is the Light of the world who lights all those who come into this world. (See John 1:9.) The tragic news is that men who were born in the light choose to walk in darkness.

This psalm begins with these words, "The Lord is my light and my salvation; Whom shall I fear? The Lord is the strength of my life; Of whom shall I be afraid?" (v. 1). When I was a child I used to sing two songs about letting your light shine and keeping the oil in your lamp burning. How do we keep our lamps lit and our hearts burning with love for the Lord? David gave the answer when he declared, "One thing I have desired of the Lord, That will I seek: That I may dwell in the house of the Lord All the days of my life, To behold the beauty of the Lord, And to inquire in His temple" (v. 4).

The house of the Lord is an eternal house that we gain entrance to when we receive Jesus Christ as our Lord and Savior. At that moment His light invades the darkness of our hearts and His glory begins to shine out of our lives. Are there people in your family or neighborhood who still live in darkness? Before you close your eyes tonight, pray this prayer for those you know who need salvation:

> *Father, reveal Jesus Christ to those who need salvation.*

February 3

Morning Wisdom: Read Proverbs 6:27–35. "Don't touch the stove! You'll get burned!" These were my constant warnings to our three sons when they were young. All three of our sons loved to hang around the kitchen when I was cooking, because they all loved to eat and were anxiously awaiting their next meal.

When our sons were older I warned them about the dangers of having sex outside of marriage. Solomon told his sons that they would be burned if they committed sexual sins. (See vv. 28–29.) Participation in sex outside of marriage will always cause someone to be burned. Paul warned against fornication and adultery when he wrote:

> Foods for the stomach and the stomach for foods, but God will destroy both it and them. Now the body is not for sexual immorality [fornication] but for the Lord, and the Lord for the body. And God both raised up the Lord and will also raise us up by His power. Do you not know that your bodies are members of Christ? Shall I then take the members of Christ and make them members of a harlot? Certainly not! Or do you not know that he who is joined to a harlot is one body with her? For "the two," He says, "shall become one flesh."
>
> —1 CORINTHIANS 6:13–16

These verses are great verses for young men and women to memorize, even before they reach puberty.

Lord, I pray for Christian parents to impress upon their children the spiritual and physical dangers of sex outside of marriage.

Evening Watch: Read Psalm 27:8–14. This passage includes some good advice for us to give our children, mates, and friends. If these instructions are followed daily, the paths we travel in life will be much smoother. Here are the instructions we should follow daily:

- Seek God's face. Take time to worship and praise the Lord.

- Ask God to teach you His ways. Read God's Word consistently.

- Cast every care upon the Lord. He promises to take care of you.

- Seek the goodness of the Lord in the events of the day.

- Wait on the Lord. Trust in Him and He will strengthen you.

Lord, help me to follow these instructions every day.

FEBRUARY 4

Morning Wisdom: Read Proverbs 7:1–5. I have a twin sister, and it is amazing how much we think alike and look alike. Solomon mentioned two sisters who also think alike. Their goal is to produce discretion and prudence in our lives. These two sisters are wisdom and understanding.

He exhorted his sons to say to wisdom, "'You are my sister,' And call understanding your nearest kin" (v. 4). If we will listen to these two sisters, we will be able to discern Satan's seductive tactics as he seeks to ensnare us.

Proverbs 7 includes the account of how the strange woman lures a foolish young man. As we look closely at this account, we will see the woman described is symbolic of Satan. Proverbs 7 opens our eyes to see both the character of the strange woman and the character of Satan. As we go through this chapter of Proverbs together, I will share some of Satan's major tactics. We will learn together how to guard ourselves against the assignments of seducing spirits to entice and lure us into sin.

Lord, teach me Your ways and also help me to learn the tactics of Satan so that I will not be ensnared.

Evening Watch: Read Psalm 28:1–9. When I was a young girl, we used to sing a song in church that I still love to sing—a song about how our hearts can ring with the melody of the Lord's love all day long. I cannot sing this song without entering into the joy of the Lord. This is why I like to sing it so often, because the joy of the Lord is my strength.

David the psalmist did not write this song, but he knew the power of singing songs of praise. He knew that as we sing songs of praise, our hearts will greatly rejoice.

Sometimes we experience slumps in our spiritual walk with the Lord when we succumb to anxiety, fear, and doubt. It is at these very times that we need to sing a lot. The melody of God's love can lift away any spirit of heaviness and can place us in a position of trusting the Lord once again. David said, "My heart trusted in Him, and I am helped" (v. 7). He declared that the Lord was his strength and his shield.

Tonight before you snuggle under your warm covers, snuggle into the position of safety that God's loving arms supply. He does have the whole world in His hands. His hands also are wrapped around you to supply you with His strength and to shield you from harm. Wow! I feel better already. How about you?

Lord, help me to keep a song in my heart all day long.

Morning Wisdom: Read Proverbs 7:6–23. We see Satan's character outlined clearly in these verses. Satan is like a woman with the attire of a harlot. The attire of a harlot is 100 percent fake, and everything about Satan is fake. He is the father of lies. He is subtle of heart, just like the seductress. The word *subtle* in Hebrew means "a man watcher." Satan and his demon agents are watching us constantly to observe our weak areas.

The word *subtle* means clever, crafty, wily, strangely suggestive, sly, hard to detect, intricate, insidious, keen, acute, and designing. *Subtle* certainly describes Satan's character.

The seductress was described as loud and rebellious (v. 11). Satan is the master of rebellion, and he seeks to seduce others to defy the authority of God. This verse also described the woman as restless. We know that Satan walks to and fro in the earth seeking to devour his prey. (See 1 Peter 5:8.)

Verse 12 mentioned the illusiveness of this woman. Satan is the master of illusion. He is the chief magician who loves to delude through illusions. He is able to make the real appear unreal and the unreal appear real.

Verse 13 described the impudent actions of this seductress. The Hebrew word *impudent* means strong, hard, and prevailing. Satan does not give up easily. The voice of the immoral woman was described as loud and pushy, and this certainly describes Satan's voice. Sometimes I feel like he is shouting in my ears.

In verse 14, the seductress offers peace offerings. Satan always offers a counterfeit peace. He usually offers the shortcut or the easy way out. Just like the evil woman, Satan is diligent (v. 15). He wears us down with his seducing thoughts.

Just as the woman enticed her victim through luring his five senses, Satan lures us through our five senses. Everything he offers us looks good, smells good, tastes good, feels good, and sounds good.

The woman convinced the young man to sin with her through her enticing speech. Satan skillfully uses words to place thoughts in our minds that will cause us to give in to his temptations. The seduction of this victim took place in the dark. Satan is the prince of darkness. He loves to allure in the night.

Lord, thank You for this picture of Satan. Help me to be on the alert.

Evening Watch: Read Psalm 29:1–11. This morning we learned about Satan's character. David described God's character and ways in this psalm. He described His voice as powerful and full of majesty, with the power to break trees into splinters, to divide fire, to shake the wilderness, and to strip the forest bare. David assured us that God is the only true peacemaker who blesses His people with peace. No matter how strong Satan may seem when he comes to tempt us, the Lord our God is stronger.

Lord, thank You for enabling me to overcome Satan with Your strength.

Exodus 23:14–25:40; Matthew 24:29–51; Psalm 30:1–12; Proverbs 7:24–27

Morning Wisdom: Read Proverbs 7:24–27. Solomon closed his description of the seductress with this warning, "Do not stray into her paths; For she has cast down many wounded, And all who were slain by her were strong men" (vv. 25–26). Whenever we depend upon our own strength to do battle against the devil, we will fail. Jesus Christ is Captain of the heavenly hosts, and He has given us the keys to the kingdom. Jesus said, "And I will give you the keys of the kingdom of heaven, and whatever you bind on earth will be bound in heaven, and whatever you loose on earth will be loosed in heaven" (Matt. 16:19).

There are three heavens. When we look at the blue sky or the nighttime sky filled with twinkling stars, we observe the first heaven. The atmosphere surrounding us is the second heaven. Satan is the prince and power of the air. If we had our eyes opened to discern spirits, we would see the demonic spirits who try to seduce us daily. The third heaven is where Paul visited. (See 2 Corinthians 12:2.) God dwells in the third heaven and Satan dwells in the second heaven. Whenever we bind demons on earth, we limit their activity. At the same time we need to loose ministering angels to come to our aid.

I pray a binding and loosing prayer every morning. You might want to join me as I pray this prayer:

> *Thank You, Father, that I am hidden in Christ in You and I am seated in Christ far above all the principalities, powers, rulers of darkness, and wickedness in heavenly places who would seek to destroy me and my family. From that position of authority, I bind in the blood of Jesus every spirit that cannot confess that Jesus Christ of Nazareth is God in the flesh. I cancel out their assignments against my family, [name each member], and I give them command in the name of Jesus to go make up the footstool of Jesus where Jesus will deal with them, and they will not return. I loose my family members and myself to the ministry of angels and the sevenfold anointing of the Holy Spirit. (See Isaiah 11:2.) I pray this all in the powerful name of Jesus Christ.*

Evening Watch: Read Psalm 30:1–12. This psalm declares two great promises. God promises to turn our weeping at night into joy when we awake, and He promises to turn our mourning into dancing. When we know without a doubt that Jesus has given us all power and authority over all the power of the devil, we can dance and rejoice. We may grieve over the loss of a loved one, but grieving is momentary. We know that death has been swallowed up in victory and the grave no longer has any sting. Praise the Lord!

> *Thank You for this day, Lord. I will rejoice and be glad in it!*

February 7

Morning Wisdom: Read Proverbs 8:1–10. Proverbs 16:32 says, "He who is slow to anger is better than the mighty, And he who rules his spirit than he who takes a city." The portion from Proverbs today compares the spirit to a great city. We are three-part beings: spirit, soul, and body. We are a spirit. We have a soul, and we live in a body. Our souls also are made of three parts—mind, emotions, and will.

Proverbs 8:3 reads: "She [wisdom] cries out by the gates, at the entry of the city." The three gates to the soul are the ear, eye, and mouth gate. Satan baits our five senses. He then tries to lure us by tempting us in the areas of our three lusts—the lust of the flesh (seeking to satisfy our five senses in an indulgent way), the lust of the eyes (greedy longing and imaginations in our minds), and the lust of the pride of life (trusting in ourselves and our own resources more than we trust in God).

Wisdom cries out at the gates of our city. If we walk in the wisdom of God, we will hear her warning cry when Satan tries to tempt us through our ear gate, eye gate, and mouth gate.

Every day of our lives we hear three voices: the voice of our flesh, the voice of God, and the voice of Satan. We also hear the voices of others who are often used to voice Satan's messages to us. Usually the first and loudest voice I hear daily is the voice of my own soul. My mind cries out, "I think." My emotions cry, "I feel." My will stubbornly speaks, "I want." The cries of my fleshly soul must be silenced so I can hear clearly the voice of wisdom. There is nothing crooked or perverse when wisdom speaks to us, but when Satan speaks to us his mouth is filled with wickedness.

Daily the wisdom of God that we glean from God's Word and from the instructions of His Holy Spirit will help us guard the gates to our souls. Nothing can compare to the wisdom from above that will keep us in peace, purity, and protection all day long. (See James 3:17.)

Lord, help me to listen to the voice of wisdom today.

Evening Watch: Read Psalm 31:1–8. We talked this morning about the voices we hear every day: the voice of our fleshly souls, the voice of God, and the voice of Satan. We also hear the voices of those we encounter daily. This psalm talks about how God longs to hear your voice every day. In fact, He bows down His ear to hear your praise and petitions.

When you awake tomorrow, He wants to hear you make the same declaration David did in this psalm. David declared, "You are my rock and my fortress…Lead me and guide me" (v. 3). David continually expressed his trust in the Lord. Wouldn't you love to hear such statements from your own children daily? I guess most of us would pass out if our children greeted us in the morning with a statement like this: "Daddy and Mom, I trust you and I want to do whatever you want me to do today." Our heavenly Father can't wait to hear such a declaration of obedience.

Father, I love and trust You, and I want to obey You.

Morning Wisdom: Read Proverbs 8:11–13. We learned in an earlier devotion that wisdom and understanding are sisters. (See Proverbs 7:4.) Wisdom has many relatives, and some more of them are listed in Proverbs 8:12: "I, wisdom, dwell with prudence, And find out knowledge and discretion."

Prudence, knowledge, and discretion are also closely akin to wisdom. A prudent person is capable of exercising sound judgment in practical matters. We exercise wisdom when we refuse to make important decisions without first consulting God's Word and hearing from a multitude of counselors.

The knowledge we gain through reading Scripture is not knowledge as the world knows it. It is the knowledge of the Holy One that leads us to fear the Lord (obey Him and honor Him). As we come to know more intimately the height, width, length, and depth of the love of Jesus Christ, we have the knowledge that even Satan will not be able to rob from us.

I have forgotten most of what I learned in college. I guess the knowledge I gained in college is still lodged somewhere deep in my brain. The knowledge of the love of Jesus, however, remains forever, because it is not head knowledge. It is heart knowledge.

Discretion is the ability to clearly separate what is evil from what is good. A discreet person is one who is very careful about what he says and does. Later in Proverbs we will see that a woman without discretion is compared to a pig with a jewel of gold in its snout. (See Proverbs 11:22.) Wisdom is far better than rubies and is not found where there is a lack of prudence, knowledge, and discretion.

Lord, help me to gain heart knowledge daily as I study Your Word.

Evening Watch: Read Psalm 31:9–18. Have you ever felt like nothing was going right in your life? Someone related a story to me about a man who got out of bed, banged his head on the bedpost, tripped on the floor on the way to the bathroom, flushed the toilet and it overflowed, cut himself while shaving, fell down the stairs on the way to the kitchen, ate soggy cereal after getting a call from someone who said his bank account was depleted, and opened the car door to discover that the car would not start. Throughout these trials, this weary man kept telling himself to cheer up.

David must have been having a day like this when he wrote: "My eye wastes away with grief…my life is spent with grief, And my years with sighing" (vv. 9–10). He felt forgotten like a dead man. However, David did not give up. Just after he confessed that he knew his enemies were scheming to take away his life, he said: "But as for me, I trust in You, O LORD; I say: 'You are my God.' My times are in Your hand" (vv. 14–15).

Lord, thank You for overcoming the world so that I can remain cheerful no matter what tribulation may come my way tomorrow.

Exodus 29:1–30:10; Matthew 26:14–46; Psalm 31:19–24; Proverbs 8:14–26

Morning Wisdom: Read Proverbs 8:14–26. We know that Jesus Christ is all wisdom. Listen to this verse: "But of Him you are in Christ Jesus, who became for us wisdom from God—and righteousness and sanctification and redemption" (1 Cor. 1:30).

Jesus is wisdom personified. As you read through Proverbs 8, you can replace the word *wisdom* with the name of Jesus. This portion of Proverbs 8 says "The LORD possessed me at the beginning of His way, Before His works of old" (v. 22). Jesus was with God in the beginning, and all the worlds were framed by Jesus, the living Word of God. I believe that anyone who truly seeks the wisdom that is from above will always find Jesus. When James exhorts us to ask God for wisdom, he is also exhorting us to ask God to reveal Jesus to us since He is all wisdom. (See James 1:5.)

I'll never forget riding in a taxi with a Muslim cab driver in Jerusalem. As soon as I got in the car I said to the driver, "You have been seeking wisdom about something." Then I told him that he needed to pray this prayer before he went to sleep: *God, if You are real and Jesus Christ is Your Son, reveal this to me tonight.* The next morning when I was walking on the streets of Jerusalem, I heard a horn honk. It was my friend, Nasar. He was so excited. He had prayed the prayer the night before and God did reveal Jesus to him. That night he received the wisdom he was looking for all of his life. It was also my birthday that day. What a birthday gift from God to see another soul born into His kingdom!

Thank You, Father, for Jesus, who is all wisdom to me.

Evening Watch: Read Psalm 31:19–24. One of my husband's lifelong dreams has been to place a gazebo in our backyard. We are blessed with beautiful dogwood and other deciduous trees on our back lot. Whenever I sit in a gazebo I experience a quiet, cozy feeling. As I gaze at the beauty of God's nature, somehow I feel safe from the storms of life. The birds' singing drown out all other sounds, and the distractions of mundane routines of life dissolve as the wind blows gently through the trees.

Most every person longs for a place of comfort, quiet, and beauty. The good news is that God has designed such a place for us and we can enter it daily. This psalm tells us that God has prepared a secret place, a pavilion far from the strife of tongues. He waits for us to enter His special gazebo every day. When we remain in His presence all during the day, we will experience His comfort, calm, joy, love, and peace. When we abide in His pavilion of love, nothing anyone says about us will offend or trouble us. Our hearts and minds will be focused on the beauty of the Lord, and nothing we see in this world that has been tainted by the devil will have the power to distract us from that holy view of Jesus. Whenever we abide in the pavilion of the presence of the Lord, He is able to strengthen our hearts, and we are filled with hope and confidence all day long.

Lord, help me to abide in Your pavilion tomorrow and every day.

Morning Wisdom: Read Proverbs 8:27–32. Wisdom was beside God as a master craftsman, and wisdom was the daily delight of God (v. 30). This verse reminds me of a passage in the Gospel of John. John wrote: "In the beginning was the Word, and the Word was with God, and the Word was God. He was in the beginning with God. All things were made through Him, and without Him nothing was made that was made" (John 1:1–3). Again we have the confirmation that Jesus is the wisdom spoken of in Proverbs 8.

The last verse in our passage reads: "Now therefore, listen to me, my children, For blessed are those who keep my ways" (v. 32). When we keep the ways of the Lord, we will be blessed. The only way we can begin to comprehend the ways of the Lord is to read the Bible daily. In the pages of this marvelous book we will find not only the ways of the Lord, but also the way we should live every day.

People are looking for answers these days, and they will find them in the Bible. Jesus is not only all wisdom, but He is also the answer to every problem. Turn whatever problems you are facing today over to Jesus. Philippians 4:6 tells us to "be anxious in nothing, but in everything by prayer and supplication, with thanksgiving, let your requests be made known to God." The word *supplicate* in Hebrew means "to transfer your burden." Today transfer every burden you may have to the Lord Jesus Christ, and He will have the wisdom needed to lead you throughout the day.

Thank You for leading me through this day.

Evening Watch: Read Psalm 32:1–11. We talked about turning our problems over to the Lord this morning. Sometimes problems flood our lives with such force that we fear we are going to drown in them. David experienced many times like this in his life. He expressed how he felt during those times when he said, "My vitality was turned into the drought of summer" (v. 4). Have you experienced days when you felt spiritually dry and physically drained of energy?

What do you do when those days come your way? David knew what to do on such days. The first thing he did was confess his own sins to the Lord. Often the problems we experience in this life are caused by our own willful sins. For example, we break the law by speeding and we get a ticket. We experience sleepless nights because we lie during the day about some of the things we have done. Our boss asks us if we have finished the project he assigned us. We respond, "Yes, I've finished it. I just haven't gotten it to your desk yet," when the truth is that we haven't even started working on the project. The moment we confess our own sins, God is faithful and just to forgive us and also to cleanse us of all unrighteousness. (See 1 John 1:9.) Confession clears the way for us to experience deliverance and peace. Confession causes our prayers to soar unhindered into God's throne room. Ask the Holy Spirit to reveal anything you may need to confess tonight before you retire.

Holy Spirit, search my heart and show me those sins I need to confess.

Exodus 32:1–33:23; Matthew 26:69–27:14; Psalm 33:1–11; Proverbs 8:33–36

Morning Wisdom: Read Proverbs 8:33–36. In the description of the tabernacle outlined in Exodus we learn the gates of the tabernacle were made of tapestry. The veil before the holy of holies was a huge tapestry curtain, intricately woven with threads of purple, gold, blue, and red.

Today's reading in Proverbs speaks about the gates that allow wisdom to enter our hearts and minds. I believe the names of these gates are instruction and obedience. Wisdom can only enter our lives if we are careful to obey the instructions God gave us in His Word.

We talked earlier about the three gates to our souls—the eye, ear, and mouth gates. We have the daily choice to open the gates of our souls either to the wisdom from above or the wisdom from below. (See James 3:13–18.) What we hear, see, smell, touch, and taste can honor God or bring us into bondage. Be careful today to open your gates to let the King of Glory come in with all of His wisdom.

Lord, help me to keep the gates of my soul open to Your wisdom.

Evening Watch: Read Psalm 33:1–11. The beautiful tapestries of God's tabernacle were mentioned in our morning devotional. The beauty of the tapestries in the tabernacle could not be seen until one entered the tabernacle. The outside of the tabernacle was covered with badgers' skins.

Our lives are like tapestries woven by God's hands. Sometimes our lives appear to us to be covered by badgers' skins. However, if we surrender our lives daily to the Lord, He can make something beautiful of our lives.

When my husband experienced the depths of a lengthy depression, I cried out to the Lord, *Do You know what we are going through?* Five minutes after I cried out this prayer of desperation, I received a call from a former prayer partner. She asked me, "Linda, is everything all right with you and Tom?" Then she said the Lord laid on her heart a verse of Scripture to give us. The verse was, "Therefore we do not lose heart. Even though our outward man is perishing, yet the inward man is being renewed day by day" (2 Cor. 4:16). David said, "Praise from the upright is beautiful" (v. 1). God has made us upright, because we believe we have been made righteous through the shed blood of Jesus on the cross. Because of the righteousness of Jesus within us, we can take heart and know that God is working something beautiful in and through our lives.

Thank You, Lord, for Your beauty that dwells within me.

February 12

Morning Wisdom: Read Proverbs 9:1–6. In my book *Around the Word in 365 Days,* I wrote a devotional on this passage in Proverbs. I shared that the seven pillars of wisdom represent the sevenfold anointing of God mentioned in Isaiah 11:2:

> The Spirit of the LORD shall rest upon Him, The Spirit of wisdom and understanding, The Spirit of counsel and might, The Spirit of knowledge and of the fear of the LORD.

The menorah described in Exodus symbolizes this sevenfold anointing of the Holy Spirit. The main branch of the menorah flares into six half-moon couplings of candles. The priests poured the oil into the main branch of the menorah, and that branch supplied the oil needed to light both the bowl of the main branch and the other six bowls of oil. The priest was instructed to put fresh oil in the golden candlestick daily.

The seven pillars of wisdom are the Spirit of the Lord, represented by the main stem that flares into the coupled branches of wisdom and understanding, counsel and might, knowledge and the fear of the Lord.

In Proverbs we learn that the fear of the Lord is the beginning of wisdom and knowledge. Daily I ask for this sevenfold anointing to operate in my life, because if I do not do this there will be days when I run out of oil. We all need a fresh filling of the Holy Spirit daily. When we do ask for this anointing, understanding and wisdom will be established in our lives. We will be able to receive the knowledge of holy things and the fear of the Lord will keep us on the right path. I know the seven pillars of wisdom will enable my body, spirit, and soul to remain strong in the Lord.

Lord, I ask for that sevenfold anointing of God today.

Evening Watch: Read Psalm 33:12–22. David wrote that God fashions our hearts individually, and He considers all our works. (See v. 15.) I am an identical twin. My sister and I have a lot of fun confusing people, which is easy to do since we look so much alike. God, however, can certainly tell the difference between us. He considers our works and knows our hearts.

My twin and I began to put our trust and hope in the Lord when we were nine years old. Even though we have had crisis times in our lives, we can both declare that our lives have been blessed because we have trusted in the Lord.

As we both enter our senior years, we have great hope for the future. We know the best is yet to come, because when we go on to be with the Lord we will be able to rejoice continually. Until that day, we have decided not to retire, but instead to be refired by the Holy Spirit. Our major goal is to accomplish every work God has designed for us to do while we are on Earth. Blessed are those who put their hope and trust in the Lord.

Lord, I trust You with all my tomorrows.

FEBRUARY 13

Morning Wisdom: Read Proverbs 9:7–8. Have you ever attempted to set someone straight? My efforts to do this have usually failed. I have come to the conclusion that most people will end up doing what they want to do. My prayer, of course, is that my friends and family will all do what God wants them to do, but this is not always the case.

There was a season when two of our sons went their own way. Our attempts to turn them from their worldly ways failed, but our prayers for them did not fail. When a person is in rebellion to God, it is difficult for anyone to tell them anything. They feel like they know everything already.

Most teenagers experience a season of rebellion. They may scoff at some of the things you believe in, but do not give up praying for them. The day will come when you will see the fruits of your prayers. That day came for us. Our two sons who went through this type of season returned to the Lord and are walking daily with Him. The Holy Spirit responded to our prayers and brought both sons to a place of repentance.

Even though we may be helpless in our efforts to convince our children not to participate in worldly activities that will bring harm to them, we have a wonderful helper, the Holy Spirit, who will be able to draw our children back on the right path. We have to remember that the persuasive power of the Holy Spirit is far greater than the seductive power of the enemy. Don't ever give up praying for your loved ones to walk in the ways of the Lord.

Lord, thank You for the persuasive power of the Holy Spirit.

Evening Watch: Read Psalm 34:1–10. I wrote a devotional on this psalm in my first book, *Around the Word in 365 Days*. In that devotional I listed eight ways we can position ourselves to receive the blessings of God. These eight ways are: have a grateful heart, brag on the Lord, make the Lord your top priority, seek the Lord and fellowship with Him daily, pray and cry out to the Lord when you are in trouble, fear the Lord by standing in awe of His goodness, and enjoy the Lord and trust in Him with all of your heart.

God is always pouring out His blessings upon this earth. Many people, however, never know His blessings, because they are idol worshipers or have the stronghold of pride in their lives. We visited India and saw the poverty and confusion that reigns there. The idolatry of that land has blocked its inhabitants from knowing God and receiving His blessings.

We also had the opportunity to visit Russia, where the people were under an atheistic government for seventy years. The root of Communism is pride, because people actually believed they could get along quite well without God. One visit to Russia disclosed how poorly the people of Russia did when they were under Communist leadership. We discovered that, although Russia was considered a world power, they were actually a third-world country.

Lord, I pray for the stronghold of pride and idolatry to be pulled down.

FEBRUARY 14

Morning Wisdom: Read Proverbs 9:9–10. Solomon wrote, "Give instruction to a wise man, and he will be still wiser; Teach a just man, and he will increase in learning" (v. 9). We fear the Lord when we have an obedient heart that honors God with our speech and actions. We fear the Lord when we stand in awe of His greatness and worship Him for who He is. Wise men fear the Lord and receive instruction.

We mentioned earlier this week about how the fear of the Lord is taught, not caught. We can do much as parents to set a godly example for our children. However, we must do more than just set the example. We must teach our children the Word of God. The Word of God contains the instructions that will empower our children to walk on the righteous path. David wrote, "Your Word I have hidden in my heart, That I might not sin against You" (Ps. 119:11).

One of the main ways we can help our children hide God's Word in their hearts is to have them memorize a verse in Proverbs every day. We can also read Bible stories to our younger children before they go to bed. There are all kinds of helps today such as videos, music tapes, Scripture cards, and other tools we can use to help imprint God's Word on the hearts of our children. The knowledge of the Holy One, Jesus, can only be discovered through reading Scripture. Today you might even consider giving your child a Valentine that includes some Scripture verses.

As a grandmother of nine young children, I stand amazed at the knowledge of the Word of God that these children have. Their parents are doing their job to teach their children to fear the Lord.

Lord, help me to teach many to fear the Lord.

Evening Watch: Read Psalm 34:11–22. Our Psalm reading begins with this invitation, "Come, you children, listen to me; I will teach you the fear of the LORD." This morning we learned many ways to teach our children the fear of the Lord, and this psalm includes even more ways. I will paraphrase in modern terms an instructive way we can talk with our children based on the verses in this psalm:

> Children, do you want to live a long life and love each day you live? Then stop speaking evil things and telling lies. Do good and seek peace. Children, do you want to be delivered out of all your troubles? Then you must pray and cast all your cares upon Jesus. Children, do you want all your sins and mistakes to be redeemed? Then give your sins and mistakes to the Lord. End of lesson. I learned something about how to fear the Lord. Did you?

Holy Spirit, teach me how to fear the Lord.

FEBRUARY 15

Morning Wisdom: Read Proverbs 9:11–12. Many years ago I did a study on the fear of the Lord. I listed all that was promised to those who fear the Lord, and the list was huge. One of the major things promised to those who fear the Lord is length of days. When we are wise and fear the Lord, we will also be wise about the way we treat our bodies.

My husband and I have made a resolution to eat healthy and exercise daily. We hope we will be able to live longer because of this discipline. However, we know that people who fear the Lord may suffer disease because of environmental influences or their lives might be cut short by an accident. At the same time, we have a responsibility to treat our temples well by not abusing them through overeating, drugs, or alcohol.

Verse 11 says that by wisdom our days will be multiplied and years of life will be added to us. When we begin to know Jesus Christ, the Holy One, more intimately, we will grow in both understanding and wisdom about how to live meaningful days. Moses wrote in Psalm 90, "Teach us to number our days, That we may gain a heart of wisdom" (Ps. 90:12). When we know our time on Earth is brief, we are challenged to live each day to the fullest. As we continue reading the wisdom found in Proverbs, we need to hear God's Word with our hearts, not just our ears. Our hearts will only be changed when we become doers of God's Word.

Lord, teach me to number my days and to daily apply Your wisdom.

Evening Watch: Read Psalm 35:1–16. This psalm is very special to me, because my husband and I prayed this psalm daily for our son when he was on drugs. The key to victory over the enemy in any situation is to declare the Word of God out loud over the situation or over relationships. David was crying out to God to be the One to do battle for him over his enemies. David knew that the battle is the Lord's, and the victory is ours.

The prayer we prayed based on Psalm 35 is in my book *Building a Family for God*. If you have something in your life that seems insurmountable or a relationship that needs restoration, put on the full armor of God and pray:

> *Father, in the name of Jesus Christ of Nazareth, I break the power of Satan over [name the person]. I speak to every principality and power and ruler of darkness and wickedness in high places that desires, designs, and devises hurt against [name the person] and me. I command these demonic forces in the name of Jesus and by the power of the blood of Jesus to be confounded, to be turned back away, and to be brought to confusion.*

Morning Wisdom: Read Proverbs 9:13–18. When we traveled to Zurich, Switzerland, our hotel was located near the train station. As I walked down the streets of that European city, I saw a demonstration of these few verses in Proverbs 9 displayed in living color. Window after picture window had women seated in seductive attire with their hands outstretched, beckoning simple men to come into their places of business to enjoy their company. In America I had often seen prostitutes waiting on street corners, but I had no idea that Europe offered the opportunity to window shop for prostitutes. Listen to these words in Proverbs 9:14–18:

> She sits at the door of her house, On a seat by the highest places of the city, To call to those who pass by, Who go straight on their way: "Whoever is simple, let him turn in here"; And as for him who lacks understanding, she says to him, "Stolen water is sweet, And bread eaten in secret is pleasant."

We live in a world where multitudes of men and women are simple-minded. They believe Satan's lies that stolen water is sweet and bread eaten in secret is pleasant. "Whoever commits adultery with a woman lacks understanding; He who does so destroys his own soul" (Prov. 6:32). Pornography is a form of adultery. Sex outside of marriage is fornication and idolatry. The price a person pays for giving in to Satan's seductive ways is death to the soul. Sexual sin is the only sin that is against our own bodies. (See 1 Corinthians 6:18.) It seems the world has gone sex crazy and many souls are dying because people believe Satan's lies.

Lord, I pray for those who have fallen prey to Satan's lies.

Evening Watch: Read Psalm 35:17–28. Last night we ended the evening with the warfare prayer found in Psalm 35.

This warfare prayer is a powerful tool against the enemy. The verses at the end of this psalm include the rest of this warfare prayer that can be used for any situation or relationship. Let's continue the prayer:

> *Father, in the name of Jesus Christ of Nazareth I command all darkness to flee. I ask You, Jesus, to assign angels to chase away the powers of darkness from [name the person]. May Satan's influence in this [relationship or situation] be destroyed and the influence of the Holy Spirit be magnified. I silence the whispers of Satan, and I ask You, Holy Spirit, to open the ears of those I know to hear God's Word. I declare that those I love will glorify Jesus Christ with their lives, extol Him with their mouths, and declare in word and deed His love to all.*

FEBRUARY 17

Leviticus 4:1–5:19; Mark 2:13–3:6; Psalm 36:1–12; Proverbs 10:1–2

Morning Wisdom: Read Proverbs 10:1–2. As I looked at the red eyes of my nineteen-year-old son, I knew he was on drugs. When he moved out of the house to live with his drug buddies, I was grieved, but I was comforted with this thought: "Now that he can be free to do what he pleases, he will find out that freedom is not much fun." Our verse today says, "A wise son makes a glad father, But a foolish son is the grief of his mother" (v. 1). I was grieved when I observed our son's foolish ways, but the Lord reminded me that our son was in His hands. I had given all of our sons to the Lord when they were very young.

When our youngest son was only a toddler, I was tormented for several weeks with the thought that I would die young and leave my children without a mother. Finally, one morning after another night of torment, I asked the Lord if He was preparing me to leave my children or if I was hearing the voice of Satan, who was trying to put fear in my heart. The Lord answered my questions with these two questions: "So what if you did die now and leave your young children? Do you trust Me to fulfill My plans for your children even if you are not on the scene?"

I realized I had not released my children to the Lord. I asked Jesus to forgive me, and I told Him I trusted Him to be the Author and Finisher of all three of our sons' faith. Our youngest son turned his heart back to the Lord when he was almost twenty-one, and he served as a missionary to Hungary for six years. When we release our children to the Lord, we may be grieved for a season as we observe their foolish ways, but God will ultimately accomplish His will in their lives.

Lord, help me to release all my loved ones to You.

Evening Watch: Read Psalm 36:1–12. I shared this morning how our youngest son did not operate in the fear of the Lord for a season of his life. This psalm shares what will happen to us if we do not abide in the fear of the Lord. The person who does not fear the Lord will manipulate through flattery, love evil, speak lies and evil things, and want nothing to do with God. Such a person has no idea of how great God is. (See vv. 1–4.)

God's greatness is also described in this psalm. David compared the righteousness of God to the great mountains and the judgments of God to the great deep. He said the loving-kindness of God was precious to him. Both the fountain of life and the light of life are found in God, who gladly shares all His light and life with all those who trust in Him. God always honors those who put their trust in the Lord. When we trust Jesus with not only our family members but also with every care, we will be overwhelmed by His loving-kindness. His loving-kindness is better than life itself, because His loving-kindness extends to every generation. Your walk in the fear of the Lord today will affect generations to come. Pray for those generations tonight before you retire.

Lord, let Your loving-kindess flow to our future family generations.

Leviticus 6:1–7:17; Mark 3:7–30; Psalm 37:1–11; Proverbs 10:3–4

Morning Wisdom: Read Proverbs 10:3–4. *Diligence* is one of the words most of us do not like to speak or read about. *Discipline* is a companion word to *diligence*, and both of these words usually carry with them a good amount of conviction. If we were honest, most of us would have to confess a lack of both diligence and discipline. Something in our souls craves to be free from the confinements that diligence and discipline demand of our lives. Yet the rewards of both diligence and discipline are great.

Proverbs 10:4 says, "He who has a slack hand becomes poor, But the hand of the diligent makes rich." Not all rich people earn their wealth by diligence and discipline. However, someone in their family probably had those two qualities. For example, my husband's mother was a saver. When she inherited her sister's money, we asked her what she would do with all that money. She declared, "I will save it, and maybe now I can afford to have my hair done once a week." My husband and I are now the recipients of the money she carefully saved, and that inheritance has enabled us to travel to many places that we could never have afforded otherwise.

Not everyone who is diligent is rich in material wealth. On our trips to Mexico we noticed many people who were both diligent and disciplined. Even though they were not able to gain material wealth, they were rich in the Spirit.

The best definition I heard for *prosperity* is "having enough to meet your own needs and to give to others." Even the poor Mexicans were disciplined in saving money to buy soft drinks for us when we came on mission trips. They were disciplined in their saving and giving to the Lord. We do not have to own much to give much. I'm reminded of the widow's mite that meant more to Jesus than a million dollars. (See Luke 12:59.)

Lord, help me to daily be diligent and disciplined.

Evening Watch: Read Psalm 37:1–11. The Mexicans I spoke of in this morning's devotional were richer than most Christians. They all seemed so meek and humble in spirit. David wrote in this psalm that the "meek shall inherit the earth" (v. 11). These poor people seemed so happy. Their life was simple and uncluttered with stuff. They did not have a lot to fret about, because they did not have a lot of material things. They had plenty of time to rest and wait upon the Lord, because they did not have to drive through traffic, make deadlines, and keep appointments.

Can we lead a simple life in the midst of all the demands a materialistic world places on our lives? I believe we can simplify our lives by just praying about everything.

When we pray, the mountains we may face in the workplace or in the family will become molehills. When we give our to-do list to the Lord in prayer each day, we will not fret if we do not accomplish all of our goals for the day. Start your simple life tonight by praying this prayer:

Lord, I give You my schedule for tomorrow. Change whatever You want to change and put me in the right place at the right time.

Leviticus 7:28–9:6; Mark 3:31–4:25; Psalm 37:12–28; Proverbs 10:5

Morning Wisdom: Read Proverbs 10:5. Just recently my husband and I have been sharing a special five-minute message called "Wake up, America" in churches all over America. In my talk I share with the congregation about an experience I had when my husband and I were visiting our son in China in 1990. We traveled thirty-six hours by train to Beijing. Shortly after settling down for the night in our sleeper car, I dreamed I was speaking to many churches in America. As I spoke, people were going to sleep. Some were even falling out of the pews on the carpet. Suddenly I stood on a chair and shouted at the top of my voice, "Wake up, America." They woke up, sat up straight, and began to read their Bibles.

For years I reflected on this dream, but I did not get the interpretation until two years ago when I read the book *The Heavenly Man*. This book was about a preacher in China who was terribly persecuted for his faith. After almost dying several times in prison, he finally escaped. He now lives in America and has the opportunity to visit many churches in America to share his message. At the end of the book, he said that many Christians in America are falling asleep during this great harvesttime. They are neglecting to read the Word of God, and they are ineffective witnesses for Jesus Christ. When I read his words, the dream I had in China came back to me, and I realized my mission was to awaken churches in America and challenge them to read through the Bible every year.

Today's passage states, "He who sleeps in harvest is a son who causes shame" (v. 5). We have all been called to be laborers in this last great harvest before the Lord returns. Don't fall asleep on the job!

> *Lord, help me to be faithful to read God's Word daily and to be a co-laborer with You in this last harvest.*

Evening Watch: Read Psalm 37:12–28. We shared this morning how we can cause shame if we fall asleep during this last great harvest. This psalm reveals how we will never have anything to be ashamed of in this life or when we are in heaven. David wrote, "The LORD knows the days of the upright, And their inheritance shall be forever. They shall not be ashamed in the evil time, And in the days of famine they shall be satisfied" (vv. 18–19).

We are living in evil times. However, as evil increases in the world, the Lord is gathering many souls to Himself. We need to be alert daily for opportunities to share the gospel with others. David wrote, "The steps of a good man are ordered by the LORD, And He delights in his way. Though he fall, he shall not be utterly cast down; For the LORD upholds him with His hand" (vv. 23–24). We do not have to fear falling during these evil days if we are daily feeding ourselves the Bread of Life—the Word of God. God protects, provides, and preserves the righteous even during these evil days.

> *Thank You for opening doors for me to witness to others tomorrow.*

FEBRUARY 20

Morning Wisdom: Read Proverbs 10:6–7. The church was packed. We listened to four different speakers share what our nephew, Sergeant Christopher Van Der Horn, meant to them. Speakers shared how Chris had invested time in them to help them along life's way. Chris was the first soldier killed in Iraq in 2006. When we leave this world, our riches, our travels, and our jobs will not be remembered. Only the relationships we have had with others will be remembered. We heard other friends share how Chris had helped them stay on the right path.

Proverbs 10:7 says, "The memory of the righteous is blessed, But the name of the wicked will rot." What we do and say daily will affect our rewards in heaven. Our conversations and actions also have the potential to daily bless people on Earth. We serve a relational God who sees every person as a worthy investment. All of our material wealth will one day rot, but people are eternal treasures. When we invest our time, talents, and money into people, we are blessing people on Earth and laying up for ourselves treasures in heaven.

Lord, help me to see every person I meet today as a treasure.

Evening Watch: Read Psalm 37:29–40. One of the verses my youngest son memorized when he was young is, "The law of his God is in his heart; None of his steps shall slide" (v. 31). Even though our youngest son experienced a season of backsliding, he came back to the Lord. God still was holding him in His hands and was ready to return him to the righteous path the very moment our son repented. God saw to it that the wicked did not destroy our son while he was in rebellion.

Our son, Ray, memorized scriptures, and the law of God was in his heart, even though his outward behavior did not display his true heart. He gave his heart to the Lord at a young age, and Jesus held his heart close to His heart even during those rebellious years. We experienced the promise David declared in this psalm. Because we trusted our son into the loving arms of Jesus, we received the promise that the Lord would help him and deliver him from the wicked. (See v. 40.)

Our nephew, Sergeant Van Der Horn, made it his goal to help people stay on the right path. After our son repented, he was able to give his testimony to young people, and he exhorted them to not veer off the right path. Whenever we warn the wicked and exhort the righteous to stay on the path God has chosen for them to follow, we make a deposit in our heavenly bank account. Both Chris and Ray made deposits in their heavenly bank accounts. Make it your prayer tonight to invest your time and yourself to help guide people to walk in the fear of the Lord.

Lord, help me to invest in people tomorrow. They are Your true riches.

Leviticus 11:1–12:8; Mark 5:21–43; Psalm 38:1–22; Proverbs 10:8–9

Morning Wisdom: Read Proverbs 10:8–9. Tom and I were leading a group of people to Washington, DC for a large prayer rally there. Our bus driver thought he knew where the hotel was, but he got hopelessly lost. We circled the city of Washington about five times before he finally decided to use his cell phone to call for directions. Once he had the correct directions, it only took us twenty minutes to arrive at our destination. Why our bus driver took so long to phone for directions was a mystery. However, I remembered one time when I was lost and was so confident that my directions were correct that I too kept following the same directions to no avail. When I stopped at a gas station, I learned that some of the street names had been changed. I soon discovered that the gas station was only two blocks away from my destination.

Today's verse says, "He who walks with integrity walks securely" (v. 9). Life is a journey, and the directions for living an abundant, fruitful life are found in the Bible. The Holy Spirit is the One who leads us in the way we should go. We can put our full confidence in the directions we find in the Bible and in the leading of the Holy Spirit, because the Bible is the Word of truth and the Holy Spirit is the Spirit of truth. When we walk in the Spirit and follow God's Word we will be walking with integrity.

Lord, thank You for directing me today and every day.

Evening Watch: Read Psalm 38:1–22. David usually rehearsed the times of victory, but in this psalm he rehearsed the negative things that were happening to him. The list was overwhelming. Here are some of the troubles he listed:

- God's hand seemed to be pressing him down.
- His flesh and bones suffered because of his sin.
- The wounds caused by his foolishness were fowl and festering.
- There was no soundness in his heart or in his flesh.
- His strength and eyesight were failing him.
- His loved ones and friends fled from him and his enemies sought his life.

If I were David I would shout out, "Stop the world! I want to get off!" However, after David poured out his complaint to the Lord, he made this amazing statement, "For in You, O LORD, I hope" (v. 15). When David declared that his hope was in the Lord, he placed the helmet of salvation firmly upon his mind, and even his emotions became anchored in that hope. He determined in his will to press forward with hope no matter what faced him in the future. David was a man after God's own heart, because he never gave up hoping in the Lord. No matter what you may face tomorrow, hope in the Lord.

Lord, I put my trust and hope in You.

FEBRUARY 22

Leviticus 13:1–59; Mark 6:1–29; Psalm 39:1–13; Proverbs 10:10

Morning Wisdom: Read Proverbs 10:10. A wink can mean many things. Some people wink to flirt with the opposite sex. On many occasions I have been talking with one person in the presence of a third person who winks at me while the conversation is in progress. That wink conveys that the third person does not trust or does not like what the person I am talking with has said. In most cases, winking is a way of signaling another person without saying a word. Whatever we are thinking at the time can be expressed by winking to another. This verse in Proverbs warns against winking and against prating. The verb *prating* in Hebrew means "speaking vain words that have no content."

Both the wink of an eye and the use of vain words can lead to trouble. Another verse reminds us that the person who keeps his lips will also keep his soul from troubles. (See Proverbs 21:23.) God does not have to see our winks or hear our words to know what is in our hearts.

Lord, forgive me for the times I have expressed myself in an unkind way, either through winking or talking too much.

Evening Watch: Read Psalm 39:1–13. We talked this morning about speaking vain words that have little relevance. David knew that his only hope of ordering his conversations aright was to ask the Lord to restrain his mouth with a muzzle. (See v. 1.) Dog muzzles are designed to keep them from barking and biting. David asked God to guard his ways so that he would not sin with his tongue. (See v. 1.) Later in this psalm David declared, "I was mute, I did not open my mouth, Because it was You who did it" (v. 9).

The only way we can control our tongues is to give the control of our tongues to the Lord. No man can tame the tongue. Only God, through the power of the Holy Spirit, can tame our tongues.

I have often wondered if mute people have less trouble than those who can speak. My theory is that they probably do have less troubles, because Proverbs 21:23 says, "Whoever guards his mouth and tongue Keeps his soul from troubles." If you ask God tonight to set a guard over your mouth and tongue, I believe you will have less trouble tomorrow. I can guarantee that your soul will not be troubled, no matter how troubling the day may seem. We bring trouble on ourselves when we use our mouths to criticize and judge others. We can see clearly that the troubles of the children of Israel were multiplied, because they murmured and complained. Pray this prayer tonight:

Lord, set a guard over my mouth and tongue. Let the meditations of my heart and the words of my mouth be acceptable in Your sight.

Morning Wisdom: Read Proverbs 10:11–12. Why is it so hard to love? My husband and I often ask this question after we counsel young married couples. A familiar saying is, "Love is blind." When couples first get married they often are blinded to the faults of their mate, but soon the blinders are removed. The couple begins to see all the failings of their mate, and all too often they begin to criticize and judge their mates. They fail to see their own sins, because they are too busy pointing their fingers at their mate.

The Bible tells us that healing comes when we confess our sins to one another and pray for one another. (See James 5:16.) When couples become judgmental and critical of one another, their love for one another begins to decrease. If they are not careful, they soon will find themselves in strife, because as our reading says, "Hatred stirs up strife" (v. 12). This couple would never admit they hated one another, but their conversations will soon reveal this hatred. Our reading today also says, "The mouth of the righteous is a well of life, But violence covers the mouth of the wicked" (v. 11).

Honesty usually comes in a marriage when the couple is able to admit the times when they resented and even hated their mate. When they come to this place of honesty, they are on the way to a healed marriage. I asked a friend once if she ever thought about leaving her husband. She replied, "Of course not, but I have thought about killing him."

Let's be honest, we have all had our moments. The only way to get strife out of a marriage is to individually ask God to show us our own sins. Then we need to confess our sins to one another and ask our partner for forgiveness. We will continue to be able to keep strife out of our marriages if we will daily ask the Holy Spirit to pour the love of God for our mate into our hearts. (See Romans 5:5.) When we see one another with the eyes of Jesus, His love will shine through us and will cover our own sins and the sins of our mates.

Lord, give me Your eyes of love to see others as You see them.

Evening Watch: Read Psalm 40:1–10. This morning we asked why it is so hard for people to love one another. This psalm lists several reasons why it is hard to love others. Before we can love others we must learn to trust and love God. When we know, understand, and receive the love of Jesus Christ into our hearts, the Holy Spirit is on duty to see to it that God's love fills our hearts to the point that our major motivation in life is to share the love of Jesus Christ with others. The person who is forgiven much can love much.

David was forgiven much in his life. When his restoration came, after he repented from adultery and murder, God put a new song in his mouth. God set him on a rock and delivered him out of the horrible pit and miry clay of sin. God does not require any sacrifice from you to earn His love. He loves you just the way you are, and He desires you to offer your body as a living sacrifice to Him.

Lord, I give You my heart, my body, and my soul.

Morning Wisdom: Read Proverbs 10:13–14. Have you ever had diarrhea of the mouth? I know I have on many occasions. I start running off at the mouth, and soon my words are polluting others. The verses today tell us that an understanding person will speak words of wisdom and that wise people store up knowledge. When we say foolish things with our mouths, we can cause destruction to ourselves and to others.

How can we get out of the cycle of hurting others by what we say? How can we cooperate with the Holy Spirit as He tries to tame our unruly tongues? We lack understanding when we have failed to store up knowledge. The knowledge spoken of in these verses is not head knowledge. It is the heart knowledge only gained through having an intimate relationship with Jesus Christ. Jesus told us that the words we speak come from what is in our hearts. (See Matthew 12:34.)

We enter an intimate relationship with Jesus Christ when we take time to spend in God's Word. The Word of God is the rod of correction that will help us gain the knowledge and understanding to speak wise words. The beginning of wisdom is understanding and knowledge of the fear of the Lord. Our tongues will only speak what we have stored in the computer of our minds. When our hearts are imprinted with the Word of God, the printout of the pages of our lives will be filled with wise words and wise actions.

Lord, help me to store up the knowledge of Your Word.

Evening Watch: Read Psalm 40:11–17. David had his moments of despondency and despair, but he did not camp out there. David was a man after God's own heart because he was honest with God. He expressed his deepest feelings to God. People go to counselors because most counselors provide a platform for people to reveal their deepest emotions and feelings. Too often, we are not able to express how we feel to those we love, because we fear they may discount our feelings by saying, "Oh get over it!"

David, however, knew he could freely express his anger, resentment, fears, and a multitude of other feelings to God. His outlet was to write songs that expressed his innermost thoughts to God.

God knows our feelings, but He wants us to freely express those feelings to Him for our sake, not for His. He knows that when we lay all of our feelings on the table, we can then enjoy the table He has prepared for us. The table God prepares for us is a table filled with the fruit of love with all of its manifestations. When we feed on what the Lord has prepared for us, we will not want to feed our fleshly lusts.

David wrote that he was poor and needy, yet he knew that the Lord thought upon him. David exhorted us all to seek the Lord and to rejoice and be thankful for His salvation. The Lord will be magnified when we admit our own feelings and lay them before Him.

Lord, magnify Yourself in my life tomorrow and every day.

Leviticus 16:29–18:30; Mark 7:24–8:9; Psalm 41:1–13; Proverbs 10:15–16

Morning Wisdom: Read Proverbs 10:15–16. Proverbs 10:16 says, "The labor of the righteous leads to life, The wages of the wicked to sin." Almost every day we hear of another corporation that was guilty of corrupt practices. Many top executives have faced jail sentences because of their unethical business practices. Greed was the engine that ran these corporations, and many received the wages of their wickedness.

Riches gained through greed eventually will cause destruction. However, the rich man who gains wealth honestly can strengthen even a city. In my city, I have observed many wealthy men contribute millions to improve our art centers, stadiums, parks, and city buildings.

Proverbs 10:15 says, "The destruction of the poor is their poverty." We have had the privilege of visiting many third-world countries where the poor are destroyed because of poor sanitation and living conditions. When we were in India we prayed for many who were sick, but our hearts were heavy for them since we knew they would return to their squalid living quarters. Those who are rich both monetarily and spiritually have a responsibility to save the poor from destruction. God has promised that whenever we invest in the poor we are lending to Him. (See Proverbs 19:17.) I am challenged by the words of our verses today to give more to the poor and to make sure that I am never motivated by greed.

Lord, forgive me for the times I have neglected the poor.

Evening Watch: Read Psalm 41:1–13. We learned this morning how important it is for us to share our wealth with the poor. The first verses of this psalm read: "Blessed is he who considers the poor; The LORD will deliver him in time of trouble. The LORD will preserve him and keep him alive, And he will be blessed on the earth" (vv. 1–2). This psalm continues to declare what God promises to do for those who extend their hands to the poor. God even promises to deliver us from the sickbed if we have a generous heart and give to the poor.

A man who gives to the poor is a man of integrity. I believe David was able to triumph over his enemies because he generously gave to the poor. You may not live in an area where you see many poor people, but you can always minister to the poor in the inner city and in other countries by sending monies to ministries that feed and clothe the poor. We all have the opportunity daily to give to those who are poor spiritually. There are multitudes of hungry and thirsty people who are just waiting for someone to feed them with God's Word. Their thirst can only be quenched by the Holy Spirit, who desperately desires us to share His anointing with others. Jesus told His disciples that we would always have the poor with us. Tomorrow let it be your goal to reach out to the poor. They are all around you.

Lord, help me to be alert to see those who are in need. May I meet their needs by supplying them with Your riches.

FEBRUARY 26

Morning Wisdom: Read Proverbs 10:17. I'm praying with someone now who has a rebellious teenager. The mother shared with me that whenever she instructs her daughter, her daughter becomes angry. So many parents who have nurtured their children and taught them the ways of the Lord find themselves in this predicament when their children reach the teen years.

It seems like something dramatic happens in the souls of teenagers that launch them into a period of rebellion. I believe that Satan uses those years to try to seduce our children to go the ways of the world. Sadly he often is successful in this tactic. The fiercest attack upon the souls of people, I believe, comes between the ages of sixteen and twenty-one.

Scientists now have the capability of looking into the brain, and they have discovered that the emotional part of the brain is not fully developed until young people reach twenty-one or older. Their ability to discern the difference between reality and fantasy is not developed, and this is why so many teenagers think they are invincible.

Proverbs 10:17 says, "He who keeps instruction is in the way of life, But he who refuses correction goes astray." We had two sons who went astray during their teen years, but they returned to the Lord. During those teen years, we prayed continually that the Lord would protect our children when they did exactly the opposite of our instructions. Those prayers paid off, because these two boys usually were caught when they did something we told them not to do. Both of these sons are teaching their own children now to obey their parents. When children honor their parents and obey their instructions, they are promised a long life. (See Exodus 20:12.)

Lord, help parents to persevere in prayer for their teenagers.

Evening Watch: Read Psalm 42:1–11. The psalmist speaks to his soul in this psalm. He says, "Why are you cast down, O my soul? And why are you disquieted within me? Hope in God, for I shall yet praise Him For the help of His countenance" (v. 5).

Self-talk is being taught in seminars today. The idea is that you can gain confidence and be more fruitful in your life if you simply keep speaking positive affirmations to yourself. No self-talk will truly change our lives unless we put our hope in the Lord and not ourselves. The psalmist put his hope in the Lord, and then he remembered God's loving-kindness in the daytime, and he sang to the Lord at night.

Self-talk is transformed into soul talk when we daily lift our souls up to the Lord. The Holy Spirit has the assignment to transform our souls (minds, emotions, and wills). He can only fulfill this assignment if we are willing to renew our minds by reading and hiding God's Word in our hearts. The Holy Spirit wants to anchor our emotions in the hope of the Lord, but He can only do this when we lift our souls up to Him. The Holy Spirit will be able to conform our wills to God's will when we are willing to listen and obey God's Word.

Holy Spirit, transform my soul.

Morning Wisdom: Read Proverbs 10:18. The Hebrew meaning of the name *Satan* is "slanderer." Jesus called Satan the father of lies. (See John 8:44.) Satan daily accuses us before the throne of God. He is called the accuser of the brethren. (See Revelation 12:10.) We do have the promise that one day Satan will be cast out, but until that time he continues to use the tongues of even saints to bring railing accusations against one another. Whenever we give a bad report about someone, whether it is true or not, we are gossiping. None of us know the whole story about why people act the way they do, so we should be careful to let people tell their own stories.

Proverbs 10:18 says, "Whoever hides hatred has lying lips, And whoever spreads slander is a fool." If we have hatred in our hearts, we usually lie to cover up our hatred. Jesus said that we could not truly love Him if we hated someone. Satan uses slander and gossip to wound others, but when we harbor unforgiveness, bitterness, and resentment, which are the fruits of hatred, we are the ones who will be wounded. My constant prayer is that I will not allow Satan to speak his words of slander and gossip through me.

Lord, forgive me for the times I have told other people's stories.

Evening Watch: Read Psalm 43:1–5. We learned this morning that the name *Satan* means slanderer. Satan loves to pass on lies about us. One of his favorite things to do is to pass on lies about God to us. He loves to besmirch God's character.

How can we silence the lies of the enemy? This psalm reveals the secret. Even when our souls are cast down, we need to praise the Lord. This drives the devil crazy. If you will begin to praise the Lord the moment you are attacked with depression or oppression, the devil will flee. Praise is the devil's death knell.

We all need to make the decision to praise God no matter what. When my nephew was killed in Iraq, I exhorted my sister to praise God seven times a day. The garment of praise is given to us by the Lord to lift the Spirit of heaviness. (See Isaiah 61:3.) What good is that garment to us if we refuse to put it on daily?

Do you want to torment the devil tomorrow? Then praise God out loud throughout the day and your soul will be lifted out of the depths. The devil's plans to keep you depressed and oppressed will be spoiled.

Lord, may my lips praise You all day long.

February 28

Leviticus 22:21–23:44; Mark 9:30–10:12; Psalm 44:1–7; Proverbs 10:19

Morning Wisdom: Read Proverbs 10:19. In an earlier devotional this month I talked about having "diarrhea of the mouth." (See February 24.) Whenever we talk too much we run the risk of wounding others by what we say. The verse today says, "In the multitude of words sin is not lacking, But he who restrains his lips is wise." Our tongues are like red carpets rolled out to receive either the King of Glory or the prince of darkness (the devil). The red carpet of our tongues can welcome either grace-filled words or strife-filled words. Imagine that your tongue is like a red seesaw. Two little demons sit on each end of your tongue. They wait patiently for you to start rapidly flapping your tongue and then they enjoy the ride. Picture these little demons laughing and flying wildly in the air as your tongue moves up and down. That picture will help you to resist being a motormouth.

David made a covenant with his mouth not to speak evil when he wrote:

> I have purposed that my mouth shall not transgress. Concerning the works of men, By the word of Your lips, I have kept away from the paths of the destroyer. Uphold my steps in Your paths, That my footsteps may not slip.
>
> —Psalm 17:3–5

When we use our tongues to speak the Word of God against Satan, we will keep ourselves from the path of the destroyer. I am convicted that I need to purpose daily not to sin with my tongue. Join me in this prayer:

> *Lord, let the words of my mouth and the meditations of my heart be acceptable in Your sight today.*

Evening Watch: Read Psalm 44:1–7. Psalm 44:5 says, "Through You we will push down our enemies; Through Your name we will trample those who rise up against us." We need to put our trust in the Lord to save us when our enemies come against us. As stated earlier, we have three enemies—the devil, the flesh, and the world. When we stand in our own righteousness instead of God's righteousness purchased for us by Jesus Christ, we will never be able to defeat the devil. The old saying, "God helps those who helps themselves," is not in the Bible. A true saying is, "The devil always defeats those who help themselves." Determination to break fleshly habits will not work unless we call upon the help of the Lord.

> *Lord, give me Your strength to break sinful habits and to pull down strongholds in my life.*

Leviticus 24:1–25:46; Mark 10:13–31; Psalm 44:8–26; Proverbs 10:20–21

Morning Wisdom: Read Proverbs 10:20–21. "He is a silver-tongued orator" is an expression used to describe speakers who are gifted in both the delivery and content of their speeches. Throughout history there have been many silver-tongued orators. Top on my list would be Abraham Lincoln. He had a way with words that conveyed not only his message but also his heart.

The passage of scripture for today compares the tongue of the righteous to choice silver. Many years ago I did a study on the tongue of the righteous and the tongue of the wicked. I discovered that people who allow the righteousness of Jesus Christ to shine through them are very careful about their speech. They do not talk about evil things, and they do not speak evil of others.

Those who commit themselves to Jesus have a great responsibility to use their words to feed others. Verse 21 of our reading says, "The lips of the righteous feed many." Before we can feed others we must feed ourselves by both meditating on and studying God's Word. Then we need to ask the Holy Spirit to help us whenever we teach others the Word of God. The Holy Spirit knows how to measure out the food of God's Word. He knows that some people will get spiritual indigestion if they are fed too much of God's Word in one sitting. One of my favorite parables is the parable of the faithful and wise servant who ruled his master's household well and gave his household food in due season. That servant will be blessed when the Lord returns and finds him giving food to his household. (See Matt. 24:45–46.) My prayer is that I will be like that servant.

Lord, help me to daily feed on Your Word.

Evening Watch: Read Psalm 44:8–26. Have you ever felt like God let you down or that He simply does not care? After such tragedies as the Holocaust, 9/11, and the tsunami, many have asked this question: "Where was God when these things happened?" The writers of this psalm were asking the same question. This psalm is a contemplation of the sons of Korah, but I think it is more appropriately the complaint of the sons of Korah. The sons of Korah were descendents of Korah who led two hundred fifty leaders to rebel against Moses and Aaron. Korah wanted to lead the people instead of Moses and Aaron. Judgment fell upon those who complained and rebelled, and they were swallowed alive by the first earthquake.

In this psalm the sons of Korah complained that they had been faithful to keep God's covenant and to praise Him continually, but they were scattered as sheep without a shepherd. It is human nature to feel like God has abandoned us when things go wrong in our lives. However, the truth is that Jesus promised never to forsake us. (See Matthew 28:20.) Jesus also made another promise when He said, "In the world you will have tribulation; but be of good cheer, I have overcome the world" (John 16:33). We serve a sovereign God who sees all and knows all. He will walk with us through the fire and through the flood. We must believe this.

Lord, help me never to doubt Your goodness.

MARCH 2

Morning Wisdom: Read Proverbs 10:22. We used to sing a song called, "Count Your Blessings." The words went something like this: "Count your blessings. Name them one by one. Count your many blessings. See what God has done."

Most of my Christian life I have kept a journal of daily activities. Just this year I was inspired by a friend to write down five ways God blessed me throughout the day. I was amazed by the many blessings showered upon me daily when I reviewed my days. Even a small thing like someone opening the door for me in a busy shopping center was a blessing.

I heard someone say that if he could not think of one thing to thank God for during the day, he could always thank God for giving him fluid in his eyeballs. We can all find something to thank God for daily, because as this verse says, "The blessing of the LORD makes one rich, And He adds no sorrow with it."

As we discussed yesterday, we all experience sorrowful times in our lives, because we live in a world that is in the process of dying. However, if we commit every day to the Lord, the blessings of the Lord will far outweigh those sorrowful times. This morning commit the day into the hands of the Lord and be on the lookout for His blessings all day long.

Lord, I look forward to counting my blessings today.

Evening Watch: Read Psalm 45:1–17. The Lord uses us all to do His work on Earth. In Isaiah 61 the ministry of Jesus is described. Jesus came to preach good tidings to the poor, to heal the brokenhearted, and to proclaim liberty to the captives and the opening of the prison to those who are bound. (See Isaiah 61:1–2.) It has been my privilege to pray for Jesus to heal many brokenhearted people.

Brokenhearted people have a poor image of themselves, because they have experienced so much rejection in their lives. As I pray for brokenhearted people, I paraphrase verses 10–15 in this psalm to help them realize how important they are to God. You may want to use this prayer below to pray for those you know who have experienced a lot of rejection:

> *King Jesus sees you as beautiful, and He greatly desires Your beauty. He sees you in robes of many colors, and He rejoices every time He sees you. Jesus loves everything about you, and He looks forward to the time you spend with Him daily. His glory shines through you.*

When brokenhearted people catch a glimpse of how God sees them through the eyes of Jesus, they will begin the process of having their hearts completely healed.

Lord, thank You for healing the brokenhearted.

Morning Wisdom: Read Proverbs 10:23. This verse could be summarized by this statement, "The sport of fools is to do evil, and the sport of the wise is to gain understanding." Psalm 14:1 says, "The fool has said in his heart, 'There is no God.'" Those who do evil believe that their actions will not be judged, because they believe there is no God. Evil men take no thought for the consequences of their evil ways.

Throughout history people have been interested in various sports. There is only one sport God is interested in, and that sport is gaining understanding through the reading of His Word. Sports heroes know the more they practice and play the game, the better they become at the sport. The more we read and ask the Holy Spirit to interpret Scripture to us, the more we will become experts at the sport of gaining understanding.

The game of life can only be understood by one who has studied God's Word. God's Word is the breakfast of spiritual champions.

Lord, help me to be a diligent student of Your Word.

Evening Watch: Read Psalm 46:1–11. We spoke this morning about gaining understanding about life through reading God's Word. This psalm tells us how we can have a peaceful life in the midst of great turmoil. Psalm 46 declares that God is our refuge and strength. He is our help in times of trouble. My husband reads the *Wall Street Journal* every morning before breakfast. The pages of this newspaper capsule the troubled economy, the troubled weather, the troubled politics, and the troubled wars. I'm surprised that my husband doesn't cry out, "Help, Lord!" after reading just a few pages of this newspaper.

If my husband only read the pages of the *Wall Street Journal*, he probably would not want to leave the house for fear that some trouble would immediately assail him. When he turns from the pages of the *Wall Street Journal* to read a portion of God's Word, however, hope begins to anchor his emotions and peace begins to flood his mind.

We do live in troubled times, but we do not have to fear anything that is going on in this world if we have a heavenly view. This psalm makes a graceful leap from Earth to heaven. Verses 1–3 describe an earth filled with turmoil where waters are roaring and mountains are being cast into the sea. Verses 4–7 describe the peaceful scene of the river of life that flows from the holy tabernacle of God. Verse 7 declares, "The LORD of hosts is with us; The God of Jacob is our refuge."

Jesus told His disciples about the troubled times that would come just before He returned to Earth. He told them, "Now when these things begin to happen, look up and lift up your heads, because your redemption draws near" (Luke 21:28). When we read the pages of God's Word, we will know "the rest of the story." When we know the end from the beginning, as recorded in God's Word, we will maintain a heavenly view.

Lord, help me to set my affections on the things that are above.

Numbers 2:1–3:5; Mark 11:27–12:17; Psalm 47:1–9; Proverbs 10:24–25

Morning Wisdom: Read Proverbs 10:24–25. A great promise is found in verse 24. God promises to grant the desires of the righteous. When we are walking in righteousness, our desires will be planted in our hearts by God. What God plants, He grants. When we turn our hearts completely over to God, He then begins to work within us both to will and to do of His good pleasure. (See Philippians 2:13.) Our own desires begin to match up with God's desires.

A good way to find out if we are walking in righteousness is to take an inventory of our desires. If you made a list of five things you desire right now, what would be on the top of your list? When we are walking in the Spirit, our greatest desire is to please God. We desire to be successful in God's sight.

Below is a list of ten things that God desires from us. During this week you may want to ask God to reveal the desires He has for your life. We are successful in God's sight when we begin to fulfill some of the desires He has for us. We are successful in God's sight when we:

- do justly, love mercy, and walk humbly with God (Mic. 6:8);
- keep His commandments (John 15:17);
- abide in Him (John 15:4);
- abide in His Word (John 15:7);
- walk in the Spirit instead of in the flesh (Gal. 5:16);
- glorify Him in word and deed (Rom. 15:18);
- submit to Him and resist the devil (James 4:7);
- draw near to Him (James 4:8);
- cast every care upon Him (Matt. 11:28–30);
- pray continually (Phil. 4:6–7).

Lord, help me to be successful today in Your sight.

Evening Watch: Read Psalm 47:1–9. When teenagers experience something good, they often exclaim, "That's awesome." The word *awe* in Hebrew means "to quiver or quake with the emotion of fear." This psalm says, "For the LORD Most High is awesome; He is a great King over all the earth" (v. 2). When God revealed Himself on Mt. Sinai, the children of Israel stood in awe. They were afraid when they heard His voice and asked Moses to speak for God, because God's voice was frightening to them.

The good news is that God is still as awesome as He was on Mt. Sinai, but now we have the Holy Spirit to channel His greatness into our lives so that we do not have to be terrified of God any longer. We only need to respect, honor, and obey Him.

Holy Spirit, thank You for transmitting God's greatness to me.

MARCH 5

Morning Wisdom: Read Proverbs 10:26. Every morning I refresh my face with cider vinegar before I put on my makeup. I have to be careful that the vinegar does not get near my eyes, because my eyes would sting and burn. In the past I used cider vinegar to aid my digestion. Every morning I drank one tablespoon of cider vinegar in a glass of purified water. I did this right after I brushed my teeth. I learned quickly that cider vinegar is great for digestion, but it is not so great for your teeth. The acid in vinegar can cause damage to the enamel of teeth.

The proverb today says that a lazy man sent to do a job is like vinegar to the teeth and smoke to the eyes of those who send him. When smoke gets in my eyes, my eyes water, burn, and temporarily blind me.

Whatever job a lazy man is sent to do will not get done. That lazy man may put up a smoke screen and tell you how great he is, but when he gets on the job you soon find out that you have been burned and blinded.

Proverbs has a lot to say about lazy people, but the message of this proverb is to warn employers about hiring lazy people. Employers need to ask for the wisdom of God before they hire anyone. They also need to ask for clear discernment and for the Lord to reveal anything that the prospective employee might be trying to hide. If you are an employer, you might want to pray this prayer before you hire someone for a job.

> *Lord, I ask for Your wisdom as I look at this resumé and interview this person. Reveal to me the truth about this person and give me clear discernment to determine whether to hire this person or not.*

Evening Watch: Read Psalm 48:1–14. We sang a chorus in our church that included verses 1 and 2 of this psalm (KJV):

> Great is the LORD, and greatly to be praised in the city of our God, in the mountain of his holiness. Beautiful for situation, the joy of the whole earth, is mount Zion, on the sides of the north, the city of the great King.

Truly God is beautiful for every situation we may face in life.

This psalm tells us about the position God has. The city He dwells in is a "forever city." This "forever city" is called Zion. We can look forward to living in this "forever city" where we will dance and rejoice before the Lord forever. Until that time we can be confident that God is our God forever and ever, and He will be our guide even to death. This makes me want to shout, "Hallelujah!"

> *Lord, thank You for being my eternal guide while I am on Earth.*

MARCH 6

Morning Wisdom: Read Proverbs 10:27–28. Two things in this life will preserve and prolong our days here on Earth. Those two things are mentioned in these verses of Proverbs. The fear of the Lord will prolong our days and hope will preserve us, because our souls will be anchored in the Lord.

We fear the Lord when we honor and reverence God with an obedient, faithful heart. God looks at our hearts, and He alone knows when we serve Him begrudgingly or willingly. We are commanded to love the Lord God with all of our hearts. We are also commanded to honor our fathers and mothers so that our days may be long on this earth. (See Exodus 20:12.) When we honor God, our heavenly Father, we are promised long days.

Our souls will be preserved for eternity when we daily walk in faith. Faith is the substance of things hoped for and the evidence of things not seen. (See Hebrews 11:1.) When we hope in the Lord and His Word, our souls will be preserved by the Lord, even in the troubled, stormy times of life. The soul of man includes three parts—the mind, the emotions, and the will. When we fear the Lord and hope in Jesus, the peace of God that passes all understanding will mount guard over our hearts and our minds. Our emotions also will be anchored, and we will be able to have the joy of the Lord no matter what our circumstances are.

We often hear it said, "Don't get your hopes up!" However, we must always keep our hopes up in the Lord, and when we do we will be strengthened by the joy of the Lord. The expectations of the righteous will make them glad, but the expectations of the wicked will perish. (See Proverbs 10:28.)

Lord, I put all my expectations in you today.

Evening Watch: Read Psalm 49:1–20. The psalmist asked this question, "Why should I fear in the days of evil?" (v. 5). We learned in our reading this morning that when we fear the Lord, we do not have to fear those things that occur in this world. Jesus exhorted His disciples to look heavenward when the turmoil of these end times reaches cataclysmic proportions.

The psalmist compared the thoughts of a foolish man with the thoughts of a wise man. Foolish men think they will live forever and that even their houses will last forever. They name their lands after themselves, but even the names of these lands will vanish eventually. They will be renamed by other proud, foolish men who want their name to be remembered for generations to come. They forget that they have an appointment with death.

We all have our appointment with death. That appointment date and time is written in the Book of Life in heaven. However, we can shorten our days if we are unwise. The psalmist was wise and knew that one day his soul would be redeemed from the grave. When we trust in our Redeemer, we do not even need to fear death.

Lord, help me to keep my eyes on my Redeemer.

MARCH 7

Morning Wisdom: Read Proverbs 10:29–30. These verses in Proverbs continue to compare the way of the righteous with the way of the wicked. Yesterday we learned that the expectations and hope of the righteous will be gladness, but the expectation of the wicked will perish.

The promises for the righteous in this reading are magnificent. Those who walk uprightly are promised strength and eternal endurance. The statement is made, "the righteous will never be removed" (v. 30). The wicked, however, will not inherit the earth. We have God's promise that the day will come when there will be new heavens and a new earth. We will enjoy living in our resurrected bodies when that day comes. The wicked will no longer be with us. We can look forward to that day when we will inhabit the New Jerusalem. Until that day we are challenged to walk every day in a righteous way.

Lord, may my words and actions today be righteous in Your sight.

Evening Watch: Read Psalm 50:1–23. Psalm 50:4 says, "He shall call to the heavens from above, And to the earth, that He may judge His people." Judgment Day is coming. The Bible is clear about this. Hebrews 9:27 tells us that it is appointed once for man to die and then comes the judgment. This morning we talked about that glorious day when there will be new heavens and a new earth. We all look forward to that day, but there will also be a Judgment Day. Christians do not have to fear the judgments that await them. True believers are not appointed to God's wrath. God will mete our judgments to give us rewards, not punishment. Our deeds and words, however, will be judged. Our words and deeds are recorded in heaven.

Nothing ever passes God's view. He sees everything on this earth, and He humbles Himself even to look into our hearts. God also owns everything. He even owns the cattle on the hills.

What can we sacrifice to a God who owns all and knows all? How can we please Him? This psalm gives the answer to these questions. God is pleased when we daily offer Him the sacrifices of our thanksgiving, worship, and praise. We are also called to offer our bodies to Him as a living sacrifice. When we do this our conduct and conversations will be pleasing to God and our eternal rewards will be great.

Lord, I offer my body to You as a living sacrifice. I offer the members of my body as instruments of righteousness, peace, joy, and love. I offer my tongue to speak of Your glory, my lips to give you praise, my eyes to see others as You see them, my hands to help others, and my feet to walk in Your ways.

MARCH 8

Morning Wisdom: Read Proverbs 10:31–32. One of my prayers every morning is, *Let the words of my mouth and the meditations of my heart be acceptable to You, my Strength and my Redeemer.*

Speaking what is acceptable to the Lord is a real challenge. So often we want to speak in haste, and if we give in to that temptation, we will usually wound the hearer. What are the acceptable words to the Lord? In Philippians 4:8 Paul gave a list of the things we should think about. This list also can be used as a "talk test" as well as a "think test." Before you open your mouth, you might want to ask if what you are going to speak is:

- True;
- Just;
- Pure;
- Lovely;
- Of good report;
- Virtuous;
- Praiseworthy.

If we will daily use this test before we speak, we will be wise and our words will be few but valuable.

> *Lord, help me to remember to take the "talk test" before I speak. Lord, let the words of my mouth and the meditations of my heart be acceptable in Your sight.*

Evening Watch: Read Psalm 51:1–19. This morning I trust you prayed for your words to be acceptable to God. If you did, I know God was faithful to guard your tongue.

Wise words will flow from our mouths when the wisdom from above fills our hearts. God is able to make us know wisdom and truth in our inner parts. David experienced the shame, guilt, and pain that sin always brings into our lives. He made a futile attempt to cover his sin, but Nathan, the prophet, confronted him.

Whenever we try to hide our sins, our fellowship with God is destroyed. When David confessed his sin and cried out to God, the cleansing came. When we are truthful and confess our sins to God rather than hiding sin in our hearts, God is quick to respond to our cries. Psalm 66:18 says that God will not even hear us if we hide iniquity in our hearts. God heard his cry and restored the joy of David's salvation. Whenever we come clean with God about our own sins, our hearts will become clean. Are there any sins you need to confess before you go to bed? Ask the Holy Spirit to shine a light into your heart and then confess any sins He reveals.

> *Lord, search my heart and reveal any hidden sin.*

Morning Wisdom: Read Proverbs 11:1–3. We learn in this psalm that pride brings shame. (See v. 2.) Pride has two forms. It causes us to either think too much of ourselves or to feel that we are unworthy and useless. Both forms of pride are a sin. When others reject us and we become victims of a spirit of rejection, we are in pride. Rejection will cause people to lose their self-esteem and feeling of worth. The spirit of rejection is a wicked spirit that will cause people to feel shame and reproach.

We have to recognize who the author of rejection is. Satan was rejected by God when pride filled his heart and he sought to exalt himself above God. Misery loves company, and ever since Satan was rejected, he has successfully captured victims in that horrible web of rejection.

The only way to be delivered from rejection is to humble ourselves and accept that Jesus was despised and rejected by men and died on the cross to set us free from all rejection. If we remain in rejection, we can become unfaithful to God, because our minds are continually upon ourselves rather than God. We even run the risk of being perverse in our ways. These truths challenge me to resist the devil whenever he tries to give me thoughts that I am not worthy.

> *Lord, thank You for taking my rejection on the cross so I no longer have to accept feelings of rejection from Satan.*

Evening Watch: Read Psalm 52:1–9. We learned this morning that whenever we think too lowly of ourselves or too highly of ourselves, we are guilty of pride. When we humble ourselves before God, He gives us eyes to see ourselves as He sees us. The words we speak daily will reveal whether we are walking in pride or walking in humility.

The writer of this psalm described the words a wicked person speaks. He speaks words of deceit and destruction. The end of such a person is destruction.

This psalm was definitely written by a person who walked in humility. His words at the end of this psalm revealed his humble dependence and trust in God. He ended his psalm by praising God. Whenever we walk in humility, our mouths will be filled with praise. He compared himself to a green olive tree in the house of God and declared that he would trust in the Lord's mercy forever. On one of our trips to Israel we observed olive trees in the Garden of Gethsemane that had been there since the time of Jesus. Even though an olive tree appears to be dead, the roots never die, and those roots give birth to more olive trees. May we all be so rooted and grounded in the love of Jesus Christ that our mouths will be filled with praise forever.

> *Lord, help me to always walk in humility, and may I praise Your name for all eternity!*

Morning Wisdom: Read Proverbs 11:4. This verse says, "Riches do not profit in the day of wrath, But righteousness delivers from death." Those who are eternally rich are those who have been made righteous by receiving Jesus Christ as their Lord and Savior. When we have that assurance that Christ has forgiven, cleansed, and dressed us in His robe of righteousness, we do not have to fear the day of wrath. Believers in Christ are not appointed to the day of wrath. (See 1 Thessalonians 5:9.) However, our words and deeds while on Earth will be judged for eternal reward.

Knowing that I have been delivered from the day of wrath should cause me to spend this day praising God. I also am challenged to share the good news of Christ with others who can also escape that day of wrath if they receive Jesus as their Savior.

> Lord, thank You for becoming sin for me so that I might become righteous through You.

Evening Watch: Read Psalm 53:1–6. David prayed, "Oh, that the salvation of Israel would come out of Zion! When God brings back the captivity of His people, Let Jacob rejoice and Israel be glad" (v. 6). God is bringing back the captivity of His people even as we speak. In the past ten years over a million immigrants have come to live in Israel. Daily planeloads of Russian immigrants and immigrants from the four corners of the earth are landing at the Tel Aviv Airport. God is gathering His people unto Himself.

Many in Israel, however, are not believers, but the day will come when all Israel will be saved in one day. That day is prophesied in Zechariah 12:9–10:

> It shall be in that day that I will seek to destroy all the nations that come against Jerusalem. And I will pour on the house of David and on the inhabitants of Jerusalem the Spirit of grace and supplication; then they will look on Me whom they have pierced; they will mourn for Him as one mourns for his only son, and grieve for Him as one grieves for a firstborn.

That day is coming sooner than you think. Are you ready?

> Lord, help me to be ready for Your return.

Numbers 15:17–16:40; Mark 15:1–47; Psalm 54:1–7; Proverbs 11:5–6

Morning Wisdom: Read Proverbs 11:5–6. These two verses declare that those who walk uprightly will receive both direction and deliverance. I often face days when I feel like I have lost my way. I call such days "muddle days." When this happens, the Holy Spirit often whispers these words of Jesus to me, "I am the way, the truth, and the life" (John 14:6). When we can meditate on one or two verses from the Bible during the day, our muddle days will quickly change into meaningful days.

I also face days that I call "help-me-Jesus days." Such days are when I feel great resistance from Satan and I know I am under attack. Those are days when I have so much to do in a day that I become overwhelmed. On such days I forget my keys or lock them inside the car, leave my checkbook or credit card at a store, or rear end someone with my car. That's when I cry, "Help me, Jesus!" and the Holy Spirit reminds me of this promise, "Many are the afflictions of the righteous, But the LORD delivers him out of them all" (Ps. 34:19). We will be attacked often by the enemy just because we are righteous, but the good news is that Jesus will deliver us.

Lord, thank You for direction and deliverance.

Evening Watch: Read Psalm 54:1–7. This morning we learned how Jesus can give us direction and deliverance by the power of His Holy Spirit. The psalmist in this passage declared that "God is my helper; The Lord is with those who uphold my life" (v. 4). The psalmist also declared that the Lord delivered him out of all his trouble and he has seen his enemies put to flight.

Just recently we had a team from our church and a few other churches hold a prayer conference in Argentina. The head of the team had some powerful supernatural experiences on prior trips to Argentina. His wife enjoyed hearing about her husband's revelations into the spirit realm, but she had never had such experiences until she accompanied him to Argentina.

While those gathered for the conference were worshiping the Lord, she saw angels in the four corners of the auditorium. Then she saw demons, and they were fleeing as the worship continued. This logical, down-to-earth servant of the Lord had her eyes opened that day to see into the spirit realm.

God purposely does not allow us to see continually the demons that are against us daily or the angels that are on our side, but we can rest assured that there are more angels than demons. When Elisha's servant was afraid, Elisha said, "'Do not fear, for those who are with us are more than those who are with them.' And Elisha prayed, and said, 'LORD, I pray, open his eyes that he may see.' Then the LORD opened the eyes of the young man, and he saw" (2 Kings 6:16–17).

Lord, open my eyes to see.

Morning Wisdom: Read Proverbs 11:7. This verse repeats Proverbs 10:28 which says, "...the expectation of the wicked will perish." The hope of the unjust will also perish. (See v. 7.) One of the downfalls of human nature is to expect and hope in the wrong things. We have counseled many young couples who run into problems just after marriage because they become disappointed in their partners. Most couples enter marriage with high expectations that being married will perhaps solve their physical, emotional, and financial needs. However, in most cases none of these problems are solved. In fact, these problems are just doubled. When we put our expectations in a man or woman, we will always be disappointed.

Our hopes also are often misplaced. Hope is in the future, and we think things will be better in our future. We play the "when–then game." We say things like: "When our children are a little older, then we will have more time to spend with one another." This scenario usually does not happen, because when the children get a little older, we end up being chauffeurs to all their activities. We find ourselves spending more time in the car with our children than with our husbands.

The only sure thing for everyone in this life is that one day we will die. You have heard the expression, "Death and taxes are the only sure things in life." This may be true for the nonbeliever, but as believers we can count on the following sure things:

- Eternity with Jesus Christ, our heavenly Father, and the Holy Spirit;
- The resurrection of our bodies one day;
- Eternal rewards for our words and deeds on Earth.

When we put all of our expectations in Jesus Christ and the Word of God, the Holy Spirit will give us a calm assurance and joy that will keep us from ever being overwhelmed with disappointment. Our brief disappointments are God's appointments with us to reveal His strength and His joy no matter how overwhelming our circumstances may seem at the moment.

Lord, I put my expectations in You today.

Evening Watch: Read Psalm 55:1–23. Have you ever cried out in desperation, "Lord, stop the world! I want to get off!" David was having one of those muddle days when all seemed to be against him. He sighed, "Oh, that I had wings like a dove! I would fly away and be at rest" (v. 6). David spent most of his life in fright and flight. He escaped from one hiding place to another.

David experienced betrayal by Saul and other companions, but David never gave up. He said, "As for me, I will call upon God, And the LORD shall save me" (v. 16). David learned to cast his burden upon the Lord and to trust in His delivering power.

Lord, I put my trust in You, and I know You will take care of my tomorrows.

MARCH 13

Numbers 19:1–20:29; Luke 1:1–25; Psalm 56:1–13; Proverbs 11:8

Morning Wisdom: Read Proverbs 11:8. This proverb gives a great promise: "The righteous is delivered from trouble." Last night as I watched the news, I saw an illustration of how the Lord delivered a righteous person from great danger. A troubled man killed four people in Atlanta as he tried to escape police after he was on trial. He held a woman hostage in her own apartment for seven hours. She tried to gain this man's trust and finally ended up reading the Bible to him and another spiritual book called *The Purpose Driven Life*.

She told him that she did not want him to kill her because she had seen her husband stabbed to death in a robbery just four years ago, and her little five-year-old daughter would be without a father or mother if he killed her. His troubled mind was somehow soothed by the Word of God, and he eventually surrendered to the police without firing a shot after the lady called 9-1-1.

We might ask this question: "Why would God allow four innocent people to be killed and then deliver another one from what looked like a sure death?" Those four people who were killed may have been righteous people also. I believe the offensive weapon of the Word of God used against the demons in this man caused the demons to keep silent long enough for this man to calm down and have a change of mind. He repented of the evil he had done and came to himself again. Some of the other victims did not have time to use spiritual weapons to pull down the strongholds in this man's mind.

If we ever find ourselves in a critical situation like this lady experienced, we need to know what our spiritual weapons are and use them. The Word of God, prayer, the full armor of God, the name of Jesus, and the blood of Jesus are just a few of these weapons. If we only have time to call upon the name of the Lord, I believe angels will come to our rescue. When I hydroplaned into a wooded area with my husband, I only had time to say out loud, "Jesus." My husband and I came out of that accident without any serious injuries, because our car was turned to hit the trees from the rear instead of the front. I don't know about you, but I will hold on to the promise in this verse: "The righteous is delivered from trouble."

Lord, thank You for Your delivering power.

Evening Watch: Read Psalm 56:1–13. This morning we learned that the skillful use of God's Word can put demons to flight.

David revealed another secret to overcoming our adversaries in this psalm. David said that his enemies hounded him all day. He had more than just physical enemies. Demonic spirits had assignments to kill David. He had much to fear, but he wrote, "Whenever I am afraid, I will trust in You. In God (I will praise His word), In God I have put my trust; I will not fear. What can flesh do to me?" (vv. 3–4). We can confront whatever enemies face us tomorrow without fear when we put our trust in God.

Lord, I put my trust in You and in the power of Your Word.

MARCH 14

Morning Wisdom: Read Proverbs 11:9–11. The comparison between the wicked and righteous continues in this passage. It is interesting that the mouth is mentioned two times in these verses. We talked earlier about the power the tongue has to destroy or create, and this passage confirms this truth.

When hypocrites open their mouths, they can destroy their neighbors. A hypocrite is a person who says one thing and does another. Whether we like it or not we are living epistles or letters read by our neighbors. If our neighbors see us go to church in our Sunday clothes, but later that week they hear us cussing when we can't start our lawnmowers, they may call us hypocrites. A lot of people use the excuse that the church is full of hypocrites and that is why they do not want to attend any church. We are capable of destroying our Christian witness by what we speak with our mouths.

Wicked people can destroy a whole city by what they say with their mouths. Recently we saw how multimillion-dollar megacorporations were destroyed by people who lied about how much money their corporations had.

The good news is that righteousness exalts a nation and righteous people have the power to exalt a nation and a city by the blessings they speak.

I am challenged by this reading to speak blessings over my city and nation daily in my prayer time. I must admit that often I forget to pray for my nation and city government. This morning join me as I pray for those in authority.

> *Father, I pray for those in authority in my nation, city, and state government. I pray that those in leadership will be blessed with Your wisdom and that they will have clear discernment as they make decisions that will affect those they lead.*

Evening Watch: Read Psalm 57:1–11. David was surrounded by people whose teeth were like spears and arrows. He compared their tongues to sharp swords. His enemies had prepared a net for him, but he was not overwhelmed by his circumstances. Instead, he declared, "My heart is steadfast, O God…I will sing and give praise" (v. 7). David wrote this psalm when he fled from Saul into a cave.

When I ask people how they are doing, I sometimes get this response, "Pretty well under the circumstances." I am tempted to ask them, "What are you doing under the circumstances?" I refrain from such a comment since it is a bit judgmental. David did not allow himself to get under the circumstances. Instead, he got under the shadow of God's wings. He made God his refuge when he was in trouble. I do not believe God has wings, but I do know for a fact that angels have wings. Angels hearken to the voice of God's Word, and when we find ourselves under the circumstances, we need to begin to declare as David did, "Be exalted, O God, above the heavens; Let Your glory be above all the earth" (v. 11).

> *Lord, thank You for being my refuge and my covering.*

MARCH 15

Morning Wisdom: Read Proverbs 11:12–13. My pastor asked me one time to give a little talk on the dangers of gossip. Rumors were flying in our church, and he wanted the gossip mill stopped. You may think that you do not gossip, but the truth is that we all gossip from time to time. Any time we pass on a negative report that reflects on a person's character, we are guilty of gossiping. We may frame the negative report as a prayer request, but it is still gossip.

A gossip is a talebearer who reveals secrets. If we have a faithful spirit, we will conceal the sins of others. Another verse says, "It is the glory of God to conceal a matter" (Prov. 25:2). All of us want to glorify God daily with the words we speak and the actions we take. One of the ways we can glorify God in our speech is to be careful not to pass on any negative reports about people.

When I gave my talk on gossip, I suggested that people not even listen to a negative report, because when you do, you are participating in gossip. When a person begins to talk negatively about someone else, reach your hands out to hold their hands and say, "Let's pray for that person right now." It is hard to stop a person who has a motormouth, but don't even give that person a chance to finish their report. After prayer, simply walk away.

Lord, help me to guard my tongue.

Evening Watch: Read Psalm 58:1–11. When we were in India we had the opportunity to see many snake charmers who placed their money baskets in front of them to earn money for their talents. Charming snakes must take a special gift, but I do not think I would want to try it. When we were in Savannah and word got out that we spoke in tongues, a member of our church who was training helicopter pilots in the marshes of Savannah said: "You and Tom should come out next week, because we are having a big snake round up." He had heard that anyone who spoke in tongues could easily handle snakes. He based this premise on Mark 16:17, which says: "And these signs will follow those who believe: In My name they will cast out demons; they will speak with new tongues; they will take up serpents."

This psalm compares wicked people to cobras, "which will not heed the voice of charmers, Charming ever so skillfully" (v. 5). The psalmist is conveying the message that a wicked person is determined to do evil, and it is hard for anyone to turn him from his wicked ways. However, we know that the Holy Spirit has the power to woo people into God's kingdom. We have a history of people in the Bible who did turn from their wicked ways because the Holy Spirit delivered the gift of repentance to them.

We spoke earlier about the murderer who held a woman hostage for seven hours, and how he finally repented of the evil he had done. This woman delivered the Word of God under the powerful anointing of the Holy Spirit, and he did her no harm and turned himself into the authorities.

Praise God for the power of the Holy Spirit.

Morning Wisdom: Read Proverbs 11:14. Our verse today says, "Where there is no counsel, the people fall; But in the multitude of counselors there is safety." Some churches have fully paid counselors on duty to help the members of their congregation and others who have problems. Part of the sevenfold anointing listed in Isaiah 11:2 is the anointing of counsel and might. Wisdom and understanding are listed together in this anointing, and knowledge and the fear of the Lord are coupled together.

I never understood why counsel and might were coupled together until I prayed about it one day. When I prayed, the Lord helped me to understand that those who seek counsel have weak areas. Their weak areas may be financial, physical, or psychological. It is the counselor's job to lead people who are weak or bound in some area in their lives to find their strength in the Lord and in God's Word. Only a relationship with Jesus Christ, understanding of God's Word, and the power and might of the Holy Spirit can set people free from whatever is troubling them.

If the body of Christ operated in these gifts, there would be far fewer people who have to go to counselors who charge a fee. Many in the church can lead others to find their answers in God's Word through counseling and teaching under the anointing of the Holy Spirit. Others in the body of Christ are intercessors who can fast and pray for individuals who are bound. Part of the chosen fast is to loose the bands of wickedness, undo heavy burdens, let the oppressed go free, and break every yoke of bondage. (See Isaiah 58:6.) Also many in the church have the gift of exhortation. We are all called to exhort one another daily.

> *Lord, help me and the body of Christ to operate in the gifts You have given us.*

Evening Watch: Read Psalm 59:1–17. How would you like to have a host of murderers prowling around the perimeters of your home? David wrote this psalm when Saul's men were surrounding his home.

Saul sent them to kill David. David described these men when he wrote, "At the evening they return, They growl like a dog, And go all around the city. Indeed, they belch with their mouth; Swords are in their lips; For they say, "Who hears?" (vv. 6–7).

You might breathe a sigh of relief and say, "Thank God I have never been in such a dangerous situation." The truth is, however, that every day we are surrounded by demonic spirits who would love to see us dead. That is not a pleasant thought, but when we do what David did when he was surrounded, we will put these demonic spirits to flight. David closed this psalm with these words, "But I will sing of Your power; Yes, I will sing aloud of Your mercy in the morning; For You have been my defense And refuge in the day of my trouble. To You, O my Strength, I will sing praises; For God is my defense, My God of mercy" (vv. 16–17).

> *Lord, keep me singing all day long.*

MARCH 17

Morning Wisdom: Read Proverbs 11:15. Securing a person's loan by cosigning on a mortgage or car payment is not a good idea. This verse warns against being a surety for a stranger. We have been asked to cosign for loans, but we have always gone back to this sound warning in Proverbs, and we have heeded this warning. I do not feel it would even be wise to cosign on a loan for family members. Many problems in family relationships can arise if we cosign for loans even with people who are related to us. When we cosign, we run the risk of our security being threatened if the other party is not able to pay his payments.

The important thing to remember is that all that we have belongs to God. We are only stewards on Earth of what He possesses. My prayer is you will be a wise steward.

Lord, help me to be a wise steward.

Evening Watch: Read Psalm 60:1–12. David wrote, "You have made the earth to tremble; You have broken it; Heal its breaches, for it is shaking" (v. 2). When David wrote this psalm, everything in his life seemed to be shaking. He had just seen many fall in battle as Joab led his troops against Mesopotamia and Syria.

There is a whole lot of shaking going on in this world today. There is no question that everything that can be shaken is being shaken in these last days. We see well-known evangelists falling away, corporate leaders going to prison, wars and even physical earthquakes occurring in many places.

Wars cause many to fall, but behind the scene of every physical war is a spiritual war. We can only see armies moving against one another with our natural eyes, but if we could have our eyes opened to view the spiritual realm, we would see warring angels coming against demonic spirits. In these last days, saints need to recognize that they are in a war. Satan is using his big guns in these last days to try to rob even mature Christians of their faith.

The good news is that in the midst of this warfare, God has given saints a banner to display. David wrote, "You have given a banner to those who fear You, That it may be displayed because of the truth" (v. 4). What is that banner? I believe that banner is God's Word. Several years ago I was given an unusual picture in my mind. I saw saints in a great stadium. They were watching the teams on the field. One team was dressed in black and the other team radiated light. The saints were exhorting and shouting, "Go, go, go," to the team that was filled with light. Those in the stadium were holding up banners with scriptures written on the banners. Satan was watching this scene, but all he could see was God's Word. The banners with God's Word covered and protected the saints he wanted to destroy.

Lord, help me to hold up Your Word daily by declaring it out loud against the enemies of my soul.

MARCH 18

Morning Wisdom: Read Proverbs 11:16–17. I have a friend who is writing a musical that will hopefully play on Broadway someday. It is about her life and the life of many women who have been physically or verbally abused by their husbands. Her story ends well because she finally recognized her codependency in her marriage relationship, and after twenty-five years of abuse, she finally got a divorce. I know God hates divorce, but I do not believe women should live in an abusive marriage.

Proverbs 11:17 says, "The merciful man does good for his own soul, But he who is cruel troubles his own flesh." Most abusive people have experienced abuse in their past. They are victims of abuse, but they can be set free from perpetrating that same abuse on others. Abusive people do have troubled souls, and my prayer is that this musical will set many people free from the unworthiness and rejection that most abused people experience.

We can trouble our own souls when we refuse to be merciful to others. I am challenged by these verses in Proverbs to show mercy to all. Jesus said, "Blessed are the merciful, For they shall obtain mercy" (Matt. 5:7).

Lord, help me to always be merciful to others.

Evening Watch: Read Psalm 61:1–8. David was overwhelmed when he wrote this psalm. In this psalm David looked back over his life and declared the faithfulness of the Lord to rescue him through the years. His life had been one of fight and fright. He remembered, however, how the Lord saw him through every troubled time. As he reviewed his life, I believe joy welled up within his soul and he began to sing this psalm and other songs to the Lord as he played his harp. David was preserved throughout his troubled days by the mercy and truth of God (v. 7). David learned the secret to obeying the Lord. He said, "I will sing praise to Your name forever, That I may daily perform my vows" (v. 8). It is hard to have a rebellious heart that desires to disobey God if you daily remain in praise.

The devil and his demonic companions daily try to woo us to go the way of the world. The best way to shut out the voice of seducing spirits is to sing praises to the Lord. Derek Prince told the story of a man who had gone his own way for years. His wife had prayed for him continually. She finally talked her husband into going to see Derek. As soon as the man entered Derek's home, he wanted to leave. The demonic spirits operating in his life did not want to have anything to do with Derek Prince, who knew exactly how to deliver this man from his oppression and depression. Derek politely asked the man to remain just a few minutes, and the man stayed. Those in the room began to sing some praise songs. As their worship and praise continued, this man was totally delivered from his depression and rebellion. He surrendered his life to Jesus.

Praise is the devil's death knell. Commit to sing songs of praise throughout your day tomorrow, and I know you will have a blessed day.

Praise the Lord!

MARCH 19

Morning Watch: Read Proverbs 11:18–19. When we look at the benefits of living a righteous life listed in Proverbs, we are challenged to walk in righteousness daily. This proverb reveals that we can do more than just walk in righteousness. We can sow righteousness, and if we do, we will reap a sure reward. (See v. 18.) As I meditated on this scripture, I remembered a time in my life when I thought my opportunities to sow righteousness into the lives of others were very limited because I did not even have a car during the day. It was on one of those days when I knew I would have to stay home that I prayed this prayer: *Lord, if there is anyone You want me to minister to today, send them to my home.*

The Lord answered that prayer when he brought a neighbor to my door who I had met at a garden club earlier that week. She shared that she knew I was a Christian, and she asked me to be her prayer partner. I answered with a quick yes. My neighbor exclaimed, "I want you to pray about this before you give me your answer." I then shared that I had already asked the Lord that morning to send someone who I could minister to that day, because I could not get out of the house. We agreed to pray weekly every Monday morning, and we saw many miracles happen in her life because of our agreement in prayer. We can sow righteousness into others when we pray with them and share God's Word with them. Today pray for opportunities to sow righteousness into the lives of others.

Lord, help me to sow righteousness into the lives of others.

Evening Watch: Read Psalm 62:1–12. This morning I reviewed a time when I asked God to send someone who needed ministry to my door, because I was without a car that day. When I prayed that prayer, I was expectant during the day to see how God would answer my request. I knew I was praying according to His will, because He desires to use us every day for His glory.

Whenever we pray, we should pray with expectation. David quieted his soul at a time when his enemies were coming against him. He told his soul to "wait silently for God alone, For my expectation is from Him" (v. 5). Our souls can remain quiet and at peace if we put all of our expectations in God. I often tell people, "Expect everything from God and nothing from people, and you will never be disappointed." Disappointment comes when our expectations are not met.

Because David put his expectations in God, he could declare with confidence that God was his rock, his salvation, his defense, his strength, and his refuge. (See vv. 6–7.) He ended this psalm with this statement, "Power belongs to God. Also to You, O Lord, belongs mercy" (v. 11–12). When we trust in God's power and His mercy and pray according to His will, we will never be disappointed. John wrote, "Now this is the confidence that we have in Him, that if we ask anything according to His will, He hears us. And if we know that He hears us, whatever we ask, we know that we have the petitions that we have asked of him" (1 John 5:14–15). Pray with expectation about how God will use you tomorrow.

Lord, I give you tomorrow, and I expect You to use me for Your glory.

Numbers 30:1–31:54; Luke 4:1–32; Psalm 63:1–11; Proverbs 11:20–21

Morning Wisdom: Read Proverbs 11:20–21. I can remember praying often for my three sons when they were teenagers that they would have nothing to be ashamed of when they saw Jesus face-to-face. I knew how peer pressure can cause young people to do things they might be ashamed of later. One day when I was praying this prayer, I heard the Lord speak these words to my heart:

> Your boys will have nothing to be ashamed of when they see Me face-to-face. I see your sons as three golden vessels that will gleam with My glory.

All my anxious thoughts about the future of my sons left me that day. I was able to see them with the eyes of Jesus, and I knew that Jesus had the power to cleanse and keep their souls. Our scripture today says, "The blameless in their ways are His delight" (v. 20). As we release those we love to the Lord, we can trust that He will cause them both to will and to do of His good pleasure. (See Philippians 2:13.) They will be blameless in their ways. Today join me as I pray for those I love with the paraphrased prayer Paul prayed in the twenty-fourth verse of Jude.

> *Now to Him who is able to keep my loved ones from stumbling, and to present them faultless before the presence of His glory with exceeding joy to God our Savior, who alone is wise, be glory and majesty, dominion and power, both now and forever. Amen.*

Evening Watch: Read Psalm 63:1–11. There is a song that came out in the 1960s by the Rolling Stones called "I Can't Get No Satisfaction." People who have not put their trust in the Lord look to drugs, sex, alcohol, money, entertainment, food, and many other things to satisfy their souls. They may find temporary satisfaction in these things, but soon they will be craving more to fill the void in their souls.

When David wrote this psalm his soul thirsted for the Lord, and even his flesh craved to be in the Lord's presence. He looked for the Lord in the sanctuary, and there he saw His power and His glory. When David was in the presence of the Lord, he was overwhelmed by the loving-kindness of the Lord. He even said that the loving-kindness of the Lord was better than life. He declared that his soul was satisfied, and he could not stop praising God. Because David's soul followed close to the Lord, the Lord's right hand always upheld him. In the presence of the Lord there is fullness of joy for you, and He holds the pleasures that will satisfy your soul forever. (See Psalm 16:11.)

Thank You for satisfying my soul.

Morning Wisdom: Read Proverbs 11:22. This is one of my favorite chapters in Proverbs. In fact, I wrote a devotional on this verse in my book *Around the Word in 365 Days.* The vision this verse portrays makes me laugh every time I read it. Imagine a huge pig with a gold ring in his snout. Solomon compared a woman who lacked discretion to this pig. Discretion is the power to discern and judge and the ability to make careful and wise decisions.

Unfortunately in my lifetime I have met several women who lacked discretion, and when I encountered them, I immediately had this mental image of the pig described in this verse. I was so thankful they could not read my mind.

We are exhorted in Scripture to ask for wisdom when we lack it. (See James 1:5.) When we ask for wisdom, God also gifts us with discretion and prudence. It has been my practice to ask for wisdom at the beginning of most days. Will you join me as I once again ask the Lord for wisdom?

> *Lord, I ask for Your wisdom today. You know the people I will meet and the problems I will encounter today. Thank You for giving me clear discernment and the ability to make wise decisions.*

Evening Watch: Read Psalm 64:1–10. David compared the tongues of his enemies to sharp swords and their bitter words to sharp arrows that wound the soul. James wrote that it is impossible for a fresh fountain to produce bitter waters. He questioned, "Does a spring send forth fresh water and bitter from the same opening?" (James 3:11). He concluded that anyone who both blessed God and cursed men with his mouth would have bitter waters within his soul. He said, "No spring can yield both salt water and fresh" (James 3:12).

What we say with our mouths reveals the condition of our hearts. I am tempted sometimes to say to people, "Please be quiet. Your heart is showing." Whenever I am judgmental and critical of others, I know right away that there is an element of fear or insecurity within my heart. I also know that if I confess my fears and give them to the Lord, He will cleanse my heart and cause my speech to reflect His love. If my words are bitter, I know to ask the Lord quickly to remove any unforgiveness in my heart. I cannot afford to allow any bitterness to take root in my heart, because if I do I will say things that will hurt those around me. (See Hebrews 12:15.)

I want my words to heal, not hurt. Before you go to bed, join me as I make a commitment to yield my tongue tomorrow to the Lord so that I will speak only those things that edify others.

> *Lord, cleanse my heart of any bitterness I may have toward anyone. Create in me a clean heart, and use my mouth to bless not wound others.*

MARCH 22

Morning Wisdom: Read Proverbs 11:23. We learned earlier that God grants the desires of the righteous. When our hearts want to please God, our desires will line up with God's desires. He plants in our hearts His desires, and what He plants He grants. This verse states, "The desire of the righteous is only good." God is good and therefore every desire He plants in our hearts is good.

Today might be a good day to review some of the things you desire. If you are seeking to please God, here are some of the desires that should be top on your list:

- The desire to have more faith—faith pleases God
- The desire to read God's Word—His Word is our daily spiritual food
- The desire to pray—communicating our every need to God
- The desire to worship—meditating on God's greatness and magnifying His name
- The desire to fellowship—when we walk in the light, we long to have fellowship with other Christians

If we lack any of these desires, it might be time to take our spiritual temperature.

Has our love for God grown cold? The Bible says that in the last days the love of many will wax cold. (See Matthew 24:12.) May we never allow our love for God to become cold.

Lord, forgive me if I have allowed other desires to crowd out Your desires. Create in me a clean heart, and renew Your righteous desires within me.

Evening Watch: Read Psalm 65:1–13. What does it mean to be chosen by God? David wrote, "Blessed is the man You choose, And cause to approach You" (v. 4). What a joy it is to be chosen by God to enjoy His presence forever! The thought that we can enter the throne room of the King of the universe every day of our lives is awesome.

David meditated on the greatness and goodness of God in this psalm. Let's review together with David some of the great things God does. God does awesome deeds (v. 5); He causes the evening and mornings to rejoice (v. 8); He waters the earth and makes it fruitful (vv. 9–10); He crowns every year with His goodness (v. 11); and He gives abundant provision (v. 12). As I meditate upon the greatness of God described in this psalm, I have a mental picture. I see God as the director of a great symphony. Every creature on Earth is part of this symphony. The music resounds through the pastureland, hills, rivers, and mountains. At the end of the symphony, everyone sings a new song filled with shouts of joy.

Thank You for choosing me to be in Your symphony.

Numbers 36:1–Deut. 1:46; Luke 5:29–6:11; Psalm 66:1–20; Proverbs 11:24–26

Morning Wisdom: Read Proverbs 11:24–26. When my husband and I took a motivational gift test, we discovered that my husband's motivational gift is giving and my motivational gift is teaching. I was so glad to find out that my husband's motivational gift is giving, because I also have another motivational gift called "spending." We have never had financial problems in our married life, because my husband is a generous giver. Proverbs 11:25 says, "The generous soul will be made rich, And he who waters will also be watered himself." We certainly have not been wealthy, but we have always had what we needed and enough to tithe and sow into the kingdom.

As a teacher of God's Word, it has been my privilege to water many souls. We are sanctified and cleansed by the washing of water by the Word of God. (See Ephesians 5:26.) I have noticed that whenever I teach the Word of God to others, my own faith is built up and my own soul is refreshed.

We are blessed whenever we give to others. One sure way to be strengthened daily by the joy of the Lord is to be a giver. Stingy people are not joyful, and they have souls that are poverty stricken. This morning think of some ways you can give to others today.

You may decide to cook a very special meal for your family or call a friend and invite them to lunch. If you work, you may want to take some cookies to share with others at work. These are just simple ways of giving, but those simple things can make someone's day more joyful. Pray and ask the Holy Spirit to give you creative ways to give to others today.

> *Holy Spirit, help me to hear Your still, quiet voice as You inspire me with creative ways to give to others.*

Evening Watch: Read Psalm 66:1–20. This morning we discussed the simple works we can do daily that will be our way of giving to others. God has given so much to us, and all of His works are awesome. One of my favorite songs is "Awesome God." The invitation is given in this psalm to "come and see the works of God" (v. 5). God truly is "awesome in His doing toward the sons of men" (v. 5).

We could label the rest of this psalm "Show and Tell," because the psalmist declares the awesome works of God. The psalmist lists the various trials God uses to test and refine his people. Then he joyfully declares how God has used even trials to deliver us and to give us rich fulfillment (vv. 10–12).

Tonight before you close your eyes to sleep, meditate on some of God's awesome works that He has done in your own life. Your heart will be filled with praise, and your mind will be flooded with peace.

> *Lord, thank You for all the awesome things You have done for me.*

MARCH 24

Morning Wisdom: Read Proverbs 11:27. This verse exhorts us to earnestly seek what is good. If we do this, we will have favor. There are many people on this planet who do good works to earn favor with God. However, whenever we do good to earn favor with God, we have already lost our reward. We will not be rewarded in heaven for our good works. We will be rewarded in heaven for the works we have allowed the only true righteous One, Jesus Christ, to do through us by the power of the Holy Spirit. No one is righteous apart from the effectual work of Jesus Christ within his soul. All of our own righteousness is as filthy rags. (See Isaiah 64:6.) On the cross Jesus exchanged our self-righteousness for His righteousness. "For He [God] made Him [Christ] who knew no sin to be sin for us, that we might become the righteousness of God in Him" (2 Cor. 5:21).

When my son was in Bogotá, Colombia, he experienced the perfect illustration of the divine exchange that took place on the cross. Ron had the opportunity to visit a drug rehabilitation center. Even the police did not go into the area where this center was located, but their brave leader decided to take a team into the center to hold a service for the men there. When Ron first entered, he was overwhelmed by the testimonies of these men. He was so touched by the dedication of these men, and he wanted to bless them. He suggested that the team wash the feet of the men who were being rehabilitated.

Many of the men were not familiar with the passage when Jesus washed the disciples' feet. Ron gave a little teaching on that passage, and then the men sat down. A member of the team had just put on a fresh, new pair of socks that morning. As he removed the filthy socks of the man in front of him to wash his feet, he had the inspiration to give this man his new, clean socks when the footwashing service ended.

The man received the new socks with joy and then handed the team member his old dirty socks. The team member put the dirty socks on and walked out of the center with those filthy socks on his feet. This is what Jesus did on the cross. He took our filthy self-righteousness and exchanged it for His glorious righteousness.

Whenever we earnestly seek to do good things, we must at that time earnestly seek the righteousness of Jesus Christ and pray that His righteousness will shine through us. (See Matthew 6:33.)

Lord, thank You for the great exchange on the cross.

Evening Watch: Read Psalm 67:1–7. Our passage this evening is also about God's righteousness. He will judge the people of all nations righteously. Only God knows what inspires us to do good works.

Only He knows whether we do good things in our own power to earn favor with others. God will do more than judge our works on Earth. He will judge the motivation of our hearts.

Lord, create within me a clean heart.

Deuteronomy 4:1–49; Luke 6:39–7:10; Psalm 68:1–18; Proverbs 11:28

Morning Wisdom: Read Proverbs 11:28. It is springtime in Atlanta. My sister is here for a visit, and she was in such hopes of seeing the dogwood and azalea in bloom. She lives in Seattle, where their springtime is not as beautiful as ours. When she arrived in Atlanta, however, she noticed that the trees were bereft of leaves. I always look forward to seeing the first signs of spring when the trees put forth their tiny yellowish, green foliage, and the stark, bare trees of winter become clothed in beauty.

The promise in our verse today is that "the righteous will flourish like foliage."

I've noticed that the leaves of spring soon turn a rich, dark green and they increase in size and amount. Soon the limbs of the trees are not even visible because of the increase in foliage during the summer. Once we have received Jesus Christ as our Lord and Savior, we are dressed in His robe of righteousness and His glory light is upon us. Proverbs 4:18 says, "But the path of the just is like the shining sun, That shines ever brighter unto the perfect day." Our paths become brighter, because the glory of the Lord within us grows brighter. God daily clothes us with the beauty of His glory light. We are trees of righteousness planted by the Lord. As His righteous trees, we are called to both increase in His glory foliage and fruitfulness. May your day be fruitful as you share with others the love of Jesus Christ.

Lord, thank You for dressing me daily with Your glory.

Evening Watch: Read Psalm 68:1–18. This psalm contains several songs that we sing in our church. "Let God Arise" is one of these songs. We also sing a song based on verse four which says, "Sing to God, sing praises to His name. Extol Him who rides on the clouds, by His name Yah, and rejoice before Him." (See Zephaniah 3:17.) I get excited whenever we sing those songs, and somehow I feel like maybe these were the songs Paul and Silas sang in jail when the earthquake came and the angel led them out of prison. I have a visual picture every time we sing these songs of Paul and Silas with their hands raised in praise to the Lord even though they were bound by chains. As they rejoiced before the Lord despite their circumstances, I believe God was tapping His foot to the beat of their joyful choruses, and this is what caused the earthquake. We know that God rejoices over us with singing. I know it just thrills our heavenly Father when we join in the choruses He is singing with Jesus in heaven over us.

I correspond with a lady prisoner who is sentenced to life in prison and has no chance of pardon unless God intervenes. She was taken away from her children when they were just seven and nine years of age. When I receive her letters, I just shout for joy, because her letters are so filled with joy and love. There is not one ounce of bitterness towards those that accused her falsely. She has learned the way to live above the circumstances is to rejoice in the Lord always. Fill your day with rejoicing in God's presence tomorrow.

Lord, help me to rejoice always.

Deuteronomy 5:1–6:25; Luke 7:11–35; Psalm 68:19–35; Proverbs 11:29–31

Morning Wisdom: Read Proverbs 11:29–31. Yesterday we talked about being fruitful and flourishing trees of righteousness. Today's reading continues with that theme. Verse 30 says, "The fruit of the righteous is a tree of life, And he who wins souls is wise." God measures our fruitfulness by the souls we touch on this earth with the love of God.

I recall a vision I had when I was praying years ago. As I closed my eyes, I saw and heard the following in my spirit.

> Come up with Me to this high mountain, and see My kingdom. Remember when Satan took Me to the high mountain and promised Me the kingdoms of this earth if I would bow down and worship him. Look at the kingdom he showed Me. Look at the fields over there. Look at that forest of trees on that mountain in the distance. Look at the sea the mountains surround.

As I looked at the fields, I saw sheaves of wheat waving in the breeze, and I heard, "The fields are ripe for harvest." Suddenly I saw those sheaves of wheat turn into faces. When I looked at the mountain, the trees seemed to be clapping their hands, and then faces appeared in place of the trees. I heard, "These are the little children who need to know the Father's love." Then I looked at the sea, and I saw the ripples in the sea turn to faces. Those faces looked so sad, and I heard, "These are the brokenhearted who need My message of forgiveness."

The kingdom Satan offered Jesus was a kingdom of souls, and this is what Jesus wanted to possess. He knew, however, that he would have to go to the cross to win this kingdom. We now are colaborers with Him to share the good news with people so they can be translated from the kingdom of darkness into the kingdom of His light.

Lord, help me to be an effective colaborer in this last harvest.

Evening Watch: Read Psalm 68:19–35. We talked this morning about the kingdom Jesus wants to possess. His treasures on Earth are not gold, silver, or jewels. His treasures are souls, and we are privileged to colabor with Him to possess the treasures He has already purchased with His blood.

Some of you may feel that this is a job beyond your strength and capability. However, this psalm assures us that God has commanded your strength (v. 28). Where we are weak, Jesus is strong. (See 2 Corinthians 12:10.) God has chosen the weak things of the world to confound the wise. (See 1 Corinthians 1:27.) God uses those who are weak so that no flesh will receive His glory. As we depend upon God's strength and not our own, we will be effective co-laborers in this last great harvest.

Lord, thank You for strengthening me as I witness to others.

Deuteronomy 7:1–8:20; Luke 7:36–8:3; Psalm 69:1–14; Proverbs 12:1

Morning Wisdom: Read Proverbs 12:1. The person who refuses to be corrected lacks wisdom. What causes people to refuse correction? People refuse correction because they think they know it all or they simply want to do their own thing. Unwise people are prideful people. Pride is the enemy of our souls, because when we are prideful we are destined for a fall.

The voice of pride speaks to us every day. I know you have heard that voice when you hear phrases like these: "You are your own boss"; "No one can tell you anything you don't already know"; or "Your way is the right way of doing things." The key to living a fruitful and joyful life is to refuse to listen and obey the voice of pride.

Wise people accept correction, and they love instruction and knowledge. Every morning I pray this following prayer. Join me this morning as I pray:

> Lord, You are all wisdom. I humble myself before You today and ask for Your wisdom throughout the day.

Evening Watch: Read Psalm 69:1–14. When I read this psalm, I feel like I am not only reading the testimony of David, but I am also reading the testimony of Jesus. There were many lonely times in David's life when he felt like even his best friends had become his enemies. He felt like a stranger in his own house. Jesus shared these same feelings. David exclaimed, "I have become a stranger to my brothers, And an alien to my mother's children" (v. 8).

Sometimes we forget that Jesus had a family. We know He had brothers, because Scripture tells us that His family asked the disciples to tell Jesus that they wanted to see Him when He was ministering one time. Jesus responded by pointing to His disciples and saying, "Here are My mother and My brothers! For whoever does the will of My Father in heaven is My brother and sister and mother" (Matt. 12:49–50).

Jesus' own brothers did not believe that He was the Messiah. In fact, they even mocked Him and told Him to go to Jerusalem to show His stuff during the Feast of Tabernacles. Jesus told them He would not go with them. However, He did go later during this seven-day feast. He stood in the shadows and watched His family joyously celebrating this feast as they ate their meals under the thatched roof of their Sukkoth. Jesus at that time felt rejected and lonely, and I'm sure He also felt like a stranger and an alien to His brothers. (See John 7.)

Jesus experienced the pain of rejection, not only on the cross but also throughout His life on Earth. He experienced this, but then He provided a way for that horrific pain of rejection to be removed when He willingly bore the sins of this world upon His body.

Lord, thank You for delivering me from rejection.

MARCH 28

Deuteronomy 9:1–10:22; Luke 8:4–21; Psalm 69:15–36; Proverbs 12:2–3

Morning Wisdom: Read Proverbs 12:2–3. My husband and I recently had the opportunity to return to our roots when my husband celebrated his fiftieth high school reunion. Classmates from the various schools visited their old grammar schools. We also visited the high school. We were amazed that these structures still looked the same, but they were much improved on the inside. Additions had been added to provide for more students. We also visited our old homes. Our homes had been modernized, but the basic structures were the same. We were so grateful that our homes and schools were still standing after all of these years.

The basic structure that forms the body of Christ is still the same also. The foundation of the body of Christ is Jesus Christ, the framework is faith, and the roof is the Holy Spirit's anointing. As members of the body of Christ, we all share the same roots, and these roots will never change or be moved.

The reading from Proverbs today says, "The root of the righteous cannot be moved" (v. 3). Once we have received Jesus Christ as our Lord and Savior we receive a kingdom that cannot be moved, because it is rooted in the love of Jesus Christ. Paul prayed that we all might be rooted and grounded in the love of Jesus Christ. (See Ephesians 3:17–19.) We begin to comprehend the love of Jesus Christ and even come to know the height (His grace), depth (His forgiveness), length (His mercy), and breadth (His truth) of His love. The roots of bitterness and rejection are uprooted as we submit and yield to the Holy Spirit. The Holy Spirit will help us to add to our faith the knowledge of the love of Jesus, virtue, self-control, perseverance, godliness, and brotherly kindness. (See 2 Peter 1:5–7.) We can look forward to having constant improvement in the body of Christ as we are willing to submit to the Holy Spirit, who will conform us to the image of Jesus Christ.

> *Holy Spirit, help me to cooperate with You as You continue to conform me to the image of Jesus Christ.*

Evening Watch: Read Psalm 69:15–36. Even though David did not see Jesus Christ in the flesh, I believe he knew Jesus in the spirit. The reproach David described in this psalm is exactly the same reproach Jesus experienced on the cross. David wrote, "They also gave me gall for my food, And for my thirst they gave me vinegar to drink" (v. 21). These exact words were used in all four Gospels to describe Jesus' condition on the cross. (See Matthew 27:34; Mark 15:23; Luke 23:36; John 19:28–30.) On the cross Jesus bore the shame and reproach we may experience in our own lives. Jesus was despised and rejected of men. He was a man of sorrows, and He was acquainted with grief. Because of the cross our reproach is rolled away once and for all, and we no longer need to live a life bound by shame and reproach.

> *Hallelujah! Lord, thank You for setting me free from shame and from every enemy of my soul.*

Deuteronomy 11:1–12:32; Luke 8:22–40; Psalm 70:1–5; Proverbs 12:4

Morning Wisdom: Read Proverbs 12:4. I can recall sitting at a table with a couple at a birthday dinner party. There were four couples at each table. One of the wives kept saying derogatory remarks about her husband. She went on and on, sharing with us all of her husband's failures. The other couples kept trying to change the subject with no success. I felt so sorry for her husband.

The verse today says that a wife who causes her husband shame is like rottenness to his bones. Two more verses talk about how the words we speak can affect bones. Proverbs 15:30 says, "A good report makes the bones healthy." Proverbs 16:24 declares, "Pleasant words are like a honeycomb, Sweetness to the soul and health to the bones."

The words we speak have the power to affect not only our own health but also the health of the person to whom we speak. An excellent wife is to be a crown to her husband, which means she is to honor and respect her husband.

We are commanded to esteem one another higher than ourselves. Wives are commanded to honor and respect their husbands. The percentage of divorces in the church is the same as the percentage of divorces in the world. This would not be true if wives would speak only those things that edify or build up their husbands. I am challenged by this verse to be more careful with the words I speak to others about my husband and also the words I speak to him directly.

Lord, help me to only speak those things that edify.

Evening Watch: Read Psalm 70:1–5. We learned this morning how our words can affect others. The words we speak also have the power to create a positive or a negative atmosphere in our homes and offices. We can magnify the presence of the Lord by the very words we speak. This psalm exhorts everyone who seeks the Lord to say continually, "Let God be magnified" (v. 4). This would be a great declaration for you to make when you get up every morning. Before you have your first cup of coffee in the morning, declare these words out loud:

Let the Lord be magnified in my home and office today! Let the Lord be magnified in my heart and life today! Let the Lord be magnified in my church today! Let the Lord be magnified in my marriage today!

Before you rest your head on your pillow, declare:

Let the Lord be magnified in my dreams tonight.

MARCH 30

Morning Wisdom: Read Proverbs 12:5–7. We have been talking about the power of words. This reading from Proverbs tells us that the mouth of the upright has delivering power. A wicked person lies in wait to ensnare and harm others. The good news is that those who are righteous can deliver those who have been ensnared by the devil. Our very prayers can pull down strongholds in another person's life and can liberate that person from bondage.

Paul told us that the weapons of our warfare are mighty through God to the pulling down of strongholds. (See 2 Corinthians 10:4–7.) We have the power through prayer to cast down vain imaginations, prideful thoughts, and every high thing that exalts itself against the knowledge of Jesus Christ. We can speak liberty to those who are held captive by Satan and his seducing spirits. Strongholds are fortresses in the mind that house rebellious thoughts that are contrary to the truth of God's Word. Strongholds are built in our minds by what we have been taught or what we have experienced in life. Pride is the major stronghold that keeps people from accepting Jesus Christ.

When we use the weapon of declaring God's Word in prayer as we intercede for those who are in bondage, we will see many delivered from the wiles of Satan.

The effective, fervent prayers of a righteous person will avail much. (See James 5:16.)

Lord, help me to pray effectively.

Evening Watch: Read Psalm 71:1–24. This psalm presents many ways that we can magnify the Lord. We magnify the Lord whenever we declare His magnificence. David declared that the Lord was his strong refuge and fortress (v. 3). David put his trust and hope in the Lord (v. 5).

David vowed to tell of the Lord's righteousness and salvation daily. He said he would praise the Lord continually, no matter what enemies he faced daily. He declared God's wondrous works to his generation and the power of the Lord to everyone who would follow his generation. The secret to David's overcoming life was his "tongue talk." He said, "My tongue also shall talk of Your righteousness all the day long" (v. 24). When we magnify the Lord with our mouths, the enemies of our souls will always be defeated.

Lord, may my mouth always magnify You.

MARCH 31

Deuteronomy 16:1–17:20; Luke 9:7–27; Psalm 72:1–20; Proverbs 12:8–9

Morning Wisdom: Read Proverbs 12:8–9. When we are in pride we think either too highly or too lowly of ourselves. When we think too lowly of ourselves, we slight ourselves. When we think too highly of ourselves, we may boast of having a lot when in reality we have nothing. Proverbs 12:9 reads, "Better is the one who is slighted but has a servant, Than he who honors himself but lacks bread." Jesus told us that He came to be both our servant and our friend.

When we realize that Jesus Christ is both our servant and our friend, we will not fall into the trap of low self-esteem. When we know that the God of the whole universe came to Earth as a servant in the form of Jesus to save and serve us and even to be our Friend, we will see ourselves as God sees us. He sees us as righteous, because He sent His righteous Son to die for us to cleanse us from all of our sins.

You will walk in true humility today if you will see yourself as God sees you. You will never think of yourself as worthless, because you were bought with a great price—the shed blood of Jesus Christ, God's only Son. We will never lack any good thing, nor will we ever have to beg for bread, because Jesus is our Provider, and most of all He is a Friend who sticks closer than a brother to us. Enjoy your friendship with Jesus today.

When you spend time daily with your Friend Jesus, you will learn meekness and lowliness of heart, and you will find rest for your soul.

Lord, thank You for being my friend.

Evening Watch: Read Psalm 72:1–20. "It's not fair! It's not fair!" How many of you parents heard that exclamation over and over again when your children got into strife. Life is not fair, and God is not fair. God is just. This psalm declares how God will bring justice to the poor and deal justly with the oppressor. This psalm was written by Solomon, and the word pictures he used are delightful.

Solomon wrote, "He [God] shall come down like rain upon the grass before mowing, Like showers that water the earth. In His days the righteous shall flourish, And abundance of peace, Until the moon is no more" (vv. 6–7). There is nothing more relaxing than a gentle, quiet rain flowing upon freshly cut grass. When rain comes down on tall grass, however, one can hear the drops of rain crashing against the blades of grass as they blow in the wind. Judgment Day will not be a quiet day. On that day, God's voice will shake the earth. The righteous will flourish on that Judgment Day, because the river of life will cause them to flourish. The contrast is clear. God's judgment of the wicked will not be peaceful or quiet. The judgment of the saints for rewards will be like gentle showers that water the earth. The rain falls on the just and the unjust. Pray for those you know who are not saved. The judgment they will face will not be peaceful.

Lord, I ask You to save [name the people].

APRIL 1

Morning Wisdom: Read Proverbs 12:10. It says, "A righteous man regards the life of his animal." We have a friend who has the gift of mercy. We always enjoy observing the tenderness he extends to his pets. He so impressed us with the care he gave his pets that we gave our dog to him. We had a problem with Ollie, our black lab, because he barked at all hours in the night. To stop the continual complaints from our neighbors, we gave Ollie to our friend who needed another hunting dog. We are convinced that our friend's loving care of Ollie converted our pagan dog to Christianity. I know Ollie thought he had died and gone to doggie heaven, because he was allowed to be an inside dog. Ollie's days were spent by the fire eating venison. He even took his baths in the shower inside the house.

God's tender love to all of His creatures exceeds any love and mercy we might extend to others or our pets. God invites us daily to abide in His home, where we can be warmed by His love and feast on His Word. Daily He seeks to wash us with His Word and shower us with His blessings. Oh, how great are the tender mercies of our heavenly Father! His mercies are new every morning. Take time this morning to let His love and mercy warm and comfort you.

Lord, thank You for Your tender care.

Evening Watch: Read Psalm 73:1–28. We learned this morning that a righteous man shows mercy and kindness to his pets. Nothing is said in Psalms about how the wicked treat their pets, but I am sure they kick their dogs often. The description the psalmist gave of the wicked in this psalm was extremely vivid. Horrible mental images popped into my mind as I read this psalm. I saw the wicked draped in garments stained with the blood from their violence. They had long tongues that slithered like snakes throughout the earth. They drooled as their tongues tasted the juicy bits of slander, gossip, and lies supplied by their gaping mouths.

The psalmist admitted that he was jealous of the wicked, because despite their violence and cruel tongues, they seemed to prosper and be at ease. Even in death, they seemed to be strong. The psalmist remained in his miserable jealousy until he went into the sanctuary. In the quietness of God's sanctuary, he understood the final end of the wicked. Destruction and desolation would be the end of the wicked.

The intimate time with God that the psalmist experienced in the sanctuary also helped him to see how good God had been to him. He recognized that only God could satisfy and strengthen his heart. Spend a few moments recounting God's goodness towards you before you go to bed tonight. This could be a nightly exercise that will be much more beneficial than counting sheep.

Lord, thank You for Your goodness towards me.

Deuteronomy 21:1–22:30; Luke 9:51–10:12; Psalm 74:1–23; Proverbs 12:11

Morning Wisdom: Read Proverbs 12:11. There are many scriptures in the Bible that describe people who lack understanding. For example, a person who commits adultery lacks understanding. (See Proverbs 6:32.) Today's verse tells us that anyone who follows after vain people is void of understanding.

How do we follow after vain people? Sometimes we give more time and attention to sports heroes and Hollywood stars than we do the Lord and our own family members. I heard that the average American spends at least four hours a day in front of the TV. I remember my mom and mother-in-law discussing for hours the lives of people who I did not know personally. I finally asked my mom, "Those people really sound mixed up. Where do they live and how do you know them?" My mom responded, "We're talking about soap opera characters, not real people." Sometimes we invest more time in the lives of people who are not real than the lives of those who live with us daily.

When our boys were younger we did without a TV for eleven years. During those years the boys' grades went up. We loved playing board games with each other and actually had eye-to-eye contact with them when we conversed together. We were able to understand our boys better because the communication lines were not interrupted by sports or movies on TV. I believe we all will grow in understanding instead of lack understanding if we limit the time we spend in front of inanimate objects like the TV or the computer. God wants us to invest our time in people, because they are His treasures.

Today, look for opportunities to invest your time in others.

> *Lord, forgive me for wasting Your precious time. Help me to invest my time in people, not things.*

Evening Watch: Read Psalm 74:1–23. We learned this morning that people who lack understanding commit many sins. Understanding is part of the anointing of God's Spirit that can only be obtained through reading and heeding God's Word. Even though every person born on this earth has a conscience that supplies them with the knowledge of good and evil, only Scripture can give people the understanding that will cause them to do good instead of evil.

The psalmist who wrote this psalm lamented, because he felt God had forsaken him. For a moment he lacked understanding and thought the wicked were winning over the righteous. He asked the question, "O God, how long will the adversary reproach? Will the enemy blaspheme Your name forever?" (v. 10). I'm sure you have had frustrating days when you felt like God was on vacation and the devil had set up camp in your household. We all on such days cannot help but cry out, "God, do something!"

The truth is that God has already done everything we need through Jesus. Praise Him!

> *Lord, thank You for never going on vacation. I know You always hear me when I cry out for Your help.*

Deuteronomy 23:1–25:19; Luke 10:13–37; Psalm 75:1–10; Proverbs 12:12–14

Morning Wisdom: Read Proverbs 12:12–14. As I listened to the testimony of my sister-in-law, I was amazed at the troubles she had experienced in her life. She is now sixty-three years old, and at this late date in her life she has finally been set free to enjoy God's kingdom here on Earth. God's kingdom is righteousness, peace, and joy in the Holy Spirit.

She divided her life into seven-year increments. Each seven-year period was full of trouble. For example, during the first seven years of her marriage, her husband was not saved. The following seven-year periods were filled with many moves because of lost jobs. With each move she faced a new set of problems. At the end of her testimony I was in awe of how she was able to get through everything she faced in her life.

When I read this morning's verses I learned her secret. Proverbs 12:13 says, "But the righteous will come through trouble." What a wonderful promise to those who have received the righteousness of Jesus Christ and who seek to walk in His righteousness daily! No matter what trials, tests, or troubles you may face today or the rest of your life, you can face them, because you know God will see you through every trouble.

Thank You, Lord, for seeing me through troubled waters.

Evening Watch: Read Psalm 75:1–10. We learned this morning that God is able to get us through any trial we may experience on Earth. The key to victory in trials is to cast every care upon Jesus. We humble ourselves before the Lord when we transfer every burden to Him. God exalts the humble and also gives sufficient grace to them to carry them through the troubled waters of this life. We learn in this psalm that exaltation and promotion do not come from the east or from the west or even from the south. Promotion and exaltation come from God.

True humility occurs when we cast every care upon the Lord and we trust Him fully with every aspect of our lives. We do not have to push ourselves up the worldly success ladder or prove our worth to others. God will open doors to promote us in His timing. Think about that tonight as you close your eyes and remember His promise to meet all of your needs according to the riches of His glory through Jesus Christ. (See Philippians 4:19.)

Lord, I humble myself before You, and I cast every care upon You. Let me exalt You both in word and deed tomorrow.

April 4

Morning Wisdom: Read Proverbs 12:15–17. There are a lot of shameful things going on in this world today. We are warned in Scripture not to ever even talk about such things. (See Ephesians 5:11–12.) Last night I heard a speaker who stopped in the middle of this sentence, "The hair on your head would stand on end if you knew..." He was about to describe the things that went on in the limousine he drove for a well-known evangelist. The Holy Spirit stopped him in the middle of his sentence and he said, "Forgive me; I almost said some things I should not."

This chapter in Proverbs tells us that the prudent man covers shame. We are prudent when we refuse to speak about shameful things, because that type of conversation opens the door for Satan to put all kinds of images in our minds and the minds of others. Another verse tells us that it is the glory of a man to cover a transgression. (See Proverbs 19:11.) Instead of talking about people's shameful sins, we need to confess our own to the Lord.

> *Lord, forgive me for the times I have shared shameful things people have done. Help me to guard my lips from ever speaking shameful things to others.*

Evening Watch: Read Psalm 76:1–12. Sometimes we forget that God's judgments are also weighted with His mercy.

Our God can express His wrath through judgment, but as believers in Christ Jesus we are not appointed to the day of God's wrath. (See 1 Thessalonians 5:9.) We are privileged to be living in the dispensation of God's grace. However, God still judges. His judgments are dispensed to deliver the oppressed on the earth.

The statement in this psalm that God girds Himself with wrath can easily be misunderstood. The only reason God would gird Himself with wrath would be to avenge those who are oppressed.

When we were in India we saw many people offering food to idols. They did this to appease the gods. There are over three hundred million gods in India that people could choose to worship. One of these gods is called Shiva, their god of destruction. We know who the destroyer is, and it is not Shiva. Satan came to destroy us, but Jesus came to destroy the works of the devil. Ultimately, Satan and all of his demons will be thrown into the lake of fire. Hell was made for the devil and his angels. One day God will judge all those who have died, as well as those who live to see His coming. God will take no pleasure when He sees the wicked perish, but because He is a just God, He will only pardon those who come to His Son for salvation. The knowledge of God's judgment stirs the burden I have in my heart for lost souls.

> *Lord, give me the opportunity tomorrow to share Your good news of grace and forgiveness with someone.*

Deuteronomy 28:1–68; Luke 11:14–36; Psalm 77:1–20; Proverbs 12:18

Morning Wisdom: Read Proverbs 12:18. We know that the Word of God is like a two-edged sword. It is able to divide asunder the soul from the spirit, and it is able to discern the thoughts and intents of the heart. (See Hebrews 4:12.) God's words are always used to heal. Our words often hurt others because the words we speak are like swords that can pierce and wound the heart of others. You have heard it said, "We hurt the ones we love the most." In a moment of strife we can say words that will wound even those we love. Those wounds can last for years if they are not exposed to the healing power of the cross.

This proverb says, "The tongue of wise promotes health." We need to pass the think test before we say a word. Philippians 4:8 tells us what we should think about:

> Finally, brethren, whatever things are true, whatever things are noble, whatever things are just, whatever things are pure, whatever things are lovely, whatever things are of good report, if there is any virtue and if there is anything praiseworthy—meditate [think] on these things.

Before I speak a word, I ask myself, "Is what I am about to speak noble, just, pure, lovely, of good report, virtuous, and praiseworthy?" If I can answer yes to the above criteria, then I speak what is on my mind. Remember when we give a person a piece of our mind, we lose some of our minds because we lack wisdom and understanding.

Lord, help me to think before I speak.

Evening Watch: Read Psalm 77:1–20. We learned this morning how important it is to think before we speak. We can trouble our own souls by what we speak. The psalmist said, "I am so troubled that I cannot speak" (v. 4). He should have kept his mouth closed in his troubles, but he complained instead. He said, "I complained, and my spirit was overwhelmed" (v. 3). We can overwhelm our spirits and our souls when we murmur and complain.

The only safe complaint department is the throne room of God. David learned the secret of pouring out his complaints to God instead of the people who surrounded him daily. The murmuring and complaining of the children of Israel kept them from entering the Promised Land. God is able to hear our complaints without prejudice or condemnation. Other people do not have these character qualities, and when we complain to them, we charge the atmosphere with negativity that will strike fear and distrust in the hearts of those listening to our complaints.

Tonight before you go to bed, pour out your complaints to God alone. He will hear your cry, and you will find relief for your troubled soul. Refuse to complain to anyone tomorrow.

Lord, help me not to murmur and complain.

APRIL 6

Morning Wisdom: Read Proverbs 12:19–20. When our sons were very young, I asked the Lord to tell me what their calling was in this life. A calling is not a vocation or even a ministry. A calling is like a golden thread that gathers many aspects of our lives together to form an invisible garment that clothes us daily. For example, the Lord revealed to me that I was called to be a voice on Earth to declare His Word. I discovered this when I asked the Lord what member of the body I was. He led me to the verse in John that described John the Baptist's calling. (See John 1:23.) He was a voice in the wilderness crying out to prepare the way of the Lord. My mission is to prepare the body of Christ for the second coming of the Lord, and this is why I have written three devotional books. When I asked the Lord about the calling of my three sons, I heard this in my spirit:

> Your oldest son is called to be a bridge between races. Your middle son is called to be a bridge between nations. Your youngest son is called to be a bridge between families. Your youngest son is a peacemaker.

The reading today says that the counselors of peace have joy. Ray, our youngest son, was called to bring peace between the two families of God—the Jewish people and Gentile believers. He served in Budapest, where he taught on Jewish roots and was able to pull down some of the walls of anti-Semitism in that city. As he fulfilled his calling, he had great joy whenever he was able to sow peace into the hearts of those who listened to his message. All of us are called to pursue peace with all people. (See Hebrews 12:14.) We don't have to go to Budapest to do this. You can sow peace into the hearts of all those you meet today.

Lord, help me to be an effective peacemaker.

Evening Watch: Read Psalm 78:1–25. One of my favorite things we do in our church is give testimonies. Whenever I hear a testimony, hope is stirred in my soul. I have hope that God can do the same thing in my life that He did for the person sharing the testimony.

Throughout the Bible God shares the testimonies of various people. Our psalm today says that God established a testimony in Jacob. He did this so that Jacob's testimony could be shared with the generations that would follow him and those generations could set their hope in God (vv. 5–7). Is your testimony one you want to be shared with the generations to come? God establishes a testimony through testing. Without a test, there is no testimony. Tomorrow you can receive the tests and trials you may face during the day with joy, because a great testimony is being established in your life. If you will endure your tests and trials with faith and patience and share with others how God brought you through, those who hear will be established in hope.

Lord, help me to share my testimony with someone tomorrow.

APRIL 7

Morning Wisdom: Read Proverbs 12:21–23. "Lying lips are an abomination to the LORD, But those who deal truthfully are His delight" (v. 22). That is an extremely strong statement. Why is lying an abomination to the Lord? As I asked myself that question I came up with the reasons why we lie and what happens when we lie. We lie because:

- we want to cover up something;
- we want to please others;
- we want to succeed in the world;
- we want to appear to be someone other than who we really are;
- we don't want God to be angry with us.

Lying produces the following:

- Those we lie to are hurt.
- One lie leads to more lies.
- When our lies are discovered, the consequences usually cause loss.
- Our fellowship with God is broken.
- No one ever will trust us.
- Lies can affect generations to come.

God hates lying because He knows what will happen to us when we lie. When we lie we are doing Satan's work. Jesus called Satan the father of lies. (See John 8:44.) I challenge you this morning to review Scripture and see the disastrous results that happened when some of our Bible heroes lied. You might look at Abraham, Isaac, and Jacob to begin your study.

Lord, help me to be truthful today with all those I encounter.

Evening Watch: Read Psalm 78:26–45. This morning we discussed the reasons why we lie and what happens when we lie. This psalm speaks about the children of Israel and what happened to their character because they lied. This psalm reveals that unbelief is one of the root causes of lying. The children of Israel saw all the wondrous works of God, but they still did not believe, and they sinned. They flattered God with their mouths, but they were lawless in their actions.

Flattery is a form of lying. Because they lied to God with their tongues, they were unfaithful and lacked steadfastness. They were ungrateful and soon forgot how God led them out of bondage. Unfaithfulness and ungratefulness always result when we do not repent of lying. The good news is that God forgave the children of Israel, and He also will forgive you if you will be honest with God and confess the times you have lied.

Lord, I confess the times I have lied, and I repent before You.

Deuteronomy 32:30–52; Luke 12:35–59; Psalm 78:46–58; Proverbs 12:24

Morning Wisdom: Read Proverbs 12:24. We were in Savannah on a tour of the city when I learned exactly how the state of Georgia was established. Our guide told us that General Oglethorpe had a friend who died in a debtor's prison. The death of his friend caused Oglethorpe to seek ways to help those who were in debt. He interviewed people who were destined to be imprisoned, because they could not pay their bills. He offered those who were skilled in building, planning, law, medicine, and other essential skills a chance to go to America to settle and begin again. The indebtedness of these people was not caused by their laziness. They all wanted a chance to have their debt removed so that they could begin again.

Our verse today says that the "hand of the diligent will rule, But the lazy man will be put to forced labor." If Oglethorpe had not offered the chance to begin again, the people he chose faced a debtor's prison and forced labor. Forced labor can be the consequence people may face even if they are not lazy.

Oglethorpe saved the day for many in England who faced forced labor. We have a Savior who has saved us from forced labor. Jesus paid the debt we owed for our own sins and then presented us the opportunity to be free from forced labor. Once we accept Jesus, we will never have to be forced to labor. We no longer have to struggle to be right with God by doing good works. We are instantly made righteous when we accept Jesus and commit our lives to His lordship. He then will begin to work through us both to give us a desire to do His will and to give us the strength to accomplish His will on Earth. (See Philippians 2:13.) We have all been spared a debtor's prison. We can have our debt removed and start again. Praise His holy name!

Lord, thank You for freedom!

Evening Watch: Read Psalm 78:46–58. This psalm continues to review the great works God did for Israel when He delivered them from Egypt. It reviews the various plagues God sent to Egypt. The children of Israel had seen God's mighty hand move on their behalf when they were delivered from the bondage they experienced in Egypt. However, they entered another type of bondage when they walked through the wilderness. They entered the bondage of ungratefulness. Soon after they had seen God's mighty miracles of deliverance, they began to worship other gods. They began to murmur and complain, and this started them down the slippery slope that ended in total idolatry. They even established places of worship in the high mountains, and God was moved to jealousy.

The downward spiral of sin most always begins with an ungrateful heart. Romans 1 describes the downward spiral of sin. First those who did know God refused to glorify Him and they were ungrateful. Their ungratefulness led to foolish thinking, idolatry, uncleanliness, and unbelief. They exchanged the truth of God for a lie and worshiped the creature rather than the Creator. Whenever we murmur and complain, we need to ask ourselves who is on the throne of our hearts. Have we traded the truth of God for a lie?

Lord, help me to always have a truthful heart.

Deuteronomy 33:1–29; Luke 13:1–22; Psalm 78:59–72; Proverbs 12:25

Morning Wisdom: Read Proverbs 12:25. Recently I took a test to determine my spiritual gifts. One of those gifts was the gift of exhortation. This is a spiritual gift that needs to be used more in the body of Christ. Our verse tells us that a good word can make a heavy heart glad. There are many heavy-hearted people today. When we ask people how they are doing, we usually receive this response, "OK under the circumstances." Few of us really want to give a listening ear to hear what circumstances are troubling the person we just asked this question. However, a listening ear and a good word are exactly what this person needs.

Jesus had the ability to see the hearts of individuals. A person might say one thing, but He knew exactly how they were feeling and what was going on in that individual's life. We do not have that ability. However, the Holy Spirit can give us keen discernment if we will ask Him for the ability to see beyond the words people speak. We are called to walk as Jesus walked on Earth, and that walk included the ability to minister to people's needs.

The Holy Spirit has helped me to discern when a person is depressed. Some of the signs of depression in a person are:

- They sigh often;
- They stoop when they walk;
- They have a grayish countenance;
- They mumble or speak with a quiet voice.

In order to speak a good word to a heavy-hearted person, we need to be alert to recognize these signs of depression. I believe if more people in the body used the gift of discernment and the gift of exhortation, Christian counseling centers would close down. Be alert today to give a good word to someone who is downcast. The Bible exhorts us to be ready to give a word in season to others. (See 2 Timothy 4:2.)

Lord, give me just the right exhortations for the people I meet today.

Evening Watch: Read Psalm 78:59–72. I am always learning more about the character of God. Since we are the body of Christ, our goal is to be the heart and hands of Jesus to others. Today's reading in Psalms talks about God's heart and hands. God's has a heart that is filled with integrity. He also has skillful hands.

We are all called to not just talk the talk, but also to walk the walk. What we say and do daily displays what is in our hearts to others. It is so easy for us to preach one thing and do another. However, a person of integrity will demonstrate the love of Jesus in word and deed. Think over your day as you retire to bed, and ask yourself this question, "Did I demonstrate the love of Jesus today in word and deed?" Make it your goal tomorrow to be Jesus' heart and hands to others.

Lord, give me a heart of love.

Deuteronomy 34:1–Joshua 2:24; Luke 13:23–14:6; Psalm 79:1–13; Proverbs 12:26

Morning Wisdom: Read Proverbs 12:26. We are warned in the Bible that in the last days seducing spirits will be on the rampage. Their goal is to lure even righteous people into doing things that will destroy their testimony. Our proverb today says that wicked people can seduce even the righteous. We need to take heed if we think we stand, lest we fall. (See 1 Corinthians 10:12.)

In the last decade we have seen great preachers and evangelists fall into all kinds of sin. We are led astray by our own lusts. However, seducing spirits have the assignment to tantalize and tempt us in the area of our lusts. They watch for our weak spots and then tempt us in those areas. If we have given in to one of the three lusts (lust of the flesh—seeking to gratify our five senses in an indulgent way; the lust of the eyes—greed, covetousness, idolatry; or the lust of the pride of life—trusting in ourselves more than we trust in God), seducing spirits will target and tempt us in that lust. These seducing spirits will usually use the same bait that worked before when we gave in to one of our lusts and sinned.

We can shut the door to their seductive suggestions if we will speak the Word out loud. A good word to speak is: "My righteousness is of Jesus Christ." (See Isaiah 54:17.)

If we try to stand against seducing spirits in our own righteousness, we will fall.

When we are tempted and the devil knocks on the door of one or more of our lusts, we need to send Jesus to the door. Jesus was tempted in all points as we are, but He was without sin. (See Hebrews 2:18.) Now, He can rescue us quickly when we call upon His name and ask for His strength to close the door in the face of the devil and his hoards of demonic spirits.

Lord, thank You for giving me authority over seducing spirits.

Evening Watch: Read Psalm 79:1–13. I have been reading a book about sheep, and now I have a better understanding of why God calls us the sheep of His pasture. Sheep are not smart animals. They cannot do anything for themselves. Their shepherds have to lead them to good pastureland and quiet, clean waters. Shepherds have to protect their sheep from pests and predators.

The psalm today talks about the predators that want to rob, kill, and destroy us. We have to remember that this is the assignment that Satan and his demons have against us.

Just recently we had an experience with predators who stole checks out of our mailbox. These predators proceeded to make counterfeit checks and were able to clean out one of our accounts. This psalm gives me hope that God will avenge this wicked deed and we will receive sevenfold in return for this reproach against us. In the meantime I will forgive these thieves and pray for their salvation.

Lord, thank You for being my Good Shepherd.

Morning Wisdom: Read Proverbs 12:27–28. God promises many things to those who walk uprightly. When we receive Jesus Christ as our Lord and Savior, we receive Jesus' righteousness. Our challenge after receiving Christ is to walk daily in a righteous way.

The verses today give an almost unbelievable promise. It sounds too good to be true. Listen to this promise again:

> In the way of righteousness is life, And in its pathway there is no death.
> —PROVERBS 12:28

What on earth does this mean? We all know the statistic that one out of one dies. We all have our appointment with death. (See Hebrews 9:27.) However, the appointment believers have with death is quite different from the appointment unbelievers have. When the believer dies, he will simply stop breathing. With his last breath, his soul and spirit will instantly go to be with Jesus. To be absent from the body is to be present with the Lord. (See 2 Corinthians 5:8.)

When Lazarus died, Jesus told His disciples that Lazarus was asleep. (See John 11:11.) Death for a Christian is like falling asleep and waking up in the arms of Jesus. We may experience pain and sorrow before death, but there will be no more pain and sorrow after we die.

It amazes me that many Christians fear death. If they knew and believed Scripture, the fear of death would be eliminated. First Corinthians 15:55 says:

> O Death, where is your sting? O Hades, where is your victory?

Lord, thank You for the victory over both death and hell.

Evening Watch: Read Psalm 80:1–19. Another rainy day in Georgia! I live in Atlanta, and we have more rain than Seattle. One bright note is that the fronts that bring rain to our city pass through quickly. The day after a good rain is bright and beautiful, because all the pollution, smog, and pollen have been washed out of the atmosphere.

Sometimes we can experience rainy days in our souls even when the sun is shining brightly outside. The psalmist who wrote this psalm must have been experiencing a rainy day in his soul. He kept asking God to cause His face to shine upon him. When we experience rainy days in our souls, the Lord can break through the clouds of depression, oppression, and despondency with His sunshine. We need to remember that during those rainy days of our souls, the Holy Spirit is doing a work of cleansing and restoration.

Lord, thank You for rainy days.

APRIL 12

Joshua 5:1–7:15; Luke 15:1–32; Psalm 81:1–16; Proverbs 13:1

Morning Wisdom: Read Proverbs 13:1. One of my constant prayers when my three sons were young was that they would all be able to hear the voice of the Lord. To receive the blessings of God we must both hear the voice of God and obey His voice.

The verse today says that a wise son hears his father's instruction, but a scorner does not hear when he is rebuked. Scripture contains all of our heavenly Father's instructions. The Word of God is a rod of correction. It is also a two-edged sword that is able to discern the thoughts and the intents of the heart. (See Hebrews 4:12.)

Some Christians have a hard time hearing from God. I believe our hearing problem could be solved easily if we would spend half an hour daily reading the Word of God out loud. We can just read out loud to ourselves, but if we read Scripture out loud to our spouse or our children, there will be a double blessing. We will be blessed and those listening will be blessed also. Faith comes when we hear the Word of God. (See Romans 10:17.)

> Lord, help me to humbly receive the correction and instructions You give me in Your Word.

Evening Watch: Read Psalm 81:1–16. This psalm contains one of my favorite verses of Scripture. In fact, I have been claiming the promise found in this verse of Scripture for years. Let me share the King James Version of one of my favorite verses.

> I removed his shoulder from the burden: his hands were delivered from the pots.
>
> —PSALM 81:6 KJV

As the only female in a house full of four hungry men, it seemed most of my waking years were spent in the kitchen. I would just finish cleaning up the breakfast dishes on Saturday mornings when the boys would ask me, "What's for lunch?" I longed for the day when the promise in this verse would be fulfilled in my life. Now that the boys have wives who are their love slaves in their own kitchen, I can almost proclaim this promise, "He has delivered my hands from the pots."

The psalmist reviewed God's warnings not to become idolatrous. The psalmist reminded them of the time God commanded, "There shall be no foreign god among you; Nor shall you worship any foreign god. I am the LORD your God, Who brought you out of the land of Egypt; Open your mouth wide, and I will fill it" (vv. 9–10). Food can become a great idol in our lives, and that is one of the reasons I believe God exhorts us to fast.

Paul warned about those who allow their bellies to become their gods. (See Philippians 3:19.) God's promise is that He will fill our mouths if we will open them wide. When we open our mouths wide to praise Him, God satisfies our every longing.

> Lord, I praise You with my lips, and I extol You with my open mouth.

Morning Wisdom: Read Proverbs 13:2–3. During World War II there was a saying, "Loose lips sink ships." This was a warning to citizens to be careful not to reveal any secrets about the war to anyone since no one was to be trusted. Proverbs 13:3 warns that loose lips have the power to destroy. If we do not guard the gates of our mouths, we can destroy another person through gossip and slander.

Another proverb says that we can trouble our own souls by the words we speak. (See Proverbs 21:23.) The very words we speak can backfire on us and wound us.

Every morning I ask God to keep the door of my lips. You might want to join me this morning as I pray this prayer:

> *Father, let the words of my mouth and the meditations of my heart be acceptable to You, my Savior and Redeemer.*

Evening Watch: Read Psalm 82:1–8. The earth is the Lord's and the fullness thereof. We have to remember that God is sovereign and His plans for the earth will be accomplished. In these last days, we are entering a period of great turmoil. Jesus told us exactly what would be happening on Earth just before He came again. He said there would be wars and rumors of wars, famines, earthquakes, and pestilences. (See Matthew 24:6–7.) He said that these are just the signs of the beginning of sorrows that will sweep the earth before His return.

Just before a baby is born, the mother experiences the greatest travail during her labor. The whole earth seems to be in travail as it awaits the second coming of the Lord.

The recent tsunami should alert us all to the fact that soon the Lord will return. This psalm says, "All the foundations of the earth are out of course" (v. 5, KJV). After the tsunami, scientists confirmed that the earth's course had shifted a little. We need to be aware of the signs of the times. When we see these signs, we can look up, because our redemption draws nigh. Are you ready for the Lord's soon return?

> *Lord, help me to be ready every day for Your return.*

April 14

Morning Wisdom: Read Proverbs 13:4. I can remember the frustration I experienced when I attempted to get my boys out of bed to go to school. Sometimes I would threaten to put a cold, wet rag on their faces if they did not get out of the bed. On several occasions I lost it and shouted, "Wake up, you lazy sluggards!" I know better than to do that today, but we all lose it at times. Proverbs has a lot to say about sluggards. After reading a few of the statements in Proverbs, I discovered the horrible consequences of being lazy.

Today's verse relates one of these consequences. It says that the soul of a sluggard has nothing. If we are diligent, however, we will have wealth. The King James Version says the "soul of the diligent shall be made fat." I much rather have a fat soul than a fat body. We have a fat soul when our souls are filled with the love, peace, and joy of Jesus. We have a fat soul when we are careful to daily feed ourselves the Word of God, which is the Bread of Life. Our souls cannot afford to go on a "low-carb diet." We need to constantly intake and digest this satisfying Bread of Life (the Word of God).

Reading and meditating on the Word of God daily will keep us from becoming lazy sluggards. Perseverance, determination, patience, and endurance will develop when we diligently digest God's Word daily.

Some people say, "Well, I just do not have time to read the Bible!" I have only heard a few people exclaim, "Well, I just do not have time to eat!" May I suggest a creative way to read God's Word? During breakfast read a chapter in Proverbs. During break time read the New Testament reading. During dinner or at the afternoon break read the Old Testament reading. At night before you go to bed read a psalm. When we divide our daily readings according to our meals and bedtime, we will be able to absorb and digest what we are reading. Inch by inch, it's a cinch! Mile by mile, it takes a while!

Lord, help me to daily diligently digest Your Word.

Evening Watch: Read Psalm 83:1–18. Almost daily, the news has some report of trouble in Israel. There are still nations who want to push Israel into the sea. I try to stay updated on reports directly from Israel by reliable sources, and the latest report I received caused me to tremble. The report I read said that a Muslim coalition was forming and planned to attack Israel as soon as the U.S. pulled its troops out of Iraq. Ezekiel 38:16–23 speaks about this coalition and actually names the countries that will be involved in this attack against Israel. The daily paper reads like the Bible, because we are seeing prophecies fulfilled in our day.

The psalmist in our reading asks God to confound or put to confusion the enemies of Israel. This is a good prayer not only to pray for Israel but also to pray for our souls. We have enemies who seek to destroy our souls. Join me as I pray against these enemies.

Lord, confound the enemies of my soul.

APRIL 15

Morning Wisdom: Read Proverbs 13:5–6. Verse 6 says, "Righteousness keeps him whose way is blameless." Righteousness has the power to keep us walking on the correct path. Psalm 23 tells us that our Good Shepherd, Jesus Christ, leads us in the paths of righteousness for His name's sake.

We are ambassadors for Christ in the foreign land of Earth. We are citizens of heaven, and as Christ's ambassadors and heavenly citizens, we are all called to fulfill our public duty.

I am writing this devotional while I am fulfilling one of my public duties. Right now I am sitting in a jury pool, because a month ago I was summoned to appear at the courthouse to serve on the jury. Fulfilling this public duty is a pleasure, because I know our justice system depends on good jurors.

Fulfilling my public duty as a citizen of heaven is also a pleasure. The public duty of every Christian is to daily walk in a righteous way. Others observe my actions and hear my words, and I do not want to bring reproach to the name of Jesus by my sinful actions or words. If I do not daily convey the love of Jesus Christ to others, I have failed in my public duty as a citizen of heaven.

Lord, help me today to fulfill my public duty as a citizen of heaven.

Evening Watch: Read Psalm 84:1–12. We talked about being ambassadors for Christ in this foreign land we call Earth. Every foreign ambassador has an embassy, a place of safety where he can conduct his business unhindered by those who would seek to gain his favor through manipulation. As ambassadors for Christ we have an embassy that provides not only a place of safety, but also a place where we can be strengthened, refreshed, and discover God's grace expressed through the presence of His glory. That place is described in this psalm.

The psalm begins, "How lovely is Your tabernacle, O LORD of hosts!" The psalmist said that even the birds seek out this sanctuary of peace and safety. Those who dwell in this sanctuary are blessed. As I continued reading this psalm, I saw the pilgrims making their journey three times a year to the temple in Jerusalem. Their journey was weary and filled with dangers, but they sang songs of praise as they made their ascent to Jerusalem. The long journey seemed but a short one because their hearts were filled with joy. Soon they would reach their destination where they could worship in the beauty of God's sanctuary.

We can enter this special embassy of our God daily. Tomorrow plan to enter His gates with thanksgiving and His courts with praise. Commune with God in the holy place and discover the foundation of faith and peace that will strengthen you throughout the day.

Lord, thank You for dwelling in the temple of my body.

Joshua 13:1–14:15; Luke 18:1–17; Psalm 85:1–13; Proverbs 13:7–8

Morning Wisdom: Read Proverbs 13:7–8. This reading tells us that the ransom of a man's life is his riches. Most of us have seen dramas on TV and in the movies that portray kidnappings. The kidnapper usually asks for a ransom, and he threatens to kill the child if the ransom is not paid. The kidnappers usually victimize children who belong to extremely wealthy people.

When we became Christians, we were adopted into the wealthiest family in heaven and Earth. Our heavenly Father owns the cattle on a thousand hills. Satan often targets this wealthy family and is able to kidnap the children who have not learned to resist him. Satan is able to capture the minds of new babes in Christ by placing thoughts of doubt and unbelief in their minds. Satan, however, will not receive a ransom for his dastardly deeds, because the ransom to rescue these babes in Christ has already been paid. It was paid two thousand years ago when Jesus died on the cross. Jesus' very own blood was the ransom payment for all those who are kidnapped by Satan.

The day Jesus died, the schemes and plans of Satan were defeated. The more mature Christians in the family of God need to use their spiritual weapons to rescue the babes who have not learned to resist Satan. (See 2 Corinthians 10:3–6.) The older brothers and sisters in the Lord need to come alongside the babes in Christ and teach them how to resist Satan by using the spiritual weapons that are mighty through God. Today think of those babes in Christ you know who are having doubts about their decision to follow Christ. Intercede for them and if possible come alongside them to teach them how to use their spiritual weapons to resist Satan.

Lord, help me to pray effectively for the new believers I know.

Evening Watch: Read Psalm 85:1–13. This morning we talked about the great ransom Jesus paid on the cross for all those who have been or will be kidnapped by Satan. We learned how it is up to the family of God to intercede and use their mighty spiritual weapons to rescue Satan's victims. When we imagine the scene of Jesus' crucifixion, we see a scene that is grotesque. We see the battered, bloody body of Jesus as He struggled to take His next breath. However, if we use our spiritual eyes and our divine imagination to picture this scene, we see a scene that is glorious. Psalm 85 paints that glorious picture.

With our spiritual eyes we can see how mercy and truth met together on that fateful day Jesus died for our sins. Righteousness and peace kissed each other and truth sprang forth. All righteousness looked down from heaven on that day and exclaimed, "Yes, the LORD will give what is good; And our land will yield its increase. Righteousness will go before Him, And shall make His footsteps our pathway" (Ps. 85:12–13). The righteous saints in heaven are still rejoicing over what Jesus did for mankind on the cross. "Worthy is the Lamb who was slain!" (Rev. 5:12).

Lord, thank You for being the perfect sacrificial lamb. Thank You for taking away my sins.

APRIL 17

Morning Wisdom: Read Proverbs 13:9–10. Proverbs 13:10 says, "By pride comes nothing but strife." Pride is one of the major sources of contention and strife. When we get into strife with another person, we are usually trying to prove our own point. We are defending our opinion, which is simply pride. Before you know it, we are arguing with that person, and if we are not careful, the words we speak could do great damage.

When we allow ourselves to get into strife, we have an audience that applauds us. I had a vivid picture of this audience when I counseled a couple who had a strife-filled marriage. As I closed my eyes and prayed for this couple, an unusual scene passed through my imagination. I saw this couple in a boxing ring. They were not wearing boxing gloves. Instead, they were striking one another with their tongues. Then my attention was drawn to the audience surrounding them. I was horrified when I saw hundreds of grotesque demons clapping their hands wildly as the couple continued their fight. I heard one yelling, "Hit her a lick! Tell her how she wounded you a year ago!"

Then I heard another one yelling to the wife, "Tell him what a lazy bum he is!"

That scene was all in my imagination, but I have never been able to get it out of my mind. When I am about to get into strife with my husband, the Holy Spirit replays that scene in my imagination, and I then am able to keep from saying hurtful things to my husband.

To win the victory over strife, we need to daily humble ourselves before the Lord. We do this when we surrender to the Lord what we think of as our own rights. In reality, when we accepted Jesus' righteousness in exchange for our own righteousness, we lost our own rights. We now possess the rights that were purchased for us on the cross. We now have the wonderful right to take authority over every demonic spirit that tries to get us into strife. Today seek peace and pursue it. If you are tempted to get into strife, remember the scene I described this morning.

Lord, help me to avoid strife today.

Evening Watch: Read Psalm 86:1–17. I talked earlier this month about the rainy days of our souls. The sun may be shining brightly outside, but our souls can be deluged with the downpour of worries and cares. The psalmist David experienced many days like this, and he learned the secret to overcoming those rainy days. He first learned to encourage himself in the Lord when he was greatly distressed. When he saw the city of Ziklag burned to the ground, he thought he had lost his entire family. At that moment of despair, Scripture records that David encouraged himself in the Lord. (See 1 Samuel 30:6.)

In this psalm, we see another way David learned to overcome his down days. On the days when his soul was cast down, he lifted his soul up to the Lord by declaring all the good things about God's character. Those declarations led Him to be immersed in worship and suddenly every care was released to the Lord.

Lord, I worship You and release every care to You.

April 18

Morning Wisdom: Read Proverbs 13:11. "Honesty is the best policy!" This is a tried and true statement that fits every situation in life. Another true statement about honesty is found in the verse for today. This proverb states that wealth gained through dishonest practices will ultimately diminish.

Just recently TV and radio news was filled with report of large corporations that dissolved because people in the company were "cooking the books." Those in charge of finances gave false reports about their earnings.

One of the wealthiest women in the US, Martha Stewart, had to go to prison for lying in court about receiving secret information about one of her investment stocks. The future of her company is very shaky now because of her dishonesty. "An honest day's work pays an honest day's wage" is a well-known saying. We may not make millions on this earth, but we will receive great rewards in heaven if we are honest in our business practices. Whenever we lie about anything, we are doing the devil's work for him, because he is the author of lies and the father of all lies. (See John 8:44.)

Evening Watch: Read Psalm 87:1–7. Did you know that your birthplace is recorded in heaven? We learn in this psalm that the Lord records where we were born in a registry. I believe the Lord records where and when we were physically born and where and when we were "born again." "Where were you born?" and "When were you born?" are two of the main questions asked on most government forms. When I am asked that question, I am tempted to write: "I was born twice in Atlanta, Georgia—once physically and once spiritually."

Where and when we are born has a lot to do with our future. For example, our Russian son, Vladimir, was born in Ukraine. When the Soviet Union dissolved, Vladimir was not accepted as a student in the top universities in Moscow, because he was a citizen of Ukraine. His mother, dad, and brother were born in Russia, but his father was transferred by the military to Ukraine where Vladimir was born. Vladimir's older brother was accepted to one of Moscow's finest universities, because he was a Russian citizen.

Vladimir came to our home as an exchange student. We saw that he was a bright student who deserved a good education, and miraculously we were able send him to Georgia Institute of Technology, where he graduated with honors. His birthplace could have held Vladimir back, but God intervened and he received a great education.

Where and when we were born physically could hold us back from accomplishing some of our goals in life. However, once we are born again by the Spirit of God, we can look forward to achieving all the most important goals in this life and the life to come. At our new birth we receive a great inheritance that far exceeds any wealth gained through an earthly inheritance. We become joint heirs with Christ, and we enter a kingdom that is rich with peace, righteousness, and joy in the Holy Spirit. Hallelujah!

Thank You, Lord, for intervening in my life to give me new life.

Morning Wisdom: Read Proverbs 12:12–14. "Don't get your hopes up!" This is the advice usually given to a person who has been diagnosed with a terminal illness. Doctors and family members usually are determined not to give false hope to a patient who has received a negative medical report. However, Proverbs 13:12 says, "Hope deferred makes the heart sick."

A person who has a terminal illness needs to hold on to hope more than ever. The hope this patient needs to hold on to is not false hope. The hope that will keep the soul of a sick person well is the hope they have in Jesus Christ. No matter what negative circumstance we may face in this life, we will be able to have peace of mind and heart when we put our hope in Jesus. We also will know the joy of the Lord, which will strengthen us for every trial we may face.

We can always keep our hopes up when the fountain of God's Word is springing from our souls. When we abide in the love of Jesus and abide in His Word, the eternal hope of Jesus Christ will anchor our souls through the many troubled waters we may experience in this life.

Thank You, Lord, for being my eternal hope.

Evening Watch: Read Psalm 88:1–18. Most of the psalms David wrote end on a positive note. This psalm is a contemplation of Heman the Ezrahite. I do not know Heman's history, but I am sure he had a melancholy temperament. People with a melancholy temperament tend to look on the dark side of life.

I struggle to cancel out negative statements spoken by others by speaking the positive. An atmosphere of negativity attracts the wrong kind of audience. That audience is a host of demonic spirits who have an assignment to keep us oppressed, distressed, and depressed.

As you read this psalm, I suggest that you write down a blessing you have received from God for every negative statement in this psalm. For example, when you read, "I am like a man who has no strength" (v. 4), write and speak, "but the joy of the Lord is my strength." When you read, "You have laid me in the lowest pit" (v. 6), write and speak, "but I know I am seated in Jesus Christ in heaven above all principalities and all pits."

Tomorrow make it your goal to turn your negative thoughts into positive thoughts. I promise you, you will have a blessed day.

Lord, thank You for all of Your positive blessings and promises to me.

Morning Wisdom: Read Proverbs 13:15–16. When we look at the life of Jesus, we see how He built a deep relationship with twelve people. His relationship with them was not based upon how much they understood about His teachings. Often His disciples did not have a clue about what He was telling them. It was not until His resurrection that His disciples finally understood many of the things He told and taught them.

The love and understanding Jesus had toward His disciples is what kept them faithful to Jesus. I came to an understanding of His compelling love when I had a vision of the face of Jesus. His eyes were like laser beams that pierced through me. He could see everything within me, and I felt naked before Him. As I looked at His eyes again, however, I saw great compassion flowing from them towards me. I knew He understood me and accepted me even with all of my shortcomings. The compassion He poured upon me in that vision actually caused my spirit to leap within me. I wanted to run and fall into His arms. I said to myself, *No wonder the fishermen on the Galilee dropped their nets immediately and followed Jesus.*

We learn in our Proverbs reading today that "good understanding gains favor, But the way of the unfaithful is hard" (v. 15). Jesus was often misunderstood while He was on Earth. However, people were drawn to Jesus because He had the ability to see into their hearts and to understand exactly where they were coming from.

When we ask Jesus to help us see people as He sees them, we also will be able to have a better understanding of those we relate to daily. We will be able to see beyond their outer appearance. When we ask Jesus to help us hear people like He hears them, we will be able to hear not only their words but also their hearts. When we begin to understand people like Jesus understands them, people will be drawn to us. We will gain favor with them even though they might not understand all that we try to communicate with them. Today ask Jesus to give you His heart, His eyes, and His ears.

Lord, help me to relate to every person I meet today with Your understanding.

Evening Watch: Read Psalm 89:1–13. One of my constant prayers is, *Lord, help me to love like You love.* The love of the Lord Jesus Christ is supernatural. We talked this morning about seeing people as Jesus sees them. We have to see others with more than our natural eyes. Our natural eyes would prejudge people and even look down on people. God is faithful, however, to shed abroad the love of Jesus Christ in our hearts. This psalm extols the faithfulness of God and exhorts all the saints to reverence and fear Him. When we remember God's faithfulness to us, we can have faith that He is uprooting everything in our hearts that would block His love from flowing through us to others. This gives me great comfort.

Lord, thank You for Your faithfulness.

Joshua 22:21–23; Luke 20:27–47; Psalm 89:14–37; Proverbs 13:17–19

Morning Wisdom: Read Proverbs 13:17–19. The first part of verse 19 reads, "A desire accomplished is sweet to the soul." The New International Version of this verse reads: "A longing fulfilled is sweet to the soul." We all have longings in our souls that we want to be fulfilled.

Yesterday I heard a radio preacher say that every soul is God-shaped. When God breathed into Adam, he became a living soul. Adam became an earthly vessel that was filled with godly desires. Adam desired to enjoy God, worship God, and glorify Him.

After the fall Adam's soul was invaded by ungodly and worldly desires: the lust of the flesh—fulfilling his five senses in an indulgent way; the lust of the eyes—greedy longings in his mind that led to covetousness; and the lust of the pride of life—trusting in himself more than he trusted in God. Adam's godly spirit died and self now was on the throne of Adam's heart. Things did not get better for mankind. In fact the worldly lusts within man took over completely and God had to destroy all but eight people in the flood.

Worldly lusts will never satisfy the longings in a soul. Worldly lusts are never satiated. Jesus made it possible for every human being who believes in Him to once again be filled with the Spirit of the living God. On the cross, Jesus made it possible for every believer to have his soul restored. Only the Holy Spirit can put a longing in the hearts of people for Jesus. Pray today for your longing for Jesus to be increased and for those you love to begin to long for Jesus. When Jesus fulfills the longing in our hearts for Him, our souls will be satisfied.

Lord, rekindle the longing in my heart for You and place in the hearts of those I love the same longing.

Evening Watch: Read Psalm 89:14–37. This psalm flows beautifully from a description of God's throne to a description of David's throne. The description of God's throne in this psalm should give us all hope. Verse 14 says, "Righteousness and justice are the foundation of Your throne; Mercy and truth go before Your face." God measures justice with mercy and His righteousness lights our paths. He is our shield and strength. These facts about almighty God should make us rejoice in His name continually.

God promises to exalt David's throne and to cause his seed to endure forever. God declared that His faithfulness would never depart from David. God said David's throne would be as the sun before Him and it would be established like the moon.

God vowed never to break His covenant with David.

All the promises God gave to David are ours also. Because Jesus lives in us, we can be assured that God will not break His covenant with us either. He will always be our strength and shield. God will always be faithful to us.

Lord, thank You for Your faithfulness.

Joshua 24:1–33; Luke 21:1–28; Psalm 89:38–52; Proverbs 13:20–23

Morning Wisdom: Read Proverbs 13:20–23. Every time my sons see me using a measuring tape in the house, they sigh and exclaim, "There goes our inheritance!" Our house is over thirty years old, and during those years we have made many home improvements. I can remember standing on our deck measuring a space when my husband asked, "What are you measuring for now?" We had agreed to add a sunroom to the house, but I thought while the contractor was there he could also give us an estimate on building a tiny apartment attached to our home. When my husband recovered from the shock, he finally agreed to both additions. We have since used that apartment to help many souls who were in need of a place to stay. Our sons will still have an inheritance, although it has been diminished a little by some of our home improvements.

Proverbs 13:22 says that a good man will leave an inheritance to his children's children. As daughters and sons of God we have an inheritance that is eternal. That inheritance will never diminish. On the cross Jesus purchased a great inheritance for us. Then He sent us His Holy Spirit to put a seal on that inheritance.

Because we have received what Jesus did for us on the cross, we are the wealthiest people in the world. The wealth of sinners is temporary, and it is stored up for the righteous. Our inheritance is everlasting. Knowing about my great inheritance should deliver me from ever worrying about my treasures here on Earth. I should be challenged to add to my treasures in heaven daily, because these treasures will last forever.

> *Lord, thank You for my eternal inheritance.*

Evening Watch: Read Psalm 89:38–52. How I enjoyed reading Psalm 89 until I reached verse 38! What happened? All the promises were so precious, but the author of this psalm suddenly began to doubt God's goodness. This psalm was not written by David. It was written by Ethan the Ezrahite. Earlier we read another negative psalm by Heman the Ezrahite. (See Psalm 88:1–18.) The Ezrahites must have all been melancholy in temperament. The authors of both of these psalms accentuated the negative and almost eliminated the affirmative.

We have to accentuate the positive and eliminate the negative. "Mr. Negativity" is the devil, who constantly tries to rain on our parade and put out the fire of God in our hearts. Evidently he had great success with the Ezrahites.

Whenever we begin to declare negative things, we cooperate with "Mr. Negativity." He will take our very words and use them against us later. Whenever we entertain negative thoughts and declare them, the devil has gained a stronghold in our minds, and he will dwell there until we get out of our pattern of negativity.

> *Lord, help me to refuse negative thoughts and speak only positive things.*

APRIL 23

Morning Wisdom: Read Proverbs 13:24–25. "If you do that one more time, Johnny, you're going to get a spanking." Parents usually use the threatening method of discipline. However, our reading today exhorts parents to use the immediate method of discipline. Proverbs 13:24 says, "He who spares his rod hates his son, But he who loves him disciplines him promptly." Prompt discipline will usually yield prompt obedience.

When my children were young, I had a hard time spanking my boys. In fact, I had dreams about trying to spank them, but as I raised the belt to spank them, I became paralyzed. I finally came to a realization that I was paralyzed by the fear of rejection. I always had this question in the back of my mind: "If I spank my boys, will they still love me?"

God miraculously delivered me from the fear of rejection when I had to keep a friend's child for three weeks while his parents went to a Campus Crusade conference. I asked permission of his parents to spank their four-year-old if he was disobedient, and they responded, "Of course." I put up with the child's disobedience, because, frankly, I lacked the courage to spank him because of my fears.

The big test came when I was rushing the boys to get in the car to go to their baseball game. Suddenly I remembered I left something in the house and I did a stupid thing. I left the motor of the car running while I ran into the house. Thank God I engaged the emergency break, because when I returned, this four-year-old boy had stepped on the gas so hard that the tubes to the radiator blew off. I shiver every time I think about what could have happened if the emergency break had not been engaged. I proceeded to give that little boy a good wearing out on his bottom. After the spanking, something happened that amazed me. The child climbed up in my lap and hugged me. I never had another problem with him after that. He obeyed me instantly. Wouldn't it be wonderful if we obeyed God instantly? God is our loving heavenly Father who will not hesitate to discipline us when it is needed.

Lord, help me to obey You quickly.

Evening Watch: Read Psalm 90:1–91:16. Psalm 90 was written by Moses. Moses recounts the good times and what seemed to him to be the bad times in his journey with the Lord. He had seen the Lord's anger poured out upon the rebellious children of Israel. He knew that no one could ever hide his or her sins from the Lord. He declared that we are promised "seventy years; And if by reason of strength they are eighty years" (v. 10). He prayed, "Teach us to number our days, that we may apply our hearts unto wisdom" (v. 12, KJV). As I enter my sixty-sixth year, I recognize how swiftly the days go by. Psalm 91 gives us hope that God can prolong our days. (See v. 16.)

Lord, may this day and every day count for You.

Morning Wisdom: Read Proverbs 14:1–2. This proverb says every wise woman builds her house, but the foolish plucks it down with her hands. The building blocks a woman uses to build her house are her words. Every day a woman has the choice to build her house with her words or to tear her house down with her words.

As a wife, a woman has the charge to honor her husband. If she tears him down with critical, judgmental words, she is coming against her very own personhood, because she and her husband are one. As a mother, a woman must become a patient exhorter who takes time to give her children plenty of praise. The self-esteem of children has a lot to do with the words their parents spoke to them. I can remember counseling a family of five whose father continually spoke negative things to his children. He even told one of his sons that he was not worth the price of a bullet to blow his own head off. Is it any wonder that all of these five children have had severely low self-esteem?

As a homemaker, a woman has the duty of not just looking after her family's needs, but she also has the privilege of charging the atmosphere of her home with her praise, her hymns, and her spiritual songs to the Lord. Her praises can fill her home with an aroma that is better than any deodorizing spray. What we say has a lot to do with our remaining filled with the Spirit. Paul exhorted us to stay filled with the Spirit by speaking to one another in psalms and hymns and spiritual songs, singing and making melody in our hearts to the Lord. (See Ephesians 5:18–19.) If women and all of us obeyed Paul's exhortation, we would not have time to use our tongues to tear down others. I daily commit my tongue to the Lord by declaring this prayer:

> *Let the words of my mouth and the meditations of my heart be acceptable in Thy sight, O Lord, my strength and my Redeemer. May everything I say today glorify You and sow good seed into the lives of others. Amen.*

Evening Watch: Read Psalm 92:1–93:5. We talked this morning about committing our tongues to the Lord so that we will speak edifying words throughout the day. We can start the process of ordering our conversations aright as we are going to bed. David wrote, "It is good to give thanks to the LORD, And to sing praises to Your name, O Most High; To declare Your lovingkindness in the morning, And Your faithfulness every night" (Ps. 92:1–2). I have a friend who thinks over her day every night, and then writes down five things that happened during the day that she can give praises to God for that evening. She reads aloud the ways God showed His faithfulness to her during the day, and then she retires to a sweet sleep. Why don't you try that tonight?

> *Lord, I choose to declare Your faithfulness every night before I retire.*

APRIL 25

Morning Wisdom: Read Proverbs 14:3–4. We are friends with a couple our age who is diligent about their health. They eat all the right things, work out at the gym every day, and walk. Sometimes I ask my husband this question, "Do they plan to live forever?" We know that none of us will live forever on Earth, because no matter what we do to preserve our bodies here, we all have our appointment with death. However, the Bible gives several ways that we can lengthen our days on Earth. For example, the only commandment with a promise is the one that commands us to honor our father and mother. If we obey this commandment, we are promised long, prosperous days. (See Deuteronomy 5:16.)

The reading from Proverbs today gives another way we can preserve our life on Earth. Proverbs 14:3 says: "In the mouth of a fool is a rod of pride, but the lips of the wise will preserve them." Whenever we speak we have several audiences that listen in on our conversations. We are only able to see the person we are speaking to, but we are surrounded by demonic and angelic beings who listen to our conversations. Demonic spirits are listening to what we say to discover ways they can ensnare us in their traps. Satan does not have the power to read minds, so his gang is always hanging around to see if they can use the very words we speak against us. On the other hand, angels are listening, and whenever we speak God's Word, they come to attention and they stand ready to perform God's Word in our lives. (See Psalm 103:20.) Angels also come to our aid quickly when we declare the name of Jesus.

We can preserve our lives when we speak only those things that edify others and glorify God. I heard recently about a lady who was trying to memorize Psalm 91. This is a great psalm to declare as a protection over us. A man attacked her, and she could not remember the verses, but she cried out several times, "He covers me with His feathers!" (See Psalm 91:4.) Her assailant thought she was crazy and ran away. Her life was preserved.

Lord, help me to keep a guard over my lips.

Evening Watch: Read Psalm 94:1–23. We talked this morning about how we can preserve our lives by being careful about what we speak. We also need to be careful to listen to and obey the Lord. This psalm tells us that people who follow God's instructions are blessed. When we are obedient to God's Word, we will be delivered and helped by the Lord. When we seek to obey God daily, He is able to comfort our souls whenever we are anxious about anything. (See v. 19.) I have experienced this comfort many times when I found myself about to get into a "worry wad." When anxiety tries to overwhelm us, we need to cry out for God's comfort and then roll every care upon Him. When we do this, peace will be established in our minds and joy will flood our hearts.

Thank You, Lord, for comforting me in my anxious moments.

Morning Wisdom: Read Proverbs 14:5–6. There are several warnings in God's Word against keeping company with scoffers. In Psalm 1 David says that the man who refuses to sit in the seat of the scornful will be blessed. (See v. 1.) Proverbs 22:10 says that when we cast out the scorner contention will cease. Someone who scoffs at others usually has a problem with pride. Pride is the source of all contention. Peter warned that in the last days there would be many scoffers. This is why we must learn how to deal with them. (See 2 Peter 3:3.) Scoffers walk according to their own lusts, and the pride of life is one of their major lustful areas. They trust in their own knowledge and wisdom and scoff at the knowledge and wisdom of others.

Proverbs 14:6 says, "A scoffer seeks wisdom and does not find it." The reason why scoffers can never find wisdom is because they are unwilling to listen to God's Word. God's Word reveals that Jesus is wisdom. Anyone who seeks Jesus will find Him, and he or she will also find wisdom. A scoffer, however, will have a hard time finding Jesus, because the stronghold of pride binds him from receiving wisdom from any other source but himself. Are there any scoffers in your life today? If there are, pray and pull down the stronghold of pride in their lives. God will be able to get His message to even a scoffer if others are praying for him.

Lord, help me to effectively pray for even those who scoff at my beliefs.

Evening Watch: Read Psalm 95:1–96:13. In this psalm David warned us not to harden our hearts as the children of Israel did. They saw God's works, but they did not know God's ways. We can observe the work of others, but unless we come to know others intimately, we will never completely know their character and what motivates them. The children of Israel were so afraid of God that they asked Moses to convey God's messages to them. They did not want to have direct contact with God.

David was a man after God's own heart, because he knew the ways of God. He had an intimate relationship with God. His relationship with God was so deep that he even felt safe when he poured out his complaints to God. He knew God loved him and he was confident that God was not against him.

How did David obtain such an intimate relationship with God? David simply asked God to teach him His ways. (See Psalm 86:11–12.) David wanted to know God's ways, because he wanted to be able to glorify God in all he said and did in this life. David was willing to listen to God as He patiently taught him His ways through the various trials David experienced in his life. We learn a lot about God's ways when we pour out our complaints to Him, rather than murmuring and complaining to others when we go through hard times.

Lord, teach me Your ways.

APRIL 27

Morning Wisdom: Read Proverbs 14:7–8. This proverb exhorts us to surround ourselves with prudent, wise people. Prudence, wisdom, and understanding are a threefold cord that will keep us from falling apart during troubled times. It is important that we watch the company we keep when we are going through trials. During trying times we usually encounter people who are eager to tell us what we are doing wrong and how we can fix whatever mess we are experiencing. Such people are like Job's friends, who accused Job of actually causing all of his trials because of his own sin. They were convinced that God was punishing Job for something he did. Proverbs 14:7–8 tells us to leave the presence of such foolish people who think they have all the answers, but in reality they are deceived.

If we feel like we are going to lose it when life gets difficult, we need to surround ourselves with prudent, wise people who understand what we are going through.

We can also cry out to God to give us wisdom in the midst of trials, and He will reveal what He is trying to accomplish in our lives through the trials. God will honor such a cry for wisdom, and He will give us the prudence, understanding, and discernment to press through whatever we face in this life.

Lord, I ask You for Your wisdom and prudence to operate through me today in whatever situations I may face.

Evening Watch: Read Psalm 97:1–98:9. This morning we discussed two things that will help us get through the trials that confront us in this life. First, we need to surround ourselves with prudent, wise people. Second, we need to cry out to God for understanding and wisdom. This psalm reading gives such hope and assurance of God's presence with us in the midst of trials.

The psalm begins with descriptions of God's great power. He has power to burn up His enemies, and the mountains melt in His presence. The Lord, the Most High, is above all the earth, and He is higher than any idol. He is able to preserve the saints and deliver them out of the hands of the wicked. God is able to sow light into our dark trials and the eyes of our understanding can be enlightened. God's right hand always gives us the victory.

If you are going through a great trial now, you will be comforted as you meditate on this psalm reading. When we meditate on God's greatness, the mountains of troubles melt, and the stormy sea of trials become a river of peace. God is great enough to carry you through whatever troubles you are experiencing now. My older sister lost her son in Iraq this year, and God's right hand and His holy arm have lifted her family and her son's wife above the storm of despair.

Both of these psalms exhort us to shout for joy, make music to praise the Lord, and sing a new song. Staying in praise and in the presence of the Lord is the way my sister's family has found comfort in the midst of their sorrow.

Lord, keep me singing "How Great Thou Art" all day long tomorrow.

Judges 8:17–9:21; Luke 23:44–24:12; Psalm 99:1–9; Proverbs 14:9–10

Morning Wisdom: Read Proverbs 14:9–10. We talked earlier about how scoffers would increase in number in the last days. (See April 26 Morning Wisdom.) I believe that mockers will also increase in the last days. Proverbs 14:9 says, "Fools mock at sin." I could not believe my ears when I heard people laughing in a movie theater when someone on the screen was murdered. Even though movies are not real life, I had a hard time understanding why anyone would laugh at someone being beaten and murdered. It seems that in these last days, people are becoming insensitive to one another.

The great progress we have made in technology has offered individuals alternatives to building relationships. I would venture to say that most people spend more time behind a computer and TV than they do talking with their family members. With the introduction of the cell phone, people walk through stores and down the street without being conscious of those around them. They carry on conversations with someone over the phone rather than conversing with the person they are with at the time. A lack of quality relationships causes people to dehumanize one another.

Jesus warned that because of lawlessness in the last days, the love of many will grow cold. (See Matthew 24:12.) There seems to be less and less respect for the law. Today the news is full of people who scoff at the law and mock at sin. What can we do to stop this downward trend? We can intercede for city and nations to receive the gift of repentance. Only the Holy Spirit can change the hearts of men. Daniel interceded for his nation, and they were delivered from the bondage of the Babylonians. God told Abraham that he would spare Sodom and Gomorrah if he could find only ten righteous men. Intercession can cause the crime rate in a city to go down. I am challenged to pray more for my city and nation.

Lord, send Your gift of repentance upon our nation.

Evening Watch: Read Psalm 99:1–9. We have been singing a chorus in our church that declares that the Lord is worthy, holy, and awesome. This song must have been inspired by Psalm 99:3, which says, "Let them praise Your great and awesome name—He is holy." Even though Israel was disobedient to God, He forgave them. God's forgiveness toward us is awesome.

Before you go to sleep tonight, try to recall the many times God has forgiven you when you disobeyed Him. I can think of many times that I have not obeyed that still, quiet voice within me, only to find out later God wanted to use me in another person's life. I remember going with my husband to visit a financial adviser who was urging us to invest in a certain stock. As I sat on the sofa next to this man, I heard the Lord prompt me to share the gospel with him. I did not obey, simply because I was afraid and didn't think I was capable of sharing. This man died two weeks later of a sudden heart attack. God forgave me for this, but I missed an opportunity to lead another to the Lord.

Lord, thank You for Your forgiveness.

Morning Wisdom: Read Proverbs 14:11–12. "There is a way that seems right to a man, But its end is the way of death" (v. 12). This statement is made more than once in the Book of Proverbs. Deception is Satan's greatest weapon against us. He is an expert at convincing us that we are going the right way, when in reality that way is leading us down the path to destruction. He can make sin look so appealing that our flesh responds to the bait his seducing spirits use to entrap us. The old saying, "The grass is greener on the other side," is one of Satan's deceiving lies. So many have fallen for that lure and have discovered the other side is full of briars and thorns.

I will never forget a dream I had that gave me a deep burden for souls. I saw blindfolded people walking a path that led to a cliff. They were falling off the cliff into a deep chasm with flames leaping from it. I was horrified. Suddenly Jesus appeared. He was in the Spirit. His spiritual form was huge. I cried out to Him, "Jesus, why don't You save them? You could stop them with one swoop of Your huge hands." Then I heard Him say, "My resurrected body is in heaven, and you are seeing My spiritual body. You are My body on Earth, and only you can save them from perishing. You are My hands and My voice on Earth." I awoke with a heavy burden for the lost. I knew that to save the lost, God has chosen to use the church, the body of Christ, to deliver His gospel. God has given us His Spirit who will enable us to be soulwinners. When we see someone today who is headed for destruction, pray for that person and also share the good news with him.

Lord, thank You for choosing me to be a colaborer with You.

Evening Watch: Read Psalm 100:1–5. My quiet times with the Lord every morning are not very quiet. I spend most of my quiet time singing songs of praise to the Lord, and then I wait to hear Him. Often I receive a new song from Him. This psalm exhorts us to come into the presence of the Lord with singing. We are told the way we can quickly enter into the presence of the Lord. We are told to:

- Enter His gates with thanksgiving. Tonight review your day and give thanks to the Lord for His help and His love throughout the day.
- Enter His courts with praise. Thanksgiving always leads to praise.
- Praise Him tonight for His mighty works and His wonderful ways.
- Bless His name. Review His names and meditate on the meaning of those names. He is Jehovah-Jireh, your Provider. He is Jehovah-Shalom, your peace. He is Jehovah-Rapha, your Healer.

Lord, thank You for Your presence with me all night and all day.

Judges 11:1–12:15; John 1:1–28; Psalm 101:1–8; Proverbs 14:13–14

Morning Wisdom: Read Proverbs 14:13–14. Proverbs 14:14 describes how individuals fill their lives. This verse says, "The backslider in heart will be filled with his own ways, But a good man will be satisfied from above." When we seek to gain satisfaction from the world we will never be fulfilled. The lusts of the world within us will constantly cry out for more, more, more.

Paul exhorted us to set our affection on the things that are above. (See Colossians 3:2.) When we understand that our lives are now hid with Christ in God, we will experience a position of security and satisfaction. I often illustrate our position in Christ by having a person reach out both of his hands. I instruct them that their thumb on the right hand represents them. Then I ask them to close their right hand and tuck their thumb so that it is hidden by the other fingers on the right hand. I share then that the other four fingers on their right hand represent Christ. They are hidden with Christ in God. I ask them to take their left hand and totally cover their right fist with their left hand. Their left hand represents God. Now their hands become united, and they are totally hidden from the world with all of its temptations.

If we could see this visual picture every time we awaken, we would not doubt our salvation or the fact that we can hide ourselves in Jesus and be free from the power and pull of our worldly lusts that are never satisfied. We will be filled full of the Spirit of God, and there will be no room to try to satisfy our own worldly lusts. When you pray this morning place your hands together in the position I described, and be reminded that Jesus won the total victory over the world, the flesh, and the devil.

Thank You, Lord, for satisfying my soul.

Evening Watch: Read Psalm 101:1–8. "Behave yourself!" How many times have we exhorted our children with this phrase? I know I just about wore that phrase out when we were training our children. We all want our children to behave, because their misbehavior is perceived as a reflection of the inadequate teaching and training of our children.

God wants His children to behave. When we misbehave, the world looks at our misbehavior and asks, "What kind of God do these Christians serve?" I can remember being in the old marketplace in Jerusalem when an Arab engaged me in conversation. He rehearsed all the recent misbehavior of various TV evangelists in America and then he exclaimed, "Your Christianity means nothing!"

David had a heart for God, and He made several vows to God. He vowed to behave wisely in a perfect way and to walk within his house with a perfect heart. He vowed never to set anything evil before his eyes. We should do the same. We need to tell ourself to sit down and shut up. If we did this we would not misbehave.

Lord, help me to be obedient.

MAY 1

Morning Wisdom: Read Proverbs 14:15–16. There was a time in my life when I believed whatever anyone told me. I had great trust in people. I got myself in a lot of trouble by believing all the words I heard with my ears. Proverbs 14:15 says, "The simple believes every word." I guess that tells me I was simpleminded. Sadly, however, the trust I had in human beings since that time has been destroyed.

Since I began to look to Jesus for wisdom, the Holy Spirit has added an amount of prudence to my daily walk with the Lord. I have learned the hard way that the only One you can depend upon is Jesus. People are fleshly vessels who will fail you from time to time.

The reason we are taking so much time in Proverbs daily is that through the reading and applying of Proverbs we will gain wisdom, discernment, and prudence. Proverbs 14:16 tells us that the wise man will depart from evil. I am so thankful that the Lord protected me during my simpleminded years. I believe that protection came from my parents' prayers. We need prudence to keep us on the right path. A good prayer to pray every day for our children and for us is:

> Lord, I ask for wisdom, understanding, and prudence to guard both my mind and my mouth today.

Evening Watch: Read Psalm 102:1–28. As we read this passage, it is apparent that David was in a deep depression. The first few verses list all the signs of depression, which are:

- The days seem to vanish into nothing—"My days are consumed like smoke" (v. 3).
- The loss of appetite—"I forget to eat my bread" (v. 4).
- The body feels heavy—"My bones cling to my skin" (v. 5).
- The days and nights are sleepless—"I lie awake" (v. 7).
- The emotions are bound by paranoia—"My enemies reproach me" (v. 8).
- The tears flow at the drop of a hat—"I mingled my drink with weeping" (v. 9).
- The feeling of abandonment takes over—"You have cast me away" (v. 10).

David told the Lord just how he felt. He poured out his complaint to the Lord. Because he humbled himself and was honest, God began to lift his thoughts off self and onto Him. David began to focus on the Lord and His faithfulness, mercy, and favor shown to those who cry out to Him in their distress. Then David looked forward to the day when he would be changed from glory to glory. He looked forward to spending eternity with God. He declared that God never changes, and this is one fact that will carry us through any depression.

Thank You for lifting up my soul to think higher thoughts.

MAY 2

Morning Wisdom: Read Proverbs 14:17–19. We as Christians have an advantage over unbelievers. We see how the world seems to be going to hell in a handbasket. However, Christians do know the rest of the story. Good will win over evil. Our God is good, and He is a winner. Proverbs 14:19 predicts that evil will bow before good, and the wicked will bow at the gates of the righteous. This proverb should encourage us all.

The character qualities of prudence, discretion, and discernment are built into our lives as we daily abide in God's Word. Only the Word of God has the power to discern the thoughts and intents of the heart. As we stay in God's Word we will be able to recognize which voice is speaking to us. We daily hear three voices—the voice of God, the voice of Satan, and the voice of our own flesh. The voice of God is heard with our spiritual ears. The voice of Satan is heard with the ears of our physical body and the ears of our soul. Whenever we hear the thoughts, *I think*, *I feel*, and *I want*, we can know for certain that those thoughts come from our flesh (our souls). Hebrews 4:12 tells us that the Word of God is sharper than any two-edged sword, and it has the power to divide the soul from the spirit, and it is a discerner of the thoughts and intents of the heart.

Thoughts come from the mind, and intents usually come from the spirit.

Clear discernment of which voice is speaking to us will help us to depart from evil and will keep us from being companions with angry men. We will be crowned with prudence and knowledge as we abide in God's Word.

Lord, help me to be faithful to abide in Your Word.

Evening Watch: Read Psalm 103:1–22. David knew how to lift up his soul to the Lord when he was at the depths of depression. First, he rehearsed the goodness of the Lord. Second, he prayed that the Lord would unite his heart to fear His name. (See Psalm 86:11.) Third, he encouraged his soul in the Lord. (See 1 Samuel 30:6.)

In Psalm 103, David reviewed the goodness of the Lord. He reviewed the blessings and benefits God had granted to him. He listed the benefits: forgiveness, healing, redemption, love, tender mercy, provision, renewal, righteousness, justice, graciousness, grace, and sovereignty.

At the end of this psalm David invited all to bless the Lord. He invited angels, the hosts of heaven, and every nation under his dominion to join him in praising the Lord. He ended the psalm as he began it, with this exhortation, "Bless the LORD, O my soul!" At the end of the day lift your soul up to the Lord by declaring all of His benefits. Your soul will be saturated with gratefulness, and your tomorrow will be filled with His grace.

Lord, thank You for all Your benefits.

MAY 3

Morning Wisdom: Read Proverbs 14:20–21. Verse 20 declares a truth that I have seen many times. Rich people have an abundance of friends because they want to share in their rich friend's wealth. The poor, however, are usually neglected and sometimes even hated.

Verse 21 warns us not to despise our neighbor because if we do, we sin. The problem in America is that most of us do not even know our neighbors. The custom of dropping in at a neighbor's house for coffee is a thing of the past because these days people are so busy. People work, come home, eat, watch TV, or work on the computer, and then go to bed. People often travel on the weekends and are involved with the sports events of their children.

My husband and I have lived in our home for over thirty-three years. Neighbors have come and gone, but we are determined to at least meet as many of our neighbors as possible. Once a year we have an open house, and I deposit an invitation in 125 mailboxes. My husband and I pray that during these events we will have the opportunity to share the love of Jesus with our neighbors. We have been encouraged by the many thanks we receive after these open houses.

You may want to host a get-together in your neighborhood. You will be surprised at how rewarding this can be.

Lord, help me to love all of my neighbors.

Evening Watch: Read Psalm 104:1–24. This psalm reviews God's wonderful works. Our works every day seem insignificant when we view God's mighty works. We dress ourselves with earthly clothing, but God dresses Himself with honor, majesty, and light. We walk from our car to our office, but God walks on the wings of the wind. We check on the weather, but God makes the clouds His chariot. We only see the people we deal with daily, but God sees the principalities and powers that surround people. He created His angels to minister to His saints. We go to the ocean to vacation and observe the sea, but God made the sea and even set up boundaries to contain the sea. We visit the mountains to get away from the mundane routines of life, but God's voice can melt even the mountains we climb. We give water to our pets, but God waters every beast on this earth. We pray that our days are fruitful, but God satisfies the earth and everything in it with the fruit of His works.

After reading the first portion of this psalm I can't help but ask the question that David asked, "What is man that you are mindful of Him and the son of man that you visit him?" (Ps. 8:4). Yet God has made us a little lower than the angels, and He crowns us with glory and honor. He has made us to have dominion over all of His works and has put everything under our feet. (See Psalm 8:5–6.) When I think of God's greatness and realize that He has chosen me to be a caretaker of His works on Earth, I am overwhelmed.

Lord, thank You for trusting and loving me.

MAY 4

Morning Wisdom: Read Proverbs 14:22–24. "Idle chatter leads only to poverty" (v. 23). Jesus warned us that at Judgment Day we will be held accountable for every idle word we have spoken. (See Matthew 12:36.) I have a friend who said she believed she would spend the first ten thousand years of eternity in the "idle word room" since she felt she had spent so many years speaking idle words. If we recorded the hours we spend on the phone just talking about nothing important, we would be amazed at the record. If we had spent those hours at a job making money, think about how rich we would be.

Idle chatter can lead not only to physical poverty, but also to spiritual poverty. If we spend our hours in meaningless chatter instead of sowing God's Word into people's lives and praying, we also will become spiritually impoverished. A great way to curb our meaningless conversations is to give ourselves the "talk test." Before we open our mouths we need to ask ourselves, "Is what I am about to say edifying, honest, of good report, virtuous, lovely, and just?"

This is the list of things Paul exhorts us to think about in Philippians 4:8. We usually speak what we think and what is in our hearts. Today use this "talk test." You will be amazed at the time you will have to really listen to others when they speak and also to listen to God when He speaks to you. God created us with two ears and one mouth so that we would listen twice as much as we speak.

Lord, help me to listen and to employ this "talk test" today.

Evening Watch: Read Psalm 104:24–35. Verse 24 declares, "The earth is full of Your possessions." All we own belongs to the Lord. The more stuff we have, the more stuff we have to take care of, so why do we spend our lives obtaining more possessions? In our effort to gain possessions, we often neglect to take care of God's most precious possessions—people.

Our son and his wife call all the stuff they accumulate *squat*. This is a good word to describe the material possessions we have. All the material stuff we accumulate in this life is not worth squat. When I was at Megiddo in Israel I observed a dig that revealed over twenty-one layers of civilization. Each layer was reduced to a relatively small pile of ash. As I observed this, I heard the Lord speak to my heart, "Linda, why do you spend so much time taking care of ashes?" I recalled the many hours I spent cleaning out squat in our basement. Everything we own belongs to the Lord, but there are only a few things we will be able to take with us to heaven. We can take the Word of God we have hidden in our hearts, the prayers we have prayed for others, the words we have spoken about the Lord on Earth, and the deeds the Lord Jesus has empowered us to do. In my book *You Can Take It With You*, I share a daily deposit we can put in our heavenly bank account. All of these daily deposits involve our relationships with people—God's most precious treasures.

Lord, help me to accumulate eternal possessions.

MAY 5

Morning Wisdom: Read Proverbs 14:25. From time to time I am notified to report for jury duty on a certain date. I usually do not mind sitting in a jury pool, because it gives me time to work on Bible lessons and devotionals. I try not to be distracted while I am writing devotionals, but just recently when I was in the jury pool, I became very distracted by a man on a cell phone.

We were instructed not to use cell phones in the pool, but this man insisted on using his cell phone, even after the manager of the pool restated that no one should use a cell phone. I could not help but overhear this man's conversation. He was talking about business, but he seemed to be encouraging his associates to lie about something. I tried to focus once again on my devotional writing. I was writing about David and how he encouraged himself in the Lord when he found all of his family gone and the city of Ziklag burned to the ground. (See 1 Samuel 30.) I wrote in my devotional that I imagined that David picked up his "cell phone" and encouraged himself in the Lord. I meant to write, "David picked up his harp and encouraged himself in the Lord." The distraction of this man's conversation on his cell phone invaded my thoughts and caused me to write "cell phone" instead of "harp."

When I read this verse I was reminded of this incident, and I was thankful the man with the cell phone was not called to be on the jury. How could he be a good juror if he encouraged lying? Proverbs 14:25 says, "A true witness delivers souls, But a deceitful witness speaks lies." Whether we like it or not, we are always on the witness stand if we daily stand up for Christ. The words we speak about Jesus Christ as we witness to others can save many souls. We have to be careful that our witness is clear and truthful. We also have to keep our mind focused on Jesus and the individual we are witnessing to, because the enemy would love to distract us and get us off the subject.

Lord, help me to be a truthful witness.

Evening Watch: Read Psalm 105:1–15. We talked this morning about being an effective witness for Christ. This psalm gives some ways we can clearly and truthfully witness to others. David wrote about having a joyful, grateful heart. When we are joyful and declare our thanks for the Lord's wondrous works in our own lives, whoever we are witnessing to will have a listening ear.

People might want to argue Scripture with you as you witness to them, but they will have no way to argue against your personal testimony. Personal testimony is one of the best ways to witness to another person. David emphasized that God was a covenant-keeping God (v. 8). We need to share with others how God has kept His covenant with us. God is faithful. David spoke about what the Lord had done for Israel. We can speak today about how God has fulfilled almost all of the prophetic words written in the Bible about Israel. One only needs to look at the land of Israel to see how God has built up the waste places and prospered the land.

Lord, help me to be an effective witness.

MAY 6

Morning Wisdom: Read Proverbs 14:26–27. Four marvelous blessings are promised to those who fear the Lord in this passage. The book of Proverbs has many verses that declare both the blessings and the benefits of walking daily in the fear of the Lord. First, however, you may be asking, "What is the fear of the Lord?" The fear of the Lord is an awesome reverence and love for God that manifests itself in a person through his obedience to God's Word. Some people think that in order to fear the Lord we must be afraid of Him. This was the problem with the children of Israel. They were afraid of God. When God revealed Himself to the people on Mount Sinai they were terrified. They heard God's mighty voice and the whole mountain shook. The people asked Moses to speak to them from that time on whatever God had to say, because they were so afraid of God's presence.

The fear of the Lord should draw us to God's presence, not away from it. As we think of God's sovereignty and His majesty, we cannot help but worship Him. We do not have Moses any longer to speak God's words to us, but we now have the Holy Spirit. He shows us the things of Jesus that are written in God's Word.

God put on an earth suit and came as flesh to dwell among us in the form of Jesus Christ. Jesus Christ taught us just exactly what it means to fear the Lord. Jesus only did what He saw the Father do, and He only said what He heard the Father say. He was in constant communion and union with the Father, and the works Jesus did on Earth manifested the Father's glory. This is exactly what we should do daily as we walk in the fear of the Lord. Daily we need to have communion with the Holy Trinity—Father, Son, and Holy Spirit. As we spend time in prayer and in God's Word, we will be empowered to walk in the fear of the Lord.

The four blessings mentioned in this passage that will come our way as we walk in the fear of the Lord are: confidence, refuge, a fountain of life, and deliverance from the snares of death. Don't you want to walk in the fear of the Lord today?

Lord, help me daily to walk in the fear of You.

Evening Watch: Read Psalm 105:16–28. Throughout history, God has raised up men and women of God to be used powerfully to deliver His people. This psalm reading describes some of these great deliverers. God sent Joseph before His people to deliver them from famine. He sent Jacob, who He renamed Israel, to increase His chosen people and to strengthen them. God sent Moses to deliver His people from slavery.

We talked this morning about walking in the fear of the Lord. When we walk in the fear of the Lord every day, we too can be instruments to deliver people from Satan.

We can help deliver people from spiritual famine every time we share God's Word with them. We can help deliver people whenever we share the gospel with them. We can help people be delivered from the strongholds that bind them when we intercede and pray for them.

Lord, help me to deliver someone tomorrow from Satan's prison.

Morning Wisdom: Read Proverbs 14:28–29. We need only look at the historical accounts of many of the characters in the Bible to discover how most of the troubles they experienced were because they not only disobeyed God, but they also acted on impulse. Some examples are Abraham, who did not wait for God's timing. Instead he went ahead of the Lord and on impulse gave in to Sarah's wish for him to have relations with her Egyptian maid, Hagar, to bear them a son. Not only was Ishmael born from this union, but the Arab-Israeli conflict was also born and it still exists today. (See Genesis 16.) Generations to this day have been affected by Abraham's impulsiveness. We see how Saul lost his position as king over Israel when he could not wait for Samuel to come and perform sacrifices to the Lord. (See 1 Samuel 13.)

Today we read, "He who is slow to wrath has great understanding, But he who is impulsive exalts folly" (v. 9). Satan is able to accomplish his plans in our lives if we are impulsive. Pride is what makes us impulsive. When we give in to the lust of the pride of life (trusting in ourselves more than we trust in God), we have played the fool, and folly will result. We need to resist the idea that we can do things without God's help or advice. Whenever we have that idea and act upon it, we have played right into the hands of Satan.

It is human nature to do things on impulse, but because Jesus now lives in us, we have a new nature. The Holy Spirit within us can help us learn to wait upon the Lord and inquire of Him before we take action on any matter.

Lord, help me never to be impulsive.

Evening Watch: Read Psalm 105:39–45. This reading in Psalms concludes a marvelous chapter that reviews the wondrous works of the Lord. We are urged at the beginning of Psalm 105 to make known the deeds of the Lord to the peoples. The verses that follow recount how the Lord provided for the children of Israel by sending Joseph ahead of them, how He raised up Moses and Aaron to deliver them, how He sent the plagues upon Egypt and brought Israel out of Egypt with silver and gold, how He provided food for them in the wilderness, and how He gave them the land He had promised them.

Has God done wondrous works in your life? Begin tonight to make a list of some of the ways God has provided, protected, and delivered you. Making this list will certainly be more fruitful than counting sheep before you go to bed.

Lord, bring to my remembrance all the wondrous works You have done in my life.

MAY 8

Morning Wisdom: Read Proverbs 14:30–31. Several years ago I asked the Lord to reveal to me what part of the body our local church was. Just as there are many members in one body in the local church, I believe each local church also is a special member of the larger body of Christ here on Earth. For example, I have always seen Baptists as hands in the larger body of Christ. Baptists help many churches in the larger body to hold spiritual conferences and retreats at their lovely retreat centers all over the world.

Each local church has a function in its community that no other church can fulfill. When I asked the Lord what part of the body our church was, I was shocked at the answer I received. I heard with my spiritual ears that the Lord considered our local church as the heart of the larger body of Christ in the community. I thought about what the heart does. The heart pumps life into the body. I believe the Lord was telling me that our church's function in the body of Christ throughout our community and worldwide was to pump life into other ministries and churches. Over the years I have seen our church fulfill this function in the body. We have sent teams out to local churches to do revivals, and we have sent mission teams all over the world to bring revival to places like Peru, Mexico, India, and many other countries.

Proverbs 14:30 reads, "A sound heart is life to the body, But envy is rottenness to the bones." I believe if every local body would busy themselves fulfilling their function in the larger body of Christ, there would be no time for jealousy and competing with one another. You might ask the Lord today to reveal to you what member of the larger body is your church. Paul told us in 1 Corinthians 12 that there are many members but only one body. Once you have discovered whether or not your local church is a hand, foot, eye, or another part, you will be able to work with your fellow members to fulfill the function in the larger body that God has called you to provide.

> *Lord, help me to work with my local body to fulfill the needs in the larger body of Christ.*

Evening Watch: Read Psalm 106:1–12. We talked this morning about discovering where we fit in a local body of Christ and in the larger body of Christ. What member of the body are you? Are you hands or feet or some other member? I discovered my calling when I asked the Lord to reveal to me what member of the body I represent. I heard in my spirit that I was a voice, which led me to the passage in Mark where John is described as a voice in the wilderness sent to prepare the way of the Lord. (See Mark 1:3.) My call is to prepare the way of the second coming of the Lord by giving God's Word voice through my writing, speaking, and singing.

Today's reading reveals several common callings we all have. We are called to keep justice, do righteousness at all times, praise Him, and to declare God's mighty acts. (See vv.1–3.)

> *Lord, help me to fulfill Your callings upon my life.*

Morning Wisdom: Read Proverbs 14:32–33. Picture a menorah in your mind. You have probably seen a menorah with seven candlesticks. There is one main stem that divides into six branches, three on one side of the main stem and three on the other side of the main stem. The priests were charged with the responsibility of keeping the candlestick forever burning. They poured oil down the main stem, which fed the other six branches. The menorah represents the sevenfold spirit of God mentioned in Isaiah 11:2, which lists: the Spirit of understanding and the Spirit of wisdom, the Spirit of counsel and might, and the Spirit of the fear of the Lord and knowledge. The main stem is the spirit of the Lord. Understanding and wisdom are coupled together, because they are so closely akin.

Proverbs 14:33 says, "Wisdom rests in the heart of him who has understanding."

Solomon was a man of great wisdom, and the book of Proverbs is helpful; but if we do not ask the Holy Spirit to give us understanding of these insights, we will not be able to apply wisdom to our everyday life. The wisdom Solomon had was supernatural. It was given to him by God, because Solomon asked for wisdom. Because Solomon was a natural man who did not have Jesus Christ living in his heart, later in life he lacked understanding. The Bible tells us that the man who commits adultery lacks understanding. (See Proverbs 6:32.) Jesus is all wisdom, and when we have Him in our hearts, we will have understanding as well as wisdom.

Lord, thank You for giving me both wisdom and understanding.

Evening Watch: Read Psalm 106:13–31. This psalm reveals the patience and mercy of God. The Israelites believed God's Word after He led them across the Red Sea, but soon they began to doubt, murmur, and complain. They forgot the exceedingly great wonders He did for them in the wilderness. They rebelled and even made idols and worshiped them. God was ready to destroy all of them, but Moses' intercession for them spared them from God's wrath. God's anger was kindled many times against His chosen, but nevertheless He regarded their affliction, heard their cry, and delivered them.

God is the "God of the nevertheless." We deserved to be wiped off the face of the earth because of our wicked hearts, but nevertheless God chose not to spare His own Son so that we could be spared from His wrath. Has God revealed His patience and long-suffering to you? Close your eyes for a moment and don't fall asleep. Think back over the times in your life when you deserved God's punishment, but He was merciful to you. I am sure you have experienced the "God of the nevertheless." Tomorrow, if you have time, look up the word *nevertheless* in the Strong's Concordance, and read some of the passages listed. Your faith will be built up as you see God's mercy manifested time and time again.

Lord, thank You for Your mercy.

MAY 10

Morning Wisdom: Read Proverbs 14:34–34. We were at Liberty Square in Philadelphia. Our friend, who is bound by a wheelchair, wanted to get close enough to the Liberty Bell to touch it. However, the crowds prevented this. We decided instead to pray in the car. Another friend had purchased small replicas of the Liberty Bell. God was leading us step-by-step as we laid hands on these small liberty bells and prayed for the foundations of righteousness to be restored to our nation. My friend has not allowed the limitations of a wheelchair to keep her from traveling throughout the world to pray that the foundations be restored.

Proverbs 14:34 says, "Righteousness exalts a nation, But sin is a reproach to any people." Psalm 11:3 reads, "If the foundations are destroyed, What can the righteous do?" In the past ten years my friend has taken over three trips to Washington and Philadelphia to pray for the foundations of righteousness that were laid by our forefathers to be restored. She has seen our country steadily go down the slippery slope of sin in the last decade. She has seen how lawlessness and the destruction of family values have brought this nation to a crossroads. Only intercession will stay the hand of God's judgment on this nation, and that is why she felt the urgency once again to return to Washington and Philadelphia. Only a return to righteousness will restore our nation and deliver it from judgment. Will you join me this morning as I pray for our nation?

> *Lord, send Your gift of repentance upon our nation and restore us to righteousness.*

Evening Watch: Read Psalm 106:32–48. We talked this morning about staying the hand of God's judgment upon this land through intercession. Evidently the children of Israel did not have many intercessors who were praying for them. Moses, their diligent intercessor, was dead. God did provide judges to deliver Israel whenever they cried out to the Lord. He always remembered His covenant with Israel and relented according to the multitude of His mercies.

This psalm records how God takes action against disobedient people. The good news, however, is that this psalm also reveals God's long-suffering with such people. If we did not have a merciful, long-suffering God, this earth would not exist today. Lawlessness and immorality seem to be rampant in most nations today. The Bible says that the last days will be just like they were in the times of Noah. (See Matthew 24:37–38.) As we know, all those who lived in Noah's day, with the exception of Noah's family, were destroyed in the flood. God promised Noah He would not destroy the earth by a flood again; but we know that the New Testament speaks of one third of the earth being destroyed by fire. (See Revelation 8:7.) These facts should cause us all to bow our knees, weep, and confess the sins of our own nation. We need to cry out for God's mercy.

> *Lord, have mercy upon our nation, and allow us to have more time.*

MAY 11

Morning Wisdom: Read Proverbs 15:1–3. Wisdom is applied knowledge, and understanding is what enables us to apply knowledge. We talked earlier about how Solomon had supernatural wisdom from God, but he often lacked understanding, because he did exactly the opposite of what He knew God wanted him to do. The world is saturated with wise fools, men and women who have worldly knowledge but who have no idea what God has said in His Word. I am convinced that no one can have the wisdom that comes from above without having a relationship with Jesus Christ. James spoke of two kinds of wisdom when he wrote:

> If you have bitter envy and self-seeking in your hearts, do not boast and lie against the truth. This wisdom does not descend from above, but is earthly, sensual, demonic. For where envy and self-seeking exist, confusion and every evil thing are there. But the wisdom that is from above is first pure, then peaceable, gentle, willing to yield, full of mercy and good fruits, without partiality and without hypocrisy.
>
> —JAMES 3:14–17

Proverbs 15:2 reads, "The tongue of the wise uses knowledge rightly."

When we daily abide in Jesus and God's Word, we will know how to use knowledge the right way. James asked this question, "Who is wise and understanding among you? Let him show by good conduct that his works are done in the meekness of wisdom" (James 3:13).

Our daily conduct will reveal whether or not we have knowledge and understanding of God's Word.

Lord, help me today to walk in the wisdom that is from above.

Evening Watch: Read Psalm 107:1–43. This morning we learned that wise people use their tongues to disperse knowledge in the right way. We live in an age where the increase of knowledge is overwhelming. The knowledge, however, that we need to understand is the knowledge of God's works and His ways. This psalm reviews God's delivering power and His ability to satisfy every longing soul. The phrase that is repeated many times in this psalm is, "Oh that men would give thanks to the LORD for His goodness, And for His wonderful works to the children of men!"

Have you praised Him for the works He has done in your life today? Take a few minutes to write down five ways that God's goodness was revealed to you today. God is good all the time!

Lord, may I never take Your goodness towards me for granted.

MAY 12

Morning Wisdom: Read Proverbs 15:4. "A wholesome tongue is a tree of life: but perverseness therein is a breach in the spirit" (Prov. 15:4, KJV). You have probably heard the expression, "He speaks with a forked tongue." In other words the person with a forked tongue has a divided tongue. *Webster's New World Dictionary* defines *perverse* as "deviating from what is considered right or acceptable." Whenever we speak words that deviate from the truth of God's Word, we are speaking with a forked tongue, and those words can cause a division in our spirit. The words we speak have the power to kill or give life to others and ourselves. Proverbs 18:21 says, "Death and life are in the power of the tongue." A wholesome tongue will inject life into the people we speak to every day.

I just received a phone call from a friend who had received nothing but word curses from her brother. When she called me she was actually fighting to breathe, because those word curses were almost physically choking her.

After doing some warfare against the accusatory and jealous spirits that caused her brother to say such things, I asked my friend to declare what the Word of God says about her. She immediately began to say, "I am accepted in the beloved. I am a queen in the Lord's court. I have the mind of Christ, and no weapon that is formed against me will prosper. Every tongue that rises against me I condemn, because my righteousness is of Jesus Christ." When she finished these declarations of what God says about her, she could breathe again and was even able to call her brother to tell him that she forgave him for everything he said to her.

Lord, help me to always have a wholesome tongue.

Evening Watch: Read Psalm 108:1–13. David used his tongue to exalt and praise God continually. This is a beautiful psalm filled with praises to God. If you ever have a difficult day when you feel depressed or oppressed, I suggest that you read this psalm out loud. As you declare the praises David wrote in this psalm, I know your spirits will be lifted. Praise God, because His truth reaches to the clouds, His glory is above all the earth, He delivers and hears your cry, and He will cause you to do valiantly, because He treads down your enemies.

When we put on the garment of praise by giving thanks and declaring our praises out loud to God, all heaviness will leave. My sister suffered from bouts of depression. She discovered if she quickly began to praise God when that dark cloud of depression began to overwhelm her, the light of God's love would flood her soul and all heaviness and depression would leave.

Lord, I sing praises to Your name.

MAY 13

Morning Wisdom: Read Proverbs 15:5–7. "The lips of the wise disperse knowledge, But the heart of the fool does not do so" (v. 7). There are many intellectual professional teachers who are experts at dispersing knowledge. Some of these intellectuals may just possess the wisdom of this world instead of the wisdom that is from above. Those who operate in the wisdom of the Lord will disperse knowledge of God's Word to others. Those who are anointed instructors of God's Word will also be able to impart the anointing of wisdom and understanding, counsel and might, the fear of the Lord and knowledge to others.

I have been in Bible studies that were merely a study of facts. It is helpful to know the facts about the authors of the Bible and the history of Bible accounts, but it is essential that we come to know Jesus, who is the Author and Finisher of our faith. The Pharisees and Sadducees knew all the law and the prophets, but they did not know Jesus as the Son of God. The knowledge of the Holy One can only be dispersed by a person who has an intimate relationship with Jesus Christ. Those who teach the knowledge of the Holy One under the power of God's anointing will see those who listen to their teachings transformed from students of God's Word to disciples of Jesus Christ.

Help me to know You better each day of my life.

Evening Watch: Read Psalm 109:1–31. We learned this morning that the lips of the wise disperse knowledge, but the knowledge we should disperse as believers is the knowledge of Jesus Christ. In this psalm David used his lips to curse his enemies. Frankly, I would not want to be on David's hit list. He actually prayed that God would do the following to his enemies:

- Cause their days on Earth to be short
- Cause their children to be rebellious and fatherless
- Cause financial ruin
- Cause their name to be blotted out in generations to come
- Cause even the memory of their mothers to be cut off

Proverbs 26:2 says, "Like a flitting sparrow, like a flying swallow, So a curse without cause shall not alight." I am sure that every curse David prayed upon his enemies did alight, because all of his curses had a cause. David said that his enemies showed no mercy, persecuted the poor, sought to slay the broken in heart, loved cursing, and did not delight themselves in blessing. He wrote that his enemies clothed themselves with curses. We reap what we sow. If we sow curses, we will reap curses.

Jesus instructed us to bless our enemies. Be careful tomorrow to sow blessings.

Lord, help me to bless others continually.

MAY 14

Morning Wisdom: Read Proverbs 15:8–10. Proverbs 15:8 says, "The sacrifice of the wicked is an abomination to the LORD, But the prayer of the upright is His delight" (v. 8). A comparison of King Saul with King David reveals that King Saul's sacrifices were an abomination to God, but King David's sacrifices were acceptable and pleasing to God. King Saul disobeyed God and offered sacrifices, because he was unwilling to wait for Samuel, the Lord's priest, to offer sacrifices. Only priests were commissioned by God to offer sacrifices. King Saul had a wicked, rebellious heart. Samuel told King Saul that his rule would be given to a man who was after God's own heart. That man was David. (See 1 Samuel 13:6–15.) God harshly disciplined Saul, because Saul forsook the way of the Lord. If Saul had received God's correction with a humble heart, his reign as king might have been restored.

These verses in Proverbs reveal exactly what pleases God. God is pleased when we walk uprightly with Him and we daily follow after righteousness. God replaced King Saul with David, who did seek to daily follow after righteousness. Even though David sinned, he humbled himself and repented. We have no record in Scripture that Saul ever repented. There is no question that we will do things in our lifetime that will displease the Lord, but if we will confess our disobedience, repent, and turn once again to the Lord, God will lift us up and help us to walk uprightly once again. God delights in the prayers of those who have humble hearts.

Lord, help me to have a repentant, humble heart.

Evening Watch: Read Psalm 110:1–7. This psalm is a good psalm to quote to your Jewish friends, who may not understand that Jesus is Lord. Most Jewish people believe that Christians serve three Gods—the Father, the Son, and the Holy Spirit. They have no concept of the Trinity and how these three are one. However, every Sabbath Jewish people always quote Deuteronomy 6:4, which says, "Hear, O Israel: The LORD our God, the LORD is one!"

The Hebrew word for "one" in this passage is *echad.* Echad means collective unity. Jesus used this psalm to prove that both He and the Father were Lord. When He taught in the temple and asked how the scribes could say that the Christ is the Son of David, Jesus quoted Psalm 110:1. Jesus skillfully used this psalm to prove that David by the Holy Spirit declared that he called someone Lord who God had appointed to defeat His enemies. Jesus was not David's son. Jesus was David's Lord. (See Mark 12:35–37.)

Christians believe in God the Father, God the Son, and God the Holy Spirit. God is a three-part being, and we are created in His image. We also have three parts—body, soul, and spirit. A simple way to understand the Trinity is that God the Father is Spirit, Jesus is the body of God, and the Holy Spirit expresses the soul of God.

Thank You for being everything I need, because You are three in one.

MAY 15

Morning Wisdom: Read Proverbs 15:11. Proverbs 15:11 says, "Hell and Destruction are before the LORD; So how much more the hearts of the sons of men." A lot of people have a hard time believing in God because they ask, "How could a loving God send anyone to hell?" God is a loving God who knows the hearts of men. He sees men's hearts, and He knows those hearts who desire to please Him. He also knows those hearts that only want to rebel against Him.

God will send no one to hell. Only those people who choose to go to hell by their own rebellious disobedience will be in hell for eternity. Because hell and destruction are always before the Lord, the Lord wants no man to perish. In fact the Bible tells us this:

> The Lord is not slack concerning His promise, as some count slackness, but is longsuffering toward us, not willing that any should perish but that all should come to repentance.
>
> —2 PETER 3:9

I can remember praying with a lady who helped me learn to evangelize through a program called Evangelism Explosion. She was my trainer, and after a visit to share the gospel with someone, she confided that she did not believe that it was God's will to save her son, because he was so rebellious and strung out on drugs. I read her this scripture in 2 Peter, and I asked her if she could now believe that God did want to save her son. She said yes, and we prayed for her son to be saved. One year later I met a young woman who introduced herself to me as the daughter-in-law of the woman who trained me in Evangelism Explosion. She joyfully reported that her husband was saved and delivered from drugs. God is faithful!

Thank You, Lord, for Your faithfulness to save the lost.

Evening Watch: Read Psalm 111:1–10. This month we have talked a lot about wisdom, the fear of the Lord, knowledge, and understanding. This psalm sums it all up in the last few verses when it says:

> The fear of the LORD is the beginning of wisdom; A good understanding have all those who do His commandments.

We walk in the fear of the Lord when we do what God has commanded. Knowing God's Word and His Son intimately will give us the wisdom we need to live every day with praise and joy. God will increase our knowledge of Him and will give us understanding of others when our hearts desire only to please Him. David wrote this psalm, and he had a heart that desired to walk in the fear of the Lord. May we all have a heart like David's.

Lord, create in me a clean heart, and renew a right spirit within me. (See Psalm 51:6.)

MAY 16

1 Samuel 18:5–19:24; John 8:31–59; Psalm 112:1–10; Proverbs 15:12–14

Morning Wisdom: Read Proverbs 15:12–14. Have you met people who always look sad? When I meet people with a sad countenance, I know that they probably have a spirit of heaviness. We open the door for a spirit of heaviness to oppress us when we refuse to release our burdens to the Lord. The heaviness of burdens can take a toll on our bodies. Proverbs 12:25 says, "Heaviness in the heart of man maketh it stoop: but a good word maketh it glad" (KJV). The New King James version reads, "Anxiety in the heart of man causes depression, But a good word makes it glad."

Proverbs 15:13 says, "A merry heart makes a cheerful countenance, But by sorrow of the heart the spirit is broken." When we see people who have dark countenances, we should be alerted to share a good word with them.

It is a challenge to bring cheer to anyone who is suffering from a heavy heart. I believe, however, if we will ask the Lord to help us speak an encouraging word to them, He will give us exactly what to say.

Isaiah 61:3 says that God has provided the garment of praise to lift the spirit of heaviness. The battle against the spirit of heaviness is won when we praise the Lord. If you know someone who is heavy-hearted, encourage him or her to begin to praise the Lord.

My friend was miles away from her daughter when her daughter called her to tell her that she was considering suicide. The Holy Spirit inspired my friend to tell her daughter to read the last five psalms in the Bible out loud and to keep reading them until she fell asleep. The daughter called the next morning with the good news that her heavy heart had been healed. Later my friend opened her Bible to see what the last five psalms said. Every one of the psalms begins with the words, "Praise the Lord!" She realized then that she had instructed her daughter to receive the garment of praise to lift the spirit of heaviness.

Lord, help me to encourage someone today.

Evening Watch: Read Psalm 112:1–10. During this month we have learned a lot about what it means to fear the Lord. Today's psalm describes the benefits and blessings we will experience when we walk daily in the fear of the Lord. When we walk in the fear of the Lord our descendants will be mighty on the earth (v. 2); we will live blessed and prosperous lives (vv. 2–3); we will prosper, and even our dark days will become light (vv. 3–4); we will experience the compassion and graciousness of the Lord, and He will give us discretion (v. 5); people will remember us when we die (v. 6); nothing will shake us, because we will be steadfast and our hearts will not be fearful even of evil tidings (v. 7); and we will have the funds to give to the poor and God will honor and exalt us (v. 9).

Lord, unite my heart to fear Your name. (See Psalm 86:11.)

MAY 17

Morning Wisdom: Read Proverbs 15:15–17. I recall seeing the movie *Babette's Feast.* If you have never seen this movie, I would recommend it to you. Babette's love was cooking, and she was very poor. She offered her services to a family for little or no salary. Later she came into an inheritance, and she ended up spending her entire inheritance upon one grand feast. She invited everyone to the feast, even those who had treated her badly. She imported food from other countries to prepare her feast. The feast was so extravagant that her guests feasted on the memory of that delicious meal the rest of their lives.

Proverbs 15:15 reads, "All the days of the afflicted are evil, But he who is of a merry heart has a continual feast." This verse reminds me of Psalm 34:19, which says, "Many are the afflictions of the righteous, But the LORD delivers him out of them all." When we experience affliction, we can rest assured that the Lord will strengthen us and deliver us. This knowledge should help us have a merry heart, even during severe trials. Paul and Silas had merry hearts when they were in prison. With their arms bound in chains, they began to sing praises to God. Their deliverance from prison came as they praised the Lord. (See Acts 16:26.) We can have a continual feast no matter what we go through in this life if we remain in praise.

Lord, thank You for Your joy that abides with me forever.

Evening Watch: Read Psalm 113:1–114:8. Psalm 113 is a psalm filled with praise. Verse 3 says, "From the rising of the sun to its going down, The LORD's name is to be praised." If you cannot think of some reasons to praise the Lord, I would suggest that you spend an hour reading the book of Psalms. Then write out a praise list. Put your praise list in you Bible, and use it on the days when you have a hard time praising the Lord. This psalm declares who God is and the works He does on Earth. Even though God is high above all nations, He humbles Himself to behold the things that are in the heavens and in the earth. God raises up the poor out of the dust and lifts the needy. He gives the barren woman a home and causes her to be like a joyful mother of children. When David penned many of the psalms, his pen became a mighty sword that we can use today to defeat the enemy. Before you go to sleep, read the last five chapters in the book of Psalms. You will have a sweet sleep and you will want to praise God's name forever.

Lord, thank You for all of Your blessings.

MAY 18

Morning Wisdom: Read Proverbs 15:18–19. In our Proverb reading today we have another comparison between the wicked man and the righteous man. A wicked man is usually wrathful and loves to stir up strife.

Causing strife is one of Satan's favorite strategies. Satan is in the middle of every strife-filled relationship. He stirs up strife by putting accusing thoughts into the minds of those who are trying to relate to one another.

We may be able to restrain ourselves from entering into strife with others, but we can entertain strife in our minds. Satan can get a foothold in our minds when we receive his accusations about others. Have you ever pictured yourself getting revenge on someone who hurt you? I have on several occasions. I even think of some juicy words to say to such people when I see them again. I want to hurt them as much as they hurt me. When we imagine strife-filled scenes like this, we have sinned in our hearts. If we allow such scenes to be played over and over again in our minds, bitterness and resentment can begin to take root in our hearts.

How can we resist Satan when thoughts of retaliation or accusation enter our minds? We first have to recognize why we think such thoughts. Is there a door in our minds that we have failed to close when strife-filled thoughts enter our imaginations? The door we open to all strife, whether it is in our minds or in our actions, is pride. Pride is the source of all contention. James had good advice when he wrote: "'God resists the proud, But gives grace to the humble' Therefore submit to God. Resist the devil and he will flee from you" (James 4:6–7).

We know that Satan is the proudest being in the universe, and he lures his prey into contention. Satan loves to sow strife. Watch out for his traps today, and make sure you humble yourself this morning and every day. You can humble yourself by releasing to God the person who offended and hurt you. Then ask God to help you to forgive that person. Take it one step further and pray for the Lord to bless that person. Only when we remain humble can we have any hope of resisting Satan.

Lord, help me to be a peacemaker instead of a strife contender.

Evening Watch: Read Psalm 115:1–18. We learned about Satan's subtle strategies to get us into strife. This morning's devotional concluded with the exhortation to humble ourselves when we have strife-filled thoughts. We learned that a good way to humble ourselves is to release to God the person who offended us, forgive them, and then pray a blessing over them. We find a good prayer to pray for others in this psalm. Psalm 115:15 says, "May you be blessed by the LORD, Who made heaven and earth." The first part of this psalm describes idol worship. As you read verses 1–8, you may think, "At least I'm not an idol worshiper." Whenever we get into strife, we become idol worshipers. The idol is ourselves.

Lord, fill me with Your love so that I will not be easily hurt and offended.

MAY 19

Morning Wisdom: Read Proverbs 15:20–21. "A wise son makes a father glad, But a foolish man despises his mother" (v. 20).

Another Proverb says, "A wise son makes a glad father, But a foolish son is the grief of his mother" (Prov. 10:1). Every parent wants their children not to bring shame upon them or their family. There was a point in my life when I was heavily burdened, because two of our sons were not serving the Lord. They both had gotten into a worldly lifestyle that could cause shame to them.

During those years, I almost daily prayed that these two sons would do nothing that they would be ashamed of when they saw Jesus face-to-face. One morning after I had prayed this prayer, the Lord spoke these words to my heart:

> *Your sons will have nothing to be ashamed of, because when they see me face-to-face they will be like me. I see all of your sons as my three golden vessels.*

The words Jesus spoke to my heart helped me to see these two sons like He saw them. My attitude and my actions toward them changed after that day. I began to thank the Lord for what He would do in the lives of the two sons who were not walking with Him. God answered my prayers, and these two sons are now serving Him.

Lord, give me eyes to see others as You see them.

Evening Watch: Read Psalm 116:1–19. This morning I shared how my heart was filled with thanksgiving when I heard the Lord answer my cry about my two sons who went through a season of rebellion. David cried out to the Lord many times. In this psalm David reviewed those times when God heard his prayers and delivered him out of trouble. He declared how gracious and merciful the Lord was towards him. He said the Lord delivered his eyes from tears and his feet from falling.

David was so filled with gratitude that he asked the Lord how he could give back to the Lord all the benefits He had given to him. He said he would pay back God by taking up the cup of salvation, continually praying, and paying his vows to the Lord in the presence of all His people.

When we think of the mercy God has extended to us in our lifetimes, we too can pay God back when we take up the cup of salvation and share the good news about how we were saved with others. How can we pay our vows to God? The answer to this question is simple. We pay our vows to God when we continually pray, listen, and obey God. Make it your goal to pay your vows to God tomorrow and all the tomorrows until He comes again.

Lord, thank You for Your continual mercy to me.

MAY 20

Morning Wisdom: Read Proverbs 15:22–23. Too few people seek out godly counselors these days. Instead, many people seek out counselors who will tell them what they want to hear instead of what God's Word says. An effective counselor does not have to have earthly degrees to qualify them. They only need a clear knowledge and understanding of the Word of God. They also need to be able to convey the Word of God to their clients in such a way that their clients will be able to apply the instructions God's Word presents them.

Proverbs 15:22 says, "Without counsel, plans go awry, But in the multitude of counselors they are established" Another scripture reads, "By the mouth of two or three witnesses the matter shall be established" (Deut. 19:15).

Before we make an important decision, my husband and I first seek counsel from someone in the body of Christ who is wise in Scripture. Then we ask the counselor, the Holy Spirit, to direct our decision. We also seek a confirmation of our decision from the counsel of the Word of God. Godly counsel has kept us from making many wrong decisions.

Lord, help us always to seek counsel from You before we make important decisions.

Evening Watch: Read Psalm 117:1–2. This is one of the shortest chapters in the book of Psalms. The author of this psalm exhorts all nations to praise the Lord for His merciful kindness and for His truth that endures forever. Take time tonight to praise and thank Him.

Lord, You are worthy of my praise. Thank You for the truths in Your Word that guide me daily. Thank You also for the mercy You extend to me even when I fail to seek counsel from Your Word.

MAY 21

Morning Wisdom: Read Proverbs 15:24–26. The kingdom of God on Earth works quite differently from the kingdom of this world. In the world's system people climb the ladder of success by pushing others down. They exalt themselves and try their best to sell themselves. Our sons have had several jobs during their lifetimes, and each time they try for another job, they send out resumés that describe all of their past job experience. The goal is to make the resumés look good to the person who reads them. I have never seen a resumé that read like this, "My only experience has been as a servant who depends upon God for my wisdom, knowledge, and strength."

In the kingdom of God the way up is the way down. God pulls down the proud and gives grace to the humble. (See James 4:6.) God promotes those who humble themselves. Jesus said, "Blessed are you poor, For yours is the kingdom of God" (Luke 6:20). Jesus said, "For whoever exalts himself will be humbled, and he who humbles himself will be exalted" (Luke 14:11).

Proverbs 15:24 reads, "The way of life winds upward for the wise." Those who depend upon Jesus are wise people who will experience a life that always winds upward. Once we have been born again, our life is no longer our own. We now have Christ living within us, and we can look forward to living eternally from that moment on with Him. When we decide to follow Jesus, our path is upward bound. We may stumble and fall from time to time, but He is always there to pick us up and carry us to a higher level of intimacy with Him.

We may not be considered wise by the world, but the wisdom we have will get us through every trial on this earth. When we tap into the wisdom that comes from above, we will live lives that are peaceable, pure, gentle, willing to yield, and full of mercy and good fruits without hypocrisy or partiality. (See James 3:17.) When we receive and walk in the wisdom from above we will be able to live above every circumstance we may face in this life. Praise the Lord!

Lord, thank You for giving me Your wisdom today.

Evening Watch: Read Psalm 118:1–18. "The LORD is on my side; I will not fear. What can man do to me?" (v. 6). Paul must have been quoting this verse from Psalms when he wrote: "If God is for us, who can be against us?" (Rom. 8:31). Everyone in life wants to be on the winning team. When we accepted Jesus Christ as our Savior, we signed up for the winning team. Jesus has already triumphed over Satan and his hoards of demons. On the cross Jesus disarmed principalities and powers and made a public spectacle of them, triumphing over them in it. (See Colossians 2:15.) When we receive all of these truths by faith, we can boldly make this declaration: "The Lord is on my side. I am not afraid. The devil has no power over me and no place in me. My righteousness is of Jesus Christ, and no weapon that men or the devil might form against me will prosper. I condemn every word of judgment spoken against me." (See Isaiah 54:17.)

Lord, thank You for the victory!

MAY 22

Morning Wisdom: Read Proverbs 15:27–28. My mother always told my sisters and me to think before we open our mouths. That was good advice, and it has served me well over the years.

Proverbs 15:28 says, "The heart of the righteous studies how to answer, But the mouth of the wicked pours forth evil." We need to think before we speak, but we also need to have our hearts tuned to another person when they ask us a question. Jesus had the ability to hear not only the words people spoke, but also the hearts of others. He knew the motivations of people when they asked Him questions. He instantly knew that the questions the Pharisees and scribes asked Him were motivated by their desire to entrap Him.

Since the same Spirit that raised Christ Jesus from the dead now dwells in our mortal bodies, we also can tap into the power of discernment. As we hear people ask us questions, we can silently ask the Holy Spirit to help us to give the right answer. The Holy Spirit knows exactly the word in season to give when we are asked a question. He can also impart the humility we might need to admit that we do not have all the answers.

Abiding in God's Word daily is the best way we can prepare ourselves to answer the questions people may have when we witness to them. The Holy Spirit can only bring to our remembrance those verses we have hidden in our hearts. Make it your goal today to memorize at least one scripture a day. You will be amazed how the verses you memorize will bounce out of your mouth at exactly the right times.

Lord, help me to be faithful to hide God's Word in my heart and to be bold enough to speak God's Word to others.

Evening Watch: Read Psalm 118:19–29. David reminded us that we enter God's presence through the gates of praise. He said he would go through the gates of righteousness and would praise the Lord. One of the best ways I have found to enter into worship is to begin to praise God and thank Him for making me righteous through the righteousness of His Son, Jesus Christ.

David praised God because He had become his salvation. God the Father put on an earth suit and came to Earth in the form of Jesus to sacrifice Himself in the flesh so that we might be set free from the sins of our own flesh. David declared, "The LORD is my strength and song, And He has become my salvation" (v. 14). He exclaimed, "God is the LORD, And He has given us light" (v. 27). Jesus is truly the light of the world, and God provided a way that all darkness can be penetrated by the light of His Son, Jesus. Praise Him tonight and give thanks to the Lord, for He is good. He extended His mercy to you and saved you when you were a sinner.

Lord, thank You for coming to Earth to die for my sins.

MAY 23

Morning Wisdom: Read Proverbs 15:29–30. There is definitely a connection between the outer body and the inner spirit. Proverbs 15:30 says, "The light of the eyes rejoices the heart, And a good report makes the bones healthy." Jesus said: "The light of the body is the eye: if therefore thine eye be single, thy whole body shall be full of light" (Matt. 6:22, KJV).

The eyes are the windows to the soul. The eyes also can reveal a lot about our physical condition. When I go to the eye doctor and he shines a light into my eyes, he can see things that reveal whether or not I am in good health.

The eye of the mind is the imagination. Images come across the screen of our minds every day. Satan even has the power to put wicked images in our minds. Our imaginations were designed to help us worship God in Spirit and in truth. After the fall, however, the imaginations of men's hearts became wicked, and all but Noah and his family were destroyed in the flood because of the wicked imaginations in people.

What we allow to capture our imaginations will capture us. Satan has had much success with capturing the minds of many through pornography. The only way to be delivered from this bondage is to begin to take thoughts captive and place the focus of the imagination upon Jesus as we worship Him.

I can usually tell by someone's eyes whether or not they are in bondage to some besetting sin. The eyes of such a person will not sparkle with light, because there are dark areas within the soul. Our souls will always rejoice when Jesus is the focal point of our lives. When we keep the eye of our minds upon the Lord, joy will fill our hearts, and even our bones will be healthy.

Lord, help me to keep my eyes focused on You.

Evening Watch: Read Psalm 119:1–16. As you read through this psalm underline the many times David spoke about the Word of God. Our reading today contains the following statements about God's Word:

- We are blessed when we walk in God's Word (v. 1).
- We are commanded to keep the precepts found in God's Word (v. 5).
- When we keep God's statutes we will never be ashamed (vv. 5–6).
- We can be cleansed when we obey or heed God's Word (v. 9).
- We can hide God's Word in our hearts, and this will keep us from sinning (v. 11).
- When we declare God's Word with our lips, we will have joy (vv. 13–14).

When we meditate and delight ourselves in God's Word, we will learn the ways of the Lord (v. 15).

Lord, help me to daily abide in Your Word.

MAY 24

Morning Wisdom: Read Proverbs 15:31–32. Most of us do not enjoy being corrected when we have said or done something wrong. Proverbs 15:32 says, "He who disdains instruction despises his own soul, But he who heeds rebuke gets understanding." *Webster's New World Dictionary* defines *rebuke* as a "sharp reprimand." I was reprimanded a lot when I was a small girl, but as an adult I try to avoid reprimands by making sure I follow instructions. I must admit that I have, on more than one occasion, received reprimands from my husband. At least he doesn't say, "How can you be so stupid!" when he reprimands me.

In the Old Testament, God gave a lot of reprimands to the children of Israel. Because they disdained God's instructions, they experienced many troubled times. Today we have God's Word as a rod of correction in our lives. If we follow the instructions in our Maker's handbook—the Bible—we will receive instruction, correction, and reproof from God throughout our lives. Too many people try to put their lives together without ever reading the Maker's handbook and the results are disastrous.

When I was a little girl I tried as much as possible to obey my parents because I did not want to be reprimanded. Whenever I was reprimanded, I experienced some amount of shame. The good news is that Jesus bore our shame on the cross, and now if God reprimands us, we can receive His reprimands with grace instead of shame, because we know He loves us and He is not ashamed of us.

Lord, thank You for gently reprimanding me through Your Word.

Evening Watch: Read Psalm 119:17–35. David prayed for God to give him understanding of His Word. David wanted God to reveal all of His wondrous works and His marvelous ways to Him as He meditated and delighted in God's Word. He knew if he held on to God's Word he would not be ashamed. He knew that God's Word had the power to revive and strengthen him during the times when his heart was heavy.

The secret to David's fruitfulness was that he abided in God's Word. He reviewed the accounts of the beginning of time and the testimonies, statutes, and laws contained in the books Moses wrote. He learned from the stories of Abraham and Joseph how God deals with those who seek to please Him. David had an intimate relationship with God, because he listened to God speak to him through the written accounts in His Word. I believe David was reading the first words in the book of Joshua when he wrote Psalm 1 and compared the man who meditated day and night on God's Word to "a tree Planted by the rivers of water, That brings forth fruit in its season, Whose leaf also shall not wither; And whatever he does shall prosper" (Ps. 1:3). Before you retire read the first chapter of Joshua and compare it to Psalm 1. I believe David had memorized Joshua 1:7–8.

Lord, help me to memorize Your Word.

MAY 25

Morning Wisdom: Read Proverbs 15:33. We talked yesterday about following the instructions in the Maker's handbook. Today's verse reads, "The fear of the LORD is the instruction of wisdom, And before honor is humility." We have discussed in earlier devotions exactly what it means to fear the Lord. (See May 6.) We have learned in our Proverbs readings this month that the fear of the Lord is the beginning of knowledge and wisdom.

The only way we can grow in the fear of the Lord (the awesome respect for God that causes us to obey God's Word) is to daily abide in God's Word. A child cannot be expected to obey his parents if his parents have failed to communicate the rules that the child needs to follow. Both what we are to obey and how we are to obey are clearly described in God's Word.

We need to have a spirit of humility when we read and heed God's Word. James shared about a humble, meek spirit as it relates to God's Word when he wrote:

> Who is wise and understanding among you? Let him show by good conduct that his works are done in the meekness of wisdom.
>
> —JAMES 3:13

> Therefore lay aside all filthiness and overflow of wickedness, and receive with meekness the implanted [engrafted] word, which is able to save your souls.
>
> —JAMES 1:21

True humility occurs when we refuse to figure things out ourselves or do things in our own strength. Instead, we look to God and His Word to help us in every situation of life.

Lord, help me to both hear and do God's Word.

Evening Watch: Read Psalm 119:36–52. David wrote, "Establish Your word to Your servant, Who is devoted to fearing You" (v. 38). Which came first: the chicken or the egg? Did David fear the Lord and then have God's Word established in him, or did David walk in the fear of the Lord because God's Word was established in his heart? The fear of the Lord is taught. It is not caught. The establishment of God's Word in David's heart, not just his head, is what caused him to daily reverence and obey God. God's Word reveals how we can sin against Him. Even though David sinned by committing both adultery and murder, it was his knowledge of God's Word that caused him to grieve and repent of his sin.

Lord, establish Your Word in my heart, so I will not sin against You.

2 Samuel 9:1–11:27; John 15:1–27; Psalm 119:53–70; Proverbs 16:1–3

Morning Wisdom: Read Proverbs 16:1–3. These verses from Proverbs contain a prayer that I pray daily: *Lord, I commit my works to You, so You will establish my thoughts.* When I have my morning quiet time, sometimes it is hard for me to stay focused upon the Lord and His Word, because I am thinking about all the things I have to do that day. Over the years I have learned what to do when my mind starts making my to-do list in the middle of worshiping the Lord. I stop striving to get my thoughts to return to worship, and I simply write down all the things I have to do that day. Often I just make a mental list. Then I commit that list to the Lord and I thank Him for setting that list in the right order of His priorities, not mine. I also ask Him to put me in the right place at the right time.

At the beginning of each day, I also try to prepare my heart to be in tune to the Holy Spirit all day long. Proverbs 16:1 clearly states that the preparations of my heart are my responsibility, not God's. To prepare my heart for whatever I may face that day, I confess whatever God shows me I need to confess, I clear my heart of any bitterness or resentment or unforgiveness, and I ask God to help me say no to my three lusts—lust of the flesh, lust of the eyes, and the pride of life. Join me this morning as I pray:

> *Lord, I commit my works to You so that You can establish my thoughts. Help me to have Your priorities today instead of my own. I confess any bitterness, unforgiveness, or resentment. Help me to walk in the Spirit today so that I will not fulfill the lusts of my flesh.*

Evening Watch: Read Psalm 119:53–70. David knew how to commit his way and his works to the Lord. At night he meditated on the names of God and His commandments (v. 55). He thought about his ways and compared them to God's ways (v. 59). It is not what we do but the way we do things that reveals our character. David praised God at midnight (v. 62). David delighted in God's law and asked God to both show favor to him and to teach him His ways (v. 66). He especially desired for God to teach him good judgment and knowledge.

God answered all of David's requests, because his requests were not selfish.

Proverbs 10:24 says that God grants the desires of the righteous. The reason He is able to do this is because God plants His desires in our hearts. God planted His own desires in David's heart, and God granted what David requested. David said that God will "fulfill the desire of those who fear Him; He will also hear their cry and save them" (Ps. 145:19). When we desire for our way to be conformed to God's way and our works to be performed by God through us, we can expect the unfailing help of the Holy Spirit to both will and to do of God's good pleasure every day. (See Philippians 2:13.)

> *Thank You for helping me to do Your works in Your way every day.*

MAY 27

Morning Wisdom: Read Proverbs 16:4–5. Proverbs 16:4 declares that the Lord has made all for Himself and that even the wicked have been made by God. When God created mankind He fashioned Adam and Eve to have hearts that longed to worship, glorify, and enjoy Him. After the fall, wicked imaginations entered mankind, and God had to destroy all but Noah and his family in the flood. Noah was a righteous man, but it was not long before Satan had success with the people on Earth and wickedness once again was made manifest through them.

People began to be proud in their hearts, and they no longer wanted to go God's way. If they refused to turn back to God they would face everlasting punishment (v. 5).

As we look at the stories in the Old Testament we see God's long-suffering with a rebellious people. Israel would serve the Lord for a season, but soon they began to depend upon themselves instead of God. They succumbed to all kinds of idolatry. However, God never gave up on Israel. He kept providing prophets, judges, and kings who led the people back to God. However, the ability to persevere in the fear of the Lord was not fully possible until after the cross. The next few verses in Proverbs reveals God's redemptive plan that finally made it possible for people on Earth to desire to continually worship, glorify, and enjoy Him. Read tomorrow's verses to learn the rest of the story.

Thank You, Lord, for the good news presented throughout Scripture.

Evening Watch: Read Psalm 119:71–80. "Thanks for the trials, Lord!" Have you ever given God thanks for the tests and trials in your life? David said, "It is good for me that I have been afflicted, That I may learn Your statutes" (v. 71). If our desire is to walk in the fear of the Lord and to do His will daily, then we can rest assured that every trial and test will be used by God for our good. How we respond to the circumstances of life will determine whether or not we will walk in the victory Jesus purchased for us on the cross. If we stand on the promise in Romans 8:28 that says all things work for the good to those who love God and are called according to His purpose, we will never lose hope. We will have an expectant, optimistic, faith-filled view of everything that comes our way in this life. We will only have this view if we abide in God's Word.

Every trial or test we experience in this life is designed by God to conform us to the image of His dear Son, Jesus Christ. We will only come out victorious in the trials if we turn to God's Word. Trials are always a test of faith, and we will not pass the test if we do not turn to God and His Word. If we fail the first test by not studying God's textbook, the Bible, we can rest assured that the Holy Spirit, our great Teacher, will give us a make-up test. He will keep giving those make-up tests until we finally pass. Remember, you cannot flunk out of the school of life, because the Holy Spirit will always come alongside you and help you eventually pass every test.

Lord, help me to always turn to Your Word when I go through trials.

Morning Wisdom: Read Proverbs 16:6–7. We learned yesterday how impossible it was for people to persevere in the fear of the Lord before the cross. I shared yesterday that we would discover the rest of the story of mankind's struggle to obey God in today's reading.

When God sent Jesus to die on the cross for us, mercy and truth kissed each other (v. 6). Atonement was provided for our iniquities, and it became possible for people on Earth to both fear the Lord and to walk continually in the fear of the Lord. On the cross Jesus won the victory over death, hell, the grave, and the devil. The enemies of mankind were defeated once and for all. Jesus triumphed over evil. We now are in a position of appropriating the victory that Jesus Christ won for us. Whether or not we will experience this victory every day of our lives depends upon whether or not we will walk in the fear of the Lord with a humble heart.

Proverbs 16:6 presents the gospel in a nutshell. Proverbs 16:6 reads, "In mercy and truth Atonement is provided for iniquity; And by the fear of the LORD one departs from evil." Unless atonement is provided for our iniquities, we will never be able to walk in righteousness. On the cross Jesus provided atonement by His shed blood. Without the shedding of blood there is no atonement for sin. (See Leviticus 17:11.) In all my years of reading the Bible through in a year, I never saw this clear presentation of the gospel in Proverbs. These verses can be a great witnessing tool when we share the good news with our Jewish friends. I think I'll spend this morning memorizing these verses.

Father, thank You for the atoning blood of Jesus.

Evening Watch: Read Psalm 119:81–95. You have probably heard the saying, "God said it, and I believe it." David spoke about how God's Word is established forever. He wrote, "Your word is settled in heaven" (v. 89). David had many enemies, but the faith he had in God's Word was the glue that kept him from falling apart. David vowed never to forget the precepts of God.

I do not know if David had a daily quiet time when he read God's Word and prayed, but his dependence upon God's Word would indicate that he read God's Word morning, noon, and night. We do know that David praised God seven times a day. I believe a lot of his praise included declaring the words he memorized as he read the books Moses wrote. It amazes me that even though David did not have the full counsel of God's Word available to him, he received all he needed from the things he learned from God's Word to face each day.

We have the full counsel of God's Word available to us today. If we will avail ourselves of God's Word daily, we can become even stronger in the Lord than David was. The advantage we have over David is that we now have the continual presence of the Holy Spirit who will teach us and help us apply God's Word to our daily lives.

Holy Spirit, help me sit in Your classroom every day.

MAY 29

Morning Wisdom: Read Proverbs 16:8–9. I have discovered over the years that planning a trip is just about as much fun as experiencing the trip. Right now my husband and I are planning a trip to Australia. My book, *Around the Word in 365 Days*, is being sold in Australia. I received an e-mail from a lady in Australia who bought my book in a Christian bookstore. She ordered forty more books and has started an e-mail devotional club based on *Around the Word in 365 Days*. Her friends e-mail one another after they read the devotionals each day. They make their comments and share what they have learned. We have always wanted to go to Australia and are looking forward to adding this to our many travel destinations. After we complete this trip we will have visited every continent in the world except Africa.

When we plan our trips, we first get brochures from the country. We look them over and map out the places we want to visit. We check to see the times and prices of air flights and other modes of transportation to reach our destinations. We make lists of all the clothes and books we want to take with us. We get travel videos about these places. I must confess that we usually make all these plans without committing our plans to the Lord in prayer. On this trip I am determined to pray about everything.

Our reading from Proverbs assures us that even if we have not submitted our plans to the Lord in prayer, He will direct our steps. Verse 9 says: "A man's heart plans his way, But the LORD directs his steps." It has been our experience in our travels to see just how the Lord has directed our steps. When my husband and I were traveling in China with our middle son and his friend, we tried to catch a train. We had only minutes to make it, and we had to cross six lanes of traffic to get to the station from the hotel where we spent the night. In all the excitement my son, his friend, and I got separated from my husband, who had all the tickets. My husband was in a panic when he did not know where to look for us. Suddenly a man appeared out of nowhere who could speak English, and he led Tom right to us. I think he was an angel. The Lord ordered our steps.

Thank You for ordering our steps.

Evening Watch: Read Psalm 119:96–112. This morning we talked about how God directs our steps. David wrote, "Your word is a lamp to my feet And a light to my path" (v. 105). David gained understanding, because he meditated on God's Word day and night. God's Word was able to keep him from going down evil paths. He was kept from the snares of the enemy because he followed the lighted path God provided for him through His Word. God's Word caused David to rejoice.

Tonight review the times that God rescued you from making wrong decisions because He led you by His Word. Think about the times God kept you from going down the wrong path because you consulted His Word before you decided to quit work or move to another location.

Lord, thank You for guiding my steps.

MAY 30

Morning Wisdom: Read Proverbs 16:10–11. Proverbs 16:11 says, "Honest weights and scales are the LORD's." We may try to get away with cheating someone out of his or her money, but the Lord is well aware when we do this. He sees when we fudge a little on our taxes to gain more money from the government. The day will come when the Lord will weigh the hearts of men. Our deeds and words will be judged for reward if we have received Jesus as our Savior. Our deeds and words will be punished if we have not trusted in Jesus to be our righteousness. God knows what is in our hearts, and even the motivation behind our words and deeds will be judged. We can try to fool others, but we cannot fool God.

I am so thankful that Jesus forgives me of all of my sins—past, present, and future. However, the cleansing of my heart will only take place if I confess my sins with a repentant heart. I don't know about you, but I desire to have a clean heart on this earth. I know that if I confess my sins, Jesus is faithful and just to forgive me of my sins and also to cleanse me from all unrighteousness. (See 1 John 1:9.) I want my motives, actions, and words to be pure on this earth.

> *Help me today to be honest with You, honest with myself, and honest with others.*

Evening Watch: Read Psalm 119:113–131. Our only hope of being honest with God and honest with others is to saturate ourselves with God's truths as found in His Word. David knew the secret of meditating on God's Word and how hiding God's Word in his heart would keep him from sinning.

God's Word is like a mirror, and if we look into it daily, we will see the flaws in our flesh. I can remember feeling horrified as a teenager when I saw a zit (a blemish) pop up on my face. We should be just as horrified when we look into God's Word and discover the blemishes in our flesh.

David said, "Do not let me be ashamed of my hope" (v. 116). David's hope was in God's Word, and he knew only God's Word could cause him to see the sin in his life so that he could confess it and receive cleansing. David declared how wonderful the testimonies of the Lord were, and he said God's commandments were better than fine gold. The entrance of God's Word gave David light and kept him walking in the light of God's love. Whenever we bring our sins to the light by confessing them, our fellowship in the light is restored, and we can walk in the light. Are there sins you need to confess tonight? Ask the Holy Spirit to reveal any hidden sin and meditate on God's Word tomorrow. As you hide God's Word in your heart, you will be delivered from many fleshly blemishes.

> *Holy Spirit, thank You for shining a light into my heart through God's Word.*

MAY 31

Morning Wisdom: Read Proverbs 16:12–13. David was a man after God's own heart because he always confessed and repented of his sin. Saul, however, just made excuses for his sin, and he never repented and turned back to God. David's reign was established, and he was promised that his seed would reign forever. Saul's reign was cut very short when Saul sacrificed to God instead of waiting for Samuel to sacrifice to God. Only priests were allowed to sacrifice to God.

Proverbs 16:12 says, "It is an abomination for kings to commit wickedness, For a throne is established by righteousness." David's throne was established. Absalom, David's own son, tried to rob David of his throne, but God never allowed this to happen.

Paul wrote that those who believe in Jesus are kings and priests. God has made us kings to rule and reign with King Jesus forever. He has also made us priests to offer the sacrifices of thanksgiving, praise, and worship to Him forever. When we believe, receive, and confess what Jesus did for us on the cross, God crowns us as kings and dresses us in righteous, priestly robes. Hallelujah!

Lord, thank You for reigning in my heart and for allowing me to reign with You forever.

Evening Watch: Read Psalm 119:132–155. David cried out to God and asked Him to let no iniquity have dominion over him.

What a great prayer! He also prayed that God would deliver Him from the oppression of men. David wept, because so many men he knew did not keep God's law. David knew the purity of God's Word, and this caused him to weep over those who lived impure lives because they refused to follow the pure precepts of God's Word.

David delighted in God's commandments because they gave him understanding and preserved his life. He rose before dawn to cry out to the Lord for help, and he meditated on God's Word day and night. He said, "My eyes are awake through the night watches, That I may meditate on Your Word" (v. 148). When was the last time you were awakened in the night to read God's Word? I have had that experience many times, and I desire to have it more times. Losing a little sleep to read God's Word and to hear from Him in prayer pays great dividends. There are no interruptions when we wake up to read God's Word in the early morning. When we are willing to be awakened in the night to read His Word, we can hear His voice clearly.

Lord, wake me up if there is anything You want me to read in Your Word tonight. You may have a special message for me that will help me through the day tomorrow.

2 Samuel 18:1–19:10; John 20:1–31; Psalm 119:156–176; Proverbs 16:14–15

Morning Wisdom: Read Proverbs 16:14–15. It was a bright, sunny day, and there was not a cloud in the sky. I was admiring the beauty of God's nature as I looked at the woods behind our home. As I prepared the table on the deck for morning breakfast, I heard a sound like rain. When I looked up, there was a pillar of rain falling in the middle of our woods. It was only about twelve feet in width, and the rain looked like diamonds as the sun shined on the water drops. I looked to the sky to see if there was a cloud above this rain shower, but there was no cloud. I asked the Lord what was happening, and I received these words:

> You are seeing a sign of My latter rain. I heard your prayers for your loved ones, and I have bottled the tears you have shed for them. In this latter rain I am pouring out the tears many have shed for their lost loved ones, and I am showering those loved ones with my blessings. They will come to know Me during this last harvest.

This strange happening led me to do a study on the latter rain. There are several scriptures in the Bible that reference the latter rain, and our reading in Proverbs today is one of them. Proverbs 16:15 says, "The light of the king's face is life, And his favor is like a cloud of the latter rain." Those words I heard that morning were so encouraging to me, because just prior to seeing this supernatural occurrence I had been praying for someone's child who needed to return to the Lord. I had been in the presence of the King of kings, and He had answered my prayer. His favor was manifested like a cloud of the latter rain. Is there someone you are praying for today who needs a breakthrough? Rest assured that God will pour out His blessings upon those you pray for, and His goodness will bring them to a place of repentance.

Lord, thank You for the latter rain.

Evening Watch: Read Psalm 119:156–176. The buzzword these days is *revival*. The foundations of faith that were established by the fathers of this nation are beginning to crumble. The first step to revival is godly sorrow that brings us to repentance. Our whole nation will never repent, but the body of Christ in our nation can repent. The exhortation in 2 Chronicles 7:14 is for the people who are called by God's name to humble themselves and pray and seek the Lord's face and turn from their wicked ways. If we heed this exhortation, God promises to heal our land. Revival begins with the individual Christian. Some of the prayers David prayed in this psalm reading are excellent prayers to pray for revival in our own hearts. David cried out, "Revive me according to Your judgments…Revive me, O Lord, according to Your lovingkindness" (v. 156, 159). David praised God seven times a day, and he loved God's law. When we have a heart like David's, revival will come.

Revive us, Lord!

JUNE 2

2 Samuel 19:11–20:13; John 21:1–25; Psalm 120:1–7; Proverbs 16:16–17

Morning Wisdom: Read Proverbs 16:16–17. We all are on a journey. The question is, Do we know where we are going?

It might be well for us to ponder these questions: Where are we going? and What are we going to do? God has called us all to be a people of destiny. To be a people of destiny we need to know our destination. Are we traveling through life aimlessly just doing the next thing? Do we see clearly our calling in the Lord, and are we fulfilling that call? Our destination is heaven, but in the meantime what we do on Earth is determined by what we focus on in this life. Are we seeking first the kingdom of God and His righteousness? Are we daily experiencing His kingdom of righteousness, peace, and joy?

Our proverb today talks about the highway we all need to stay on as we travel though life. Proverbs 16:17 says, "The highway of the upright is to depart from evil; He who keeps his way preserves his soul." We have the responsibility of keeping ourselves on the heavenly highway. Let's take a look at that highway. The name of the highway is faith. This highway leads into the throne room of God, and we can travel it as we climb into the vehicle of prayer. The roads in heaven are paved with gold, but the highway of faith is paved with hope. We will not have a bumpy ride if we hold on to our faith in Jesus Christ and our hope of glory, which is Christ in us. The Holy Spirit will be able to make the rough places smooth as we travel if we will abide in God's Word.

The promises in God's Word supply us with the smooth pavement called hope.

Lord, help me to stay on the highway of faith.

Evening Watch: Read Psalm 120:1–7. David expressed his dependency upon God's Word in almost every verse in Psalm 119. Now we begin to read several psalms that are called the Songs of Ascents (Ps. 120–134). The pilgrims sang these songs as they traveled up to Jerusalem three times a year to celebrate the Lord's feasts. On our trips to Israel we try to sing some of these songs as we travel from Jericho up to Jerusalem. David cried out in this psalm for peace. He said, "My soul has dwelt too long With one who hates peace. I am for peace" (v. 6–7). David was surrounded by enemies and was a man of the sword. Nathan prophesied that the sword would never depart from David. He was betrayed by his own family and his closest friends, but David knew where to go to find peace. That place was in the presence of the Lord.

Thank You for Your peace.

JUNE 3

Morning Wisdom: Read Proverbs 16:18. Pride is deadly. When we are prideful we have two enemies—God and Satan.

James wrote: "But He gives more grace. Therefore He says: 'God resists the proud, But gives grace to the humble'" (James 4:6). James probably based this verse on Proverbs 3:34, which says: "Surely He scorns the scornful, But gives grace to the humble." When we are prideful, God will resist us until we finally humble ourselves. Satan's fall came because he thought too highly of himself. He was distracted from the beauty of the Lord when he considered his own beauty. He was convinced that he could do a better job than God. Whenever we think we can do a better job than someone else, we are in pride. Satan's pride led to rebellion, and he was rejected by God. Ever since his fall he has been trying to get people to join his "self-pity club." Rejection is one of the most viscous tools of the enemy. The ruling spirit over rejection is pride.

Notice that pride always draws our attention from God to ourselves. Before the fall, Adam and Eve's attention was only upon God. The serpent, however, drew Eve's attention to the forbidden fruit. The fruit was pleasant to her eyes, and the serpent told her how she would become wise if she ate the fruit. (See Genesis 3:6.) When Eve ate the fruit, God's Spirit within her died. Her desire to glorify God died, and the lust called the pride of life developed. She began to trust in herself more than she trusted in God, and she worshiped the creature and creation rather than God.

Proverbs 16:18 reads, "Pride goes before destruction, And a haughty spirit before a fall." A haughty spirit was birthed in Eve, because her focus was on herself rather than God. The lust of the pride of life ruled mankind until Jesus died to give us new life. Jesus made it possible for us to have the victory over the lust of the pride of life. Jesus came to teach us meekness and lowliness of heart. (See Matthew 11:28.) It is now possible for us to learn humility from Jesus. True humility occurs when our attention is upon Jesus and what He has done for us on the cross, instead of on us and what we can do in our own strength. Whenever we cast every care upon Jesus, we have humbled ourselves. (See 1 Peter 5:5–6.)

Lord, I humble myself and cast every care upon You.

Evening Watch: Read Psalm 121:1–8. We learned this morning how the lust of the pride of life developed in our natures. I remember observing my son in his play school. The mothers sat behind a one-way mirror and watched the interaction of their two-year-olds with one another. I was careful not to identify which child was mine, because my son was grabbing all his playmate's toys. I kept hearing his little voice scream, "Mine, mine, mine!" It was quite clear to me that day that we are all born with a selfish nature, and our focus remains on ourselves until we are born again. When we are born again, we can lift up our eyes to the Lord and trust Him to win the victory over our selfish natures.

Lord, thank You for helping me win the victory over pride.

JUNE 4

Morning Wisdom: Read Proverbs 16:19–20. We used to sing a song when I was growing up about trusting the Lord. "Trust and obey for there is no other way to be happy in Jesus than to trust and obey" was one of the verses of this song. The person who wrote this song probably received his inspiration from Proverbs 16:20, which says, "And whoever trusts in the LORD, happy is he."

Verse 19 exhorts us to have a humble spirit. People who trust in the Lord will also be humble, because they are totally dependent upon the Lord. They have learned to cast every care upon the Lord, because they know He cares for them. They have also learned to obey God's Word. When we trust and obey the Lord, we will never be shaken by the circumstances we experience in this life. We will be able to face every day with the confidence that God is in control and He will work everything for our good even though, at the time, things may not look so good.

There is a sustaining joy that wells up within us when we trust and release every care to the Lord. I learned also that the Lord rejoices when we cast every care upon Him.

One day when I was releasing all of my cares to the Lord, I had a vision of those cares ascending to heaven. They were wrapped in silver and gold. Jesus was catching those "care packages." With my spiritual eyes I saw Him hold those cares close to His chest and dance around heaven with them. He was going from mansion to mansion showing everyone these "care packages." After I released my cares through prayer, I heard the following with my spiritual ears, "Now I can do something about these cares, because Linda has released them to Me." Are there cares today you need to release to the Lord? Wrap them up in prayer, and send them heavenward.

> *Lord, I release every care to You today. I refuse to take these cares upon myself again.*

Evening Watch: Read Psalm 122:1–9. Psalm 122:6 exhorts us to "Pray for the peace of Jerusalem." I try to remember every day to pray for the peace of Jerusalem. Why should we pray for the peace of Jerusalem? Whenever we pray for the peace of Jerusalem we are also praying for the soon return of the Lord when at last there will be peace on Earth.

The war clouds are thundering over Israel even as I write this. Ezekiel prophesied that the day would come when there would be a Muslim coalition to come up on the Golan Heights to war against Israel. (See Ezekiel 30:4–5.) When you have time, read Ezekiel 30–38 and you will see how close we are to the second coming of the Lord.

The Muslim coalition is already in place, and the spoil they want to take is Jerusalem. Pray for the peace of Jerusalem today.

> *Lord, I pray for the peace of Jerusalem.*

JUNE 5

Morning Wisdom: Read Proverbs 16:21–23. Yesterday we talked about remaining humble by casting every care upon Jesus. Pride is what keeps us from releasing our cares. We feel like we can work everything out in our lives without God's help. When we are burdened with cares, we put up the umbrella of pride that blocks the showers of God's grace and blessings from saturating our souls.

The tongue often is used as the rod that holds the umbrella of pride open. We are exhorted in this reading to have a wise heart that draws from a wellspring of understanding and flows into a fountain of pleasant, prudent, and sweet words. When we speak only those things that will edify, we can receive learning. Every day God wants to teach us things, but usually we are running our mouths so much that we don't have time to listen.

Jesus said that what we say with our mouths reveals what is in our hearts. If we speak strife-filled, hateful, critical, and judgmental words, then we have unforgiveness and resentment in our hearts.

Yesterday I had a cardiogram taken of my heart. The doctor looked at it and said, "All is well." Maybe this morning would be a good morning to ask the Holy Spirit to take a spiritual cardiogram of your heart. He may even want to heal your heart this morning. I remember during my visits to the doctor when I was a child, the first thing he said to me was, "Stick out your tongue." As my doctor placed a tongue depressor in my mouth, he searched my mouth and throat with a small flashlight. He immediately could tell the condition of health by this examination. If you want to have a healthy spiritual life, you need to allow the Great Teacher, the Holy Spirit, to add learning to your lips. He can only do this if you stay in His classroom and study the material found in His textbook, God's Word.

Lord, help me to submit my tongue daily to You. May the words of my mouth and the meditations of my heart be acceptable in Your sight today.

Evening Watch: Read Psalm 123:1–4. David said his soul was filled with contempt for the proud. Prideful people slandered and betrayed David. I'm sure David felt like he was drowning under the sea of word curses and accusations that prideful people had spoken. The trying circumstances David experienced often submerged his soul, but David knew how to come up for air. He lifted his hands in praise and his eyes heavenward as he swam to the surface. When he lifted his eyes to the Lord, he received a humble spirit. He looked to the Lord like a servant looks to his master with the desire to obey him even in the small things. He looked to the Lord like a maid looks at her mistress with the longing to please her. When you feel like your soul is submerged under troubled seas, lift your hands to praise the Lord and swim into the arms of Jesus.

Lord, my eyes are fixed upon You.

JUNE 6

1 Kings 1:1–53; Acts 4:1–37; Psalm 124:1–8; Proverbs 16:24

Morning Wisdom: Read Proverbs 16:24. We talked yesterday about how the words we speak will reveal whether or not we are spiritually healthy. The words we speak can actually affect our physical condition.

Proverbs 16:24 says, "Pleasant words are like a honeycomb, Sweetness to the soul and health to the bones." We can trouble our own souls by the words we speak. Proverbs 21:23 says, "Whoever guards his mouth and tongue Keeps his soul from troubles." When there is resentment or bitterness in our souls, our physical condition can be affected. Toxins are released into our bloodstream, and the very marrow of our bones can be infected. People who carry resentment can become arthritic, and their skeletons can become brittle.

I'll never forget hearing the testimony of a young man who took this word in Proverbs 16:24 and acted upon it. He and his wife had been having a lot of strife because he was judgmental and critical of her. When he went to the dentist, the dentist said, "Young man, your teeth are beginning to crumble." Later that day he read about the power of pleasant words to bring health to his bones. He thought, "My teeth are bones, so, Lord, I ask You to help me say only pleasant words to my wife." He went to the dentist later and the dentist was amazed at the strength of his teeth. Jesus is not only the great Physician, but He is also a wonderful dentist.

Lord, help me to speak words that are sweet.

Evening Watch: Read Psalm 124:1–8. We were observing people as they walked down the aisles of the auditorium to claim their seats. Most of them looked dejected and depressed. Only a few had smiles on their faces. We were in St. Petersburg, one of the most beautiful cities in Russia. A friend of ours was participating in a music festival. The music festival was open to the public with the hope that many Jewish people would attend. Those who participated as performers were all Jewish people who had come to know Jesus as their Messiah. In between the songs, the performers gave their personal testimonies of how Jesus had changed their lives.

One of the songs our friend sang was, "If It Had Not Been for the Lord on My Side." As I watched the audience during this song, I thought of the years of persecution God's chosen people have faced. My heart grieved over the treatment of many so-called Christians who had persecuted the Jewish people. So many horrific things happened to the Jewish people, and I am sure that many people blamed God for what they had been through. If it had not been for the Lord, there would not be one Jew left on this earth. Even now their enemies are planning to push them into the sea. The ocean would have swallowed them alive years ago if it had not been the Lord who was on their side.

Lord, I pray for the peace of Jerusalem. Protect Your people.

JUNE 7

1 Kings 2:1–3:2; Acts 5:1–42; Psalm 125:1–5; Proverbs 16:25

Morning Wisdom: Read Proverbs 16:25. It says, "There is a way that seems right to a man, But its end is the way of death." This warning is found several times throughout Proverbs. We may think the way we are going is right, but it may end in death. One of the major deceptions of Satan is to convince us that we are going the right way and doing the right thing. We will only be able to discern whether or not what we say and do is right if we continually abide in the Word of God.

I can remember ministering to a lady who came up for prayer after I spoke at a meeting. She said, "I need prayer to know what God's will for my life is." I asked her, "Do you read God's Word?" She replied, "Oh, I read the Bible years ago." I then told her that God's will unfolds day by day, and she will never know what His will is unless she unfolds the pages of her Bible to read it every day. God reveals His will in His Word, and we will be able to discern the right way to go if we daily abide in God's Word. God will never reveal the full map of our lives with all the details, but He will reveal the next step as the lamp of His Word lights our path.

Thank You for showing me the right way today.

Evening Watch: Read Psalm 125:1–5. We were in the place many believe is the Upper Room—the place where Jesus shared His last Passover meal on Earth with His disciples. Tourists walked in and out of the room as our tour group began to sing. Suddenly our voices joined in beautiful harmony as we sang in the Spirit and the tourists stopped to listen. We were on the top of what is known as Mt. Zion. We sang Psalm 125:1–2:

> Those who trust in the Lord are like Mt. Zion which cannot be moved,
> but abides forever. As the mountains are around; are around Jerusalem,
> so the Lord is around His people for ever more.

The feeling of comfort and support that I experienced in that Upper Room returns to me every time I read this psalm. The land we were standing on that day was holy ground, and it was a land allotted for the righteous to stand upon for all eternity. (See v. 3.) The wicked plots of nations that seek to throw Jerusalem and Israel into the sea will not work. God surrounds His people and will continue to protect Israel. We should daily pray for the peace of Jerusalem. Every time we pray for the peace of Jerusalem we are asking the Lord to return quickly. Peace will not be established in Israel until the Lord comes again, but until that time we should daily pray for God's protection over Israel. I have many friends who live in Israel, and I pray for their safety daily.

Lord, surround Israel with Your mighty warring angels.

JUNE 8

Morning Wisdom: Read Proverbs 16:26–27. Once again our reading speaks about the mouth and lips. Proverbs 16:26 says that the mouth of a hungry man drives him to labor for himself. My husband just called me to tell me he was hungry and asked what was for lunch. He was disheartened when I told him we would just have a protein shake for lunch. He had labored all day at the church without pay, and now he was going to get a protein shake for lunch. He was not a happy bear. You have heard the saying, "The way to a man's heart is through his stomach." The hungry mouth can drive people to even steal food. Hunger can lead people to do many evil things God forbids in His Word.

One of the most evil things a person can do is gossip. Gossip is passing on an evil report. Proverbs 16:27 says that ungodly men dig up evil and then spread it like fire. James compared the tongue to a forest fire that is out of control. (See James 3:6.) If we have a hunger and thirst after righteousness, the Word of God can fill us so that we can have both our hunger and our tongues under control.

> Lord, thank You for helping me control my appetite for food by giving me a hunger and thirst for Your Word.

Evening Watch: Read Psalm 126:1–6. Years ago I used to sing a song about bringing in the sheaves. I never knew what I was singing about. This psalm helped me understand all about sowing, reaping, and gathering in God's harvest.

This psalm begins with these words, "When the LORD brought back the captivity of Zion, We were like those who dream" (v. 1). This Song of Ascents reviews the time Israel was captive. Then the Lord liberated them, and their mouths were filled with laughter and their tongues with singing about the great things God had done. (See v. 1–3.)

Our mouths will be filled with laughter, and our tongues will sing when we see people who have been held captive by the devil set free. Have you ever wept for souls?

Whenever we sow in tears, the promise is that we will reap in joy. We are in the time of the last great harvest, and we are exhorted to cry out for the latter rain when God's Spirit will be poured out in great measure.

The tears we shed as we pray for our loved ones and friends who are not saved will cause them to receive the showers of blessings that come when they receive Jesus Christ as their Lord and Savior. We will see many souls in heaven who are there because of the tears we shed when we cried for the Lord to save them. These souls are the sheaves that the Lord will bring with Him when He returns to Earth. Before you go to bed, pray once again for those friends and relatives that you know need salvation. Weep for their souls, and your tears will not be wasted.

> Lord, thank You for hearing my cries for souls.

JUNE 9

Morning Wisdom: Read Proverbs 16:28–30. We have learned in June's devotionals the results of pride. Pride is the root of all contention, and it is what stirs up strife. Proverbs 16:28 says, "A perverse man sows strife, And a whisperer separates the best of friends." A person who is prideful often is perverse in his ways. He thinks he is in control of his life, and he does what he pleases instead of what God pleases. Such a lifestyle often leads to perversion. Perversion occurs when a person seeks to fulfill his or her version of life. A perverse person has no idea what God requires and has no desire to follow the rules expressed in God's Word. The major argument a perverse person has is that God does not care, so why should he or she care?

Perversion causes a breach in the spirit. The perverse person will be double minded. A perverse person has no respect for friendship and often seeks to divide friends, because he wants attention for himself. A perverse person is a "hit man for Satan" who wounds others with his tongue. A perverse person can separate friends by whispering behind their backs. We do have the power to bind a perverse spirit in another person. Use that power if you ever encounter a perverse person.

Lord, help me to use my authority against the enemy.

Evening Watch: Read Psalm 127:1–5. We discussed how pride can cause a spirit of perversion to develop in a person. Pride makes us think we can build our own houses and guard our own lives, when only God can do these things.

You have probably heard the expression, "A house divided against itself cannot stand." Psalm 127:1 reads, "Unless the LORD builds the house, They labor in vain who build it." We are spiritual houses that can be filled with God's Spirit or filled with our own sinful nature. When we try to build and guard our spiritual houses with our own self-effort, we will not be able to stand against the wiles of the devil. Whenever we are double minded, our earthly tabernacles are vulnerable to destruction.

We are called to guard our hearts and to seek God's wisdom so that our minds and hearts will not be divided. People who are double minded are miserable people. Part of them wants to do the will of God, and the other part of them seeks to rebel against God. Double-minded people eat the bread of sorrows and lose sleep at night. (See v. 2.) Peace only comes to those who have their mind stayed upon the Lord. Stay your mind upon the Lord tonight, and you will have a sweet sleep.

Lord, help me to never be double minded.

JUNE 10

1 Kings 7:1–51; Acts 7:30–50; Psalm 128:1–6; Proverbs 16:31–33

Morning Wisdom: Read Proverbs 16:31–33. Proverbs 16:31 says, "The silver-haired head is a crown of glory." I heard the eighty-five-year-old mother of our pastor's wife say, "I will be a redhead as long as the drugstores are open!" When I heard this I responded, "I will be a blonde as long as there are beauty shops on Earth!" Silver hair is a sign of aging, but when God looks down from heaven on silver heads, He sees His glory reflected on those silver heads that have followed the way of righteousness. Those who have walked uprightly with Him for many years are His glory. I hope He doesn't count me out, because I am a blonde by choice.

God has a special call on older people. He has often chosen to work through older people. Think of Moses and how he began to fulfill his call at the ripe old age of eighty. Then there was Abraham and Sarah, who finally had their promised son when Abraham was one hundred years old and Sarah was in her nineties. Simeon and Anna were used of the Lord mightily. Simeon was allowed to remain on Earth until He saw His promised Messiah. Anna spent years in the temple praying for the coming of the Messiah, and then she was allowed to see Him in person. Scriptures reveal that she was at least one hundred seven years old and maybe older. (See Luke 2:25–38.)

I believe those who walk in righteousness are able to live many years on this earth, because they are not easily provoked. They are not stressed out. No matter what circumstances they face in life, they refuse to be upset or angry about it. They recognize that every decision is the Lord's, because they have submitted themselves to His lordship over their lives. I pray that I will live to see the second coming of the Lord. I want to live as long as possible so I can continue to prepare the body of Christ for His return.

> *Thank You for adding years to our lives so that we might labor in Your vineyard here on Earth.*

Evening Watch: Read Psalm 128:1–6. Once a year my husband and I arrange a little family retreat when all three of our sons and their families can spend a day or two together. I so look forward to those times.

What a joy it is for me to see my sons with their precious children gathered around the table as we share breakfast, lunch, and dinner together. I am reminded of this psalm on those occasions. This psalm lists some of the blessings that come to those who fear the Lord. The husband will eat the fruit of his labor and be happy. The wife will be like a fruitful vine in the heart of her home. Their children will be like olive plants all around their table. Olive plants bear much fruit and never completely die. I always prayed for our three sons to be effective laborers in this last great harvest. I prayed that God would cause them to bear much fruit. God has answered my prayers. Tonight, you might want to pray for your children and grandchildren and even their offspring for generations to come to be fruitful laborers in God's harvest.

> *Lord, use my children and their generations to come for Your glory.*

JUNE 11

Morning Wisdom: Read Proverbs 17:1. Have you ever walked into a house and been overwhelmed by the smell of fish?

You know without a doubt that fish was served for dinner. I have walked into homes shortly after the family had their evening meal, and I knew right away that more than food was served for dinner. There was a large plate of strife that was served to the members of that household. Strife charges the atmosphere of any household with negative vibes that can be felt by discerning visitors. Sadly many families attack one another at mealtime. They may pray, *Lord, be present at our table,* but if they get into strife with one another during mealtime, the Lord excuses Himself from the table and Satan takes His chair.

Proverbs 17:1 says, "Better is a dry morsel with quietness, Than a house full of feasting with strife." During my childhood I never saw my mother and father argue with one another. Of course there were disagreements, but voices were never raised and peace reigned in our household. People do not believe me when I tell them about my childhood, but our home was a little piece of heaven on Earth because peace reigned in our home.

The Lord would love for every household to be like this. Our household was peaceful because my mother prayed and asked the Lord to help her have a peaceful home.

She came from a home where there was continual strife, because both her mom and dad were alcoholics. Alcohol and anger are closely related. Whenever someone drinks to the point where they lose control, guess who is in control? Demonic spirits take over the person who is in a stupor, and he begins to do stupid things.

The woman of the house has the responsibility to set the atmosphere in her home. Pray today that your home will be filled with the peace of the Lord. We are all exhorted in God's Word to seek peace and pursue it. Peace does not just happen. It only happens when the Prince of Peace feels welcome in our home.

Lord, give me a peaceful home.

Evening Watch: Read Psalm 129:1–8. I lived in Savannah, Georgia, during the "Jesus Movement." Many young people at that time left their jobs and began to live in communes, because they thought the Lord was going to return soon. They tried to copy the lifestyle of the early church and had all things in common. They daily broke bread together. I had the opportunity to visit the Bible study held in one of these group homes. I was impressed by the boldness of the people I met there. When I left the Bible study many in that home said, "Good-bye, and God bless you." I was so bound by the fear of man at that time, and I prayed, *Lord, one day I would love to be as bold as they are. I would love to say, "God bless you," to everyone I meet.* This psalm contains this beautiful blessing we can speak to others: "The blessing of the *Lord* be upon you" (v. 8).

May the blessings of the Lord be upon you always.

JUNE 12

Morning Wisdom: Read Proverbs 17:2–3. "Class, we're having a pop quiz today." I used to dread those words when I was in school. Those pop quizzes forced me to be up on my homework assignments. I had to review my notes every morning just in case my teacher decided to give me a pop quiz.

Proverbs 17:3 says the Lord tests the hearts. Could you pass a pop quiz if God decided to test your heart today? The only way you could pass His test would be to do your assignments and review your notes.

God has assignments for us to do daily. Ephesians 2:10 says, "For we are His workmanship, created in Christ Jesus for good works, which God prepared beforehand that we should walk in them." We discover those assignments when we pray, *Lord, put me in the right place at the right time, and let me fall short in no good work that You have prepared for me today.*

God wants you to review your notes today. Those notes are found in His Word. Today you might want to look up the word *heart* in *Strong's Concordance* and read everything in Scripture about the heart. When you finish reading your daily Bible readings today ask the Lord if there are other passages He wants you to read. He may have a special word for you today.

You will pass God's heart test if you commit yourself to do what is written in Ephesians 4. God instructs us in Ephesians 4 to: grow up in Christ; speak the truth in love; put off your old man; be renewed in the spirit of your mind; put on the new man; put away lying; do not let the sun go down on your anger; give no place to the devil; do not steal; let no corrupt word proceed out of your mouth; speak only those things that edify; do not grieve the Holy Spirit of God; let all bitterness, wrath, anger, clamor, and evil speaking be put away from you; and be kind to one another, tenderhearted, forgiving one another, even as God in Christ forgave you. Review those notes daily, and you will be ready for God to test your heart.

Lord, help me to pass Your heart test today.

Evening Watch: Read Psalm 130:1–8. We talked about being a good student of God's Word this morning. David the psalmist certainly was a good student of God's Word. David wrote, "I wait for the LORD, my soul waits, And in His word I do hope" (v. 5). The secret to living a peaceful, blessed life is found in the declaration David made in verse 5. David certainly did not live a life of peace. His life was filled with fight or flight. He spent a good part of his life running from Saul. However, David found the secret to inner peace. David experienced many desperate days when nothing seemed go right in his life. Have you experienced such days? When we encounter such days, we need to do as David did. We need to put our hope in God's Word and allow our souls to wait upon the Lord. David was confident that the Lord would forgive him, redeem him, hear him, and show mercy to him. His confidence was based upon God's Word.

Lord, help me daily to hope in Your Word.

JUNE 13

Morning Wisdom: Read Proverbs 17:4–5. The two verses in our reading today talk about evildoers. Evildoers like to lie and enjoy listening to someone who speaks spitefully. People with an evil heart even rejoice at the calamity others experience. Evildoers mock the poor. God will punish such people.

I wrote in my devotional book *Around the Word in 365 Days* about people who mock the poor. Evildoers mock the poor, because they think they are better off than the poor, but in reality they are the poorest people on Earth. Anyone who has an evil heart is bound by demonic spirits. Only when an evil person repents and gives his life to the Lord will he have access to the riches available to him through Christ Jesus.

The poor are very precious to the Lord. Throughout our travels all over the world we have met many poor people who did not even have running water available to them. They were not only dirt poor, but they had no way of washing the dirt off their skin every day. You would think such people would be heavy hearted and burdened because of their living conditions. However, the poor people we met in Mexico, the Philippines, Colombia, and Peru rejoiced in the Lord and praised Him with all of their hearts. These people were some of the most joyful and spiritually rich Christians I have ever met.

The question I had in my heart as I read about evildoers was, what does God think about evildoers? As I pondered this question I heard the Lord speak this to my spirit:

> I died for the whole world. I even died for evildoers. I do not want any to perish. Pray for those who have evil hearts. I have the power to change the hardest heart.

Someone was praying for Saul of Tarsus before he had his Damascus Road experience when he was touched by the Lord and became a new man. Today pray for those you know who seem to have evil hearts. Pray for them to have a Damascus Road experience.

> *Lord, I pray for all those who need to be translated from the kingdom of darkness into Your kingdom of light.*

Evening Watch: Read Psalm 131:1–3. Last evening we looked at Psalm 130 and discovered David's secret to living a life of peace, even when evildoers surrounded him both day and night. We learned that David allowed his soul to wait upon the Lord, and he put his hope in God's Word. Today's reading reveals exactly how David allowed his soul to wait upon the Lord. He wrote, "Surely I have calmed and quieted my soul, Like a weaned child with his mother; Like a weaned child is my soul within me" (v. 2). A weaned child no longer cries for food, because he trusts that his parents will feed him. When we trust in the Lord and put all of our hope in Him, the desperation in our souls is transformed into trust.

> *I trust You, Lord.*

JUNE 14

Morning Wisdom: Read Proverbs 17:6. Years ago the Lord promised to give me ten grandchildren before He came again. I have shared that promise with many of my friends, and they all have been counting.

The custom in Bible days was for the bridegroom to build a home for his espoused bride. After the bridegroom finished constructing a home for his bride, his father had to inspect the home. If the home passed his precise inspection, he announced that it was time for his son and his espoused bride to be married. Only our Father in heaven knows when the house is ready for the Bridegroom and His bride to take occupancy. I believe we are in the season of the latter rain when the last great harvest will be gathered unto the Lord. We must be in the season, because we just announced the birth of our ninth grandchild.

The verse today reads, "Children's children are the crown of old men, And the glory of children is their father." As I watch my husband interact with our grandchildren, I can almost see that crown of glory on his head. His silver hair shines with God's glory light as he stoops to tie the shoes of one of our little grandchildren.

It seemed like forever before our three sons would finally marry. They all married almost ten years ago, and we now have nine grandchildren ages eight and under. Our middle son, Ron, has been quite fruitful. We gave nicknames to his children. We called his firstborn "Sunshine," his second "Sunflower," his third "Sunbeam," and his fourth "Sunlight." Ron's father-in-law suggested that we nickname their fifth child "Sunset."

I know God delights as He watches these little ones sing their memory verses from His Word and dance in His presence. His delight is even greater when He sees the fruitfulness in our lives as we share the gospel with others. Every day we have the opportunity to add to God's family on Earth. Look for those opportunities today to share your faith with others so that they also can be fruitful laborers in this last great harvest.

Lord, help me to share my faith boldly with others.

Evening Watch: Read Psalm 132:1–18. We shared this morning how God calls us all to be fruitful and multiply. Even single people can fulfill this call, because when they share the gospel with others, they add to God's family. God promised David that the fruit of his body would be on the throne forever. God has prepared a dwelling place for His Son. That dwelling place is Jerusalem. He chose Zion, the city of David, to be the place where His Son would be enthroned forever. Jesus Christ is from the house of David. Even though Jesus never had children, His fruitfulness has been and will be great.

The psalmist wrote that God would make the horn of David grow and He would prepare a lamp for His anointed. You are the lamp God has prepared to shine for His anointed.

Lord, let my light shine tomorrow and every day to bring You glory.

JUNE 15

Morning Wisdom: Read Proverbs 17:7–8. The way people speak often reveals both where they are from and what their position in life is. Proverbs 17:7 says, "Excellent speech is not becoming to a fool, Much less lying lips to a prince." I have always been impressed with the monarch in England.

Whenever I hear Queen Elizabeth or Prince Charles speak, both their accent and their skill in using the English language is quite evident. I would be shocked to hear either of them use any slang in their speech.

We are called kings and priests in God's Word. Peter wrote, "You also, as living stones, are being built up a spiritual house, a holy priesthood, to offer up spiritual sacrifices acceptable to God through Jesus Christ" (1 Pet. 2:5). In 1 Peter 2:9 Peter declared the kind of language we should always speak when he wrote:

> You are a chosen generation, a royal priesthood, a holy nation, His own special people, that you may proclaim the praises of Him who called you out of darkness into His marvelous light.

As priests we should offer daily the spiritual sacrifices of praise, thanksgiving, and worship. We no longer have to offer animal sacrifices on an altar. Instead, we are to offer our bodies daily to the Lord as a living sacrifice. As priests we are called to offer the sweet incense of praise and worship daily to the King of kings and Lord of lords. Our speech should be seasoned with grace and should always edify. Our excellent speech daily should reveal that we are seated with Christ in heavenly places far above those principalities, powers, and rulers of darkness and wickedness in heavenly places. Today make it your goal to speak only those things that are fitting for a king. David wrote that whoever orders his conversation aright glorifies God. (See Psalm 50:23.)

Lord, help me today to speak the language of a king and priest.

Evening Watch: Read Psalm 133:1–3. We were gathered in a small group fellowship in Israel. As we prayed together one of the pastors spoke the words of this psalm: "Behold, how good and how pleasant it is For brethren to dwell together in unity!" David wrote this psalm as one of the Songs of Ascents that the pilgrims sang as they made their journey three times a year to worship in Jerusalem. David compared unity to the oil running down the beard of Aaron and the dew of Hermon descending upon the mountains of Zion. We had just seen Mount Hermon in all of her majesty. The top part of Mount Hermon is often capped with snow. When spring comes, the dew of Mount Hermon mixes with the melting snow to supply fresh water, which flows down into the headwaters of the Jordan. When we make it our priority to dwell with fellow Christians in unity, we will always have the fresh oil of God's anointing and the flowing river of God's Spirit.

Lord, help me never to sow discord.

JUNE 16

Morning Wisdom: Read Proverbs 17:9–11. These verses convey three important lessons about life that we all need to learn:

> He who covers a transgression seeks love, But he who repeats a matter separates friends.
>
> —PROVERBS 17:9

We should cover others' sins instead of gossiping about them. We gossip whenever we give a negative report that involves another person. Even if that negative report is true, we should never repeat it. When we discover the sins of another person, it is not our responsibility to tell others about that sin.

> Rebuke is more effective for a wise man Than a hundred blows on a fool.
>
> —PROVERBS 17:10

We waste our time when we try to correct a foolish person, because fools hate instruction and they despise rebukes.

> An evil man seeks only rebellion; Therefore a cruel messenger will be sent against him.
>
> —PROVERBS 17:11

We never have to fret ourselves about evildoers, because God will take care of them. God is our advocate who always causes us to win over evil. Vengeance belongs to the Lord, not us. We should always let God handle our adversaries.

Lord, help me to learn and follow these lessons of life.

Evening Watch: Read Psalm 134:1–3. This psalm is one of the Songs of Ascents that the pilgrims sang as they traveled up to Jerusalem to celebrate the feasts. God required that every man would come to worship and sacrifice at the temple during the Feast of Unleavened Bread, the Feast of Tabernacles, and the Feast of Pentecost. The pilgrims prepared for their time of worship and sacrifice as they journeyed the dusty roads of Israel. They lifted their hands and blessed the Lord with their singing. By the time they reached the temple, their hearts were prepared to continue their worship.

The complaint we hear often as leaders in our church is that the worship service was not anointed. The singing was too loud or the songs were too new, so people could not join in the singing. If the congregants prepared themselves to worship the Lord before the Sunday morning service, it would not matter how loud the music was or whether or not we sang a familiar hymn or two. They would be absorbed in worshiping the Lord in Spirit and in truth with prepared hearts. Their focus would be on the Lord, not the person next to them who was singing off-key or the sound system that was too loud.

Lord, help me to come to worship with a prepared heart.

JUNE 17

Morning Wisdom: Read Proverbs 17:12–13. Foolish people do foolish things, and if we keep company with foolish people, we may end up doing foolish things also. Our youngest son had friends who did foolish things, and it was not long before he ended up doing the same things. He was very committed to the Lord before this happened, and people used to make fun of him because of his commitment. By the time he reached high school, he was severely persecuted for his faith. He was not strong enough at that time to stand in faith. He came to the place of wanting friends so badly that he turned to worldly friends who influenced him. He went through a season of folly, but after several years of this lifestyle he saw that his activities were not fulfilling and he returned to the Lord. We are warned in this reading not to even meet with a fool in his folly.

> *Lord, I pray that my children, grandchildren, and all of my family members will keep godly company rather than the company of fools.*

Evening Watch: Read Psalm 135:1–21. The Songs of Ascents prepared the hearts of the people to worship in the temple. If you ever have a hard time entering into worship during your quiet times with the Lord, I suggest that you read the Songs of Ascents found in Psalm 120–134. When you read these psalms out loud, you will soon find yourself worshiping God in Spirit and truth. This is a good way for you to prepare your heart for the corporate worship you will experience on Sunday mornings.

I believe this psalm was sung once the people of Israel reached the temple. They sang this song as they stood in the house of the Lord. The psalm declares:

> Praise Him, O you servants of the Lord! You who stand in the house of the Lord, In the courts of the house of our God, Praise the Lord, for the Lord is good; Sing praises to His name, for it is pleasant.
>
> —Psalm 135:1–3

It truly is pleasant to praise the Lord. I believe David had no trouble ever worshiping the Lord, because he always prepared his heart through praise. He declared that he praised the Lord seven times a day. You might try to praise the Lord seven times tomorrow and even seven times every day this week. When you go to church on Sunday to worship God corporately, your heart will be prepared.

> *Lord, help me to praise You seven times every day.*

1 Kings 19:1–21; Acts 12:1–23; Psalm 136:1–26; Proverbs 17:14–15

Morning Wisdom: Read Proverbs 17:14–15. One day when I was running water in my kitchen sink, the faucet fell off and a geyser of water shot upward towards the ceiling. At first I was in such a state of shock that I didn't know what to do. Water was going everywhere, and I was drenched. Then I heard that still, quiet voice inside of me say, *Turn off the water.* Why didn't I think of that? I reached for the two handles of the faucet and turned off the water.

Proverbs 17:14 says, "The beginning of strife is like releasing water; Therefore stop contention before a quarrel starts." The fact that the faucet on my sink was loose and I had the water on full force is what caused the flood in my kitchen. When we are forcefully trying to prove our point to someone, we will soon find ourselves in strife, and before you know it we have a full-fledged quarrel.

I have learned over the years a secret that helps avoid strife. When my husband begins to disagree with me and I can see we are headed into a quarrel, I say to him, "You just might be right. I need to think over what you have said, and I'll get back with you."

That response usually puts a damper on what was developing into a flood of hurtful words.

Lord, help me to avoid strife.

Evening Watch: Read Psalm 136:1–26. When I was meditating on Paul's description of the love of God found in Ephesians 3:17–19, I received an insight about four aspects of the love of God.

In that passage Paul said we could comprehend the width, length, depth, and height of the love of God. I asked the Holy Spirit what this meant, and I received this answer:

- The width of His love is His truth—His truth sets us free.
- The length of His love is His mercy—His mercy endures forever to every generation.
- The depth of His love is His forgiveness—He reaches deep into our hearts to forgive.
- The height of His love is His grace—His grace is poured out from above.

I compared this Ephesians passage with Exodus 34:6–7 and discovered that God used those four aspects of His love to describe Himself. He said, "The LORD, the LORD God, merciful and gracious, longsuffering, and abounding in goodness and truth, keeping mercy for thousands, forgiving iniquity and transgression and sin." Our psalm today has the continual response, "His mercy endures forever," and it does endure forever to every generation who believes in Christ. God extended His mercy to us when He poured out His wrath upon Jesus on the cross.

Father, thank You for sending Your Son to pay the penalty for my sin.

1 Kings 20:1–21:29; Acts 12:24–13:15; Psalm 137:1–9; Proverbs 17:16

Morning Wisdom: Read Proverbs 17:16. There are some things money can't buy, and wisdom is one of those things. Proverbs 17:16 asks this question: "Why is there in the hand of a fool the purchase price of wisdom, Since he has no heart for it?" We talked earlier about how foolish people do foolish things, and one of the foolish things they do is spend thousands of dollars to obtain wisdom. The wisdom they seek is worldly wisdom. Many foolish people pay money to go to mediums or fortune-tellers to receive wisdom about their future. They may pay stock market gurus to advise them on investments. Worldly wisdom will only lead to strife, confusion, and every evil work. James said that people who seek worldly wisdom are self-seeking and have bitter envy in their hearts. (See James 3:14.)

The wisdom that will help us face this life with confidence, peace, and joy is godly wisdom. James described this wisdom that comes from above when he wrote that it is "first pure, then peaceable, gentle, willing to yield, full of mercy and good fruits, without partiality and without hypocrisy" (James 3:17). This is the wisdom money cannot buy, because Jesus already purchased this wisdom for us on the cross. When Jesus died on the cross He paid the price with His own blood to give us all the hidden treasures of wisdom in Himself. To gain the wisdom from above, all we have to do is receive Jesus Christ as our Lord and Savior, and then His wisdom will begin to flow through our lives. Today pray for those you know who need the wisdom from above, and pray for laborers to go to them and share what Jesus did for them on the cross.

Lord, I pray for all those I know who desperately need Your wisdom.

Evening Watch: Read Psalm 137:1–9. It is hard to sing when we are bound either by prison walls or by an occupying army that has taken us captive. Yet, singing is the way to pull down the walls within us that keep us from having hope for the future and joy and faith in the present. Paul and Silas knew the secret to being liberated from all bondage. They sang praises to God when they were in prison, and they were supernaturally released.

Our psalm today recalls the time when the children of Israel were in captivity in Babylon. They sat by the river and wept when they remembered Zion, their homeland. Their captors asked them to sing. They responded, "How shall we sing the LORD's song In a foreign land?" (v. 4).

We are living right now in a foreign land. This world is not our home, because we are citizens of heaven. Some Christians are held captive by their own vain imaginations and high thoughts that exalt themselves against the knowledge of God. The way to restore joy, peace, and liberty is to sing to the Lord no matter what our circumstances. The garment of praise has been given to us to lift the spirit of heaviness. (See Isaiah 61:3.) End your day and begin your tomorrow with singing.

Thank You for the garment of praise.

Morning Wisdom: Read Proverbs 17:17–18. There are several warnings in the Bible against cosigning, and our reading from Proverbs today is just one of them. These verses warn against making a pledge to become a surety for a friend. Whenever we cosign we run the risk of having to pay someone else's debt. When the person we cosign for does not fulfill his obligation and we are forced to fulfill it, we could develop a root of bitterness against that person. The Bible says we are to owe no man but to love him. (See Romans 13:8.) Even cosigning for relatives can later cause our relationship with that relative to be strained or even broken.

We want to have understanding in all of our dealings with money. I pray every morning for a double portion of the anointing of the Holy Spirit. That anointing includes the spirit of wisdom and understanding, the spirit of counsel and might, and the spirit of knowledge and the fear of the Lord. (See Isaiah 11:2.) We need the anointing of the Holy Spirit even for the practical decisions in life. We especially need it to make good decisions about money matters. Ask for a double portion of the anointing of the Holy Spirit this morning.

> *Lord, I ask You to anoint me with a double portion of Your wisdom and understanding, counsel and might, and Your knowledge, which will enable me to operate in the fear of the Lord this day.*

Evening Watch: Read Psalm 138:1–8. We concluded our morning reading by asking for a double portion of the anointing of the Holy Spirit. David must have asked the Lord for His special anointing every day. David wrote, "I will praise You with my whole heart" (v. 1). David was able to praise the Lord with his whole heart, because he gave his heart daily to the Lord. David was a man after God's own heart, because he confessed his sins and received cleansing for his heart. He asked the Lord to create in Him a clean heart and to renew a right spirit within him. (See Psalm 51:10.)

Because David gave his heart to the Lord every day, he was able to receive a fresh anointing from the Holy Spirit that enabled him to praise the Lord with a whole heart.

We can receive that fresh anointing from the Holy Spirit if we daily confess our sins before Him and receive His glorious cleansing. A whole heart is a clean heart, and only Jesus can cleanse our hearts, and only the Holy Spirit can stir up His Spirit within us.

> *Lord, I give You my heart. Search my heart and show me the sins I need to confess to You before I go to bed. Then create in me a clean heart and renew a right spirit within me so that I can praise You with my whole heart tomorrow.*

JUNE 21

2 Kings 1:1–2:25; Acts 13:42–14:7; Psalm 139:1–24; Proverbs 17:19–21

Morning Wisdom: Read Proverbs 17:19–21. I recently spoke on spiritual warfare at our church. I shared with the audience that the mind is the battlefield where Satan wants to enter. However, he can only enter through the gates to the mind. These gates are the ear gate, the eye gate, and the mouth gate. We can guard these gates if we are careful to hear no evil, see no evil, and speak no evil. Proverbs 17:19 reads, "He who loves transgression loves strife, And he who exalts his gate seeks destruction." Second Corinthians 10:5 tells us that there are high things that exalt themselves against the knowledge of God. Those high things are prideful thoughts, greedy longings in our minds, and vain imaginations. We exalt the gates to our minds when we allow high things to enter our minds. Pride is the source of all strife and contention, and when we allow the fiery darts of prideful thoughts, covetousness, and vain imaginations to enter our minds, we can destroy our very own souls. This is why we need to pull down those strongholds in our minds quickly.

Jesus taught that a man speaks what is in his heart. (See Luke 6:45.) Proverbs 17:20 confirms that a man with a deceitful heart will also have a perverse tongue. The mouth gate will only be protected when our hearts are right with God and our fellow man. If we have bitterness or unforgiveness in our hearts, we will speak bitter, hateful words to others. David purposed not to transgress with his tongue. (See Psalm 17:3.) Ask the Holy Spirit to help you guard the gates to your mind.

Holy Spirit, I need Your help to guard the gates to my mind today.

Evening Watch: Read Psalm 139:1–24. We learned about the gates of our minds this morning. We can only guard the gates of our minds if we daily read God's Word. The mind is renewed by the Word of God. When we daily read God's Word we understand as David did that nothing goes past God's sight or His hearing. He sees all, hears all, and knows all about our ways. We can declare as David did that "Such knowledge is too wonderful for me; It is high, I cannot attain it" (v. 6). To think that God knows me through and through can be quite disturbing if I am living in open sin or even sin in my thought life. It is ridiculous for us to ever try to hide our sins from God instead of confessing them. When we confess our sins, we are not telling God anything that He did not already know. We are simply agreeing with Him that we have sinned and that we desire His cleansing.

David cried out, "Where can I go from Your Spirit?" (v. 7). Even the darkness cannot hide from God, because He dwells in the midst of darkness. God formed us in our mother's womb, and we are fearfully and wonderfully made. (See v. 14.) The members of our bodies and our days are written in the Book of Life. This knowledge causes me to give my life afresh and anew every day.

Lord, I give You my days. Use me for Your glory.

Morning Wisdom: Read Proverbs 17:22. It is a known fact that people who are able to laugh even when they are going through hard times receive their healing much faster than those people who have a fearful, negative attitude. In fact, in recent years doctors have even used "laugh therapy" as part of their recovery program for patients. I heard about a person who was healed through laughter. This person's doctor prescribed a heavy dose of *The Three Stooges* and other comedy movies. The doctor instructed his patient to watch these movies daily for a season. The prescription worked, and this person was healed.

Our verse today reads: "A merry heart does good, like medicine, But a broken spirit dries the bones." When we laugh endorphins are released in our body, and they enhance healing.

When I saw a vision of Jesus many years ago, I remember the expression on His face. It conveyed total peace, but at the same time His smile transmitted unspeakable joy. Someone portrayed Jesus in a painting called *The Laughing Jesus.*

When Jesus laughed, I believe He threw His head back and gave huge belly laughs.

Not too long ago there was an outbreak of "holy laughter" in many charismatic churches. Some people judged this and said it was not of the Lord. However, after seeing the face of Jesus, I believe those laughter manifestations are real. Many people I know who experienced this holy laughter phenomenon were emotionally and physically healed. After reading this verse today there is certainly scriptural basis for healing through laughter. The joy of the Lord is our strength, and that joy heals.

Lord, may my day be filled with laughter and Your joy.

Evening Watch: Read Psalm 140:1–13. This morning we learned that laughter is good for the soul. Did you laugh at yourself today? Did you laugh at the devil today? David was on the devil's hit list all of his life. The devil wanted to polish him off, because he knew that the Messiah would come from the line of David. David never allowed the devil to disturb his inner peace. David revealed his secret to inner peace when he wrote, "Whenever I am afraid, I will trust in You" (Ps. 56:3). David continually declared that the Lord was his strength and that He heard his supplications. He knew that the Lord would help him in every battle and that He would destroy every scheme of the devil. David concluded this psalm with these words, "I know that the LORD will maintain The cause of the afflicted, And justice for the poor" (v. 12). David dwelt in the presence of the Lord, and I am sure David could laugh at the devil. Every time David praised the Lord, he was laughing at the devil. Praise is the devil's death knell. If you want to torment the devil, just start praising the Lord out loud.

Lord, help me to praise You and torment the devil tomorrow and always.

JUNE 23

2 Kings 4:18–5:27; Acts 15:1–31; Psalm 141:1–10; Proverbs 17:23

Morning Wisdom: Read Proverbs 17:23. We just recently voted to have our city become independent of our county government. As a new city we will be able to have our own city council and services. The reason yesterday's vote was an overwhelming yes for our city to have its own government is because we were not happy with the way zoning was enforced. It seems that those who wanted their special building projects to go through the county council were giving special favors and money to council members. We pray this will not happen to our new council, but the temptation to accept a bribe is always present.

The verse today sums up why people accept bribes. It says, "A wicked man accepts a bribe behind the back To pervert the ways of justice." It is easy to point the finger at county council members who have accepted bribes, but we need to understand that we are also subject to similar temptation.

Satan is the wicked man in our lives who is always trying to bribe us. He offers special favors to us if we will accept and act upon his temptations. He lies and says, "If you will do this, you will succeed." He often uses this phrase: "You need to pamper yourself, and a little indulgence won't hurt." Satan knows that the way to ensnare people in his trap is to persuade them that they will be better off if they accept his offer to partake of things that are forbidden. He did this in the garden when he told Eve that she would be like God, knowing good and evil, if she ate from the tree of knowledge. (See Genesis 3:5.) Don't accept Satan's bribes delivered by seducing spirits to you today. Be alert, because Satan is like a roaring lion, seeking whomever he might devour. (See 1 Peter 5:8.)

Lord, help me to resist the devil today.

Evening Watch: Read Psalm 141:1–10. We shared this morning that Satan tries to seduce us through flattery and bribes. He bribes us by saying, "If you do this, you will not be caught. No one will know it, and no one will be hurt." He never shares the truth, which is that someone will get hurt when we sin and it will most likely be us. We often are used as hit men for the devil. The negative and judgmental words we speak are like bullets that fly out of the double barrel of our lips to wound others. Often those word curses backfire, and we are the ones who are wounded.

David knew the power of his own tongue, and he prayed, "Set a guard, O LORD, over my mouth; Keep watch over the door of my lips" (v. 3). He also asked God to keep his heart from evil and his hands from practicing wicked works. (See v. 4.) That's a great prayer for all of us to pray daily, and when we do the devil will not be able to use us as his hit men.

Lord, guard my mouth, and keep watch over the door of my lips. Cleanse my heart, and help me to walk in Your ways.

JUNE 24

Morning Wisdom: Read Proverbs 17:24–25. When we lack understanding we are vulnerable to Satan. Wisdom is applied knowledge, and it is understanding that helps us apply wisdom. Proverbs 17:24 says, "Wisdom is in the sight of him who has understanding." Paul talked about how the understanding of people can be darkened and how they can be alienated from the life of God because they are ignorant. Their hearts have been blinded by the prince of darkness. Such people are past feeling, and they even have given themselves to lewdness to work all uncleanness with greediness. He said that we as believers have not so learned Christ. Paul said that if we have been taught by Christ, we will put off that old man, corrupted by deceitful lusts, and be renewed in the spirit of our minds. (See Ephesians 4:18–23.)

Right now our family is praying for a person who has been blinded by Satan. He was born again, but because he did not gird up the loins of his mind with the truth of God's Word, he is walking in darkness. He did not learn Christ. The only way we can learn Christ is to spend time in the classroom of the Holy Spirit. The Holy Spirit is the great Teacher who leads us into all truth and who takes the things of Jesus Christ and reveals them to us. We are praying that the Holy Spirit will open the eyes of this person's understanding. Proverbs 17:25 says, "A foolish son is a grief to his father, And bitterness to her who bore him." This young man's parents are grieving because of their son's sins. Join me as I pray for those who have been blinded by Satan.

> *Lord, I pray that the God of our Lord Jesus Christ, the Father of glory, may give to this person the spirit of wisdom and revelation in the knowledge of Him. Let the eyes of his understanding be enlightened so that he might know what is the hope of his calling, what are the riches of the glory of Your inheritance in the saints, and what is the exceeding greatness of Your power toward those who believe. (See Ephesians 1:17–19.)*

Evening Watch: Read Psalm 142:1–7. We were blessed to have a Russian young man stay with us for seven years. He came as an exchange student, but miraculously he was able to go to college here. When Vladimir first came to us he was not a Christian, but he told us he was a principled young man. His favorite expression was "Who cares?" He had lived in communist society where few did care. After Vladimir became a Christian he learned as the psalmist David did that there is One who cares enough to answer our prayers. That One is Jesus Christ. David wrote, "Bring my soul out of prison, That I may praise Your name" (v. 7). The Lord heard his cry. When David wrote this psalm he was overwhelmed with trouble, so he poured out his complaint to the Lord and supplicated. The word *supplicate* means "to transfer your burdens." Tonight give your cares to the One who cares.

> *Lord, I cast every care upon You.*

JUNE 25

2 Kings 8:1–9:15; Acts 16:16–40; Psalm 143:1–12; Proverbs 17:26

Morning Wisdom: Read Proverbs 17:26. It says, "To punish the righteous is not good." I spoke yesterday of how our Russian son lived in a society where no one seemed to care. Many Christians in Russia were persecuted for their faith. Some of them even lost their lives.

Besides having a Russian live with us, we also had a Chinese girl live with us for five years. She was unaware when she came to us of the provinces in China where there was still severe punishment of people who stood up for their Christian faith. She knew that when she became a Christian she might be discriminated against, but she had no idea that she could be punished for her faith.

Even as I write this devotional there are people being martyred daily for their faith. Several years ago a representative of Voice of the Martyrs came to our church and shared some of the stories of people who have recently been martyred for their faith. One story in particular made a lasting impression upon me. She shared how the mother of a family saw her husband and five children killed by rebels in Sudan. The rebels left and thought the mother was also dead, but she survived. She left Sudan only to bury her husband and children in the U.S. She then returned again to serve in Sudan with the hope that she could bring her persecutors to the Lord.

Proverbs 17:26 says that it is not good to strike princes for their uprightness. Jesus is the Prince of Peace who was struck many times for His uprightness. His death on the cross purchased us the peace that passes our understanding. (See Philippians 4:7.) That peace was what enabled the mother of five to return to Sudan. Those who suffer for Christ's sake have inherited the peace that the world cannot give (John 14:27), and they will continue to be peacemakers as long as they live.

Lord, help me to sow peace.

Evening Watch: Read Psalm 143:1–12. Have you ever had a "sinking spell"? David had many sinking spells throughout his lifetime, but he knew exactly what to do when he had one of these spells. When he wrote this psalm he was having one of those sinking spells, and he revealed exactly what we all should do when we experience them.

What does a person do first when he is sinking in water? He raises his hands upward so people can see him, and then he cries for help. David wrote, "I spread out my hands to You (v. 6)." Then he cried out, "Answer me speedily, O LORD; My spirit fails!" (v. 7). Not only did David raise his hands toward the Lord and cry out to Him, but He also remembered the times when God came to His rescue in the past, and he meditated on those times. David lifted up his soul to the Lord and asked God to cause him to know the way he should walk and to teach him to do God's will. He asked the Lord to revive him.

The next time you feel like you are sinking, stretch your hands heavenward, and cry out to God in prayer. A good prayer to pray is:

Lord, I lift up my mind, my emotions, and my will to You.

JUNE 26

Morning Wisdom: Read Proverbs 17:27–28. This reading has special meaning to me, because it agrees with the training my mother gave us when we were growing up. I can almost hear her voice saying, "Girls, if you do not have something good to say, then say nothing at all."

A person who spares his words is knowledgeable, understanding, peaceful, and perceptive. Proverbs 17:28 says, "Even a fool is counted wise when he holds his peace; When he shuts his lips, he is considered perceptive."

We have the Great Teacher, who desires to train and teach our lips to speak only those things that will bring glory to God. Have you ever heard His gentle voice say, "Don't say that"? I am so glad when I heed that still, small voice within me.

Satan is unable to read our minds, but he can place accusatory, critical, judgmental, bitter, unforgiving, and slanderous words in our minds. The key to victory is not to speak those thoughts Satan gives us. My husband and I would not be married today if I spoke all the thoughts Satan gave me. I learned to recognize the voice of the accuser and refused to cooperate with him. Whenever Satan gave me negative thoughts about my husband, I said out loud, "Satan, if you think I am going to speak out loud your thoughts, you have another thing coming." I decided not to receive Satan's "stinking thinking."

When I was counseling a couple who had much strife in their marriage, I received a mental picture while I prayed for them. I saw the couple in a boxing ring. They were using their tongues instead of boxing gloves to deliver devastating blows to one another. I heard jeers from an audience of demons who were yelling, "Hit her a lick. Hit her a lick! Tell her what she did to you yesterday!" They cheered as the husband struck heavy blows with his tongue. Then I heard, "Hit him a lick. Hit him a lick! Tell him how he has failed you and how he does not know how to love you!" Wisdom requires us to hold our tongues in a resting position until the Holy Spirit gives us permission to speak.

Holy Spirit, help me to hold my tongue today.

Evening Watch: Read Psalm 144:1–15. We talked this morning about holding our tongues and speaking only those things the Holy Spirit gives us to speak. David prayed a prayer to protect his family from evil tongues. He asked the Lord to rescue his family from lying words so that his sons may be plants grown up in their youth and his daughters may be as pillars sculptured in palace style (v. 12). The negative words spoken about our children can cause them to be bound by low self-esteem.

We need to ask the Lord to help us see others as He sees them. We then need to pass those word pictures from the Lord to those we encounter daily. When we do this, our speech will be edifying.

Lord, help me to praise and not criticize others.

2 Kings 10:32–12:21; Acts 18:1–21; Psalm 145:1–21; Proverbs 18:1

Morning Wisdom: Read Proverbs 18:1. We talked yesterday about one of Satan's tactics to get us to speak the thoughts he gives us. Today's verse reveals another strategy of Satan. Satan seeks to isolate us. He wants us all to himself. Proverbs 18:1 says, "A man who isolates himself seeks his own desire; He rages against all wise judgment." Satan loves it when people are offended and leave their place of fellowship. He knows that if we become lone rangers, we will not have sound judgment because we will have no accountability. John revealed exactly why staying in fellowship is so important when he wrote:

> If we say that we have fellowship with Him [Christ], and walk in darkness, we lie and do not practice the truth. But if we walk in the light as He is in the light, we have fellowship with one another, and the blood of Jesus Christ His Son cleanses us from all sin.
>
> —1 JOHN 1:6–7

We are forgiven instantly for our sins, but the cleansing process depends upon our staying in fellowship. If we isolate ourselves, Satan can easily pick us off. It is much easier to target a person when he is alone and not surrounded by other people. Accountability is one of the key ingredients to overcoming temptation. This is why we have so many support groups, such as Alcoholics Anonymous.

When we give in to Satan's temptation to withdraw from fellowship, we soon will begin to believe the lies he daily sends us. The body of Christ is designed to function in unity. Each member is necessary. We will never have the full revelation of Jesus Christ if we refuse to function in the body of Christ. Too many Christians get offended by fellow church members and they leave the church. Until they resume fellowship again they are open targets for Satan. Pray for those you know who are no longer in fellowship, and exhort them to stay in fellowship.

Lord, bring the lost sheep back into Your fold.

Evening Watch: Read Psalm 145:1–21. David purposed not to transgress the Lord with his mouth. (See Psalm 17:3.) He also purposed to glorify God with his mouth. This psalm reveals how David used his mouth to glorify God. He extolled, blessed, and praised the Lord. He declared His mighty acts and wondrous works. He declared His greatness and sang of His righteousness. He spoke of the glory of God's kingdom and His glorious majesty. This psalm ends with these words, "My mouth shall speak the praise of the LORD, And all flesh shall bless His holy name Forever and ever" (v. 21).

Lord, may I use my mouth like David.

JUNE 28

Morning Wisdom: Read Proverbs 18:2–3. Solomon had a lot to say about wicked men and fools in the proverbs he wrote. Solomon described one of the character qualities of a fool in today's reading.

Have you ever been around people who insisted on expressing their opinions about everything? Proverbs 18:2 says, "A fool has no delight in understanding, But in expressing his own heart." People who interrupt conversations with their own opinions have no delight in understanding. They are not willing to listen to what the other person thinks. They only want to prove their point.

Any time we seek to prove our point we are in pride. Satan loves for us to remain in pride, because he knows that pride will prevent us from receiving the blessings of God. "God resists the proud, But gives grace to the humble" (1 Pet. 5:5). We need to pray daily for God to give us an understanding heart. If we persist in delivering our own opinions, people will not honor us, and we even run the risk of becoming contemptible in their sight. Today make it your aim to have a listening ear and an understanding heart.

Value the opinions of others and resist the habit of trying to prove your own point. Pull down the stronghold of pride and humble yourself before God by asking Him to help you communicate with others.

Lord, help me not to be so opinionated that I discount the opinions of others.

Evening Watch: Read Psalm 146:1–10. David was a man after God's own heart, because he learned to trust in the Lord.

In the psalm for today David warned against putting our trust in man. I tell people never to expect anything from anyone and to expect everything from the Lord. When we put our expectations and trust in the Lord, we will never experience disappointment. People often are not faithful, but God is always faithful. People are often not trustworthy, but God is always trustworthy. We will live happy lives if we first look to God for help before we look to people for help.

Christians are exhorted to minister to and help one another. However, before we even go to someone in the body of Christ for help, we should first go to the Lord in prayer. David gives many reasons in this psalm for us to seek the Lord's help before we go to another person with our need. David said our hope is in the Lord, and the Lord keeps His truth forever. He executes justice for the oppressed and gives food to the hungry. He gives liberty to the prisoners and even opens the eyes of the blind. He lifts those who are bowed down, and He relieves the fatherless and the widow. The Lord reigns forever. I receive so many calls for prayer every day. I have been sorely tempted to leave a message on my answering machine that says, "If you are calling for prayer, take time right now to talk to Jesus about your concern. If He is unable to handle the problem, call me back."

Lord, help me to trust You more.

JUNE 29

Morning Wisdom: Read Proverbs 18:4–5. I can remember being in a prayer group many years ago when the Lord gave me a word of prophecy to deliver to the group. The response surprised me. One lady came up to me and said, "Deep waters abide in you." At that time I did not understand what she meant, but after I read this chapter in Proverbs I have a better understanding. Proverbs 18:4 says, "The words of a man's mouth are deep waters; The wellspring of wisdom is a flowing brook."

The words we speak do reveal the depth of what is in our hearts. Bitter waters flow out of a pool of bitterness within a person. James wrote:

> Out of the same mouth proceed blessing and cursing. My brethren, these things ought not to be so. Does a spring send forth fresh water and bitter from the same opening.
>
> —JAMES 3:10–11

Sometimes when I hear people speak negative, critical words I am tempted to say, "Watch out! Your heart is showing." Negative, critical words come from a heart that contains a root of bitterness. The only thing that can sweeten bitter waters is the Holy Spirit. Pray for those you know who are always judgmental and critical. Ask the Holy Spirit to reveal the bitterness in their souls and pray that they will confess the sin of bitterness and receive the cleansing stream of the living water, the Holy Spirit.

Lord, help me never to become bitter, and I pray for those who have a root of bitterness to be cleansed.

Evening Watch: Read Psalm 147:1–20. I usually stay up to see the late news so I can get an update on the weather for the next day. This evening's psalm sounds like a weather report. No one can read this psalm without recognizing God's greatness and how He controls the weather. Listen to the words found in verses 16–18:

> He gives snow like wool; He scatters the frost like ashes; He casts out His hail like morsels; Who can stand before His cold? He sends His word and melts them; He causes His wind to blow, and the waters to flow.

God is the weatherman, and He can predict the weather with accuracy, because He creates it and controls it. He also creates and controls the heavens. He counts and numbers the stars and names each one of them. (See v. 4.) He covers the heavens with clouds and prepares rain for the earth. (See v. 8.) Knowing these great things about our God should cause us to humbly trust Him with every aspect of our lives.

Lord, I give You my life tonight. Take control over everything in my life.

JUNE 30

Morning Wisdom: Read Proverbs 18:6–7. I shared earlier about the mental picture I had of the couple who were in strife. I saw how they delivered devastating blows to one another with their tongues. Demons were in the audience, and they were cheering and enjoying the fight. Proverbs 18:6 says, "A fool's lips enter into contention, And his mouth calls for blows." A wise person will pursue peace and avoid strife.

We can even destroy our own souls by the words we speak. Proverbs 18:7 says, "A fool's mouth is his destruction, And his lips are the snare of his soul." Just as a spider weaves a web to ensnare insects, we can weave a web with our words that will ensnare our very souls.

We can use words that will edify our souls or words that will depress our souls.

We can even speak curses over ourselves. Whenever we say, "I can't do anything right," we have spoken a curse over ourselves. We need to be wise and refuse to speak anything negative about others or about ourselves. If we followed this simple rule, we would continually live in the joy of the Lord.

Lord, help me only to speak words that edify.

Evening Watch: Read Psalm 148:1–14. One of the ways we can make sure that we do not speak negative, critical words or any words that will harm others and ourselves is to stay continually in praise. This psalm is all inclusive, as it declares that everything living on Earth should praise the Lord.

Paul wrote, "For we know that the whole creation groans and labors with birth pangs together until now" (Rom. 8:22). Even though the earth is in labor right now awaiting the return of the Lord, every creature and believer can remain in praise knowing that his or her redemption is drawing near.

Years ago a book came out called *Praise the Lord Anyhow.* We know that wickedness will increase more and more as we get closer to the time of Jesus' return, because Satan will be working overtime. Praise, however, is the devil's death knell. If we continue to praise the Lord no matter what tribulations we might be going through, we will experience the peace and joy of the Lord. The Lord's peace will be our shelter, and His joy will be our strength. When we remain in praise we build a pavilion where we can dwell in the presence of the Lord when all hell may be breaking loose outside our pavilion. That secret hiding place provides a place of safety in the midst of every storm. We can enter that pavilion far away from the strife of tongues every day. Before you retire climb into that pavilion of praise, and stay in it tomorrow and every day until the Lord returns.

Lord, I commit to praise You continually every day.

JULY 1

Morning Wisdom: Read Proverbs 18:8. Have you ever played the game when one person will tell a story and each person in the circle tries to repeat exactly what the first person told? By the time the story gets to the last person in the circle, it usually is quite different from the original story. Proverbs 18:8 reads: "The words of a talebearer are like tasty trifles, And they go down into the inmost body." We are guilty of gossiping whenever we repeat something negative about someone without permission. We need to be on guard against passing on negative reports about people to others, even for prayer in a prayer group. I learned the hard way to let every person tell his or her own story. Whenever we attempt to tell another person's story we most likely will throw our opinion on top of it and also get the facts confused.

As you study the Gospels you will discover that Jesus was a skillful storyteller. He used stories to illustrate His points. Jesus never used names in His stories. He spoke in parables. I have noticed as a speaker that my audience really wakes up when I tell my own personal story. Testimony is one of the most powerful weapons against Satan, because people can disagree about things in the Bible, but they cannot dispute your testimony. Revelation 12:11 says, "And they [the saints] overcame him [Satan] by the blood of the Lamb and by the word of their testimony."

You have probably heard the saying "juicy bits of gossip." That expression must have come from this chapter in Proverbs, because the words of a talebearer are like tasty trifles. Those juicy bits of gossip can severely wound the person whose story you are telling. Usually if we pass on a negative report about someone, that person will eventually discover what we have said. You might want to join me as I pray this prayer:

Lord, set a guard over my tongue, and let me only say edifying things.

Evening Watch: Read Psalm 149:1–9. We talked about gossip this morning. Why do people gossip? The answer to that question is found in this psalm. A person who gossips does not live in praise. This psalm exhorts all the saints to rejoice in their Maker, to sing praises to Him with the timbrel and harp, and to sing a new song and praises to His name. When we spend our days praising the Lord, our tongues will be cleansed, and we will not have time to gossip.

People gossip because they have a stronghold of pride in their lives. Pride causes us to look down on people instead of esteeming them higher than ourselves. Why don't you ask the Lord, "Do I speak against God's anointed preachers, and do I tell my friends about the sins of others?" We all have been guilty of prideful gossip. God takes pleasure in those who humble themselves, and He is able to beautify them. Do you need a face-lift? Then lift your heart up tonight, and ask the Lord to remove all pride from your heart.

Lord, remove any pride in my heart.

182

JULY 2

Morning Wisdom: Read Proverbs 18:9–10. The book of Proverbs includes many warnings against slothfulness. Proverbs 18:9 says, "He who is slothful in his work Is a brother to him who is a great destroyer."

When we were in India we discovered that there are over three hundred million gods worshiped there. Two of the main gods are Vishnu, the god of wisdom, and Shiva, the god of destruction. We know that Satan came to kill, steal, and destroy. He is the god of destruction, and we do not want to become a brother to this destroyer by being lazy. Satan's main strategy is to destroy our testimony and rob us of time. He is putting a spirit of slumber upon many in the body of Christ. Peter exhorted us to resist the devil when he wrote:

> Be sober, be vigilant; because your adversary the devil walks about like a roaring lion, seeking whom he may devour. Resist him, steadfast in the faith, knowing that the same sufferings are experienced by your brotherhood in the world.
>
> —1 PETER 5:8–9

Satan wants us all to become lazy and complacent in these last days. However, Paul exhorted us to "walk in wisdom toward those who are outside, redeeming the time" (Col. 4:5). To be an effective witness to those outside the body of Christ, we must redeem the time. Satan wants us to stay in front of the TV and computer so our time is wasted, and we will not even know our neighbors. How can we love our neighbors as we love ourselves if we do not even know our neighbors? Satan knows his time is short, so he is using every tactic in his battle plan to distract us from our mission, which is to fulfill the Great Commission. We cannot afford to be slothful in these last days. There is only one place we need to remain during these days and that is in the strong tower of Jesus' name (v. 10). When we use the name of Jesus to resist the devil, we will be effective laborers in this last-day harvest. Have you used the name of Jesus today to resist the devil?

Lord, help me to resist Satan.

Evening Watch: Read Psalm 150:1–6. Before sunrise yesterday I discovered a bird's nest in the window box outside our computer room. My attention was drawn to the window when I heard the tiny little tweets of baby birds. As I carefully looked through the screen I saw baby cardinals in the nest. Even though they were small, they were able to join their mother as she sang her good-morning song to Jesus.

I always get up before the sun rises, because I love to hear the symphony of bird songs as they harmonize to praise the Lord. Psalm 65:8 says that God makes the evenings and the mornings to rejoice. The psalm today speaks of how everything that has breath should praise the Lord. Wake up tomorrow and join the symphony.

Lord, thank You for the sounds of praise!

July 3

2 Kings 22:3–23:30; Acts 21:37–22:16; Psalm 1:1–6; Proverbs 18:11–12

Morning Wisdom: Read Proverbs 18:11–12. We talked yesterday about the god of destruction, Satan, and how his plan is to rob us of time and distract us from our call to fulfill the Great Commission. Unfortunately, Satan is accomplishing his battle plan, because too many in the body of Christ are asleep, and they are not resisting Satan. Another tool of Satan is to keep us prideful. All of us have a lust called the pride of life, and Satan loves to appeal to that lust. Whenever we think we can do things ourselves and do not pray and rely totally upon God and His power, we are in pride. We have done Satan's work for him when we have a haughty heart and an independent spirit. When we succumb to the lust of the pride of life, we can expect the god of destruction to have his way in our lives. Just as Proverbs 18:12 says, "Before destruction the heart of a man is haughty."

Satan wants to distract us from having our intimate times with the Lord, who can teach us meekness and lowliness of heart. (See Matthew 11:28.) Jesus was totally dependent upon the Father when He walked on Earth, and He wants us to follow His example. Satan wants us to be independent people who seek their own will instead of God's will.

Spend time this morning in the presence of the Lord, and ask Him to teach you meekness and lowliness of heart.

Lord, teach me humility.

Evening Watch: Read Psalm 1:1–6. In my first devotional book, *Around the Word in 365 Days,* I talked about walking in the ways of the Lord, standing in His righteousness, and sitting in His presence. The only way that we can do all three of these things is to meditate on God's Word day and night. This psalm tells us that those who meditate on God's Word day and night shall be like a tree planted by the rivers of water that bring forth fruit in its season.

Several years ago we had a willow tree in our yard, and its roots were always clogging our sewer pipes. One day I cursed that willow in the name of Jesus and two weeks later it was struck by lightning and died. We had someone come out and cut the dead tree down and grind the stump. However, a few roots of that willow survived the trauma, and a month later I saw a young willow that sprang up in our creek bed. In Isaiah 44:3–4 God promises to pour out His Spirit on our descendants to bless them, and they will spring up among the grass like willows by the watercourses.

If you are going through a dry time, take comfort, because the Holy Spirit is able to water the seed of God's Word within you and cause you to spring up with joy and be fruitful once again.

Holy Spirit, rain on me.

JULY 4

Morning Wisdom: Read Proverbs 18:13. Listening is an art that few are willing to learn. We need to listen to God first, and then we also need to listen carefully to others. When we receive prophesies or counsel from others in the body of Christ, we need to consult the Word of God to see if what we have heard lines up with Scripture. Too many of us jump ahead of God and do our own thing without laying our problems in the lap of Jesus. Proverbs 18:13 says, "He who answers a matter before he hears it, It is folly and shame to him."

Every day we are faced with decisions. However, our ability to make wise decisions is based on keen discernment. There are many voices daily shouting to us, "Do this," or "Do that." The four voices we usually hear each day are: the voice of Satan, the voice of our own flesh, the voice of God, and the voice of others who seek to give us counsel. We receive the voice of God when we read and meditate on God's Word. God's Word is the only tool by which we can have keen discernment. Hebrews 4:12 says:

> For the word of God is living and powerful, and sharper than any two-edged sword, piercing even to the division of soul and spirit, and of joints and marrow, and is a discerner of the thoughts and intents of the heart.

Our thoughts on a matter can come from our flesh or from the devil, but the intents of our hearts usually come from God if we are walking His way. We need to filter every matter through God's Word and listen carefully to Him as He speaks to our hearts. Research what God's Word says concerning the decisions you may have to make today.

Lord, give me a listening heart.

Evening Watch: Read Psalm 2:1–12. Yesterday we began to read Psalms again. I'm looking forward to seeing new things as we enter our second reading of Psalms. This psalm reveals that God has a Son who He has made King. Verse 6 tells us that God has set His King on His holy hill called Zion. Verse 7 declares that God does have an only begotten Son. God declares that He will rule over nations and break them with a rod of iron. God exhorts kings to fear the Lord and to kiss the Son. (See vs. 12.) After reading this psalm I cannot help but ask the question, "How do Jewish people interpret this psalm?" This psalm so clearly reveals both the Father and His Son, Jesus Christ. How could a Jewish person miss these truths?

The only explanation is that the veil is still over their eyes. Pray tonight for your Jewish friends who have not yet had their eyes opened to the truth of the gospel.

Lord, I ask You to open the eyes of my Jewish friends.

JULY 5

Morning Wisdom: Read Proverbs 18:14–15. We talked yesterday about listening with our hearts, releasing every problem to the Lord, and then researching what the Word of God says about the matter. When we do this we will make wise decisions. Today's reading confirms yesterday's exhortation. It reads, "The heart of the prudent acquires knowledge, And the ear of the wise seeks knowledge" (v. 15).

I can remember doing research papers when I was in school. We had to first look up what has been written about our subject in the library. Then we had to write quotes and other information that we found about the subject on separate index cards with the source of that information written at the bottom of each card. The same technique can be used when we need to make an important decision or face a difficult problem. We can get out the *Strong's Concordance* and write down what God's Word has said about the matter. The knowledge we should seek is the knowledge of God's Word, because God's truth and wisdom is revealed in His Word.

As we research God's Word, we will also be feeding our spirits. So often as I peruse *Strong's Concordance* to find scriptures about a matter, I find myself reading the content of each verse. Before I realize it, I have spent an hour or more in Scripture. Proverbs 18:14 says, "The spirit of a man will sustain him in sickness, But who can bear a broken spirit?" When we feed our spirits the Bread of Life, the Word of God, our spirits will become strong enough to sustain us through sickness. However, if we neglect feeding our spirits daily with the Word of God, we will have emaciated spirits that will easily be broken in times of trial.

Lord, help me to be faithful to read Your Word.

Evening Watch: Read Psalm 3:1–8. Verse 3 says, "But You, O LORD, are a shield for me, My glory and the One who lifts up my head." God is both a shield and a sustainer. David wrote, "I lay down and slept; I awoke, for the LORD sustained me" (v. 5). I am sure that fear often tried to overwhelm David when he faced his enemies in battle. However, he was able to conquer those fears, because he relied on these truths about God. Sometimes our greatest battles with the enemy occur in the night. I recall when our middle son was paralyzed with fear when a presence entered his room in the night. He could not see this demonic spirit, but his heart was overwhelmed with fear. He wanted to scream, "Mom!" but when he opened his mouth nothing came out. Finally he was able to cry out, "Jesus, Jesus!" The presence left. There is sustaining power in the name of Jesus.

Lord, thank You for sustaining me in the night.

JULY 6

1 Chronicles 2:18–4:4; Acts 24:1–27; Psalm 4:1–8; Proverbs 18:16–18

Morning Wisdom: Read Proverbs 18:16–18. All three of the verses in our reading today contain lessons that will be helpful to us. The first verse reads, "A man's gift makes room for him, And brings him before great men" (v. 16). Shortly after Jesus ascended, the Holy Spirit came in power, and the disciples received special gifts that were to be used to witness to the world. (See Acts 2.) When we receive these gifts and use these gifts, we can be brought before great men. The demonstration of the gifts of the Holy Spirit can make a great impact on the world and even on world leaders. We know a South American evangelist who was invited to meet the leaders of his country, because they heard about the miracles God did through him. Herod heard about Jesus and was exceedingly glad when he was able to meet Jesus in person, because he had heard many things about Him, and he hoped to see some miracle done by Him. (See Mark 6:14; Luke 23:8.) The gifts of the Spirit are meant to be used not only in the church but also in the world as a means of evangelism.

The second verse reads, "The first one to plead his cause seems right, Until his neighbor comes and examines him" (v. 17). We need to remember that out of the mouth of two or three witnesses matters need to be confirmed, and in a multitude of counselors there is safety. (See Matt. 18:16; Prov. 11:14.)

Proverbs 18:18 approves of casting lots since contentions will cease if we do this. We know that contentions ceased among the disciples when lots were cast for the disciple who was to take the place of Judas. (See Acts 1:26.)

Lord, help me to learn the lessons taught in Proverbs.

Evening Watch: Read Psalm 4:1–8. David learned the secret to overcoming fear. He said, "Whenever I am afraid, I will trust in You" (Ps. 56:3). We discovered that David relied on the truths of God's Word to sustain him both in the night and in the day. David was able to have a peaceful sleep, because he practiced the art of meditation. No, he did not do New Age meditation that simply involves picturing a calm scene or repeating some mantra. When he was in his bed, he meditated on God's Word in his heart. Tonight, try that type of meditation, and your sleep will be sweet.

Lord, help me to hide Your Word in my heart, so I can meditate on Your Word both day and night.

JULY 7

Morning Wisdom: Read Proverbs 18:19. Paul wrote that love suffers long and is not easily provoked. (See 1 Cor. 13:4–5.) Wouldn't it be wonderful to be in a church where no one ever left because of offense? In our thirty years in one church we have seen countless people leave because they were offended. Proverbs 18:19 reads, "A brother offended is harder to win than a strong city, And contentions are like the bars of a castle."

When we dissolve relationships because we have been offended, we have not allowed the Holy Spirit to pour out the love of God in our hearts. (See Rom. 5:5.) Until we allow our hearts to be softened by the love of God, we will always be subject to offenses and broken relationships.

When we are secure in the love of Jesus, we will not be easily offended. We will not repeat the childhood saying, "Nobody loves me. Everybody hates me. I guess I'll go eat worms." Instead, we will say, "Somebody loves me unconditionally, and that somebody is Jesus, and He thinks I'm wonderful."

Thank You for loving me.

Evening Watch: Read Psalm 5:1–12. David prayed some excellent prayers in this psalm. I believe he prayed these prayers in the morning, because he said, "My voice You shall hear in the morning, O LORD; In the morning I will direct it to You, And I will look up" (v. 3). We can also pray these prayers tonight as we think about tomorrow. The prayer below sums up David's prayer in this psalm. Before you go to bed join me as I pray:

Lord, lead me in Your righteous path, and help me be aware of the perfect path You have prepared for me tomorrow. I rejoice, because You will give me victory over every enemy I may face tomorrow. Thank You for blessing me and surrounding me with Your shield of favor tomorrow and every day.

July 8

Morning Wisdom: Read Proverbs 18:20–21. You have probably heard the expression, "Be careful what you say, because later you may have to eat your words." I think that saying had its roots in Proverbs 18:20, which says, "A man's stomach shall be satisfied from the fruit of his mouth, From the produce of his lips he shall be filled." Whenever we speak bitter, angry, resentful, critical, and judgmental words, both the emotional and physical part of our bodies can be affected. We were told as children to never argue at the table because our mother said it would affect our digestion.

> *Lord, help me to speak words that edify.*

Evening Watch: Read Psalm 6:1–10. When we do not release our cares to the Lord before we go to bed, we can experience some sleepless nights. David experienced such a night when he wrote this psalm. He described the weariness of his body, the trouble he felt in his soul, and the grief that caused him to weep. He finally remembered how the Lord had heard his prayers and supplications in the past, and I believe this helped him to finally release all of his burdens to the Lord. When we know the Lord hears and answers prayer, we can transfer every burden to Him. Peter exhorted us to humble ourselves under the mighty hand of God by casting all of our cares upon Him, because He cares for us. (See 1 Peter 5:6.) Jesus wants to be our Caretaker, but He cannot be this for us if we refuse to give our cares to Him. Tonight roll every burden upon the Lord and cast all your cares upon Him. I guarantee that you will sleep well.

> *Lord, I cast these cares upon You.*

July 9

Morning Wisdom: Read Proverbs 18:22. I wrote a devotional on this verse in my first book, *Around the Word in 365 Days.* I shared how most women would resent being called a thing, but this verse says, "He who finds a wife finds a good thing." When God created Adam He saw how it was not a good thing for Adam to be alone. God even said, "It is not good that man should be alone" (Gen. 2:18). God made Adam a helper and companion.

God the Father knew there was a need for Adam to have a companion, because God had experienced companionship for all eternity. God enjoyed sharing with His Son and the Holy Spirit. He desired to see people on Earth experience the same sweet fellowship. Of course, after the fall relationships became strained, and the hope of having relationships redeemed and restored was not fulfilled completely until after the cross. When Jesus died we died, and we are now hid with Him in God. Because Jesus lives within us, we have hope that His love demonstrated through us can cause our relationships on Earth to be renewed, redeemed, and restored. Is there a relationship in your life that needs healing? Pray with me as I believe for a healing of a relationship in my own life.

> *Lord, I pray that Your love will melt hearts and heal broken relationships.*

Evening Watch: Read Psalm 7:1–17. As we travel through the book of Psalms together, keep in mind that we are reading songs. Songs are meant to be sung, and David sang most of the psalms he wrote. This psalm is a meditation of David, which he sang to the Lord concerning one of his enemies. David set forth his own righteousness as a basis for God to deliver him from his enemies. I am amazed at the security in the Lord that David had. He told the Lord to deliver him to his enemies if he was guilty of plundering his enemies. He asked the Lord to judge him according to His own righteousness and integrity.

Could you pray such a prayer? Because we are believers in Jesus Christ and we stand in the righteousness of Jesus Christ, not our own, we can pray such a prayer. God has promised to deliver us from all affliction and troubles. David wrote, "Many are the afflictions of the righteous, But the LORD delivers him out of them all" (Ps. 34:19).

Thank God we do not have to depend upon our own righteousness to give us the right for God to deliver us from every affliction.

> *Lord, thank You for Your deliverance.*

Morning Wisdom: Read Proverbs 18:23–24. We sing a song in our church called, "I am a Friend of God." I love this song, because it reminds me of my eternal relationship with God the Father. In the Old Testament Moses was called a friend of God, because he was able to talk to God face-to-face like a friend. (See Exodus 33:11.)

Proverbs 18:24 says, "A man who has friends must himself be friendly, But there is a friend who sticks closer than a brother." We all want to have friends who will stick with us through thick and thin. The good news is that every believer has such a friend. His name is Jesus.

We are not able to talk to God face-to-face like Moses did, but we can talk to Jesus, our Friend, every day. You might say, "Well, I can't see Jesus." We do not have to see Jesus face-to-face to know He is present with us. I know several believers who put a coffee cup in front of the vacant chair in front of them while they drink their morning coffee. They have a little talk with Jesus before the day speeds past like a bullet train. Many times when I am in the car alone I will simply imagine Jesus is sitting next to me. I share with Him all my burdens and often even ask Him questions and wait for answers. To establish a friendship relationship with anyone there has to be good communication. Try communicating with Jesus all day long today as you go through your various activities. I know you will experience the joy of the presence of the Lord with you all day long.

Lord, help me to talk with You throughout the day.

Evening Watch: Read Psalm 8:1–9. People with low self-esteem need to read this psalm and believe it. God's view of mankind is conveyed in this psalm. God's description of us should help all of us see ourselves as people of infinite worth. Listen to some of these descriptions:

- We were created a little lower than the angels (v. 5).

- We are crowned with glory and honor (v. 5).

- We have dominion over all of creation (v. 6).

Meditate on this psalm, and recognize that you are the apple of God's eye. When Jesus looks into the pupil of your eye, He sees a reflection of Himself. You are His glory and praise.

Lord, help me to see myself as You see me.

Morning Wisdom: Read Proverbs 19:1–3. Just yesterday in Sunday school we were discussing what it means to walk in integrity. We came to the conclusion that a person who walks in integrity is a person who never pretends to be who he is not and never lies to cover his own faults and sins. A person who has integrity will be honest in his dealings with others and will be the same person at home as he is in church. He will be the same person in private that he is in public. Proverbs 19:1 says that it is better for a poor man to walk in integrity than one who is perverse in his lips and is a fool.

Perverse people do not walk in integrity, because they twist the truth. Often people will pervert the truth in order to make their actions acceptable. Perverse people are usually nervous and fretful, because they fear their lies will be discovered. Proverbs 19:3 says, "The foolishness of a man twists his way, And his heart frets against the LORD."

You may sigh with relief and say, "Thank God, I am not a perverse or a foolish person." However, whenever we become fretful and agitated, our hearts fret against the Lord. We are foolish when we worry and fret instead of trusting the Lord. When we trust in the truth of God's Word we are wise and peace reigns in our hearts.

This morning as I read the words I wrote in this devotional, I was convicted. So many times I have had a heart that frets against the Lord. I know when I am in that state of mind, because my emotions are vulnerable to Satan, and I can easily fall short of the glory and grace God intends for me to walk in daily.

Lord, help me to trust more in Your truth.

Evening Watch: Read Psalm 9:1–12. I've been looking for scriptures to include in a pamphlet to encourage our troops in Iraq. Today's reading contains several scriptures that I will use as I write this pamphlet. They are:

> When my enemies turn back, They shall fall and perish at Your presence.
>
> —PSALM 9:3

> The LORD shall endure forever.
>
> —PSALM 9:7

> The LORD also will be a refuge...in times of trouble.
>
> —PSALM 9:9

These scriptures will also strengthen you for any battle you may face tomorrow or in the days ahead.

Lord, thank You for the sword and shield of Your Word.

JULY 12

Morning Wisdom: Read Proverbs 19:4–5. My husband and I live in a moderately priced home in an extremely wealthy area of Atlanta. Sometimes we pass by homes that look more like institutions than houses. High walls with iron gates encircle the manicured lawns of these homes. As we pass by I often remark, "The people who live there are filthy rich, but I bet they are not happy."

Proverbs 19:4 reveals a reason why rich people may not be happy. Proverbs 19:4 reads, "Wealth makes many friends." The rich may have many friends who befriend them to get a portion of their money. I imagine that wealthy people are daily harassed by various organizations and individuals who are seeking substantial sums of money for their special projects.

There are wealthy people who have sincere friends who love to fellowship with them. I am one of those wealthy people. My riches are stored in heaven, and my treasures are the Christian friends I have who accept and love me just the way I am. Every believer in Christ can experience true happiness and joy, because their heavenly Father owns the cattle on a thousand hills, and their elder brother, Jesus Christ, is a friend who shares His entire inheritance with them.

Thank You, Lord, for Your eternal friendship.

Evening Watch: Read Psalm 9:13–20. Psalm 9:17 says, "The wicked shall be turned into hell, And all nations that forget God." According to Scripture there will be a day when all nations will stand before the judgment seat of God. Matthew 25:32 says, "All the nations will be gathered before Him, and He will separate them one from another, as a shepherd divides his sheep from the goats." The measuring rod that will determine the eternal destiny of nations will be how nations have treated others. The four categories of people mentioned in Matthew 25:32–46 that Jesus wants us to treat well are the Jewish people, the poor, strangers, and prisoners.

One of my joys has been the opportunity to correspond with prisoners on death row in Zambia. Even though you may not be able to go into prisons to visit, you can write them. We are called to minister to both the physically poor and the spiritually poor. Tomorrow look for opportunities to share the riches of God's glory with someone who is poor in spirit.

Lord, give wisdom to our president concerning our dealings with Israel.

JULY 13

Morning Wisdom: Read Proverbs 19:6–7. Proverbs 19:6 says, "Many entreat the favor of the nobility, And every man is a friend to one who gives gifts." Proverbs 19:7 says that even the relatives of the poor abandon them.

Yesterday we discussed the four categories of people who Jesus wants us to treat well. They are the Jewish people, poor people, strangers, and prisoners. (See Matt. 25:32–46.) According to this passage in Matthew 25, those who feed the hungry and give drink to the thirsty will be rewarded, but those who do not will be punished. Jesus said we will always have the poor with us. (See John 12:8.)

One of my favorite things I used to do every Christmas was help a needy woman who had six children. I gave her a party and invited all of my friends to come. This woman was anointed and could pray heaven down to Earth. She prayed for every woman in the group. Many of these women were extremely rich, but they had great spiritual needs.

Some had broken hearts, and some had broken homes. I always set a love basket out for the people to give her a gift. My friend joyfully gathered the love offering and exclaimed, "I plan to use this money to give Christmas to some of the poor families in my neighborhood who have no money to buy presents."

This lady seemed poor by our standards, but by God's standards this saint was wealthy. She had all the gifts of the Spirit and used them to bless others. When she received money she kept nothing for herself but passed it on to others in need.

Lord, help me to always give generously to the poor.

Evening Watch: Read Psalm 10:1–15. In the past few devotions we have shared how nations and individuals will be judged. Christians will be judged to receive rewards, but the unbelievers and the wicked will be judged to receive punishment. Psalm 10:13 says that the wicked renounce God, because they believe there will be no accounting for their deeds.

The truth is that both the wicked and just will be accountable for their words spoken and deeds done on Earth. That sobering fact makes me want to daily pray the following prayer:

Lord, let the words of my mouth and the meditations of my heart be acceptable in Your sight, O Lord, my Strength and my Redeemer.

July 14

Morning Wisdom: Read Proverbs 19:8–9. Proverbs 19:8 says, "He who gets wisdom loves his own soul; He who keeps understanding will find good." There are two kinds of wisdom and understanding. Daily we have a choice to operate in the wisdom and understanding that comes from above or the wisdom that comes from below. James clearly contrasted both kinds of wisdom and understanding when he said that the wisdom from below is self-seeking and causes confusion and every evil work. The wisdom from above is pure, peaceable, gentle, and full of good fruits. (See James 3:13–17.)

When we receive and keep the wisdom and understanding that comes from above, our souls will be at peace, and we can expect good to come out of every circumstance or trial we may experience in this life.

Lord, help me to daily walk in the wisdom and understanding that comes from above.

Evening Watch: Read Psalm 10:16–18. Often preachers will pray a prayer like this at the beginning of a service: *Lord, prepare the hearts of the people to receive Your Word.* Whether or not our lives will be impacted and changed by God's Word depends upon how we hear God's Word.

The parable of the sower in Luke 8 is all about listening and the condition of our hearts. We need to have hearing hearts.

Psalm 10:17 gives us the promise that the Lord will prepare our hearts if we have a humble, teachable spirit. The parable of the sower describes four heart conditions: the callous heart—the Word fell on stony ground; the careless heart—the Word was received but did not take root; the cluttered heart—the Word was choked out by the cares of this world; and the contrite heart—the seed took root and produced fruit. Ask the Holy Spirit to prepare and soften the soil of your heart so that the seed of God's Word will always germinate and be fruitful.

Lord, help me to have a hearing heart that is uncluttered and contrite.

July 15

Morning Wisdom: Read Proverbs 19:10–12. Proverbs 19:11 says, "The discretion of a man makes him slow to anger, And his glory is to overlook a transgression." Sometimes my husband has unintentionally done things that irritate me, and he usually has no idea how I was offended or irritated by something he said or did. I have learned over our nearly fifty years of marriage not to make an issue out of those things. Instead, I overlook them and am careful not to mention them. In my alone times with the Lord, I pour out my complaints to Him instead of my husband.

When someone transgresses against us, it means they have done or said something that has hurt us or caused us loss. People transgress against us when they offend us in some way. Isaiah 44:22 tells us that God has blotted out, like a thick cloud, our transgressions and our sins. If God is able to cover our transgressions, then we also should cover the transgressions of others. Whenever we are offended by another person, it is vital that we not speak of that offense to anyone else. If we do talk about this offense to others, they may take up our offense and have strong feelings against those who have hurt us.

The next time someone transgresses against or offends you, take that offense to the Lord and pray about it instead of mentioning that offense to others. Ask the Lord to help you completely forgive the person who offended you and also ask the Lord to bless that person.

Lord, help me always to pray before I say.

Evening Watch: Read Psalm 11:1–7. I used to tell my three boys, "You think no one is watching you when you do something bad, but God is always watching." At least that statement made them think a little before they were disobedient. I used to have a childlike image of Jesus. When my mother told me that Jesus lived in my heart, I pictured a Valentine-shaped heart. I saw Jesus at a desk, and He was writing on a two-columned tablet. One column was titled "The Bad Things Linda Does." The other column was titled "The Good Things Linda Does." I had a Santa Claus view of Jesus. He was checking the list twice to find out if I was naughty or nice. At least that childlike picture kept me from being a disobedient, rebellious child. I wanted the nice things I did to outweigh the bad things.

This psalm gives another view of why God watches us. It says, "His eyelids test the sons of men. The LORD tests the righteous" (vv. 4–5). The Lord truly is watching us, but He watches us to test us. Whether or not we pass the tests God gives us depends on our dependency upon God as we go through various tests. If we try to pass God's tests in our own strength, we will fail every test. This is why we should quickly turn our tests over to the Lord and allow Him to help us make a passing grade. If we refuse to do this, God will give us a make-up test.

Lord, I want to pass the tests the first time.

JULY 16

Morning Wisdom: Read Proverbs 19:13–14. Prudence and discretion are two qualities every Christian should desire. We learned yesterday that a person has discretion if he covers another person's transgression and is slow to anger. We display the character quality of prudence when we are able to judge matters logically and are careful about how we manage our finances and other aspects of life. When we are prudent we are discreet about matters, and we are careful not to gossip. The bottom line is that we are prudent when we are both sensitive to others and sensible about matters. Proverbs 19:14 says, "A prudent wife is from the LORD." I heard the testimony of a great Bible teacher who asked the Lord the names of his two guardian angels. As he waited in silence for the answer, he heard these words in his spirit, "One angel is named Prudence, and the other angel is named Discretion." I pray that my two guardian angels have names like that.

The absence of prudence and discretion in our lives will cause us to be contentious. Proverbs 19:13 says, "The contentions of a wife are a continual dripping." How would you like for your husband to call you a "drip"? The last thing on Earth a husband needs is a contentious woman who nags him and batters him with critical, judgmental words. It is hard for a man to go to bed with a porcupine who has needled him throughout the day. As wives we need to ask the Lord to help us not to be drips, and we need to cooperate with the Holy Spirit as He seeks to form the character qualities of prudence, wisdom, and discretion in us.

Lord, help me not to be a drip.

Evening Watch: Read Psalm 12:1–8. After a busy day when a multitude of things went wrong have you exclaimed, "Lord, come quickly! Stop the world; I want to get off"? We all have days like that. I call those days "muddle days." David must have had a muddle day when he wrote this psalm. He cried out, "Help, Lord!" He had witnessed the activities of ungodly men who gossiped and flattered and were double minded. He had seen the oppression of the poor. I believe David was just about to end his muddle day in complete despair, but then he remembered God's Word.

David ended his muddle day with this meditation, "The words of the LORD are pure words, Like silver tried in a furnace of earth, Purified seven times" (v. 6). He spoke of God's faithfulness to preserve His Word from generation to generation. (See v. 7.)

If you had a muddle day today it might be good to read out loud verses 6 and 7 of this psalm. When we end our muddle days by meditating on God's Word and His faithfulness, we will be able to have sweet dreams.

Lord, help me to recount Your faithfulness to me before I retire.

July 17

Morning Wisdom: Read Proverbs 19:15–16. Earlier this month we talked about the four kinds of heart conditions and how to prepare our hearts to receive the Word of God. We can know the Word of God from cover to cover, but for the seed of the Word of God to take root and bear fruit in our lives, we must have prepared hearts. The four heart conditions listed in the parable of the sower found in Luke 8 are: the callous heart, the careless heart, the cluttered heart, and the contrite heart. (See Luke 8:11–18.) We concluded that most of us do not bear the fruit we should, because our hearts are cluttered and choked by cares, riches, and pleasures of this life.

Today's reading speaks about the careless heart. Proverbs 19:15–16 says, "Laziness casts one into a deep sleep, And an idle person will suffer hunger. He who keeps the commandment keeps his soul, But he who is careless of his ways will die." Laziness leads to carelessness. We are exhorted in God's Word to stay alert and watchful, because our adversary the devil is like a roaring lion seeking whom he may devour. (See 1 Peter 5:8.) Jesus gave two main exhortations to the church before He ascended to heaven. He told us that we must watch and pray if we want to stand guard against temptation. (See Mark 14:34.)

There are too many Christians watching but not praying. I heard recently the staggering statistic that over 25 percent of the pastors in this nation are involved with pornography. The devil has successfully used the tool of distraction to keep the church from praying. A spirit of slumber has fallen on the church, and we have become lazy and ineffective. We are right where the devil wants us to be. David made a covenant to set no evil things before his eyes. (See Psalm 101:3.)

Lord, forgive me and help me to watch and pray in this last day.

Evening Watch: Read Psalm 13:1–6. When we read the psalms David wrote, one might conclude that David was bipolar. One moment he was up, and the next he was down. I think his problem was that he was only human, as we are. We all have our ups and downs. What impresses me about the psalms of David is that he usually talks or sings himself out of whatever misery he is experiencing. Many of his psalms begin on a sad note and end on a happy note.

This psalm is one that begins, "How long, O LORD? Will You forget me forever? How long will You hide Your face from me?" (v. 1). Have you ever had a day like that when you cried out, "God, I know You have forgotten where I live and what I am going through"? David ended this psalm on this positive note, "But I have trusted in Your mercy; My heart shall rejoice in Your salvation. I will sing to the LORD, Because He has dealt bountifully with me" (vv. 5–6). When we truly trust the Lord, our days will end on a positive note.

Lord, thank You for always getting me out of the depths of despair.

JULY 18

Morning Wisdom: Read Proverbs 19:17. I wrote about this verse in my first devotional book, *Around the Word in 365 Days.* I made the comment that most banks are more than happy to lend us money, because they know they will receive interest when they are paid back. Proverbs 19:17 says, "He who has pity on the poor lends to the LORD, And He will pay back what he has given."

God has an open heart toward the poor, and He delights to bless the poor. Whenever we have pity on the poor and give to them, we become bankers who lend money to the Lord. God will pay His bankers back all we have lent to Him.

My husband and I are on the mission committee at our church. I have always exhorted the mission committee to be sure we support missionaries who are giving to the poor in their countries. I know how much it pleases God for us to bless the poor all over the world.

Lord, may I always be faithful to give to the poor.

Evening Watch: Read Psalm 14:1–7. "Does anybody care? Is there anyone who does good? Is there anyone out there who is walking with the Lord?" Sometimes when I have to be in the marketplace doing errands most of the day, I ask myself these questions. I see the rudeness of the clerks and the hurried drivers who cut in and out of traffic or impatiently honk their horns. Can you imagine what God faces every day as He looks down on Earth to see wars, genocide, famine, and so many horrific troubles. He also humbles Himself to see into the hearts of men, and He beholds wicked hearts that scheme to murder and steal.

Foolish men do abominable things, and the Lord looks down from heaven to see if there are any who seek Him. He can't help but feel at times that no one is living in fear of Him. People are just selfish and do corrupt things. I believe the prayer line to heaven is never busy, because so few are calling out to God in prayer.

There is an open line to heaven tonight. God is longing to hear the voice of someone who desires to do His will tomorrow and every day. Why don't you give God great joy tonight by reaffirming your faith and telling Him how much you love Him? I believe God experiences the same joy an earthly father experiences when a little child says, "Thank you, Daddy. I love you, Daddy."

I love You, Abba.

1 Chronicles 28:1–29:30; Romans 5:3–21; Psalm 15:1–5; Proverbs 19:18–19

Morning Wisdom: Read Proverbs 19:18–19. Have you ever heard a parent exclaim to their disobedient child, "I'm going to beat the daylights out of you"? I am so thankful that my parents never said that to me when I was a disobedient child. However, we hear reports daily of child abuse when children have been severely beaten.

Proverbs 19:18 says, "Chasten your son while there is hope, And do not set your heart on his destruction." I have heard parents angrily say to their disobedient children, "I'm so mad at you, I could just kill you!" Such words should never come out of our mouths when we are dealing with children. Discipline should be delivered with confident authority instead of wrathful tirades.

Proverbs 19:19 says, "A man of great wrath will suffer punishment; For if you rescue him, you will have to do it again." The punishment wrathful men will suffer may not come in their lifetime. However, the day of judgment will come, and God will deliver the correct punishment on that day.

Lord, I pray for my own children to discipline their children wisely.

Evening Watch: Read Psalm 15:1–5. David asks the question, "LORD, who may abide in Your tabernacle?" Jesus instructed us to abide in Him, His love, and His Word. Jesus promised that if we abide in Him and His words abide in us, we may ask what we desire, and it shall be done for us. (See John 15:7.) A lot of people have asked me the question, How can I abide daily in the Lord? I share with them that we abide in the Lord the same way we abide with our family. To have a functional family we must be committed to one another in love. Our communication with one another should be for the purpose of edification and instruction, not criticism and judgment.

In this psalm David mentions several requirements people must fulfill in order to abide in His tabernacle. The person who desires to abide in God's tabernacle must do the following:

- Walk uprightly and do righteousness
- Speak the truth in his heart and refuse to backbite
- Commit to do no evil to his neighbor
- Commit to never take up a reproach against his friend
- Honor those who fear the Lord
- Keep his vows
- Commit to never put his money to usury or bribe the innocent

Lord, help me to abide continually in You.

2 Chronicles 1:1–3:17; Romans 6:1–23; Psalm 16:1–11; Proverbs 19:20–21

Morning Wisdom: Read Proverbs 19:20-21. During my many years as a Christian I have heard this statement, "God laughs when we make our plans." I guess that statement is based on Proverbs 19:21, which says, "There are many plans in a man's heart, Nevertheless the LORD's counsel—that will stand." We do have to make plans in this life. However, Psalm 37:5 exhorts us to commit our way to the Lord and to trust in Him. When we do this, the Lord will bring His will to pass in our lives. Proverbs 16:3 counsels us to commit our works to the Lord. The promise is that if we do this, the Lord will establish our thoughts.

My husband and I sit down at the beginning of every week with our calendars and write down the things we both have to do that week. We share a car, so each week does take some special planning. After we write down the various appointments we have to keep, engagements we have to attend, and errands we have to run, we submit the week to the Lord. We pray a prayer committing the week to the Lord. You might want to join me this morning as I pray this prayer:

> *Lord, You know the appointments, engagements, and errands I have on my list today. Right now I hold this list up to You, and I commit the day to You. I want to do Your will today, not my own. Alter my day according to Your way, and put me in the right place at the right time. Amen.*

Evening Watch: Read Psalm 16:1–11. Did your teacher ever tell you that the essay you wrote was excellent? Do you remember any time when your mom or dad told you that you were an excellent child? I think we all have had very few times in our lives when people have told us that something we have done or something we have said was excellent. There is a reason why people hesitate to give this accolade to someone. Teachers fear that if they tell a student this, that student will begin to slack off and not work as hard. Parents fear that if they tell a child this, that child might expect special privileges.

David declared that the saints who are on Earth are the excellent ones in whom God delights. God does not ever hesitate to call us excellent. God sees us always as excellent in His sight, because the excellent One dwells in our hearts. We can rest in the hope, as David did, that God will show us the path of life. We will all experience excellent lives when we set the Lord always before us as David did. David knew that fullness of joy was in the presence of the Lord and that His right hand was full of pleasures. If you want to be called excellent by God and want to live an excellent life before God, give yourself and your life to Him afresh tonight.

Lord, I give You my life.

JULY 21

Morning Wisdom: Read Proverbs 19:22–23. There is something about the word *satisfied* that makes me think of the times my grandmother used to come over to cook dinner and clean for my mother. Grandmother saw to our every need. She fixed a beautiful meal for us all and then even cleaned up afterwards. People usually experience satisfaction when others do things for them. Some people find satisfaction when they complete a project or an assignment and they know they did a good job. I know I always was satisfied when I got a good grade report.

Proverbs 19:23 says, "The fear of the LORD leads to life, And he who has it will abide in satisfaction; He will not be visited with evil." What a promise! We fear the Lord when we honor God by both our words and deeds. When we walk in the fear of the Lord, we will not visit places where we know evil things occur, and this will protect us from being visited by evil.

When we abide in the fear of the Lord, we will remain satisfied. We will be able to sit at the table the Lord has prepared for us and partake of the Bread of Life (God's Word). Jesus will be able to clean the rooms of our hearts, and He will also do battle for us against the evil one. Jesus is faithful to do through us what He has called us to do. He is the Author and Finisher of our faith, and by the power of His Spirit we will be able to complete every assignment and hear His words at the end of time, "Well done, my good and faithful servant." Now that is satisfaction!

Lord, thank You for satisfying my soul.

Evening Watch: Read Psalm 17:1–15. We see throughout the Bible how God gave tests to those He chose. When we are chosen to go to "God's School of Life and Learning," we can rest assured that there will be pop tests and exams in His school. God tested Abraham, Joseph, Paul, Peter, and a host of other saints.

David said in this psalm that God had tested his heart. He even gave a test to David in the night, and David passed the test. God found nothing in David that would cause him to flunk the test. The reason David passed God's tests was because he purposed not to transgress with his mouth. When we are tried, we need to remain in thanksgiving and praise no matter what. If we begin to murmur and complain to others, we will flunk the test. David also was careful to walk in God's ways. David said, "I shall be satisfied when I awake in Your likeness" (v. 15). Now that's satisfaction!

Thank You for the knowledge that when we see You we will be like You.

JULY 22

Morning Wisdom: Read Proverbs 19:24–25. It is interesting how the Scripture divisions of *The One Year Bible* often couple two verses in Proverbs together that do not seem to relate. Yet, if we examine the two verses closely we usually can discover that they both present principles that harmonize in their meaning. Today's reading in Proverbs reveals the characteristics of an unfruitful person.

Habit patterns can prevent us from cultivating the fruits of the Spirit in our lives. One of these habit patterns is laziness.

Proverbs 19:24 says, "A lazy man buries his hand in the bowl, And will not so much as bring it to his mouth again." Now that is lazy! The lazy person does not put his life in the hands of Jesus. Instead he just wallows in self-pity and blames his laziness on others. Proverbs 19:25 warns against rebuking a scoffer, because they will not receive the rebuke. Pride is the stronghold that causes a pattern of laziness and scoffing in our lives. When we exhibit either of these patterns, our focus is on ourselves, and we will not receive a rebuke. The stronghold of pride will always cause us to live unfruitful lives.

Lord, help me not to ever be lazy or proud.

Evening Watch: Read Psalm 18:1–15. It sounds like David was whirling in the downward spin of depression, but he cried out to the Lord. (See v. 6.) The Lord responded instantly to David's cry. He literally moved heaven and Earth to go to David's defense. After David cried out to the Lord the earth shook and trembled, the foundations of the hills quaked, smoke went up out of God's nostrils, a devouring fire came out of His mouth, He bowed the heavens, and He thundered from heaven (vv. 7–9). Then the Lord sent from above and took David and drew him out of his whirlpool of distress, and He defeated David's enemies.

Lord, thank You for hearing me and moving on my behalf.

2 Chronicles 8:11–10:19; Romans 8:9–23; Psalm 18:16–34; Proverbs 19:26

Morning Wisdom: Read Proverbs 19:26. When our sons were teenagers, they wanted to be independent. They did not like it when we told them what to do. They wanted to make their own decisions, and often when we held our ground on certain issues, they rebelled. Those teen years were difficult, but our three sons never disrespectfully tried to push us out of their lives.

Proverbs 19:26 describes the rebellious son who causes shame and brings reproach upon his family. There are several verses in Proverbs that speak about how a rebellious child brings grief and shame to his parents. I am so thankful my husband and I got through the teen years without any regrets about our sons. Granted, they did get into some worldliness that was not wise, but God had a way of always catching them before they got too far from His path. I am also thankful that I am not rearing children in this day and age. My heart goes out to the parents of teenagers today. This morning I just want to pray for them. You might want to join me in this prayer.

> *Lord, strengthen the parents who have teenagers. I pray that You will impart Your anointing of wisdom and understanding, counsel and might, and knowledge to them as they deal daily with their teenagers.*

Evening Watch: Read Psalm 18:16–34. Once again David began a psalm with negative words and ended his psalm on a positive note. God heard David's cry and drew him out of the waters of despair. God delivered him from his enemies. David felt like the Lord recompensed him because of his own righteousness. (See v. 24.) Surely David did not actually believe that he had led a blameless life. After all, he had committed adultery and murder. Was David blind to his sins?

I believe David was quite aware of his own sinfulness, but he also was aware of God's righteousness. When David discovered how wicked his own heart was after he committed those grievous sins, I believe he also discovered the forgiveness and cleansing God offers freely to those who confess their sins. God was able to create within David a clean heart.

> *Lord, I confess my sins. Create in me a clean heart.*

JULY 24

Morning Wisdom: Read Proverbs 19:27–29. These three verses in Proverbs describe what will happen if we refuse to listen and heed instructions. We can hear instructions, but if we do not heed instructions, we will stray off the fruitful path God intends for us to walk in this life. We even run the risk of doing and saying foolish things that can cause us to experience dire consequences. The judgment of scoffers and fools described in Proverbs 19:29 is something we do not want to experience.

Just reading the Bible through every year will not keep us on God's path. We have to apply the knowledge we gain through reading God's Word. Wisdom is applied knowledge. The Bible is the instruction book for life. Too few read it, and often the few who do read it do not heed it.

We had a Bible teacher in our church who always exclaimed, "What if the Bible is true and all the instructions in it can help us? What if we acted like it was true and did what it told us to do? How would our lives be then?" I can almost hear his voice now. This teacher has gone on to his heavenly reward, but the instructions he shared with us from God's Word will continue to change lives if those who hear also do what they are taught.

Lord, help me to daily follow Your instructions.

Evening Watch: Read Psalm 18:35–50. We shared this morning that our lives would be blessed if we followed the instructions given in God's Word. When we obey God's Word, we can enter the place of security that David described in this psalm. He wrote, "You have also given me the shield of Your salvation; Your right hand has held me up, Your gentleness has made me great. You enlarged my path under me; So my feet did not slip" (vv. 35–36).

God's Word is a light to our path, and when we heed God's Word, we will not slip. God's Word becomes a shield of faith whenever we declare it out loud. This shield of faith will protect us from the fiery darts of the enemy. When we meditate on God's Word, we recognize that God's right hand is holding us up. The security system of God's Word is better than any security system we could purchase to protect our homes. With any security system, however, we need to engage it before it can work. Have you engaged God's security system, His Word, today? Have you obeyed the instructions given in His Word? Pray that you will not fail to engage God's special security system tomorrow.

Lord, help me to apply my heart to the wisdom found in Your Word. Help me to both hear and do Your Word.

2 Chronicles 14:1–16:14; Romans 9:1–24; Psalm 19:1–14; Proverbs 20:1

Morning Wisdom: Read Proverbs 20:1. Christians have different views about drinking. I'll never forget hearing a preacher share what happened to him in Italy. He was offended because all the Italian Christians drank wine. When he shared his offense with an Italian saint, the Italian asked, "Is it true that the Christians are addicted to caffeine in America?" The cultures and customs of different countries vary. Some Christians vow never to take a drink, and they keep that vow because they feel it would be sinful to take a drink. Such Christians could be compared to Nazarenes who took a vow never to drink anything from the fruit of the vine during his days of separation. However, after his days of separation were completed and he was consecrated to the Lord, the Nazarene was able to drink wine. (See Numbers 6:20.)

Other Christians feel that it is all right to drink one glass of wine on occasion. Evidently Jesus drank wine since He was accused of being a glutton and a winebibber. (See Luke 7:34.) Jesus clearly said that He came both eating and drinking.

No matter where you stand on this issue of drinking, the verse for today gives a sound warning to us all. Proverbs 20:1 says, "Wine is a mocker, Strong drink is a brawler, And whoever is led astray by it is not wise." If we drink too much wine, we can lose both our equilibrium and the control of what we say and do. If we drink strong drinks, we open ourselves up to brawls. I have heard people say that some drunks are sweet and some are mean. You may not know which kind of drunk you might be, so my advice and the counsel of the Bible is to never get drunk. Whenever we are out of control, it is important to remember someone else is in control, and it is usually the devil and his demons.

Lord, help me to follow the counsel of Your Word.

Evening Watch: Read Psalm 19:1–14. I love this psalm, because our church used to sing several verses of it. This psalm describes the Word of God. The Word of God includes laws, testimonies, statutes or principles, commandments, judgments, and promises. The testimonies found in God's Word can make us wise. The statutes of the Word can cause us to rejoice. The judgments of the Lord reveal God's true character.

Whenever we keep God's Word, God's Word is able to keep us. Keeping God's Word also entitles us to great rewards. The greatest reward we can receive as we daily read God's Word is the reward of knowing Christ. Paul declared that his only goal in life was to know Christ. Is that your main goal in life? It is mine.

Lord, help me to know You in a deeper way tomorrow as I study Your Word.

July 26

Morning Wisdom: Read Proverbs 20:2–3. It is not a sin to be angry, but the Bible exhorts us not to sin when we are angry. Paul wrote, "'Be angry, and do not sin': do not let the sun go down on your wrath, nor give place to the devil" (Eph. 4:26–27). Proverbs 20:2–3 talks about anger and quarreling. We can be angry, but we are cautioned in Scripture not to provoke anger in another person. (See Colossians 3:8, 21.) Proverbs 20:2 warns against provoking those in authority to anger, because if we do this we sin against our own life. We need to pray for, submit to, and respect those in authority over us. Paul wrote to Timothy:

> Therefore I exhort first of all that supplications, prayers, intercessions, and giving of thanks be made for all men, for kings and all who are in authority, that we may lead a quiet and peaceable life in all godliness and reverence.
>
> —1 Timothy 2:1–2

I know better than to argue with a police officer who is making the decision whether or not to give me a ticket. I would be foolish to start a quarrel with an officer of the law. Proverbs 20:3 says, "It is honorable for a man to stop striving, Since any fool can start a quarrel." Quarreling is really a sign of immaturity. Children squabble and quarrel a lot, because they have not learned to control their emotions. As Christians we are called to be peacemakers who pursue peace with all people. (See Hebrews 12:14.)

Many things can make us angry in life. I have heard sermons on the difference between anger and righteous indignation. One time when I called my mother on the phone and asked her what she was doing, she replied, "I am boiling!" I asked her, "What are you cooking?" She exclaimed, "I am just boiling about how that person accused you of lying!" One of the things that can trigger anger in us is taking up another person's offense or being personally offended by another person. We give place to the devil every time we allow the emotion of anger to control us. Instead, we should take charge over this volatile emotion. If we do not confess our anger and pour it out to the Lord rather than others, we give the devil an open door to do damage to our own soul and the souls of others. Today take up the challenge to seek peace with all men, and tonight before you go to bed, confess any anger or resentment you had towards others, God, or yourself.

Lord, help me to always seek peace with all men.

Evening Watch: Read Psalm 20:1–9. Psalm 20:5 says, "We will rejoice in your salvation, And in the name of our God we will set up our banners! May the LORD fulfill all your petitions." During sports events fans wildly wave the banner that represents their team. One of the names of God is Jehovah-Nissi, which means "The Lord My Banner." We can rejoice, because Jesus is our banner, and His banner over us is love.

Lord, thank You for being my banner.

2 Chronicles 19:1–20:37; Romans 10:13–11:12; Psalm 21:1–13; Proverbs 20:4–6

Morning Wisdom: Read Proverbs 20:4–6. Proverbs 20:6 asks the question: "Who can find a faithful man?" Jesus asked this question: "When the Son of Man comes, will He really find faith on the earth?" (Luke 18:8). Jesus will find faith on the earth if those who believe in Him will remain faithful. Faithfulness is one of the most needed fruits of the Spirit in these last days. (See Galatians 5:22.) A faithful person is:

- Diligent—He is willing to labor in the field of the Lord's kingdom no matter what the conditions or the circumstances he is presently experiencing (v. 4).
- Understanding—He is able to draw to the surface what is in the heart of the person he counsels (v. 5).
- Humble—He glorifies God instead of glorifying himself (v. 6).

Jesus exhorted the church at Ephesus with these words: "Be faithful until death, and I will give you the crown of life" (Rev. 2:10).

The crown of life is promised to those who are faithful and to those who endure temptation. James wrote, "Blessed is the man who endures temptation; for when he has been approved, he will receive the crown of life which the Lord has promised to those who love Him" (James 1:12). We will remain faithful as long as we love Jesus with all of our hearts, souls, and minds.

Lord, help me to always be faithful.

Evening Watch: Read Psalm 21:1–13. Yesterday we looked at Psalm 20, which contains a beautiful blessing that we can pray over those we love. I have summarized several verses from this psalm into this blessing: "May the Lord answer you in the day of your trouble, and may He defend and strengthen you. May He give you your heart's desire and fulfill His purposes in you. May He grant all your petitions."

Psalm 21 is a summary of the many blessings David experienced. One of my favorite praise songs is "Look What the Lord Has Done." David exclaimed with joy that the Lord had given him his heart's desire and answered his requests. The Lord gave him length of days, honor, and majesty. The Lord made him exceedingly glad with His presence. The Lord defended him. We reap what we sow. I am sure David prayed the beautiful blessing in Psalm 20 over many, and David received the very blessings he prayed for others.

Lord, help me to bless others always.

JULY 28

Morning Wisdom: Read Proverbs 20:7. Today is my husband's birthday. Today's verse describes his life. Proverbs 20:7 says, "The righteous man walks in his integrity; His children are blessed after him." My husband does have his faults, as we all do, but he has consistently walked in integrity all of his life. Our children have been blessed in many ways because of my husband's integrity. The main blessing our three sons have received from their father is a desire also to walk in integrity. They love God's Word and walk in His truths. Third John 1:4 says, "I have no greater joy than to hear that my children walk in truth."

Lord, thank You for giving me a man of integrity to marry.

Evening Watch: Read Psalm 22:1–18. This psalm previews what happened on the cross. The very words that Jesus spoke on the cross when He felt God had abandoned Him are found in the first sentence of this psalm. Both Jesus and David cried out "My God, My God, why have You forsaken Me?" (v. 1). David wrote "All those who see Me ridicule Me; They shoot out the lip, they shake the head, saying, 'He trusted in the LORD, let Him rescue Him; Let Him deliver Him, since He delights in Him!'" (vv. 7–8). When I read that verse I could almost hear the taunting cries of those gathered around the cross as they shouted, "You saved others; now save yourself!"

David continued describing almost word for word what happened to Jesus on the cross. Was David a psychic or a fortune-teller? He was neither. I believe that David was in the Spirit when he wrote this psalm, and he was able to journey through time to that scene on the cross. With God there is no time or space. When we are in the Spirit, we can look down the portholes of time and see things others cannot see.

Lord, reveal to me anything in the future that I need to know.

JULY 29

Morning Wisdom: Read Proverbs 20:8–10. King David learned the hard way that he could not cover his own sin. When Nathan the prophet confronted him with the fact that he had committed adultery and murder, David confessed his sins and repented. (See 2 Sam. 12:1–15.) Shortly after that he wrote, "Create in me a clean heart, O God, And renew a steadfast spirit within me" (Ps. 51:10). Proverbs 20:9 asks the question: "Who can say, 'I have made my heart clean, I am pure from my sin'?" God knew David's heart, even though David's heart probably condemned him many times. When our own heart condemns us we have to remember that God is greater than our hearts. (See 1 John 3:20.)

David was a man after God's own heart, because he was a man of integrity who learned to be honest with God, himself, and his fellowman. David was not like the king described in Proverbs 20:8 who scatters all evil with his eyes. After David sinned, he made a covenant with his eyes not to behold evil. The Lord did cleanse David's heart. The Lord will do the same for you if you confess your sins and repent.

Lord, help me to always be honest with You, others, and myself.

Evening Watch: Read Psalm 22:19–21. This psalm ends with David's prophetic words that describe the time when Jesus will reign on Earth. The time will come when there will be a great assembly before the throne of God. That assembly will include the poor in spirit who were satisfied on Earth with God's Word, the Bread of Life. The assembly will include all nations and families, and they will bow down and worship the Lord. The generations that served the Lord will be around His throne. What a scene that will be, and one day we all will see it!

Lord, thank You for Your perfect sacrifice that paved the way for me to be in the great assembly gathered around Your throne.

JULY 30

Morning Wisdom: Read Proverbs 20:11. We are exhorted in Scripture to judge a man by his fruits. (See Matt. 7:20.) We cannot judge a person's motives, but we can judge their actions. Proverbs 20:11 makes it clear that even a child is known by his deeds. You have heard the expression, "Actions speak louder than words." We might try to appear righteous before others, but unless we walk in righteousness both our words and our deeds will reveal the truth about us. We may fool others for a while, but we will never fool God. Jesus said that what we say reveals what is in our hearts. (See Matt. 15:18.)

The day will come when all we said and did on Earth will be judged. Even our idle words will be judged. However, if we have confessed the times when we have sinned with our words and our actions, those words and actions are washed from God's memory. When we have a heart to do the will of God daily and to walk in His ways of righteousness, we can trust the convicting power of the Holy Spirit to show us those things we need to confess to the Lord. We can be assured that if we confess our sins, God is faithful and just to forgive us of our sins and to cleanse us from all unrighteousness. (See 1 John 1:9.) Once we have confessed our sins, we do not have to confess them again. When we confess our sins, God drops our sins in the ocean of His forgiveness and puts up a sign that says, "No fishing."

Lord, examine my heart and show me any ways I have sinned by my words and my deeds. I want to confess these sins to You.

Evening Watch: Read Psalm 23:1–6. Good shepherds will lead their sheep to fresh pastureland daily. A good shepherd only allows his sheep to graze to a certain level of the grass in the pastureland, and then he leads them to a new pastureland. He knows that if he allows the sheep to graze until the grass is stubby and short, that pastureland will no longer be fit for them to return to for their food.

Sheep are totally dependent upon their good shepherd to right them and set them on their feet again when they are cast down. Fat sheep who have not been shorn are the ones who always become cast down. I can picture these huge sheep on their backs with their legs flaying wildly as they try to right themselves. In that position they are open prey for wolves and other predators who seek to kill them and eat their flesh. A good shepherd makes sure his sheep never get too fat or heavy with wool. He provides a good diet for them and shears them regularly.

Our Good Shepherd will not allow us to remain in the same place spiritually. He prepares exactly the measure of fresh manna to feed our spirits each day. However, we must come to the table He has prepared for us. When you open your Bible tomorrow, ask the Lord if He has a fresh word for you, and then wait for Him to speak to your heart.

Lord, thank You for being my Good Shepherd.

JULY 31

2 Chronicles 29:1–36; Romans 14:1–23; Psalm 24:1–10; Proverbs 20:12

Morning Wisdom: Read Proverbs 20:12. Proverbs 20:12 says, "The hearing ear and the seeing eye, The LORD has made them both." I have noticed that people who are blind usually have a keen sense of hearing, and people who are hearing impaired use their eyesight to communicate through sign language.

Most of us know the story of Helen Keller, who was both blind and deaf. Her story reveals a true fact about us all. We have more than physical ears and eyes. God created us with both physical and spiritual ears and eyes. The lady who taught Helen was able to awaken Helen's spiritual ears and eyes.

Jesus often said, "He that has ears to hear, let him hear." Most of the people in the crowds He spoke to were not hearing impaired. They had physical ears. Jesus wanted the words He spoke, however, to be heard with their spiritual ears. If we do not hear God's Word with our hearts, there will be no change in our lives. We can read the Word through each year, but if we do not incline our ears to hear God's Word with our hearts, our minds will not be renewed by the Word of God.

We must depend upon the Holy Spirit to give us insight into God's Word so that we can have eyes of faith to apply what we have read in God's Word. Both our spiritual ears and eyes have to be operating at full capacity for us to be able to receive and apply God's Word in our lives. Proverbs 2:2 exhorts us to incline our ear to wisdom and to apply our hearts to understanding.

Lord, awaken my spiritual ears and eyes.

Evening Watch: Read Psalm 24:1–10. Psalm 24:7 says, "Lift up your heads, O you gates! And be lifted up, you everlasting doors! And the King of glory shall come in." What are the gates we need to lift up? When I did a study on how Satan is able to find entrance to our souls, I discovered the gates we daily must lift up to the Lord. There are three gates in the head part of our bodies that, if not guarded, will give Satan entrance to our souls. Those gates are the ear gate, the eye gate, and the mouth gate. We see from the beginning of time how Satan's strategy was to tempt us through what we hear, what we see, and what we speak. The old saying, "Hear no evil; see no evil; and speak no evil," is good advice. If we will guard the gates of our souls daily by lifting our souls up to the Lord, we will be able to overcome temptation.

We must recognize that we cannot close these gates without first releasing these gates to the Lord so that He then can help us when we are tempted. Our Good Shepherd will be able to help us guard these three gates to our souls, and He will also send His glory through these gates. We will glorify Jesus daily when we commit to hear, see, and speak no evil.

Lord, I lift up my soul to You today. Help me to guard these three gates.

2 Chronicles 30:1–31:21; Romans 15:1–22; Psalm 25:1–11; Proverbs 20:13–15

Morning Wisdom: Read Proverbs 20:13–15. Proverbs 20:13 says, "Do not love sleep, lest you come to poverty." When my children were in the first grade, something unusual happened. Both my older son and middle son had the same first-grade teacher. She gave the assignment to my older son to write down what his dad and mom loved to do. Four years later she gave the same assignment to my youngest son when he was in first grade. Both of my sons wrote this: "What my mom loves best to do is to sleep." I'm sure their first-grade teacher thought I was the laziest woman in town. The reason why they thought I just slept all the time was because when they left for school I was in my robe and when they returned from school I was still in my robe. It was my custom to have breakfast in my robe and then get dressed after the kids left for school to run errands and do housework. Just before they returned from school I took a nice, relaxing, hot bath, put my robe on, and rested for a few minutes while the house was quiet. This gave me the energy to cook dinner and enjoy my sons the rest of the afternoon and evening.

The warning in these verses is not to sleep all the time. You have heard the statement, "All work and no play makes Johnnie a dull boy." This could be rephrased to say, "All sleep and no work makes Johnnie a poor boy."

Proverbs 20:14 talks about how buyers force sellers to reduce their price. When we were in Israel we loved to go through the old marketplace in Jerusalem. We made sure we took someone with us who could speak both Arabic and Hebrew and also someone who was skilled in bargaining. Often they used the technique described in this verse. When they saw something they wanted to purchase, they usually asked the storekeeper, "How much do you want for this piece of junk?" The price was quoted, and our skilled bargainer would then exclaim, "Too much!" Then he began to walk away and usually the storekeeper would run shouting after him, "What will you pay for it?"

Proverbs 20:15 compares lips of knowledge to precious jewels. It is human nature to be lazy sometimes and also to be a little deceptive when we are trying to strike a bargain, but people who know the Lord and walk in righteousness will redeem the time and also deal honestly with others.

Lord, help me to walk in righteousness.

Evening Watch: Read Psalm 25:1–11. This psalm describes some of the character qualities of a person who fears the Lord. We fear the Lord when we have an awesome, reverent respect for the might and power of God and we walk in daily obedience to God's Word. A person who fears the Lord will lift his soul up to the Lord (v. 1); wait upon the Lord (v. 3); be led by the Spirit (v. 4); learn God's truths (v. 5); and humble ourselves and trust in God's mercy and forgiveness (vv. 6–11).

Lord, help me always to walk in the fear of the Lord.

Morning Wisdom: Read Proverbs 20:16–18. Proverbs 20:16 says, "Take the garment of one who is surety for a stranger, And hold it as a pledge when it is for a seductress." This verse reminds me of the story of Tamar and Judah described in Genesis 38. Tamar pretended to be a seductress. She requested that Judah leave a token with her as a pledge that Judah would return with a goat. Judah left his signet ring, chord, and staff. Those tokens proved that Tamar was pregnant with Judah's child. If you have time today, read this story in Genesis.

Proverbs 20:17 says, "Bread gained by deceit is sweet to a man, But afterward his mouth will be filled with gravel." Even though deception was involved in the story of Tamar and Judah, the motivation behind Tamar's deception was to raise up seed for her father-in-law, Judah, which she did. If her plans had been established by wise counsel, perhaps this deception could have been avoided. (See Proverbs 20:18.) Now you must know the rest of the story. Tamar gave birth to twins, Perez and Zerah. The son of Perez produced the Messianic line of David. Jesus Christ was from the line of David and the tribe of Judah. God saw to it that Judah finally gained a son so that the Messianic line of David would birth Jesus Christ. (See 2 Chronicles 2:4–15.)

Lord, I can trust Your plans for me.

Evening Watch: Read Psalm 25:12–22. Psalm 25:12–13 says, "Who is the man that fears the LORD? Him shall He teach in the way He chooses. He himself shall dwell in prosperity, And his descendants shall inherit the earth." Tamar feared the Lord, and her descendants truly were great on the earth. Her eyes were toward the Lord, and He was faithful to pluck her feet out of the net when her family was ready to burn her because they thought she had committed adultery. (See vv. 14–15.)

Lord, thank You for Your faithfulness.

Morning Wisdom: Read Proverbs 20:19. We have talked several times about how the mouth can be compared to a double-barreled gun. The bullets fired from this gun are words and the trigger is the tongue.

Today's verse talks about two kinds of ammunition we can supply Satan to wound even those we love. The two kinds of ammunition are talebearing and flattery.

Satan wants to use us as hit men to fire his accusations at others. Whenever we pass on a negative report, we are guilty of being a talebearer. We need to stop and think before we pull the trigger of our tongue. We need to ask ourselves this question, "Will what I am about to say build up the image of the person I am speaking about or tear it down?" I know whenever I have heard a negative report about a person, it changes how I look and act around that person the next time I see them.

Flattery is a more subtle way of wounding a person. When we flatter we are guilty of giving compliments to another person with the motive of manipulating that person. The words we speak should be sincere, and our motivation should always be to edify others.

Before you pull the trigger of your tongue today, count to ten and ask the Lord to order your conversation aright. If we will pray this prayer before we speak anything, we will resign our position as a hit man for Satan. The person who orders his conversation aright glorifies God. (See Psalm 50:23, KJV.)

Lord, may my conversations glorify You.

Evening Watch: Read Psalm 26:1–12. David was a man after God's own heart because he was so open and vulnerable in his dealings with God. He asked God in this psalm to examine him and prove him. He wanted God to try his mind and heart. Would you be willing to tell God to put you on His examining table so He could dissect your heart and reveal all the wickedness in it?

I know I would be a little afraid to do this, but I only have that fear because I think he might uncover something I don't want Him to see. How ridiculous to even think that God does not know me through and through and nothing at all would surprise Him as He searched my heart.

David was able to be vulnerable to God because he hid nothing from Him. He knew also that God was filled with loving-kindness and that He would deal gently with his heart. David loved to dwell in the presence of the Lord, and he knew God stood ready to forgive him when he confessed his sins. David wrote, "My foot stands in an even place; In the congregations I will bless the Lord" (v. 12).

Lord, thank You for making it possible for me to stand in righteousness.

2 Chronicles 35:1–36:23; 1 Corinthians 1:1–17; Psalm 27:1–7; Proverbs 20:20–21

Morning Wisdom: Read Proverbs 20:20–21. These two verses speak about honoring our parents. The only commandment with a promise is the commandment to "Honor your father and your mother, as the LORD your God has commanded you, that your days may be long, and that it may be well with you in the land which the LORD your God is giving you" (Deut. 5:16).

It concerns me that many of the cartoons and other children's programs teach children to disrespect their parents. Proverbs 20:20 warns against cursing our fathers and mothers. Children do not have to use curse words to curse their moms and dads. Whenever they speak negatively about their moms and dads to others, those negative words are released into the atmosphere and Satan can use those words as bullets to harm both their parents and the children who speak those words. For example, I have heard teenagers say, "I wish my parents were dead." Such statements can be used by Satan.

Proverbs 20:21 warns us not to be greedy to gain our inheritance quickly, because such an inheritance will not be blessed. My husband and I can rest assured that our children are not anxious for us to die to gain their inheritance, because they already have the greatest inheritance any parent could offer. That inheritance contains all the riches in glory through Christ Jesus. Since our three sons have accepted Jesus Christ as their Lord and Savior, they are joint heirs with Christ to their heavenly Father's inheritance, and He owns the cattle on a thousand hills.

Lord, thank You for our great inheritance through Jesus Christ!

Evening Watch: Read Psalm 27:1–7. Our morning reading in Proverbs 20 warned that the light of the child who does not honor his or her parents will grow dark. This cannot happen to children who fear the Lord, because they will honor both their earthly parents and their heavenly Father.

David walked in the fear of the Lord, and he recognized that the Lord was the light of his salvation. The Lord shielded him from his enemies and strengthened him through every trial. When trouble came the Lord hid David in the secret place of His tabernacle, and He set David on a high rock. God's faithfulness to deliver David through every trial gave David great joy. Psalm 27 captures David's overflowing joy. God never hid His face from David, and He always lit David's path.

I'm reminded of a song we used to sing when we taught a junior-high group in a church. That group was named The Lamplighters. The theme song of that group was a song about letting our lights shine for Jesus in our hearts, families, neighborhoods, churches, towns, cities, lands, and the whole wide world. Jesus is the Light of the world who lights every man who comes into the world. (See John 1:9.) Make it your goal tomorrow to let His light shine through you.

Thank You for being my Great Light.

Ezra 1:1–2:70; 1 Corinthians 1:18–2:5; Psalm 27:8–14; Proverbs 20:22–23

Morning Wisdom: Read Proverbs 20:22–23. The doorbell rang. I rushed to open the door, and to my shock the sheriff greeted me. He handed me a piece of paper and said, "You need to sign here to indicate that you have received this." With trembling hands I signed and then sat at my kitchen table to read this document. I learned quickly that I was being sued for three hundred thousand dollars for the injuries that occurred when I hit a neighborhood child with my car. The child miraculously was healed, but his family was suing me for three hundred thousand dollars, which would have taken all we owned. I was falsely accused and was tempted to be angry with this boy's family, but I realized that their lawyers had talked them into this lawsuit.

Later I got a call from my insurance company asking me to get an additional lawyer since they felt this case would be difficult. I told the insurance company that I already had a lawyer. They did not know that my Lawyer was Jesus Christ, my marvelous Advocate. The case was dismissed and settled out of court years later.

Proverbs 20:22 warns against recompensing evil and exhorts us to wait for the Lord to save us. Whenever we are falsely accused, we need to wait upon the Lord to defend and save us. He is faithful to be both Judge and Advocate.

Dishonesty is something God hates. Proverbs 20:23 says that dishonest scales are an abomination to God. In the days when this was written, the exchange for goods was measured by scales. A stone was placed on one side of the scales, and the buyer had to put enough silver coins on the scales to level the scales. Often merchants would put a larger stone on one side of the scales to cheat their customers. Whenever we are dishonest, we need to recognize how much this displeases God, and then we need to confess our dishonesty and repent.

Lord, help me to always be honest.

Evening Watch: Read Psalm 27:8–14. David acknowledged the Lord's saving power in this psalm. He said that even if his mother forsook him, he was confident that the Lord would take care of him. God always lived up to the trust David put in Him. David asked the Lord to lead him in a smooth path and to deliver him from false witnesses and all of his enemies. God delivered me from false witnesses when I was sued. David did not lose heart, because he trusted in the goodness of the Lord. I trusted in the goodness of the Lord when I was sued, and we can all trust in the goodness of the Lord.

Lord, I trust in Your goodness.

August 6

Morning Wisdom: Read Proverbs 20:24–25. When I read our Proverbs reading for today, my heart sank as I thought about the many marriages that have ended in divorce. I heard recently that the divorce rate among Christians is even higher than the divorce rate in the world. Then I heard a remarkable statistic that 60 percent of the divorces in Christian homes are initiated by the wives.

Proverbs 20:25 says, "It is a snare for a man to devote rashly something as holy, And afterward to reconsider his vows." Marriage is the holy union between a man and a woman, and the vows taken on the wedding day should not be reconsidered and broken.

There are many reasons for divorce, but Jesus said, "What God has joined together, let not man separate" (Matt. 19:6). I believe if couples fully understood God's view of marriage, there would not be this high divorce rate in the body of Christ. It seems that many divorces occur in less than five years of marriage. This statistic could be changed if both partners would release their expectations to the Lord instead of expecting so much of one another. I have counseled many people to expect nothing of other people and everything of God. Only God has the ability to perfectly fulfill our desires and expectations.

Proverbs 20:24 says that our steps are ordered by the Lord, and it is difficult for us to understand our own way. It is even more difficult for us to understand the ways of our spouse. Therefore, it would be prudent for both husband and wife to commit their ways to the Lord and trust Him to do the changing in each individual life. Often what we want to change in our spouse is not what God wants to change. God's way is perfect, and we can trust Him to perfect those things that are a concern to us. (See Psalm 138:8.) God can touch and change whatever concerns you about your spouse. Do not ever believe the lie that things in your marriage will never change. According to God's Word, we are daily being changed from glory to glory. (See 2 Corinthians 3:18.)

Lord, change me.

Evening Watch: Read Psalm 28:1–9. I'll never forget the time when our grandson and his little sister climbed into the trunk of their dad's car as he was about to load the car with their bicycles. Our granddaughter suddenly jumped out of the trunk into the arms of her dad. Her brother decided to do the same thing, but when he jumped, his dad was not watching, and his son fell flat on the asphalt driveway. I can remember my grandson raising his arms to his dad as he cried out, "Daddy, Daddy, why didn't you catch me?"

In this psalm David exclaimed, "When I cry to You, When I lift up my hands toward Your holy sanctuary. Do not take me away with the wicked" (vv. 2–3). Later David said, "Blessed be the LORD, Because He has heard the voice of my supplications!" (v. 6). We can trust that God will always be there to catch us and to hear our cry.

Lord, thank You for always being there for me.

AUGUST 7

Morning Wisdom: Read Proverbs 20:26–27. In our morning reading yesterday we talked about how difficult it is for us to understand our own way, much less the ways of our spouse. There, however, is a way that we can gain understanding of our ways, the ways of our spouse, and the ways of the Lord. We can gain that understanding through depending upon the Holy Spirit to give us insight and even revelation knowledge of God and the people in our lives. I think more marriages could be saved if the husband and wife would ask the Holy Spirit to help them better understand their mate. Part of the anointing of the Holy Spirit is understanding. (See Isaiah 11:2.)

Proverbs 20:27 says, "The spirit of a man is the lamp of the LORD, Searching all the inner depths of his heart." When we are born again of the Spirit of God by the Word of God, we then become vessels that contain the anointing of the Holy Spirit. That anointing abides in us continually. (See 1 John 2:27.) If we will ask the Holy Spirit to give us understanding, His light will light our spirit and the dark places in our hearts can be revealed. The Holy Spirit will be able to sift out any wickedness in our own hearts, so we then can confess our own sin and be cleansed. When we have dealt with our own sins, we will definitely have a better understanding of others and the reasons they do and say certain things.

Lord, thank You for the Holy Spirit who is my daily Helper. May He reveal to me today anything in my own heart that needs cleansing.

Evening Watch: Read Psalm 29:1–11. My mother-in-law asked me years ago how God could hear every prayer and how He could speak to people. I responded, "The communication we have with God is like a short wave or two-way radio." Then I continued describing how a short-wave radio works. I shared that signals on a two-way radio can be picked up thousands of miles away, because voices can travel on the airwaves. Both the sender and the receiver of a short-wave conversation have to be tuned to the right frequency in order for their voices to transmit. God can clearly communicate with people who are tuned to the right frequency.

Psalm 29 describes the power of God's voice. God's voice is described in this psalm. David wrote, "The voice of the Lord is full of majesty" (v. 4). His voice is able to shake a wilderness and divide fire. His transmission to us is powerful and clear. However, we often are not tuned to the right frequency. There is static on our end of the line. If we have prideful, rebellious hearts, the Lord will not hear us, and we will not hear Him.

Lord, help me to stay tuned to Your frequency daily.

AUGUST 8

Morning Wisdom: Read Proverbs 20:28–30. "Let's get all the grey out and you'll look years younger," my hairdresser exclaimed as she mixed the hair dye. We can do things to our appearance to make us look younger, but none of us prevent the aging process. Even though our bodies will grow weaker with time, our spirits can become stronger with each day.

Solomon wrote, "The glory of young men is their strength, And the splendor of old men is their gray head" (v. 29). There are three things that will preserve our spirits and souls as we age. Those three things are stated in verse 28, which says, "Mercy and truth preserve the king, And by lovingkindness he upholds his throne." When we obtain mercy by showing mercy to others, our spirits and souls will be strengthened. Abiding in God's truths and demonstrating loving-kindness toward others will also cause strength to come into our inner man. The joy of the Lord is our strength. Christ in us is our hope of glory, and those who believe in Him have only more glory to experience.

Glory, the best is yet to come!

Evening Watch: Read Psalm 30:1–12. David was well aware that his life would be brief on this earth. However, David was fruitful in the years he was on Earth. This psalm reveals why David had many fruitful days during his lifetime. He learned that the Lord's anger was only for a moment, but His favor was for life. He also knew that even though weeping might come at night, joy would come in the morning. David knew where to go when the going got rough, and at those times he made his supplications to the Lord.

When we grow older, we cannot lift the amount of weight we used to be able to lift when we were young. The burdens we hold on to in our old age will seem like they weigh a ton. This is why we need to quickly release our burdens to the Lord as David did. Jesus invited all those who are weary and heavy laden to come to Him with their burdens. (See Matthew 11:28.) When we give the Lord our burdens, we will find rest for our souls.

Lord, I commit every care to You.

August 9

Morning Wisdom: Read Proverbs 21:1–2. Proverbs 21:1 is a verse I use often in prayer. Whenever I have to go before authorities, I declare, *Lord, the king's heart is in Your hands, and I know You will turn it in the way you wish it to go.* I have never had to appear before a judge, but I am praying for someone now who is in prison for life for a crime she did not commit. We became pen pals when she wrote that she had received my book. Somehow my first book, *Around the Word in 365 Days,* got into her prison library. She not only is my pen pal, but she also is my prayer partner. I know I can tell her things to pray for that I could not tell anyone else, because she has no way to communicate with people I know.

Right now she is working with an appeals lawyer to appeal her case. I have been praying the above prayer for her, because I know God will be her Advocate, and He will turn the hearts of the kings in the way He wants. The letters she writes me inspire me, because each sentence is filled with such joy. Her joy comes from trusting her future completely into the hands of the Lord. She said whether she is freed or not she knows God will accomplish His perfect will in her life. She can say that with confidence, because she has had her mind renewed by the Word of God, so she is able to prove what is the good and acceptable and perfect will of God in her life. (See Romans 12:2.)

The Lord knows my friend's heart, and He also knows your heart and mine. Proverbs 21:2 says. "Every way of a man is right in his own eyes, But the LORD weighs the hearts." Because God does know our hearts, we can trust Him to lead us in His right path, not the one we think is right. With confidence I can say the best is yet to come for you, my friend, and me, because God's will is always best.

Lord, thank You for always having only my best on Your heart.

Evening Watch: Read Psalm 31:1–8. We talked this morning about trusting our future into the hands of the Lord.

We can be confident that God's will is the best for our lives. I pray those I know who are serving in Iraq will have that strong confidence and trust in the Lord. Just this week I have been preparing a brochure for the soldiers in Iraq. Included in the brochure are scriptures that I know will strengthen them during this time of trial in their lives.

Psalm 31:1–8 contains some of the thoughts expressed in my brochure. So many of David's psalms talked about how God was his fortress and defense. He declared that God was his refuge and the Rock of his salvation. David knew who gave him the strength to do battle. The Lord of hosts is who does battle for us every day, so we do not have to fear. The Lord is on our side. We can trust that we will always triumph in Christ Jesus. (See 2 Corinthians 2:14.) You might want to pray for the soldiers you know who valiantly serve our country.

Lord, be a shield around our troops. Let them know Your strength.

August 10

Morning Wisdom: Read Proverbs 21:3. When the Pharisees complained about how Jesus ate with tax collectors and sinners, Jesus said, "But go and learn what this means: 'I desire mercy and not sacrifice.' For I did not come to call the righteous, but sinners, to repentance" (Matt. 9:13). I am sure the Pharisees had read Proverbs 21:3, which says, "To do righteousness and justice Is more acceptable to the LORD than sacrifice." They were familiar with the writings of the prophet Micah who wrote, "He has shown you, O man, what is good; And what does the LORD require of you But to do justly, To love mercy, And to walk humbly with your God" (Mic. 6:8). The Pharisees knew these scriptures, but they had not learned to apply these scriptures to their everyday lives. We all know what we should do according to Scripture, but are we doing it?

Lord, help me to do Your works today, not my own.

Evening Watch: Read Psalm 31:9–18. David was looking down the corridor of time as he wrote verses 9–13 of this psalm. David was in the Spirit when he wrote this psalm. He described much of what Jesus experienced on the cross. The only verse that does not line up with what Jesus experienced just before and during His crucifixion is verse 10, which says, "My strength fails because of my iniquity." David had iniquity, but Jesus had none. However, Jesus bore the sins and infirmities for the whole world on the cross. The weight of the sins of the world broke Jesus' heart. Jesus died of a broken heart. He truly was a broken vessel. (See v. 12.)

When Jesus died on the cross, God not only laid upon Jesus our iniquities and sins, but He also laid His goodness upon Jesus. David spoke about His goodness when he wrote, "Oh, how great is Your goodness, Which You have laid up for those who fear You" (v. 19). The demonstration of God's goodness was manifested when the King of glory willingly gave Himself as a sin sacrifice for the whole world.

Lord, thank You for Your sacrifice.

Nehemiah 1:1–3:14; 1 Corinthians 7:1–19; Psalm 31:19–24; Proverbs 21:4

Morning Wisdom: Read Proverbs 21:4. As I read this verse I had a visual picture of a farmer plowing to prepare the soil of his fields for planting his next crop. There are many scriptures in God's Word about planting, plowing, sowing, and reaping. Today's verse is about plowing. Proverbs 21:4 says, "A haughty look, a proud heart, And the plowing of the wicked are sin."

We have the opportunity every day to be farmers in the field of the Lord. We are told in Scripture to plow up or break up the fallow ground in our hearts and sow righteousness. (See Jeremiah 4:3.) If pride is in our hearts, we will not be able to prepare the soil of our hearts to receive the seed of God's Word. Our hearts will be filled with rocks of resentment and roots of bitterness.

Whenever we look down on another person, we need to ask the Holy Spirit to shine a light on our hearts. If we gossip and criticize others, we have a root of pride in our hearts. Our speech always reveals what is in our hearts. (See Matthew 12:34.) We will reap what we sow. The very judgments we make upon others will be exactly the judgments that will come upon us. (See Matthew 7:1–2.) This morning ask the Holy Spirit to examine your heart, and if He reveals roots of pride, ask for Jesus to cleanse you.

Holy Spirit, shine Your light on my heart, and show me if there is any wicked pride in my heart. Cleanse me and renew a right spirit within me.

Evening Watch: Read Psalm 31:19–24. We need courage these days. The threat of terrorism or nuclear attack is real. David faced one battle after another, and I am sure he was terrified at times. However, he was able to overcome his fear and terror whenever he pictured himself in the safety of God's special pavilion. That pavilion was the presence of the Lord. The Lord was truly his hiding place where he could find peace in the midst of great trouble. He exhorted us to discover that secret hiding place, and he told us how to remain in it when he wrote, "Oh, love the LORD, all you His saints! For the LORD preserves the faithful, And fully repays the proud person. Be of good courage, And He shall strengthen your heart, All you who hope in the LORD" (vv. 23–24).

There are two conditions we must fulfill if we want to remain in the Lord's secret hiding place. First, we must love Him, and second, we must place all of our hopes in Him.

In 1990 the Lord woke me up and gave me a word that changed my whole family. He told me that He had opened the floodgates. There would be a flood of evil and a flood of good in the days ahead. He said that only those who hide themselves in Him by putting their trust and hope in Him would find safety from the flood of evil.

Lord, I put my trust and hope in You.

August 12

Morning Wisdom: Read Proverbs 21:5–7. We talked yesterday about how we are like farmers who are tending the Lord's fields. We plow, sow, and reap. When we break up the fallow ground of our hearts by clearing out the rocks of pride and the roots of bitterness, resentment, and unforgiveness, the seed of God's Word will be planted deep in the soil of our hearts.

Proverbs 21:5 says, "The plans of the diligent lead surely to plenty, But those of everyone who is hasty, surely to poverty." If we are diligent in the preparation of the soil of our hearts, we can look forward to a good harvest.

Proverbs 21:6–7 describes the plowing of the wicked. The wicked get treasures by lying, and they refuse to do justice. David said that he was envious when he saw the prosperity of the wicked, because they were at ease and increased in riches. (See Psalm 73:3, 12). However, when he went into God's sanctuary he understood the end of the wicked. They would one day be cast down and destroyed. (See Psalm 73:17–19.) Both the wicked and the just will reap what they sow.

Lord, help me to be a diligent farmer in Your fields.

Evening Watch: Read Psalm 32:1–11. We have learned through our readings this year that we cannot hide from God.

God is able to invade every secret room in our hearts. He knows if we have deceit in our spirit and secret sins in our hearts. Verse 1 tells us that we will be blessed when our sins are forgiven. Let's take a tour this evening through the rooms of our own hearts.

First we see Jesus sitting by the fire in the library of our hearts. He is there every morning. He waits eagerly to have fellowship with us. He hopes we will take the Bible off the library shelf and read it. He wants to warm our hearts with the fire of His love and ignite our hearts with the firepower of His Spirit. The scene continues and Jesus walks toward the closet. Jesus asks us to open the door, and we stand in His way. Without any condemnation in His voice, Jesus says, "I know there are some dark, dirty things in this closet. Won't you open the door and let Me help you clean it out?" We begin to weep, because we see that all Jesus wants to do is remove darkness and filth out of our closets filled with sin. Will you open the closet door of your heart tonight and ask Jesus to cleanse your heart from all hidden sins?

Lord, shine Your light on my heart and reveal my sins.

AUGUST 13

Morning Wisdom: Read Proverbs 21:8–10. Throughout this chapter in Proverbs we see the devastation wickedness causes in this life. It is easy for us to read these proverbs and not be convicted about the wickedness in our own hearts. However, Jeremiah wrote, "The heart is deceitful above all things, And desperately wicked; Who can know it?" (Jer. 17:9). We can deceive ourselves to such an extent that we are blinded to the sin in our lives. We have minds that are capable of excusing every sin and reasoning away the convicting power of the Holy Spirit. As we read these verses about the wicked, I suggest that we not look down at the wicked. Instead, we should look up to God and pray, *Lord, reveal any wickedness in my own heart.* You may want to join me as I confess my sins.

Proverbs 21:8 says, "The way of a guilty man is perverse; But as for the pure, his work is right." I have to ask myself, *Have I ever been bound by condemnation and guilt about something I did or said?* Jesus died to forgive me of my sins, and when I confess my sins He forgives and cleanses me. *Forgive me, Lord, for being burdened with guilt.*

Proverbs 21:9 is a verse that challenges me not to allow strife to rule my life.

I do not want to be that contentious woman who corners her husband and her family through manipulation and nagging. *Forgive me, Lord, for the times I have been contentious.*

When I read Proverbs 21:10, I was convicted about the many times I have complained and murmured about our next-door neighbors. This verse clearly states that a wicked person will always find fault with his neighbor. *Forgive me, Lord, for my murmuring and complaining.*

Evening Watch: Read Psalm 33:1–11. This morning we cleaned our spiritual houses and asked the Lord to forgive us of several sins. It is good to have "confession sessions" with the Lord. These are times that benefit us. God already knows our sins, but He wants us to recognize our sins so that we can confess them and receive both forgiveness and cleansing.

Nothing will rob us of our joy quicker than willfully living in sin. The moment, however, that we confess and repent of our sins, the joy of our salvation is restored. Psalm 33:1 says, "Rejoice in the LORD, O you righteous! For praise from the upright is beautiful." If you are having difficulty entering into praise, it might be time to do a heart cleaning. Ask the Lord to show you what you need to confess. Confession truly is good for the soul, and it will change both your inner heart and beautify and lighten your outer countenance.

Lord, search my heart.

Nehemiah 7:61–9:21; 1 Corinthians 9:1–19; Psalm 33:12–22; Proverbs 21:11–12

Morning Wisdom: Read Proverbs 21:11–12. Verse 11 promises that scoffers will be punished, and verse 12 says that the wicked will be overthrown for their wickedness. When others criticize and even scoff at us, we must be careful not to judge our accusers or those who mock and scoff at us. We need to recognize that the people who come against us are not our enemies. Paul revealed to us who our true enemies are when he wrote, "We do not wrestle against flesh and blood, but against principalities, against powers, against the rulers of the darkness of this age, against spiritual hosts of wickedness in the heavenly places" (Eph. 6:12). The accuser of the brethren is Satan, and he uses people to voice his accusations.

We will be wise when we do not allow the voices of our accusers to drown out the voice of the Lord, who gives us the wisdom, knowledge, and instructions needed to complete every task. Satan's strategy is always to deceive and distract. When Satan tries to gain a toehold in our lives through the accusations and judgments of others, we need to resist him by saying out loud, "No weapon that is formed against me will prosper, and I condemn every word of judgment against me. My righteousness is of the Lord." (See Isaiah 54:17.) Satan would love for us to become bitter against our critics, but if we do we have fallen into his trap.

Lord, help me to release all judgments to You.

Evening Watch: Read Psalm 33:12–22. Just recently we experienced a successful shuttle mission and return. When the astronauts were being interviewed, many of them commented about how beautiful the earth is. The view God has from His dwelling place in heaven is not only beautiful, but it is also detailed. God definitely has more than 20/20 vision. He can see the hairs on our heads and even what is in our hearts. This psalm says, "He fashions their hearts individually" (v. 15). This fact is beyond my finite comprehension.

God's eyes are especially upon those who fear Him. Verse 18 says, "Behold, the eye of the LORD is on those who fear Him, On those who hope in His mercy" (v. 18). We can rejoice because we know that God is watching out for us. He is able to deliver our souls from death and keep us alive in famine. (See v. 19.) God truly is our help and our shield. (See v. 20.) I cannot help but think of those who are suffering great famine in Africa right now. Many of these people do not know that God can help them. I am challenged to pray for those who are starving both physically and spiritually.

Lord, be a shield and help for those who are experiencing famine.

AUGUST 15

Nehemiah 9:22–10:39; 1 Corinthians 9:20–10:14; Psalm 34:1–10; Proverbs 21:13

Morning Wisdom: Read Proverbs 21:13. This very day our city is considering a law that will prohibit people from begging on our streets. I am praying that this city ordinance will not pass, because I feel our city will be shutting their ears to the cry of the poor. Proverbs 21:13 says, "Whoever shuts his ears to the cry of the poor Will also cry himself and not be heard." Panhandlers can annoy people on the street, but I believe they are guaranteed freedom of speech in our constitution.

It is important that we hear from the Holy Spirit when people request money. Sometimes when we give money to others, we only enable them to remain unemployed. However, many times people are just without funds temporarily because of the loss of a job or other circumstances. I can remember when a lady who worked for a Christian organization called me to ask for money since she was short at the end of the month. As I prayed, the Lord spoke to my heart to tell her to come to my house and get whatever groceries she might need. She did and continued to do this whenever she ran short of funds. She thought I ran a food pantry, but my pantry had been opened just for her. At this time we had a Chinese daughter who lived with us. Whenever I told her my friend was coming to get groceries from the basement, she ran quickly downstairs to gather up all her favorite food items so my friend would not take them. I hope her actions would not be considered closing your ear to the poor. We will always have the poor with us, but as much as possible I believe we should never shut our ears to their cries.

Lord, help me to answer the cries of the poor.

Evening Watch: Read Psalm 34:1–10. We spoke earlier about how living in sin darkens our countenance. This psalm tells us that those who look to the Lord will be radiant, and their faces will never show shame. (See v. 5.) Our countenance will also be darkened if we do not hear and answer the cry of the poor. We learned this lesson this morning.

The key to living a joyful, fruitful life is to praise Him at all times and look to Him for help when we are in need. (See v. 1.) Our lives will count for the Lord when we count on Him. We walk in the fear of the Lord when we trust the Lord with all of our hearts, refuse to lean on our own understanding, and magnify the Lord in both our words and actions. When we walk in the fear of the Lord, the angels of the Lord will encamp around us. We will never lack anything, and we will see long and fruitful days.

Keep me in the fear of the Lord tomorrow and every day.

AUGUST 16

Nehemiah 11:1–12:26; 1 Cor. 10:15–11:2; Psalm 34:11–22; Proverbs 21:14–16

Morning Wisdom: Read Proverbs 24:14–16. These three verses challenge us to be people of integrity who walk in the way of understanding. Proverbs 14 speaks about the types of gifts we should give. If we give a gift as a bribe to gain favor, that gift will cause strong wrath when someone discovers what was done.

Jesus exhorts us to give our charitable gifts in secret with the promise that His Father will reward us openly. (See Matthew 6:4.) Proverbs 21:14 says, "A gift in secret pacifies anger."

I am so thankful for the Holy Spirit, who enables us to walk in the way of understanding. When we walk justly and with understanding we will always be joyful.

Those who lack understanding will encounter destruction. (See vv. 15–16.) Today I am challenged to ask for the spirit of understanding to flow through me so that I can do justly, love mercy, and walk humbly with my God. (See Micah 6:8.)

Lord, help me to be a person of integrity.

Evening Watch: Read Psalm 34:11–22. This morning we learned how important it is for us to walk in the ways of the Lord. When we walk in the ways of the Lord, we will walk in truth and understanding. We will be able to keep our tongue from evil and our lips from speaking lies. The ways of the Lord are ways of peace, healing, and deliverance. This psalm presents some powerful promises to those who walk in God's truths and who remain on His righteous path. When we walk in the light and in the fear of the Lord we are promised:

- provision;
- prayer lives that are effective;
- peace of mind and heart;
- protection and deliverance;
- preservation—long lives.

Lord, help me to always walk in Your ways.

AUGUST 17

Morning Wisdom: Read Proverbs 21:17–18. Gas prices are soaring. At first there was no effect on the economy, but now people who are wise are trading their gas-guzzlers in and finding other means of transportation to go to work. Many are carpooling. Those who are wise are also drastically cutting the entertainment portion of their budget. Those who are rich usually do not tighten the belt of their spending. They continue to enjoy the pleasures of life and love to wine and dine. The time will come, however, when they could lose everything. Proverbs 21:17 says, "He who loves pleasure will be a poor man; He who loves wine and oil will not be rich." The wine we should seek is the new wine of the Holy Spirit. The oil we should seek is the anointing of the Holy Spirit. When we seek after the Holy Spirit's wine and oil, we will always be rich, and we will prosper in those things we set our hands to do.

Proverbs 21:18 talks about how the wicked and unfaithful will be a ransom for the righteous and upright. A ransom is paid to gain back something that was lost. When we walk uprightly we may suffer loss for a season, but the promise of God is that whatever Satan has stolen from us will be repaid to us seven times. (See Proverbs 6:31.) Jesus has already paid the ransom that guarantees we will have all that has been stolen from us returned to us either in this life or the next.

Lord, thank You for Your restoration power.

Evening Watch: Read Psalm 35:1–16. We have an Advocate, an accuser, and an adversary in this life. Our Advocate is Jesus Christ and our accuser and adversary is Satan. Sometimes I picture a court scene before the throne room of God. Satan, the accuser of the brethren, continually accuses us before the throne of God, but our Advocate, Jesus Christ, pleads our case before the Father. David probably imagined this scene when he wrote, "Plead my cause, O LORD, with those who strive with me; Fight against those who fight against me. Take hold of shield and buckler, And stand up for my help" (vv. 1–2). He continued throughout this psalm to describe ways the Lord could come against his enemies.

David was confident that the Lord would come to his aid. David said that he was able to rejoice in the midst of adversity, because he knew the Lord would do battle for him. I'm sure James remembered David's words in this psalm when he exhorted us to count it all joy when various trials happen in our lives. (See James 1:2.) We can have joy in the midst of trials when we know our Advocate, Jesus Christ, will do battle for us.

Lord, thank You for being my Advocate.

AUGUST 18

Esther 1:1–3:15; 1 Corinthians 11:17–34; Psalm 35:17–28; Proverbs 21:19–20

Morning Wisdom: Read Proverbs 21:19–20. Proverbs has much to say about women. Proverbs 31 describes the virtuous woman. Proverbs 7 describes the immoral woman. This chapter of Proverbs includes two verses about contentious women. Proverbs 21:19 says, "Better to dwell in the wilderness, Than with a contentious and angry woman."

I have a theory that contention is caused by tension. Whenever people are tense and their nerves are on edge, they can easily become contentious. It is a woman's responsibility to set a peaceful, loving atmosphere in the home. During a busy day a career woman or even a homemaker will encounter many circumstances that can cause her to be tense and anxious. We are wise when we take time during our days to relax and get a fresh infilling of the oil of the Holy Spirit's anointing so our nerves will not be on edge when we interact with others. Our family members are treasures who deserve to have a home where the Lord's peace reigns. We are called to be peacemakers also in our workplaces.

Proverbs 21:20 says that oil is in the dwelling place of the righteous. When the oil of the Holy Spirit is flowing freely in our homes and workplaces, peace and joy will abound.

Lord, help me to see my family and others as Your treasures.

Evening Watch: Read Psalm 35:17–28. We talked this morning about the contentious woman. David was surrounded with contentious enemies who strove continually to defeat him. Pride is the source of all contention, and prideful Saul sought David's life because he was jealous. David cried out to the Lord to cause the proud who came against him to be ashamed and brought to confusion. David had many physical enemies, but he had many more spiritual enemies—demonic spirits that sought to kill him.

David cried out, "Let the LORD be magnified Who has pleasure in the prosperity of His servant" (v. 27). The Lord takes no pleasure in watching ungodly men do wicked things to the righteous. He takes no pleasure in seeing demonic spirits try to oppress our souls. Our holy Father took pleasure, however, when He saw His Son become the perfect sacrifice for our sins when He died on the cross. On the day Jesus died, our Father was magnified in all the earth, and the enemy was defeated. The way for our souls to prosper was purchased on that day.

Lord, thank You for dying for me.

AUGUST 19

Esther 4:1–7:10; 1 Corinthians 12:1–26; Psalm 36:1–12; Proverbs 21:21–22

Morning Wisdom: Read Proverbs 21:21–22. Don't we all want to live righteous lives that bring honor to the Lord? Proverbs 21:21 reveals how we can obtain such a life. We simply have to follow righteousness and mercy. Jesus said, "Blessed are the merciful, For they shall obtain mercy" (Matt. 5:7). Psalm 23 promised us that our Good Shepherd would lead us in paths of righteousness for His name's sake. (See Psalm 23:3.) When we follow righteousness and mercy we will not only obtain mercy, honor, and an abundant life filled with love, joy, and peace, but we will also be able to pull down every stronghold in our lives. (See Proverbs 21:22.) I don't know about you, but this knowledge makes me want to shout, "Hallelujah!"

> *Lord, thank You for clothing me in Your righteousness and for giving me the authority to pull down every stronghold in my life.*

Evening Watch: Read Psalm 36:1–12. Some people are scared of heights, and many are afraid to fly. I believe if they read this psalm, their fears would leave. Whenever I have to fly I quote Psalm 36:5–6:

> Your mercy, O LORD, is in the heavens; Your faithfulness reaches to the clouds.

As I quote these verses, I picture the mighty hand of God reaching through the clouds to support my plane.

I did not always feel that way. I can remember when my husband was considering taking the whole family on a trip to Israel. My prayer partner just happened to call before the final decision about this trip was made. She said she had a beautiful dream about our family. She saw my husband and me dressed in white with crowns on our heads. We were riding in a chariot. You would think a dream like that would make me rejoice, but it paralyzed me with fear. I knew our plane was going to go down into the ocean and we all would perish. I wrestled with this fear for several weeks and even told my husband that he could go on to Israel with the two oldest boys. I told him that I would be happy to stay behind with the youngest child.

One day when I was driving the perimeter road, I heard what I knew was the Lord's voice. He said, "Where does fear come from?" I thought for a moment and realized that God never sends the spirit of fear. Then I heard, "The devil is trying to rob you of a great blessing." I gave my fears to the Lord at that moment and went to Israel.

The plane ride was uneventful, and I enjoyed it. The blessing came when I saw my husband and two oldest sons baptized in the Jordan River. Don't ever allow fear to rob you of the blessings of the Lord.

> *Lord, I give You all my fears.*

Morning Wisdom: Read Proverbs 21:23–24. Verse 23 says, "Whoever guards his mouth and tongue Keeps his soul from troubles." We can trouble our own souls by what we say. When we talk we have to be aware that there are more listening ears than we can see with our natural eyes. Demonic spirits are also listening to our conversations to gather information that they can later use as ammunition against us. Satan cannot read our minds, but he has familiar spirits and other spirits that have the assignment to listen to what we say. God is also listening to our conversations. In fact, whenever we speak about the Lord, it is recorded in a book of remembrance in heaven. (See Malachi 3:16.)

Proverbs 21:24 describes the scoffer. We are warned in Psalms 1 not to sit in the seat of the scornful. Scoffers have a spirit of pride, and they are ultracritical of everything and everyone. Whenever we speak critical, judgmental words we are in pride. Before you open your mouth today, you might want to consider all the listening ears that are tuned to your conversation, and you also may want to confess any pride you may have in your heart.

Lord, help me to guard my mouth.

Evening Watch: Read Psalm 37:1–11. This is one of my favorite psalms, because it reveals what our part is and what God's part is to produce a fruitful life. We all want to live fruitful, meaningful lives, but so often we fail to understand how we can cooperate with the Holy Spirit to make this happen in our lives.

This psalm lists seven things we can do to cooperate with the Holy Spirit as He performs God's will and produces fruit in our lives. We are instructed to:

- trust in the Lord;
- delight ourselves in the Lord;
- commit our way to the Lord;
- rest in the Lord;
- wait patiently for Him;
- refrain from being anxious or fretful;
- cease from anger.

If we will be faithful to do these seven things, God will be faithful to grant the desires of our hearts, and He will also increase our fruitfulness. I like to think of these seven instructions as the "magnificent seven," because when we follow these instructions the Lord will be magnified in our lives.

Lord, help me to do these seven things daily.

August 21

Morning Wisdom: Read Proverbs 21:25–26. There are two types of people in the world—dreamers and doers. Proverbs 21:25–26 says, "The desire of the lazy man kills him, For his hands refuse to labor. He covets greedily all day long, But the righteous gives and does not spare." When I read this, I pictured a man laid back in his easy chair with his feet propped up. He was watching TV, and with each commercial greedily exclaimed, "I just have to have that." He continued to dream about all the things he could have if he had the money, but he was unwilling to work to earn that money.

When we are lazy we suffer physically and spiritually. We know that if we refuse to exercise, soon our bodies will become flabby, and we even run the risk of having our muscles atrophy. You know the old saying, "If you don't use it, you will lose it."

If we refuse to use the God-given abilities we have to make a living and to have enough to give to others, we will begin to die spiritually. God is a giver, and He has designed us to be givers. When we are generous givers God will provide all the resources we need to give even more. God is able to give us more than we could ever think, hope, or imagine. He wants to fulfill our dreams, but He cannot fulfill our dreams when we are lazy. God loves for us to dream His dreams, but He also requires us to do our part to fulfill those dreams.

Lord, help me to resist being lazy.

Evening Watch: Read Psalm 37:12–28. David often compared the wicked to the righteous in his psalms. This psalm contains some revealing comparisons. Here are just a few:

- The small wealth of a righteous man is worth much more than the riches of many wicked men.
- God upholds the righteous man, but He breaks the arm of the wicked.
- The inheritance of the righteous will be forever, but the wicked shall perish.
- The wicked borrows and never repays, but the righteous gives.
- The wicked receive curses, but the righteous receive blessings.
- The wicked are cut off, but the righteous are preserved.

The steps of the righteous will be directed by the Lord, and he will never be cast down, because the Lord will uphold him. The righteous will never be forsaken. These comparisons make me so grateful that God enabled me to become righteous in His sight, because I received the righteousness of His Son Jesus Christ.

Lord, thank You for becoming sin for me so that I might become righteous in God's sight.

Morning Wisdom: Read Proverbs 21:27. We talked yesterday about how God has designed us to be givers. Some people can be givers, but the intents of their hearts do not please God. If we give with the intent to gain favor from God, the motivation of our hearts is wrong. Proverbs 21:27 reads, "The sacrifice of the wicked is an abomination; How much more when he brings it with wicked intent!" God is not impressed with our gifts. He is impressed with what is in our hearts. A giving heart is a heart that has been filled with the love of God. Only the Holy Spirit has the ability to shed the love of God abroad in our hearts. (See Romans 5:5.)

If we have roots of bitterness and resentment in our hearts, our gifts are not acceptable to the Lord. We cannot win favor from God by our gift giving if we have unforgiving hearts.

Lord, help me to give with the right heart motivation.

Evening Watch: Read Psalm 37:29–40. When the law of love is in our hearts our gifts will be acceptable to God, and we will be protected from falling away. I am convinced that if Christians were rooted and grounded in the love of Jesus Christ, they would never fall away. If our hearts are cluttered with the rocks of pride, bitterness, or resentment, the love of God will not be able to take root deeply in the soil of our hearts.

David had seen the wicked prosper and often wondered why they did, but he concluded that the wicked would ultimately be judged for their deeds. He knew one day the wicked would be cut off, but those who had the law of love written on their hearts would be exalted to inherit the land. He declared that the future of the blameless man is peace. (See v. 37.)

David was not a man of peace, but he experienced the inner peace of God even after he sinned grievously because he knew the Lord forgave him. God removed David's transgressions and sins after David humbled himself, confessed his sins, and repented of them. David also experienced the strength of the Lord in his troubled times, and he knew God's delivering power. When we confess our sins and trust in the Lord to forgive us we will be at peace because the guilt and condemnation will be removed. We will be able to experience perfect peace daily no matter what trouble we may encounter tomorrow or in the days to come.

Lord, may I always trust in You.

August 23

Morning Wisdom: Read Proverbs 21:28–29. The comparisons between the wicked and the righteous man are woven throughout the book of Proverbs. Proverbs 21:29 says, "A wicked man hardens his face, But as for the upright, he establishes his way." The willful flesh within us sometimes causes our faces to harden toward others. If we remain with hard hearts, we follow our own way rather than God's way. Our way leads to destruction.

The wicked man continues on the sure path of destruction, because he hardens his face and resists the will of God. However, the steps of a good man are both ordered and established by the Lord. (See Psalm 37:23.) We can trust Jesus, our Good Shepherd, to keep us on the righteous path if we yield our will to Him daily. He will use the Word of God as His rod of correction to get us back on the path He has prepared for us to travel. Jesus will use His staff, the Holy Spirit, to convict us when we choose to go our own way temporarily. Once we have chosen to commit our lives to the Good Shepherd, He will move heaven and Earth to keep us moving forward on the path He has prepared for us.

Lord, thank You for keeping me on Your path. I yield my will to You today.

Evening Watch: Read Psalm 38:1–22. David was greatly distressed when he wrote this psalm. He felt like God had pressed him down because of his iniquities. He was overwhelmed by the flood of guilt and shame. Even his body manifested the destruction caused by his own foolishness. He said, "There is no…health in my bones Because of my sin" (v. 3). He added, "My wounds are foul and festering Because of my foolishness" (v. 5), and "My loins are full of inflammation" (v. 7). Some scholars think David had a venereal disease. This is only a theory, but we do know that sin brings destruction upon both our physical and spiritual lives.

The good news is that David knew what to do with his sin. He knew to confess his sin to God and repent of his foolish ways. David wrote, "I will declare my iniquity; I will be in anguish over my sin" (v. 18). David was a man after God's own heart, because he grieved over his own sin. He mourned before God. David's godly sorrow brought him to repentance. Perhaps the body of Christ today needs to grieve, mourn, and weep when we go our own way instead of God's way.

Lord, forgive me for my willful sins.

Morning Wisdom: Read Proverbs 21:30–31. The anointing of the Holy Spirit described in Isaiah 11:2 includes the spirit of wisdom, understanding, and counsel. Isaiah 11:2 reads:

> The Spirit of the LORD shall rest upon Him, The Spirit of wisdom and understanding, The Spirit of counsel and might, The Spirit of knowledge and of the fear of the LORD.

Proverbs 21:30 says, "There is no wisdom or understanding Or counsel against the LORD." Whenever we are determined to have our own way, we refuse the wisdom, understanding, and counsel that the Holy Spirit can give us.

Lord, help me to be more dependent upon Your anointing.

Evening Watch: Read Psalm 39:1–13. My husband tried to keep a vow of silence for one day. He was unable to fulfill that vow. The reason why he decided to do this was because he wanted desperately for the Lord to cleanse his speech and put the law of kindness upon his tongue. He felt he had offended others by some of the things he had said.

David must have felt the same way when he wrote, "I will guard my ways, Lest I sin with my tongue; I will restrain my mouth with a muzzle" (v. 1). No matter how much we try, we all are so weak in our flesh, and that unruly member called the tongue can wound others. David recognized how frail his flesh was, and he asked the Lord to allow him to know his end. David expressed what we all feel when we grow older when he wrote, "Every man at his best state is but vapor" (v. 5). He talked about how we busy ourselves day by day, but our days in God's sight are only a handbreadth. David expressed that his only hope was in the Lord. Without Jesus we would have no hope in this life or the next.

Lord, help me to depend upon You more as I live each day.

Job 16:1–19:29; 1 Corinthians 16:1–24; Psalm 40:1–10; Proverbs 22:1

Morning Wisdom: Read Proverbs 22:1. I was just speaking to a friend this morning who has been divorced for several years. She has a great need for loving favor in her life. Proverbs 22:1 reads, "A good name is to be chosen rather than great riches, Loving favor rather than silver and gold."

There is a great need in every person's life to daily have others praise them and to appreciate their unique value in this world. When people live alone, they miss having a warm voice greet them in the morning. They miss hearing the praise of someone from the opposite sex who thinks they are beautiful. I believe the body of Christ falls short in recognizing the needs of those who live alone.

Single women especially need single men friends in their lives who they feel are safe and who will take them out for an occasional dinner and movie. Sometimes we forget that Jesus was single, and He experienced lonely times. However, Jesus was careful to surround Himself with many women friends, and those friends knew they could trust Jesus because of His purity. His women friends added richness to His life, and He was able to make them feel like they were of great value. We should pray more for the singles in our churches and ask the Holy Spirit ways we can show them loving favor.

Lord, help me to reach out more to those who are lonely.

Evening Watch: Read Psalm 40:1–10. As I read this psalm I recalled that we sang a song that included verse 3 of Psalm 40. We joyfully sang together the verse, "He has put a new song in my mouth—Praise to our God; Many will see it and fear, And will trust in the LORD." Something I love to do in the morning is sing to the Lord. He is faithful to give me many new songs as I begin to sing to Him. I start my worship time in the morning by singing some of my favorite hymns, and then I continue to sing the melody of those hymns using the new words the Holy Spirit sings to me.

I believe Jesus had one of the most beautiful voices any man on Earth could have. Even though the gospels do not include His songs, I believe He sang many songs. Many of the psalms David wrote are probably songs Jesus sings in heaven now. The Bible tells us that God rejoices over us with singing.

You might want to try singing to the Lord tomorrow, and then step out in faith and wait to hear the new song He will sing to your heart. Join the melody in your heart, and begin to voice those new words. You'll be amazed how the Holy Spirit will rejoice over you with singing.

Lord, give me new songs in my heart.

AUGUST 26

Morning Wisdom: Read Proverbs 22:2–4. In my first devotional book, *Around the Word in 365 Days*, I highlighted this reading for August 26. I talked about the benefits of humility. Proverbs 22:4 says, "By humility and the fear of the LORD Are riches and honor and life."

All of us want to have riches, honor, and an abundant life. The riches spoken of here do not necessarily mean monetary wealth. However, I believe if we humble ourselves and have a heart that desires to obey the Lord, we will always be prosperous. My definition of prosperity is having enough to meet your own needs and enough to sow into God's kingdom here on Earth.

Proverbs 22:2 says, "The rich and the poor have this in common, The LORD is the maker of them all." In our travels throughout the world, some of the richest people I have met have been the poorest monetarily. The wealth we have as joint heirs with Christ does not compare with the monetary wealth the world offers. I can remember a poor Mexican Christian talking about giving his one and only blanket to an elderly woman, because her body was so frail that she could not maintain warmth. This Mexican man was one of the most joyful Christians I ever met. I believe God allows the poor to be always with us simply because He wants us to enter into His joy by sharing what we have with them.

Proverbs 22:3 says, "A prudent man foresees evil and hides himself, But the simple pass on and are punished." We are prudent when our ears are tuned to the Holy Spirit, who often warns us about the days ahead. There will be troubled days ahead, because we are entering the period in history that Jesus called "the beginning of sorrows." (See Matthew 24:8.) Jesus will be our Provider and Protector in the days ahead. Be sure to listen carefully to the Holy Spirit in the days ahead.

Holy Spirit, help me to hear and heed Your warnings.

Evening Watch: Read Psalm 40:11–17. We talked this morning about the treacherous times we live in today. It would be impossible for us to live a life free from fear. Fears will always try to overtake us as they did David, but David knew what to do when he was afraid. The moment he felt fear, he cried out to the Lord. David cried out, "Innumerable evils have surrounded me; My iniquities have overtaken me, so that I am not able to look up; They are more than the hairs of my head; Therefore my heart fails me" (v. 12). What a desperate cry! We have all experienced days when fear came knocking on the door of our hearts. The Bible tells us that men's hearts will fail them because of fear in these last days.

Our hearts will not fail us if we give our fears to the Lord. We need to remember His promise to deliver us out of affliction. "Fear not" is an exhortation that is given over 365 times in the Bible. We can follow that exhortation daily when we give all of our fears to the Lord.

Lord, when I am afraid I will trust in You.

AUGUST 27

Morning Wisdom: Read Proverbs 22:5–6. Proverbs 22:5 reads, "Thorns and snares are in the way of the perverse; He who guards his soul will be far from them." We all have thorns in our flesh that provide Satan with the opportunity to tempt us and lead us astray. Jesus shared in the parable of the sower about the seed that never brought fruit to maturity. Listen to His words:

> The ones that fell among thorns are those who, when they have heard, go out and are choked with cares, riches, and pleasures of life, and bring no fruit to maturity.
>
> —LUKE 8:14

John described the three lusts that are like thorns in our flesh when he wrote:

> For all that is in the world—the lust of the flesh, the lust of the eyes, and the pride of life—is not of the Father but is of the world.
>
> —1 JOHN 2:16

The lust of the flesh is seeking to pleasure our five senses in an indulgent way. The lust of the eyes is covetousness that causes us to have vain imaginations and greedy longings in our minds. The lust of the pride of life is trusting in ourselves more than we trust in God. We do not have to be a perverse person to be led astray by our own lusts. This is why we need to guard our souls.

Proverbs 22:6 instructs us to "Train up a child in the way he should go, And when he is old he will not depart from it." The seed of God's Word lay dormant in the lives of two of our sons when they experienced a season of rebellion, but the water of the Holy Spirit later caused that seed to bear fruit. We should be challenged to keep sowing God's Word into lives. Even though it may seem that the seed of God's Word does not take root, it is still there, and the day will come when it will spring up and bear fruit.

Lord, help me to be faithful to sow Your Word.

Evening Watch: Read Psalm 41:1–13. David did not have an easy life. His life was one of fright and flight. Even his closest friends betrayed him and accused him. How was David able to remain faithful and fruitful? David learned what to do when he felt despair. He reviewed his past and saw God's faithfulness to deliver him. He spoke of God's sustaining and delivering power in this psalm. Somehow when we review God's faithfulness, hope and faith are stirred within us, and we can enter into the joy of the Lord despite the circumstances.

Lord, thank You for Your faithfulness!

Job 28:1–30:31; 2 Corinthians 2:9–17; Psalm 42:1–11; Proverbs 22:7

Morning Wisdom: Read Proverbs 22:7. It says, "The borrower is servant to the lender." We have a nation filled with servants. The availability of credit today invites people to incur a lot of debt. One financial adviser counsels people to take all of their credit cards, put them on a cookie sheet, and melt them in the oven. This is good advice, because when we do not pay our monthly balance on credit cards, the interest incurred can be astronomical.

The Bible tells us to "owe no one anything except to love one another" (Rom. 13:8). When we become servants to the lenders we are distracted from being servants of the Lord. Our thoughts can become occupied with getting out of debt, and our minds are no longer stayed upon the Lord. We lose our joy, because our emotions become filled with the fear that we may never get out of debt. When we incur debt, we need to transfer that burden to the Lord quickly and ask Him to reveal the steps we can take to begin to cancel that debt. Once we get our focus on the Lord and not on the debt, His joy will give us the strength to overcome the feelings of fear and frustration.

Lord, thank You for paying my debt on the cross.

Evening Watch: Read Psalm 42:1–11. David was a man after God's own heart, because he never gave up. We discussed yesterday how his life was filled with challenges and trials. His soul would be disquieted from time to time, but David knew how to encourage himself in the Lord.

Psalms 42–72 are contemplations of the sons of Korah. Many of these psalms reveal the secret to overcoming "soul slump days." We are exhorted in this psalm to pour out our souls to the Lord when negative feelings flood our souls. We are encouraged to remember the majesty and power of God, who floods us with loving-kindness. After we pour out our souls, we can sing to our God and pray. (See v. 8.) As we praise the Lord anyhow, those "soul slump days" become "soul jump days" when our spirits are uplifted to reign over our souls. We enter the faith realm instead of the feeling realm, and joy is restored to our souls. If you are having a "soul slump day," remind your soul to hope in God.

Thank You for showing me how to overcome my "soul slump days."

August 29

Job 31:1–22:33; 2 Corinthians 3:1–18; Psalm 43:1–5; Proverbs 22:8–9

Morning Wisdom: Read Proverbs 22:8–9. Verse 8 says, "He who sows iniquity will reap sorrow, And the rod of his anger will fail." *Iniquity* means gross injustice or wickedness. Iniquity is sin, and sin is what stands between us and God.

Psalm 66:18 says, "If I regard iniquity in my heart, The Lord will not hear." When we do not confess our iniquities and hide them in our hearts, we cannot experience the full power of God in our lives. Our prayers will go unanswered, and there will be a lack of victory in our lives. Ephesians 5:3–7 lists the iniquities that will hinder our spiritual growth. Ephesians 8 exhorts us to walk as children of the light.

Our own iniquities can affect generations to come. (See Exodus 34:7.) This is why it is so important for us to confess our sins and to receive God's forgiveness and cleansing. We do not want to sow iniquity into future generations. Proverbs 22:9 tells us how we can sow blessings and not curses upon future generations. Proverbs 22:9 says, "He who has a generous eye will be blessed, For he gives of his bread to the poor." Whenever we are generous in our giving, especially to the poor, we will experience God's blessings, and those blessings can be passed on to future generations.

Lord, show me today anything I may need to confess to You.

Evening Watch: Read Psalm 43:1–5. This psalm continues the exhortation to hope in God and to praise Him no matter what we are experiencing in this life. I just received a call from Beijing. Our Chinese daughter, who lived with us for five years, called to tell us that her father's lung cancer has spread. I am so thankful that her father accepted the Lord when he visited us for six months in America. Now her father has more than just earthly hope. He has the eternal hope that will carry him right into heaven, should he not recover from his illness. We are praying, however, that he will be healed.

This morning as we talked with our Chinese daughter, we told her that her whole family would feel the prayers of many in the United States. She shared how God had shown her to transfer the victories of the past to this situation. God is faithful all the time to come to our aid no matter what we may experience tomorrow. God is the God of yesterday, tomorrow, and eternity. His faithfulness will never fail, and this is why we can lift our voices in praise and tell our souls to hope in the Lord.

Lord, I trust in Your faithfulness.

August 30

Morning Wisdom: Read Proverbs 22:10–12. In the August 20 devotional we learned that scoffers have a root of pride. Proverbs 22:10 says, "Cast out the scoffer, and contention will leave; Yes, strife and reproach will cease." Pride is the source of all contention. (See Proverbs 13:10.) If the scoffer is cast out, the contention and strife will cease. Whenever we get into strife, we need to examine ourselves to see if there is an area of pride in our own hearts.

We need to always be on the alert to resist pride, because when we are prideful we have two enemies. "God resists the proud, But gives grace to the humble" (James 4:6).

Satan also has an open door to harass us if we are prideful.

I heard the testimony of a drug addict who finally got delivered of drugs. He desperately wanted to stay clean the rest of his life. He asked the Lord to show him how he could daily cooperate with the Holy Spirit to enable him to never return to drugs. The Holy Spirit shared a strategy that we all could apply to our lives daily. He was led by the Holy Spirit every morning to remain in the position of praise. He said he lifted one hand to the Lord in surrender to His will and one hand to the Lord in trust in the power of the Holy Spirit to keep him from giving in to temptation. As he lifted both hands up to the Lord, he said, "Lord, I humble myself before You." You may have daily morning exercises that you do, but the spiritual exercise of humbling ourselves as this former drug addict did is one exercise that will keep pride from entering our souls. I am challenged to try this exercise this morning. Will you join me?

> *Lord, I lift one hand up to You in trust and one hand to You in surrender. I humble myself before You and praise You.*

Evening Watch: Read Psalm 44:1–7. This psalm exhorts us also to trust in the Lord. God's faithfulness to deliver Israel from their enemies is reviewed in this psalm. The declaration was made that only through the Lord's strength and delivering power was Israel able to conquer their enemies. Whenever we trust in our own strength we will fail. Tonight before you retire, make a list of the times you have experienced God's hand of deliverance in your own life.

> *Lord, help me to remember all the times You have delivered me and given me the strength to overcome my circumstances.*

Morning Wisdom: Read Proverbs 22:13. We all know the dangers of crying "wolf" too many times. When we do this, those around us will not pay any attention to us if we truly are in danger. This verse conveys another thought when it says, "The lazy man says, 'There is a lion outside! I shall be slain in the streets!'" When I read this verse I pictured a lazy man propped up in his easy chair saying, "There is a lion outside." This man makes no effort at all to get up out of his chair to lock his door to protect himself.

Peter warned us to be sober and vigilant, because our adversary the devil walks around like a roaring lion, seeking whom he may devour. (See 1 Peter 5:8.) We cannot afford to be lazy in our spiritual walk. We must resist the devil and stand steadfast in the faith. The moment we fail to discipline ourselves by reading God's Word and praying daily, we make ourselves vulnerable to the attacks of the enemy. Make it your aim today to submit yourself to God and to resist the devil.

Lord, forgive me for the times I have had a lazy spiritual life.

Evening Watch: Read Psalm 44:8–26. This psalm begins with this declaration:

In God we boast all day long, And praise Your name forever.

Instead of complaining about whatever we may encounter daily, it might be well for us to boast about what the Lord has done in the past. When we take time to look at what the Lord has done and begin to boast about it to others, we will be too busy to criticize, murmur, and complain to others.

Lord, I praise You for what You have done in my life.

Morning Wisdom: Read Proverbs 22:14. Years ago I had a haunting dream. This proverb reminded me of the dream. I saw young men standing around a trap door. Suddenly the trap door opened and these arms reached out and grabbed these men. They fell into this deep chasm. I approached the pit and looked into it. What I saw still chills me. There was a red hue coming from the pit and what looked like women's arms suddenly turned to flames.

Proverbs 22:14 reads, "The mouth of an immoral woman is a deep pit; He who is abhorred by the Lord will fall there." That is a hard word, but I believe the men who are seduced by immoral women are abhorred by the Lord. Why would the Lord abhor such men? God abhors any idolatry. He is a jealous God, and He desires for us to have no other gods in our lives. Sexual immorality is idolatry. Whenever we allow ourselves to be seduced to commit sexual sins, we are guilty of idolatry as well as adultery.

When we understand how serious it is to give in to the lust of the flesh or the lust of the eyes, we should have godly sorrow that will lead us to repent. However, too many who are involved with pornography or other sexual sins excuse themselves and say, "That's just a habit I have." Such a statement reveals that they have been deceived. Immoral actions today will affect generations to come. We need to confess our sins, grieve over them, and ask God's strength to overcome them.

I can remember praying for a young man who made a practice of going to houses of prostitution. Before I prayed for him I asked him if he hated that sin. He said he did, and he was delivered from that sin. We have to hate what we are doing before we can be set free. Pray for those you know who are hooked on pornography, and confront them with how grievous this sin is. You may be the only one who cares enough to confront or pray for them.

Lord, I pray for those who have fallen prey to seducing spirits.

Evening Watch: Read Psalm 45:1–17. God loves righteousness and hates wickedness. (See v. 7.) God's hatred of wickedness is a demonstration of His love toward us. He knows that if we are seduced by the wicked one, we will be in danger of losing everything. If we give in to temptation, we have opened the door to seducing spirits who will not give up easily.

Soon the toehold that Satan has in our lives will become a foothold, and finally a stronghold develops and we are deceived.

God desires to have princes and royal daughters. (See vv. 13, 16.) He desires to crown each one of us with His glory and gleaming robes of righteousness. This is why God is grieved when we miss the glory He has for us by remaining in willful sin. The King of glory holds the scepter of His righteousness out to you at this moment. All you have to do is turn away from the glitter of this world and receive the glory of His kingdom by holding on to that scepter.

Lord, help me to remain faithful.

September 2

Ecclesiastes 1:1–3:22; 2 Corinthians 6:1–13; Psalm 46:1–11; Proverbs 22:15

Morning Wisdom: Read Proverbs 22:15. Why is foolishness bound up in the heart of a child? We only have to observe a four- or five-year-old for a few minutes to discover that they lack wisdom. We have a grandson who believes he is invincible. We can all remember our childhood days when we thought we could fly, and some of us even used our superman capes as wings to try to jump off roofs. Proverbs 22:15 tells us that the rod will drive foolishness out of the heart of children.

When our three sons were young, we used a wooden spoon as a rod of discipline. I am still finding wooden spoons that my sons hid when they were children. We do not have to be children to do foolish things. I know I have done a few foolish things in my adult life. I am so thankful God does not use a wooden spoon to discipline me, but He does have a rod of correction. His rod of correction is the Bible. When we fail to obey God's Word, He may use another means of correction. Often He will allow circumstances to cause us to turn to Him and receive His correction. Frankly, I prefer to look into God's Word daily. His Word is designed to correct, reprove, and instruct me in righteousness. God's Word will prevent me from doing foolish things.

Lord, help me to discipline myself in Your Word so that I will not lack wisdom.

Evening Watch: Read Psalm 46:1–11. God has provided us a safe, unmovable place that we can run to in times of trouble. God's presence is our very present help in troubled times. We live in a day when more and more catastrophic events will be manifested on Earth. Jesus predicted these days when He warned, "There will be famines, pestilences, and earthquakes in various places. All these are the beginning of sorrows" (Matt. 24:7–8).

During these days we need to declare, "The LORD of hosts is with us; The God of Jacob is our refuge" (v. 7).

Thank You for being my refuge.

SEPTEMBER 3

Ecclesiastes 4:1–6:12; 2 Corinthians 6:14–7:6; Psalm 47:1–9; Proverbs 22:16

Morning Wisdom: Read Proverbs 22:16. Many warnings are given in the book of Proverbs about what will happen to us if we oppress the poor. Proverbs 22:16 says, "He who oppresses the poor to increase his riches, And he who gives to the rich, will surely come to poverty." Several years ago I saw this verse manifested in the life of one of my elderly friends. She was a Russian lady in her 80s. She had been in the United States for ten years, but she still was naïve about our culture.

She loved to watch TV evangelists, and one evangelist had a special offer. He said for a gift of one hundred dollars he would send a special gift that would insure that her prayers would be answered. She took the bait and sent one hundred dollars. The gift she received in the mail was a shower cap with the handprint of the TV evangelist on it. The instructions read, "Put this cap on when you take a shower, and the anointing you will receive from my handprint will cause showers of blessings to come your way."

When my friend told me about this I was horrified that someone who claimed to be a Christian would take advantage of poor people this way. My friend did not have much to begin with, and she lost much of what she had because she was repeatedly taken advantage of by people who just wanted her money.

This verse states clearly what will happen to those who oppress the poor. They may obtain wealth temporarily, but eventually they will lose everything and even run the risk of losing their own souls.

Lord, help me to always bless the poor.

Evening Watch: Read Psalm 47:1–9. This psalm extols our awesome God. Verse 2 says, "For the Lord Most High is awesome; He is a great King over all the earth." We are exhorted to praise the Lord with understanding. (See v. 7.) When we begin to understand the greatness of our God, we will not hesitate to praise Him every day. What amazes me most about our awesome God is that He chose to tabernacle Himself in these vessels of flesh. He identified with mankind when He became Immanuel, God with us.

Lord, thank You for choosing us to be Your temple.

Morning Wisdom: Read Proverbs 22:17–19. As we read through the Bible each year, we need to ask the Holy Spirit to tune our ears to hear the message God wants us to receive. Sometimes I get frustrated when I lose a good station on the radio while I am traveling in the car because I have driven out of the range of that radio tower. God has a huge radio tower. He knows no time or space. He stands ready to communicate with us continually, but all too few of us have ourselves tuned to receive what He is transmitting.

To tune in to God's personal messages to us for each day, we must offer both our ears and our hearts to Him. We are exhorted in these verses to incline our ears to hear God's Word and to apply our hearts to His knowledge. (See v. 17.) He also wants us to declare what we hear to others. We are God's broadcast stations who have the great privilege of sharing His good news with others. When we hear God's Word with our hearts and ask the Holy Spirit to be our narrator as we read God's Word, we will be ready to transmit the gospel to those we meet each day. Our trust level will increase as we spend time hearing, hiding, and heeding God's Word.

Lord, help me to apply Your Word to my everyday life diligently.

Evening Watch: Read Psalm 48:1–14. I prefer the King James translation of verses 1 and 2 of this psalm. These verses read: "Great is the LORD, and greatly to be praised in the city of our God, in the mountain of his holiness. Beautiful for situation, the joy of the whole earth, is mount Zion, on the sides of the north, the city of the great King." These verses describe the holy mountain of the Lord and the city of our great King. When I read "beautiful for situation," I instantly want to praise God, because He has truly revealed His beauty to me in all the situations I have faced in my sixty-five years here on Earth.

When we can see God's beauty in every situation, every day will be a good day. I keep a daily journal of my activities, and I usually start each new page with, "Thank You, Lord, for a good day!" People who will read my journals after I am gone will probably think I was a Pollyanna who lived in denial. Quite the contrary! I am fully aware of the tribulations I have encountered in this life, but I have been able to be of good cheer during those tribulations simply because the King of glory held my hand through each one of my trials. In fact, as I think back over my life, I saw God's beauty most clearly during the horrific trials I experienced.

Lord, thank You for revealing Your faithfulness and mercy to me even in the hard times. Your presence beautifies every day of my life.

SEPTEMBER 5

Ecclesiastes 10:1–12:14; 2 Corinthians 8:1–15; Psalm 49:1–20; Proverbs 22:20–21

Morning Wisdom: Read Proverbs 22:20–21. Just recently I spoke at a Bible study kickoff for a church. The ladies gathered for brunch and sign-up lists were presented for the various Bible studies that would be offered that year. The title of my talk was "A Mind-Altering Substance." I began the talk by confessing that I had been addicted to a mind-altering substance for most of my life. The women looked shocked, but when I explained that the mind-altering substance was the Word of God, they seemed relieved.

Proverbs 22:20–21 reads:

> Have I not written to you excellent things Of counsels and knowledge,
> That I may make you know the certainty of the words of truth, That you
> may answer words of truth To those who send to you?

The excellent things of counsels and knowledge are found in God's Word. As we hide God's Word in our hearts, the Lord is able to give us a word in season for those who seek counsel from us. We begin to know the certainty of the words of truth as we commit ourselves to study God's Word. Paul exhorted Timothy: "Be diligent to present yourself approved to God, a worker who does not need to be ashamed, rightly dividing the word of truth" (2 Tim. 2:15). When the Word of God is interpreted to us by the Holy Spirit, it has the power not only to alter our minds but also to change our lives and the lives of the people we counsel and teach.

Lord, help me to rightly divide Your Word.

Evening Watch: Read Psalm 49:1–20. Life can change in a moment of time. We were made well aware of that fact when Hurricane Katrina hit the gulf area of the United States. Psalm 49:11–12 reads: "Their inner thought is that their houses will last forever, Their dwelling places to all generations; They call their lands after their own names. Nevertheless man, though in honor, does not remain; He is like the beasts that perish." People in a moment of time saw their homes and everything they owned destroyed when the floodwaters inundated their cities. For the unbeliever there is only one thing sure in this life and that is death. However, for the believer the sure thing they can hold on to in the midst of horrific trials is that God will redeem their souls from the power of the grave, for He shall receive them. (See v. 15.)

Lord, You and Your Word provide me security in this life and the next.

Song of Solomon 1:1–4:16; 2 Corinthians 8:16–24; Psalm 50:1–23; Proverbs 22:22–23

Morning Wisdom: Read Proverbs 22:22–23. As I write this devotional, there are many afflicted who desire entrance into the gates of many cities. Hurricane Katrina has devastated the Gulf Coast. People are being ordered out of New Orleans because of the polluted water caused by the flooding. The news is full of the grief-stricken faces of many who have loved ones who are missing and homes that have been totally destroyed. Many cities have opened their gates wide to receive those who have been displaced because of the storm. My own city, Atlanta, is one of these host cities. The citizens of Atlanta have stretched out their arms to those who must now start all over again.

Proverbs 22:22–23 warns us not to rob the poor or oppress the afflicted at the gate, for the Lord will plead their cause, and plunder the soul of those who plunder them. In the midst of this great suffering in the Gulf Coast there are looters who are even using weapons to rob stores. We can rest assured that God will plunder such souls who have no mercy upon the afflicted.

Lord, help me to always have open arms to the poor and afflicted.

Evening Watch: Read Psalm 50:1–23. People are always asking me, "When will the Lord come again?" No one knows the day or the hour, but we can know the season. We do know that Jesus predicted that there would be wars, famines, earthquakes, and many troubles just before He makes His descent out of heaven. He called these times the "beginning of sorrows." We have always had earthquakes, famines, and wars, but the intensity and the frequency of these troubles will increase just before the Lord comes again.

We can look back on these past years and see how this earth seems to be reeling like a drunk man just before he falls flat on his face. We mentioned Hurricane Katrina this morning as just one example of the signs of the times. The tsunami, famines in Africa, and mass earthquakes in Pakistan are also signs of the times. Labor always intensifies just before a woman delivers a baby. There is no question that the labor pangs of this earth are intensifying and becoming more frequent.

This psalm describes the tempestuous times that will surround the Lord's Second Coming. Verse 3 says, "Our God shall come, and shall not keep silent; A fire shall devour before Him, And it shall be very tempestuous all around Him."

What should we be doing as the day of the Lord's Second Coming approaches? Verse 23 gives us this exhortation, "Whoever offers praise glorifies Me; And to him who orders his conduct aright I will show the salvation of God." The King James Version says, "And to him that ordereth his conversation aright will I shew the salvation of God." Until the Lord returns we are to be careful that both our conduct and our conversations reflect His glory.

Lord, help me to glorify You daily.

Song of Solomon 5:1–8:14; 2 Corinthians 9:1–15; Psalm 51:1–19; Proverbs 22:24–25

Morning Wisdom: Read Proverbs 22:24–25. When one of our sons was in high school, he had a friend who continually had fits of anger. That friendship concerned me. As I read today's verses I realize that my concerns were well founded. Our reading from Proverbs for today says, "Make no friendship with an angry man, And with a furious man do not go, Lest you learn his ways And set a snare for your soul." I am thankful that my son did not go the way of his angry friend and that his friendship with this person finally dissolved.

The two root causes to anger are pride and jealousy. Proverbs 13:10 says that pride is the source of all contention. Anger wells up within us when we believe we are right and the other person is wrong. We end up in contention when we try to prove our point. Jealousy causes such wrath that it can lead to murder. Cain killed Abel in a fit of anger, because he was jealous of Abel. Abel's offering was received by God, and Cain's offering was not. (See Genesis 4:8–9.) Jealousy caused Saul to try to kill David on many occasions. (See 1 Samuel 18:11; 20:33.)

If we become angry, we need to ask God to show us why we became so angry. When God reveals the root, we can lay the ax of God's Word to that root by confessing our sin of jealousy or pride to God. (See 1 John 1:9.)

Lord, cleanse me of any root of pride or jealousy.

Evening Watch: Read Psalm 51:1–19. David wrote this psalm just after Nathan confronted him with the sin David committed with Bathsheba. David had committed both adultery and murder. He had failed to confess his sins to the Lord, and the days and nights he experienced after he sinned were miserable. Some of those nights and days are recorded in previous psalms.

I experienced sleepless nights after I lied to my husband. I lied to protect a friend, but I was miserable until this sin was discovered. Like David, I should have confessed my sin to God and to my husband, but I tried to cover it and the lie just got worse. You have probably heard this expression, "Oh, what a tangled web we weave when in our hearts we try to deceive." My husband did find out and confronted me. I was relieved when my lie was uncovered, because I no longer had the fear that it would be discovered.

When Nathan confronted David with his sins, David cried out to the Lord and asked Him to cleanse his heart and create a clean heart within him. He asked the Lord to renew his faithfulness to the Lord and to restore the joy of his salvation. God had been pleased with David in the past, because David continually offered up the sacrifices of praise and thanksgiving to Him, but God was even more pleased with David when he offered Him the sacrifice of a contrite heart.

Lord, help me to be honest about my sins.

Isaiah 1:1–2:22; 2 Corinthians 10:1–18; Psalm 52:1–9; Proverbs 22:26–27

Morning Wisdom: Read Proverbs 22:26–27. Over the years we have loaned money to people. We have yet to have any of this money paid back to us. We never loan money with the expectation of receiving anything in return. However, people are usually too proud to ask for money outright. When we hand them the money they usually say once again, "Now this is just a loan you know. I plan to pay you back."

Proverbs 22:26–27 reads, "Do not be one of those who shakes hands in a pledge, One of those who is surety for debts; If you have nothing with which to pay, Why should he take away your bed from under you?" Many in America are having more than just their bed taken out from under them. They are having their homes and cars taken away, because they are in so much debt.

We live in a have-to-have-it-now society that has lost the art of saving. When I was young we did not even own a car until my teen years. We did not have the money to invest in a car, so we waited until we could pay cash for a car before we purchased one.

It is so easy just to get a loan, but if we do not have the money to repay that loan and do not see that we will have that money in the future, we should never borrow money.

God is not in the loan business. He did not loan us His kingdom to enjoy when we received Jesus Christ as our Savior. He gave His only begotten Son so that we might enter into His kingdom, and now we are His stewards who take care of the great inheritance we have through Jesus Christ. God so loved the world that He gave. We should so love others that we give and expect nothing in return. When we do this we enter into the joy of His kingdom on Earth.

Lord, help me to always freely give.

Evening Watch: Read Psalm 52:1–9. This psalm is a contemplation of David when he was on the run from Saul. David feigned himself to be insane and was welcomed into the camp of Ahimelech. David thought he would be safe in the enemy camp. However, Doeg the Edomite told Saul where David was. In this psalm David declared how Doeg would be uprooted from the land of the living and how the righteous would laugh at his demise. Doeg was a wicked man who trusted in the abundance of his riches. David, however, did not trust in his riches. He declared, "I trust in the mercy of God forever and ever. I will praise You forever, Because You have done it" (vv. 8–9). When we trust in the Lord we can wait upon Him and know without a doubt that God will reveal His goodness to us in every situation.

Lord, thank You for Your mercy.

SEPTEMBER 9

Morning Wisdom: Read Proverbs 22:28–29. The name of our church is Landmark Church. We decided upon this name, because we wanted our church to be on the piece of property we bought until the Lord's return. The families in our church built our first church building. We gathered every Saturday for a year and worked on the church. We did have some members of our church who were skilled in building, and they guided the less knowledgeable members each step of the way.

When we built our first building, the street our church faced was a two-lane road with nothing but a few homes on either side. Now this street is a bustling four-lane highway with apartment and office buildings on both sides of the street. We have been offered a great deal of money for the property, but whenever we consider selling, the elders of our church quote Proverbs 22:28, which says, "Do not remove the ancient landmark Which your fathers have set."

My husband and I have been members of Landmark Church for over thirty years. During these years we have been able to support and send missionaries all over the world. We have seen many of our members excel in the building of God's kingdom. Proverbs 22:29 says, "Do you see a man who excels in his work? He will stand before kings; He will not stand before unknown men."

There is only one King that we will all stand before at the end of our days. King Jesus will judge the words and deeds we have said and done on Earth, and we will receive our just rewards. Pray for the Lord to direct your speech and actions today.

> *Lord, I commit my works to You so that You may establish my thoughts. Help me to follow the lead of Your Holy Spirit and yield myself to You throughout the day. My works will only be excellent if I allow You to both will and do of Your good pleasure.*

Evening Watch: Read Psalm 53:1–6. Do you think God gets frustrated? I have often thought that God surely must get frustrated when He sees so many corrupt men on Earth. He must have days when He asks Himself, "Is there anyone on Earth who understands and seeks Me?" This psalm expressed David's frustration with the condition of men's hearts on Earth, but I do not believe God is ever frustrated. Frustration is a fruit of pride, and God is humble. God humbles Himself to look into the hearts of men. When He sees men who say in their hearts that there is no God, I believe God is grieved, not frustrated.

Wouldn't you be grieved if you had given a rich and wonderful gift to someone who proceeded to throw the unwrapped gift into the trash? God gave the gift of salvation to the whole world when He sent His Son to Earth to die for our sins. Multitudes on Earth have never opened the gift of salvation.

> *Thank You for Your gift.*

Morning Wisdom: Read Proverbs 23:1–3. Have you ever noticed how many times discussions at mealtime center around food? People either discuss their newest recipes or the diet they plan to use after they finish the meal they are eating. Today's verses would probably not be appropriate to share while you are eating with friends. Proverbs 23:1–3 says:

> When you sit down to eat with a ruler, Consider carefully what is before you; And put a knife to your throat If you are a man given to appetite. Do not desire his delicacies, For they are deceptive food.

The custom of kings throughout the ages has been to have food testers who taste what is set before a king to make sure the meal is not poisonous. Even the president of the United States has his secret service men check out restaurants and taste food before he eats a meal when he travels to various cities.

We can be food testers every day. We can taste and see that the Lord is good. We can daily enjoy the fresh Bread of Life, God's Word. God wants us to do more than just test His Word; He wants us to live by it. Whenever we test God's Word, we will discover that His Word provides delight for our souls. Suddenly, we develop a hunger for more of His Word, and we realize we cannot live without it.

Years ago the Lord promised that my whole family would come to the place in their lives when they would consider His Word more necessary than their daily food. When I heard this word from the Lord, I had a hard time believing it, because I spent my days in the kitchen preparing meals for four hungry men. God proved faithful, however, and my husband and three sons love to devour God's Word.

Lord, may my hunger for Your Word increase daily.

Evening Watch: Read Psalm 54:1–7. When David wrote this psalm, he was hiding from Saul, who was pursuing him. He wrote, "For strangers have risen up against me, And oppressors have sought after my life; They have not set God before them" (v. 3). Saul was no stranger to David, and Scripture reveals that David had great respect for Saul, because Saul was the Lord's anointed. Both friends and strangers betrayed David. This psalm was written when the Ziphites revealed David's hiding place to Saul.

David kept his eyes continually on the Lord during his great trials. He was able to praise the Lord even when he was in great distress. He wrote, "I will freely sacrifice to You; I will praise Your name, O LORD, for it is good" (v. 6). When we keep our eyes upon the Lord, no matter what we may experience in a day, our hearts will not be fearful of evil tidings, because our hearts and eyes will be fixed upon the Lord. (See Psalm 112:6–8.)

Lord, help me to fix my eyes upon You every day while I am on Earth.

September 11

Morning Wisdom: Read Proverbs 23:4–5. The reading today provides excellent advice:

> Do not overwork to be rich; Because of your own understanding, cease! Will you set your eyes on that which is not? For riches certainly make themselves wings; They fly away like an eagle toward heaven.

Riches on this earth will fly toward heaven, and they will add nothing to our eternal rewards in heaven. In my second devotional book, *You Can Take It With You*, I challenged the readers to make daily deposits into their heavenly bank accounts. Those daily deposits of words and deeds that will have an eternal impact on the lives of others provide rewards not only in heaven but also on Earth.

Lord, help me to make eternal investments.

Evening Watch: Read Psalm 55:1–23. Our morning reading stated how riches have wings like eagles that fly toward heaven. Sometimes we experience such trials on Earth that we no longer care about riches. Our only thought is to escape this earth. David felt that way when he said, "Oh, that I had wings like a dove! I would fly away and be at rest. Indeed, I would wander far off, And remain in the wilderness" (vv. 6–7).

We have all had those moments in life when we wish we could fly away from the circumstances we are experiencing. David was betrayed by one of his closest companions. However, David released this companion to God's judgment. He decided not to dwell on his betrayal or to hold on to his hurt. David made the quality decision to call upon the Lord to save him. He committed the matter to God in prayer and trusted God to deal justly with his enemies. David exhorted us to do what he did when he wrote, "Cast your burden on the LORD, And He shall sustain you; He shall never permit the righteous to be moved" (v. 22).

Lord, I cast my burdens upon You. Thank You for hearing my prayer.

SEPTEMBER 12

Morning Wisdom: Read Proverbs 23:6–8. Our reading today warns against eating with someone whose heart is not with you. Have you ever been invited to dinner only to discover that the host and hostess had an agenda in mind when they gave you the invitation? Just after the dessert is served, your hosts begin to discuss some pyramid business they are promoting. The reading today warns us against eating a meal with a miser whose heart is not with you. Not everyone involved with pyramid schemes are misers, but providing a free dinner to someone only because you want them to help your business is not honest. I must admit that I have had hidden agendas before when I gave invitations to people to enjoy a meal in my home. The gift of hospitality is meant to be given with agape love. We should expect nothing in return whenever we open our homes to others.

There was no hidden agenda when Jesus offered everyone this invitation, "Behold, I stand at the door and knock. If anyone hears My voice and opens the door, I will come in to him and dine with him, and he with Me" (Rev. 3:20). Our Lord's only agenda when we sit at the table He has prepared for us is to love us unconditionally and to enjoy fellowship with us. You might want to linger at His table this morning as you partake of the bread of His Word and enjoy conversing with Him in prayer. I know there are special things He wants to share with you this morning.

Lord, thank You for desiring to have fellowship with me. Help me to linger at your table every morning.

Evening Watch: Read Psalm 56:1–13. The Philistines had just captured David in Gath. It was a time when David could have totally succumbed to fear, but he knew how to resist that temptation. One of the greatest weapons Satan uses against us is fear. Fear is the devil's anesthesia, which he often uses to paralyze us so that he can do his diabolical surgery on us. Twice in this psalm David made a declaration that we should all make when fear knocks at our door. He declared:

> Whenever I am afraid, I will trust in You. In God (I will praise His word),
> In God I have put my trust; I will not fear. What can flesh do to me?
> —PSALM 56:3–4

We can resist fear successfully by declaring the very same words David declared.

Satan will never cease knocking on the door of our hearts with fear, but we can quickly close that door when we put our trust in the Lord.

Lord, help me to never open the door to fear. Help me to resist fear by declaring these words out loud: "I will trust the Lord and not be afraid."

September 13

Morning Wisdom: Read Proverbs 23:9–11. Verse 11 talks about the Redeemer of the fatherless who pleads their cause. We have a Redeemer who not only pleads the cause of the fatherless, but who also pleads our cause before His heavenly Father. When our heavenly Father sent Jesus to die on the cross for us, God fulfilled His plan to redeem and restore mankind.

In times past people often became slaves to pay off the debts they owed. They were willing to work as a slave for someone until their debt was fully paid. Many times people who owed debts were spared slavery, because a loved one would offer to pay their debt in full. That type of payment was called the "redemption payment." Jesus paid our debt to sin, which is death, when He died on the cross. The redemption payment was His shed blood, which is more precious than gold.

Jesus not only freed us from our debt to sin, but He also positioned Himself to become our perfect intercessor who daily pleads our cause before the Father. The accuser of the brethren accuses us daily, but our Advocate, Jesus Christ, declares that we are free from condemnation. Through the blood of Jesus we have been justified before God. We now can stand without condemnation before our righteous and holy heavenly Father, who has purer eyes than to behold evil.

Lord, thank You for paying my debt in full.

Evening Watch: Read Psalm 57:1–11. David trusted in God's grace and mercy even before God's complete mercy and grace was given to us through Christ Jesus. Because of God's gift of grace, we do not have to be performance oriented anymore. God now works within us both to will and to do of His good pleasure. (See Philippians 2:13.)

David wrote, "I will cry out to God Most High, To God who performs all things for me" (v. 2). David did not feel like he had to perform for God. He knew God performed all the things in his life, and he was confident that whatever God did in his life would ultimately be for his good.

Nothing happens in our life except what God has either ordained or allowed. We can rest assured that God does all things well. He is able to perfect everything that is a concern to us, and He is able to perform His will through us as we yield to Him. David's heart was steadfast, and he was able to sing praises to God, because he knew that God's mercies reached unto the heavens and His truth unto the clouds. (See v. 10.) When God presented His gift of grace to us in the form of Jesus Christ, mercy and truth met together and we beheld God's glory full of grace and truth.

Lord, thank You for Your gift of grace.

Isaiah 15:1–18:7; Galatians 1:1–24; Psalm 58:1–11; Proverbs 23:12

Morning Wisdom: Read Proverbs 23:12. God desires for us to hear with our hearts, not just our ears. Proverbs 23:12 says, "Apply your heart to instruction, And your ears to words of knowledge." While Jesus walked on Earth He often ended His messages with these words, "He who has ears to hear, let him hear" (Matt. 11:15). Of course most everyone Jesus taught had the capability to hear His words. Only the hearing-impaired could not hear with their physical ears. Why then would He exhort us to have ears to hear? Jesus wanted us to listen to His words with both our spiritual ears and our physical ears.

When we hear God's Word preached or listen to a tape, we need to listen with both sets of our ears, because faith comes by hearing and hearing by the Word of the Lord. (See Romans 10:17.) Even when we read God's Word to ourselves, we need to listen with our spiritual ears.

When I was in college I received a lot of instruction but very little wisdom. I could not apply the knowledge I received. Wisdom is applied knowledge. I listened to my professors with my physical ears, but my mind was mulling over another subject. The words of the professor were not mentally absorbed, so the benefit I received from that instruction was minimal. God wants us to absorb His Word with our hearts. When we listen to God's Word with our hearts, we are listening with our spiritual ears, and both our hearts and lives will be changed.

Lord, help me to always listen to Your Word with both sets of ears.

Evening Watch: Read Psalm 58:1–11. Many of David's psalms express his righteous indignation against the wicked.

He tells God what he wants God to do to the wicked. David asked God in this psalm to break the teeth of the wicked. He desired that the wicked never see the light of day again. He wanted God to burn the wicked up in His wrath.

One day the wicked will be judged, and God will be just in His punishment of the wicked. Until that time, I will pray for those who are living wicked lives. Jesus asked for us to bless and pray for our enemies. When we intercede for wicked men, they are given a space to repent. Saul was a wicked man, and those he persecuted I am sure were praying for him. Saul was given a space to repent on the Damascus road, and he repented. The fruit that came out of Paul's life far outweighed the wickedness he committed before he repented. Pray for those you know who are not walking with the Lord.

Lord, I pray for those who are going their own way. Give them a space to repent and draw their hearts to You.

SEPTEMBER 15

Morning Wisdom: Read Proverbs 23:13–14. The exhortation not to withhold correction from a child is repeated several times in Proverbs. In today's society parents can be accused of child abuse if they spank their children.

God uses various means to chasten or discipline His children. His first preference is to discipline us through His Word. However, if we do not submit ourselves to His Word and apply His instructions to our hearts, He resorts to other means of discipline. He may allow tests and trials in our lives that will cause us to humble ourselves and submit to His instructions. Frankly, I try to continue in God's Word daily, because I much prefer to be disciplined by His Word rather than by the trials He allows.

Have you ever been around the same mountain more than one time? Sometimes God will allow similar trials to be repeated in our lives, because we did not seek Him and His Word the first time we had a certain trial. God always disciplines us as a loving father disciplines his own children. The writer of Hebrews exhorts us not to despise the chastening of the Lord or be discouraged when He rebukes us, because God only chastens those He loves. (See Hebrews 12:5–6.) I try to remind myself of God's love when I am undergoing His chastening. If we will endure our chastening with the right spirit, the peaceable fruit of righteousness will result from God's love-filled chastening.

Lord, help me not to go around the mountain more than once.

Evening Watch: Read Psalm 59:1–17. David's enemies surrounded him continually. The overwhelming fear David felt during the moments when it looked as if his enemies would kill him was real. I'm sure David's heart pounded, his stomach churned, and his body became numb and paralyzed. When those moments of fear came upon David, David cried out to the Lord. As the battles raged, I can hear David declaring, "You are my shield, Lord! You are my strength!" (Ps. 28:7).

David knew with confidence that the day would come when God would laugh at those who came against him. He knew God would let him see his desire on his enemies. He knew the very mouths of the wicked would be their demise. The curses they spouted would cause them to be cursed. The fiery taunts they shouted at David would cause them to be consumed.

David decided not to dwell in fear. Instead, he was determined to sing of God's power. He knew that God dwells in the midst of the praises of men. If you are under the attack of the enemy, begin to praise the Lord. Every demonic spirit will be confused and will flee.

Lord, Your praises will be continually in my mouth.

SEPTEMBER 16

Morning Wisdom: Read Proverbs 23:15–16. We talked yesterday about applying wisdom to our hearts. This reading talks about having a wise heart. Proverbs 23:15–16 says, "My son, if your heart is wise, my heart will rejoice—indeed, I myself; Yes, my inmost being will rejoice when your lips speak right things."

My husband and I just had lunch with our oldest son. When he was younger someone prayed over him and declared that he would be a man of wisdom. We are now seeing this prophecy fulfilled in his life. He was taught the Word of God when he was young. He is now applying the knowledge of Scripture to his everyday life. He shared with us that the knowledge of Scripture had to drop from his brain to his heart. This is the problem most of us have. We can memorize and meditate on Scripture, but that knowledge has to travel at least twelve inches from our brains to our hearts. When we have a wise heart, we will speak right things. Jesus taught that what we say reveals what is in our hearts when He said: "For out of the heart proceed evil thoughts, murders, adulteries, fornications, thefts, false witness, blasphemies. These are the things which defile a man, but to eat with unwashed hands does not defile a man" (Matt. 15:19–20).

Lord, help my children and grandchildren to apply the Word of God to their hearts.

Evening Watch: Read Psalm 60:1–12. Verse 4 says: "You have given a banner to those who fear You, That it may be displayed because of the truth." Just yesterday I was watching a football game, and I noticed the many people who were holding banners over their heads. Above the crowd was a blimp with a camera taking pictures of the game. I realized that the camera in the blimp could not see the people in the stadium. Those in the blimp only could see the colored banners.

I believe God has given us two banners to display daily. He has given us the banner of His love and the banner of His Word. If we hold these banners high by loving others and declaring His Word, the enemy will not be able to see us, and his demonic spirits will be put to confusion.

Lord, thank You for giving me these two banners. Help me to hold them high today.

SEPTEMBER 17

Morning Wisdom: Read Proverbs 23:17–18. This reading reveals the secret to life. Proverbs was written by Solomon to give wise counsel to his sons. However, towards the end of his life Solomon did not follow his own counsel. In the book of Ecclesiastes, Solomon reviewed his life. He realized much of his life was spent in vanity. When he concluded his review, he defined what was really important in life when he wrote:

> Let us hear the conclusion of the whole matter: Fear God, and keep his commandments: for this is the whole duty of man.
> —ECCLESIASTES 12:13, KJV

As wise as Solomon was, he stopped applying his heart to wisdom and temporarily lost the chief purpose of life. Proverbs 23:17–18 says, "Do not let your heart envy sinners, But be zealous for the fear of the LORD all the day; For surely there is a hereafter, And your hope will not be cut off." We will always have hope if we continue walking daily in the fear of the Lord. We fear the Lord when we obey His Word out of love, not duty.

Lord, help me to live in the fear of the Lord all day long.

Evening Watch: Read Psalm 61:1–8. We sing the first part of this psalm in our church. "Hear my cry, O God; Attend to my prayer. From the end of the earth I will cry to You" (v. 1–2). This is a good psalm to memorize today. We are now in the period of time that Jesus called "the beginning of sorrows" (Matt. 24:8). There is no doubt that we will face many horrific events in the days to come. If we shelter ourselves under the wings of the Lord, we will be able to face whatever the future holds.

Lord, I hide myself under the shelter of Your wings.

Isaiah 28:14–30:11; Galatians 3:23–4:31; Psalm 62:1–12; Proverbs 23:19–21

Morning Wisdom: Read Proverbs 23:19–21. These verses warn against being associated with gluttons and winebibbers. Jesus was accused of being both, and He responded to these accusations by saying:

> The Son of Man came eating and drinking, and they say, "Look, a gluttonous man and a winebibber, a friend of tax collectors and sinners!" But wisdom is justified by her children.
>
> —MATTHEW 11:19

Jesus attended many parties given by tax collectors and publicans, because He was a physician who healed sinners. He loved to be with people who were not self-righteous.

He knew that if a person trusts in his own righteousness, it will be hard for such a person to ever trust in Him. Jesus enjoyed a good party, but I am confident He never gave in to the temptation to become a glutton or a drunkard.

As Christians we can attend secular parties and be a shining light at such parties. If we only hang with Christians, how can we fulfill our call to be the salt of the earth and the light of the world? We will be able to mix with worldly people and not be influenced by their worldliness if we stay filled with the Spirit of God. Staying filled with the Spirit is a simple assignment. It includes speaking to one another in psalms and hymns and spiritual songs, giving thanks always for all things of God the Father in the name of our Lord Jesus Christ, and submitting to one another in the fear of God. (See Ephesians 5:19–20.) When we complete this assignment every day, we never have to fear becoming drunk with wine or living a dissipated lifestyle.

Lord, help me to partake of the new wine of Your Spirit and the food of Your Word today.

Evening Watch: Read Psalm 62:1–12. Most children want to never displease their parents, and most Christians always want to please God. This psalm begins with these words, "O God, You have cast us off; You have broken us down; You have been displeased; Oh, restore us again!"

The other night when my weekly prayer group met at my home, one of the members kept saying how she felt the Lord was displeased with her. It took all of those present to convince her that no matter what she did, God still loved her.

Whenever we get under condemnation, we can rest assured that we are under the attack of the enemy. What a diabolical enemy Satan is! He first tempts us, and if we give in to his temptation, he then proceeds to tell us that we have lost the approval of God and we might as well go our own way, because God will never forgive or love us again. When Satan condemns us we need to say out loud, "No weapon formed against me will prosper, and I condemn every word of judgment against me, because my righteousness is of the Lord." (See Isaiah 54:17.)

Praise the Lord!

SEPTEMBER 19

Morning Wisdom: Read Proverbs 23:22. The only commandment with a promise is "Honor your father and mother, as the LORD your God has commanded you, that your days may be long, and that it may be well with you in the land which the LORD your God is giving you" (Deut. 5:16). Today's verse says, "Listen to your father who begot you, And do not despise your mother when she is old." I cannot comprehend how anyone could despise his or her mother no matter what age she is.

Just recently I found some notes written by my mother to my grandmother. My mother praised my grandmother for being such a wonderful mother and a friend to her. Mother wrote these notes to her mother when her mother was in her seventies. After my mother had successfully trained her three daughters, she appreciated more than ever the training and love her own mother gave to her. I had a similar experience after my children were grown and married. The appreciation I had for my mother increased, because I realized how many sacrifices she had made for me throughout my growing years.

As I grew older I also listened and followed the advice of my mother, because I knew she had a lot more wisdom than I did. This verse also exhorts us to listen to our fathers who begot us. Jesus was the only begotten Son of the Father, and He set the example for us to listen carefully and follow the instructions our fathers give us. As we learn to listen and obey our heavenly Father, we will grow in our appreciation for Jesus' sacrifice on the cross for us. Jesus died so that we might be reconciled to our heavenly Father. Jesus opened the door for us to hear the wise instructions of our heavenly Father.

Lord, thank You for obeying Your Father always even when it meant suffering on the cross for our sakes.

Evening Watch: Read Psalm 63:1–11. David wrote this psalm when he was in the wilderness. We all go through our wilderness experiences, but what we do during those times will determine how long we will stay in the wilderness. David was in a dry place in his life. He wrote, "O God, You are my God; Early will I seek You; My soul thirsts for You; My flesh longs for You In a dry and thirsty land Where there is no water" (v. 1). David could have chosen to murmur and complain as the children of Israel did when they went through their wilderness experience. Their murmuring and complaining kept them bound in the wilderness for forty years. David knew that the only way he could get out of the dry place he experienced in his soul was to praise God no matter how he felt.

Lord, help me to always praise You.

Isaiah 33:13–36:22; Galatians 5:13–26; Psalm 64:1–10; Proverbs 23:23

Morning Wisdom: Read Proverbs 23:23. I usually like to purchase all my Christmas presents before the end of October. This verse has encouraged me to purchase Bible memory and educational games, art materials, and learning aids instead of toys for our nine grandchildren. Proverbs 23:23 says, "Buy the truth, and do not sell it, Also wisdom and instruction and understanding."

This year my goal is to buy things for my family and friends that will inspire them to draw closer to the Lord and to learn from His Word. The truth is revealed to us in God's Word. Jesus said, "I am the way, the truth, and the life. No one comes to the Father except through Me" (John 14:6). The textbook for life that will give us wisdom, instruction, and understanding is the Word of God. The great Teacher is the Holy Spirit, who takes the things of Jesus Christ and reveals them to us. (See John 14:26.)

We have the choice daily to attend the "school of learning" that God offers or the "school of hard knocks" that the world offers. I prefer the first choice, and I pray you will take time daily to open the textbook of life, the Bible, and learn from the great Teacher, the Holy Spirit.

Lord, thank You for providing me the best education available. Help me to daily take advantage of the marvelous curriculum You offer.

Evening Watch: Read Psalm 64:1–10. When we take time to attend God's classroom daily, we will soon learn that we have nothing to fear in this life. The lessons David the psalmist learned from spending time in the presence of the Lord caused him to have a victorious view of life. So many psalms David wrote began with a discouraging review of how his enemies had attacked him and how even his friends had betrayed him. However, most of these psalms end with the victorious declaration that those who trust in the Lord have nothing to fear. Psalm 64 is an example of such a psalm.

David reviewed how his enemy had plotted against him. He spoke of how his enemies encouraged themselves to lay snares for him and devised shrewd schemes against him. However, David was confident that his enemies would be defeated and they would even stumble over their own tongues. David knew that the righteous would always be victorious, because they put their trust in the Lord. He wrote, "The righteous shall be glad in the LORD, and trust in Him. And all the upright in heart shall glory" (v. 10). This last verse of Psalm 64 is one we should all memorize. When we declare this verse out loud, we will put the enemy to flight.

Lord, thank You for the victory!

Morning Wisdom: Read Proverbs 23:24–25. We just spent two days away with our youngest son, his wife, and their two children. This morning I was thanking the Lord for our three sons, who love the Lord and seek to please Him. When I observed how our youngest son and his wife were training their children in the ways of the Lord, I praised the Lord. I remembered the days when I cried out to God for this youngest son when he was on drugs. I used to pray, *Lord turn the glitter of this world into gloom, and shine the light of Your glory upon this son.* God heard my cry.

Proverbs 23:24 says, "The father of the righteous will greatly rejoice, And he who begets a wise child will delight in him." My husband recently spent a weekend with our oldest son. Our oldest son also went his own way instead of God's way for a season in his life. My husband expected to share the wisdom of the Lord with our son during that weekend, but instead my husband said he learned and gained much wisdom from our son.

Proverbs 23:25 says, "Let your father and your mother be glad, And let her who bore you rejoice." I do rejoice daily as I thank the Lord for what He has done in the lives of our three sons. If you have children who are going the way of the world, do not give up on them. Keep praying, and God will honor your prayers.

> *Lord, thank You for Your Holy Spirit, who is more powerful than the seducing spirits who seek to ensnare our children.*

Evening Watch: Read Psalm 65:1–13. I shared this morning how the Lord heard and answered our prayers for our two sons who got involved with the things of this world for a season in their lives. This next year I want to keep a prayer diary to record my daily prayers and the answers to those prayers. I wish I had done this in the past, because I know I would be amazed at how God has been so faithful to answer my prayers.

David was also in awe of how God had heard his prayers. He wrote in this psalm, "O You who hear prayer, To You all flesh will come" (v. 2). He praised God for the atonement God provided for his transgressions. (See v. 3.) David declared that God would not only hear our prayers, but He would also answer by awesome deeds done in His righteousness. (See v. 5.) David continued extolling the Lord for His greatness, His wondrous signs in the earth, His provision, and His rain. He wrote, "You crown the year with Your goodness, And Your paths drip with abundance" (v. 11). I know when I review my prayer diary at the end of next year I will also see how God has crowned the past year with His glory.

> *Praise You for Your goodness!*

Morning Wisdom: Read Proverbs 23:26–28. The reading today warns against the harlot who is seeking her victim:

> My son, give me your heart, And let your eyes observe my ways. For a harlot is a deep pit, And a seductress is a narrow well. She also lies in wait as for a victim, And increases the unfaithful among men.

Seducing spirits can be compared to harlots who are on the prowl to capture their next victim. Paul warned Timothy to be on the watch for seducing spirits when he wrote:

> Now the Spirit speaketh expressly, that in the latter times some shall depart from the faith, giving heed to seducing spirits, and doctrines of devils; Speaking lies in hypocrisy; having their conscience seared with a hot iron.
>
> —1 Timothy 4:1–2, kjv

Seducing spirits are the demonic scouts Satan sends to observe us. They look for our weak points. We reveal our weak points to them by what we say and what we do.

They cannot read our minds. We can easily conquer these wicked spirits who seek our demise by praying daily that our mouths and our actions will glorify God. When we ask the Holy Spirit to put a guard over our mouths and commit our works to the Lord daily, seducing spirits will not have any opportunity to capture our minds through their tempting thoughts.

Proverbs 26 reveals the strategy we must employ if we are going to win the battle when seducing spirits tempt us. We are exhorted in this verse to give our hearts to the Lord and observe His ways. When we do this daily we will never fall victim to the traps seducing spirits lay for us.

Lord, help me to stay filled with Your Spirit today.

Evening Watch: Read Psalm 66:1–20. This psalm reveals another way we can overcome seducing spirits and put to flight every demonic spirit that seeks to victimize us. The author of this psalm exhorts us to praise the Lord in several different ways. We are instructed to make a joyful shout to God, sing and honor His name, make His praise glorious, and declare to God all of His mighty works. When we do this all of our enemies will have to submit themselves to God. Praise is the death knell of the devil. Remain in praise all day long and you will win the victory.

Lord, help me to praise You continually every day.

SEPTEMBER 23

Morning Wisdom: Read Proverbs 23:29–35. Wherever, whoever, or whatever you run to for comfort is your god. There is so much pain in this world, and many people self-medicate themselves to cover the pain. The self-medication can take many forms, such as alcohol, drugs, sex, overeating, TV, pornography, and spending sprees. There are many ways to escape dealing with the root of pain in our lives, and Satan would love for us to try every way but God's way.

Today's reading in Proverbs describes those who linger long at wine. There are conflicting stands on whether or not a Christian should drink wine. If we seek wine or anything else as an escape or as a comfort, we are treading on dangerous ground. We see how those who self-medicate with an overdose of alcohol can enter a state of stupor where they feel nothing. Proverbs 23:35 says, "They have struck me, but I was not hurt; They have beaten me, but I did not feel it. When shall I awake, that I may seek another drink?" The person described in this verse has imbibed much more than just one glass of wine. He has lingered long at the wine. (See v. 30.)

God has sent His Holy Spirit to us as our Comforter. God has sent His only Son to heal the brokenhearted. The pain most addicts seek to cover is usually some form of rejection. God desires for us to call upon His Holy Spirit to comfort us when we feel the emotional pain of rejection. Instead of escaping or trying to cover our pain, we need to run to the arms of Jesus and allow Him to give us the oil of joy for mourning and the garment of praise to lift the spirit of heaviness. Most addicts are bound by the spirit of heaviness. Proverbs 31:6 says, "Give strong drink unto him that is ready to perish, and wine unto those that be of heavy hearts" (KJV).

The question we need to ask ourselves is where, who, and to what do we run for comfort? If we will answer this question honestly, we will discover the idols in our lives.

Lord, help me to always run to You when I am in pain.

Evening Watch: Read Psalm 67:1–7. *El Shaddai* means the "all sufficient One." This Hebrew name for God is derived from the word *fields*. It conveys the message that God is the One who gives us productivity and abundance in this life. God is more than enough to meet our needs in every situation. He is the One who we should seek first to comfort us when we are in pain.

This psalm reveals the secret to tapping into all of God's blessings and living a productive, fruitful life. Psalm 67:5–6 says, "Let the peoples praise You, O God; Let all the peoples praise You. Then the earth shall yield her increase; God, our own God, shall bless us." If you lack anything, God is the One who can supply whatever you lack. God cannot wait to bless you. Come to Him and ask Him to supply all of your needs according to His riches in glory through Christ Jesus. (See Ephesians 3:16.) Begin to praise Him!

Lord, I praise You for being El Shaddai in my life.

Morning Wisdom: Read Proverbs 24:1–2. Sometimes when we observe unrighteous people who have gained worldly wealth, prestige, and power by implementing evil schemes, we may be tempted to envy them. Proverbs 24:1–2 warns against being envious of evil men because their hearts devise violence and they speak about making trouble for others.

The psalmist David sometimes envied the wicked. He noticed how wicked, ungodly people seemed to be always at ease and increase in riches. He felt like he had cleansed his own heart in vain. However, when he went into the sanctuary and poured out his complaint to the Lord, he finally understood the rest of the story. He learned that God had set evil men in slippery places, and their end would be destruction and desolation. Evil men would be judged, and all their riches would avail nothing in eternity. (See Psalm 73:11–19.)

We truly have nothing or no one to envy in this life. Because we believe and have accepted Jesus Christ as our Lord and Savior we have received the greatest inheritance anyone could ever hope to receive. All of our needs can be supplied now by the riches of our heavenly Father's glory by Jesus Christ. (See Philippians 4:19.)

Lord, thank You for our great inheritance!

Evening Watch: Read Psalm 68:1–18. We learned this morning about the great inheritance we have through Jesus Christ. Our heavenly Father is not only able to provide for our financial needs, but He is also able to defend us and bring us into prosperity. Our heavenly Father is the Father of the fatherless and the Defender of the widows. He is able to set the solitary in families. Our heavenly Father confirms His inheritance to us by providing for the poor, leading captivity captive, and giving gifts to men.

Paul told us exactly how our heavenly Father has led captivity captive when he wrote:

> But to each one of us grace was given according to the measure of Christ's gift. Therefore He says: "When He ascended on high, He led captivity captive, And gave gifts to men.
>
> —EPHESIANS 4:7–8

Because of Jesus' death, burial, resurrection, and ascension, everything that has held us captive has been taken captive. We are now free to receive all of our inheritance, because the poverty has been broken. When Jesus became a curse for us, we were redeemed from the curse of the law. (See Galatians 3:13.) Before you retire tonight read Deuteronomy 28:16–68 to discover the curses that came upon those who broke God's law. Jesus Christ has redeemed us from every one of those curses. This makes me want to shout, "Hallelujah!" How about you?

Lord, thank You for being my Redeemer.

Isaiah 45:11–48:11; Ephesians 4:1–16; Psalm 68:19–35; Proverbs 24:3–4

Morning Wisdom: Read Proverbs 24:3-4. In my first devotional book, *Around the Word in 365 Days*, I wrote about these verses. I talked about the one house we built during our married life. It was so exciting to be able to pick out the light fixtures, the flooring, and even the type of doors and molding we desired for each room. After the builders finished our house I realized that it was just a house. It would not become our home until we moved in and filled the rooms with all of our furniture and treasures. Once we had all the pictures and mirrors hung and the furniture placed, I recognized that the true treasures that made our house a home were the people in our home. Proverbs 24:3-4 defines what makes a house a home: "Through wisdom a house is built, And by understanding it is established; By knowledge the rooms are filled With all precious and pleasant riches."

The foundation of a home that will not only stand the test of time but also will last for an eternity is Jesus Christ. Jesus Christ is all wisdom. Through an intimate knowledge of Him, we gain the understanding needed to establish an eternal home. The treasures and riches in our homes are our children and others to whom we have opened our homes. We do not have to be wealthy to have a home filled with rich treasures. Whenever we invest in people with our time, prayers, or money, we fill the rooms of our homes with God's riches. Whenever we share the gospel with others, we are adding to those riches stored in the rooms of our spiritual homes in heaven.

We have had the privilege of not only filling our home with the treasures of our own children, but we have also housed a Chinese daughter for five years, a Russian son for seven years, and an American girl for almost four years. The chambers of our home also have been filled with many guests who have caused our lives to be enriched. People are God's treasures, and even if you are single and do not have natural children, you can fill the chambers of your dwelling place by being hospitable to others.

Lord, thank You for all the treasures You have given us.

Evening Watch: Read Psalm 68:19–35. My husband spent the last few years before he retired designing benefit plans for the top managers in his company. He had no idea that one day he would benefit from those plans. He was offered early retirement with great benefits, and he took it. We have a benefit program that God has designed for us that is unending. We do not have to wait until our retirement to receive that benefit plan.

Psalm 68:19 says, "Blessed be the Lord, Who daily loads us with benefits, The God of our salvation!" Daily the Lord delights in loading us with His benefits. Before you retire tonight, think of just a few of the benefits He loaded you with today. Write them down and review them from time to time.

Lord, Your benefit plan is marvelous. Thank You.

Isaiah 48:12–50:11; Ephesians 4:17–32; Psalm 69:1–14; Proverbs 24:5

Morning Wisdom: Read Proverbs 24:5. During a visit to Russia in 1992 we were able to talk to several parliament members in Moscow. The iron curtain had just fallen, and what was the Soviet Union now faced tremendous challenges in the days ahead. We were touring Russia with a group of students from a Christian college. We asked the parliament members what we in the West could do to help them during this transition period. They encouraged us to have Russian exchange students in our home, because they needed to see how a democracy and a free economy works. One of the parliament members was a Christian, and he said that if we hosted exchange students, they could experience faith in action, and their lives could be changed.

As soon as we returned from Russia, I got a call from one of my prayer partners who told me another friend we prayed with on occasion was placing Russian exchange students. She asked if we would be interested in housing one of these students for a year.

We agreed to host a student. We were given several essays written by students, and we finally made a decision to choose a young man named Vladimir. I really wanted to have a girl student since I lived in a household of men and wouldn't have minded someone to help me in the kitchen. However, instead of receiving a student who could cook, we received a student who could eat. Vladimir was a bodybuilder, and he saw food as fuel for his body, and his consumption of fuel was amazing.

When Vladimir came to us he was not a Christian, but in less than a year with us he made a decision for Christ. Vladimir stayed with us for seven years, because we were able to get a waiver for his visa so he could go to college in the United States.

Today's verse reminds me of our years with Vladimir. Proverbs 24:5 says, "A wise man is strong, Yes, a man of knowledge increases strength." He truly was a man of knowledge who increased in both physical and spiritual strength when he was with us.

> *Lord, help me to share the gospel with many so that they too can become men and women with great spiritual strength.*

Evening Watch: Read Psalm 69:1–14. As I read the first part of this psalm, I thought of all those who experienced the devastating hurricanes on the Gulf Coast. When the levies broke in New Orleans just after Katrina made landfall, the houses were covered with water. When helicopters flew over the ninth parish in New Orleans, one could only see rooftops. David wrote, "I sink in deep mire, Where there is no standing…Where the floods overflow me" (v. 3). David was not speaking of a physical flood when he wrote this. His soul was flooded with despair as he saw his enemies and even his relatives turn against him. However, David did not give up. He continued to pray and cried out for God's mercy. He wrote, "Deliver me out of the mire, And let me not sink" (v. 14). When you have a sinking spell, this would be a good prayer to pray:

> *Lord, don't let me sink! Deliver me!*

September 27

Morning Wisdom: Read Proverbs 24:6–7. Verse 6 says, "For by wise counsel you will wage your own war, And in a multitude of counselors there is safety." Whether we like it or not we have to wage war daily against the principalities, powers, rulers of darkness, and wickedness in heavenly places. (See Ephesians 6:12.) If we could have our eyes open to see the armies of demonic spirits that seek our destruction, we would not even want to get up in the morning. However, the armies of God are much greater in number than the armies of Satan. Elisha's servant had his eyes opened to see the armies of God when the Syrian army surrounded Israel. Elisha told his servant, "Do not fear, for those who are with us are more than those who are with them" (2 Kings 6:16).

God has also set people in the body of Christ who are anointed with the Spirit of counsel. (See Isaiah 11:2.) Whenever we find ourselves in a spiritual battle we can go to these counselors, who will give us the wisdom from God's Word that we need to declare to defeat the enemy.

As you begin your day today, you do not have to fear anything. Satan may have plans to destroy you, but those plans will be put to confusion if you will take your authority over demonic spirits in the name of Jesus. The weapons of warfare, such as prayer, the word of our testimony, the declaration of the blood of Jesus, and the Word of God, are truly mighty. Every stronghold in our lives can be overcome if we will employ those mighty weapons daily. Ask the Holy Spirit today to help you to be alert to the enemy's strategies, and then call on His counsel to share with you which weapon to use against those demonic forces.

Lord, thank You for providing wise counselors to help me do battle.

Evening Watch: Read Psalm 69:15–36. When we are in a spiritual battle we should employ our mighty spiritual weapons against the enemy and offer the sacrifices of praise and thanksgiving to God. David's cry for help and deliverance in this psalm ends with this declaration, "I will praise the name of God with a song, And will magnify Him with thanksgiving" (v. 30). When we offer the sacrifices of praise and thanksgiving to God we will put the enemy to flight. It is easy to praise the Lord in the good times, but it takes determined discipline to offer thanksgiving and praise to God when we are in the thick of a spiritual battle. The sacrifice we make when we give thanksgiving and praise to God during the great trials of our lives involves laying our own cares, fears, anxieties, and worries on the altar. When we turn our fears and cares into prayers of thanksgiving and praise, we will be able to win every spiritual battle.

Lord, help me to praise You always at all times.

September 28

Morning Wisdom: Read Proverbs 24:8. Today's verse reads, "He who plots to do evil Will be called a schemer." Our carnal nature always wants to scheme to cover up the sins that we have committed. The carnal nature simply does not want to be caught and have to pay the penalty for its disobedience to God's Word. Whenever we play the blame game or lie to cover our sins, we have given in to flesh and are guilty of being schemers.

You might say, "Well, I have never been guilty of plotting to do evil." I said this also, but then I thought about the many times I had played over and over again in my mind how I could get back at someone who had done wrong to me. Even David the psalmist played these scenarios in his mind and put those thoughts on paper.

Whenever we have those thoughts of retaliation or resentment, we need to confess those thoughts as sin and take those thoughts captive to Jesus Christ. First Corinthians 13:5 says, "[Love] thinks no evil."

Lord, help me to release any judgments and criticisms of others to You.

Evening Watch: Read Psalm 70:1–5. David's fleshly nature is revealed in this psalm when he spoke to God about his enemies and said, "Let them be ashamed and confounded" (v. 2). This was a prayer telling God the punishment he felt his enemies deserved. However, at the end of this psalm David prayed a prayer that was in the spirit, not the flesh. He said, "Let God be magnified" (v. 4). What a great prayer to pray whenever we encounter a trial and especially when others have wronged us. We need to release all judgment to God and say, *Lord, You be magnified in this situation.*

Lord, be magnified in every situation I may face tomorrow and in all my tomorrows.

Isaiah 57:15–59:21; Philippians 1:1–26; Psalm 71:1–24; Proverbs 24:9–10

Morning Wisdom: Read Proverbs 24:9–10. Some people scoff when you tell them that the adversities occurring throughout the world were prophesied in the Bible. Within less than a year we have seen the tragedy of the tsunami, two giant hurricanes that hit the Gulf Coast of America, and terrorist bombings all over the world.

Proverbs 24:9 says that scoffers are an abomination to men. When we encounter such scoffers all we can do is sow God's Word in hopes that one day the Word will produce fruit in their lives.

Verse 10 says, "If you faint in the day of adversity, Your strength is small." We will never faint in the days of adversity that face us in the future if we depend upon the Lord's strength and not our own.

Lord, help me to depend upon Your strength in the days ahead.

Evening Watch: Read Psalm 71:1–24. We talked this morning about the increase of adversity in these last days. David declared our only place of safety when he wrote, "Be my strong refuge, To which I may resort continually; You have given the commandment to save me, For You are my rock and my fortress" (v. 3).

Lord, thank You for being my rock and my fortress in these last days.

SEPTEMBER 30

Isaiah 60:1–62:5; Philippians 1:27–2:18; Psalm 72:1–20; Proverbs 24:11–12

Morning Wisdom: Read Proverbs 24:11–12. "But I didn't know any better!" is often the excuse children give their parents when they do something wrong. They usually add, "But, Mom and Dad, you never told me!" We all have a human nature that does not want to admit that we have been disobedient. We seek to cover up our sins or we make excuses. The reading today states clearly that our excuses may work with others, but they will not work with God, because God knows our hearts. Proverbs 24:12 says:

> If you say, "Surely we did not know this," Does not He who weighs the hearts consider it? He who keeps your soul, does He not know it? And will He not render to each man according to his deeds.

Paul wrote about "the day when God will judge the secrets of men by Jesus Christ, according to my gospel" (Rom. 2:16). When I understand that God knows my heart, I no longer can fish for excuses when I sin. I only can confess my sins and ask God to cleanse my heart.

Lord, know my heart and show me if there is any wicked way within me. Create within me a clean heart, O God.

Evening Watch: Read Psalm 72:1–20. This morning we were reminded that God weighs the hearts of men. He even knows the secrets of their hearts. The knowledge that God knows my heart would cause me to tremble if I did not also know that God judges His people with righteousness.

Solomon wrote in this psalm, "He will judge Your people with righteousness, And Your poor with justice" (v. 2).

David said the righteous would flourish and that God "shall come down like rain upon the grass before mowing, Like showers that water the earth" (v. 6). David continued to declare how God would defeat all of His enemies and all nations would serve Him. He declared that God's name would endure forever and all nations would call Him blessed. The psalm ends with these words, "Blessed be the LORD God, the God of Israel, Who only does wondrous things! And blessed be His glorious name forever! And let the whole earth be filled with His glory. Amen and Amen" (vv 18–19). When we know the rest of the story we do not have to fear Judgment Day.

Lord, thank You for Your righteous judgment through Jesus Christ.

Isaiah 62:6–65:25; Philippians 2:19–3:3; Psalm 73:1–28; Proverbs 24:13–14

Morning Wisdom: Read Proverbs 24:13–14. Psalm 19 speaks about the Word of God being more precious than fine gold and sweeter than honey and the honeycomb. (See Psalm 19:10.) The reading today compares the knowledge of wisdom to the sweet taste of honey and the honeycomb. We obtain the knowledge of wisdom when we read God's Word. Proverbs 24:14 says that when we discover the knowledge of wisdom we will have both prospects for the future and hope.

The promises of God found in His Word supply the foundation of our hope. Whenever I teach on prayer I exhort the audience to "pray the promise, not the problem." It is so easy for our souls to become discouraged if we keep reviewing the problems in our lives. When we constantly talk about our problems to others we are providing food for Satan and his demons who seek to devour us. By turning every problem over to the Lord in prayer and declaring the promise that is tailor-made for that problem, we furnish our souls with the sweet diet of God's Word instead of the bitter diet of despair.

Faith is the substance of things hoped for and the evidence of things not seen. (See Hebrews 11:1.) Faith comes by hearing and hearing by the Word of God. (See Romans 10:17.) Hope is a sure anchor for our souls that keeps our emotions on a steady keel, even when we experience horrific trials. (See Hebrews 6:19.) God's promises give us both perspective and the prospect that everything we experience in this life God will work for our good. I think I will spend this morning praying the promise instead of the problem.

Lord, thank You for fulfillng all Your promises.

Evening Watch: Read Psalm 73:1–28. "But what about me, Lord?" Have you ever asked that question of the Lord when you see ungodly people prospering. My son had a friend in high school whose father was the porn king of the South. When Ray described this man's house, I could not help but ask the same question David asked in this psalm, "Why do the wicked prosper?"

David's description of an ungodly man in verses 4–12 was vivid. In my mind's eye I pictured the wicked man with eyes bulging from a puffy, swollen face. He was dressed in an expensive T-shirt with the words written in red, "Violence Pays." He wore a solid gold necklace with the word *Pride* spelled in diamonds. I imagined overhearing his conversation as he scoffed at Christians and boasted about himself. He kept saying, "Nobody will ever know. I got away with murder." He rested himself in a velvet lounge chair. In his lap were bundles of cash that he counted as a leisure sport.

David thought he had cleansed his hands in vain until he went into the sanctuary and discovered that God will punish the wicked and ultimately they will perish.

Lord, I don't have to envy the wicked, because I know You deal justly.

Morning Wisdom: Read Proverbs 24:15–16. One of the fears many older people have as they age is the fear of falling. This fear is well founded since as we age our bones become more fragile. The reading today has helped me to overcome this fear. Proverbs 24:16 says, "For a righteous man may fall seven times And rise again, But the wicked shall fall by calamity."

I may fall, but the promise is that I will always get up. No bones will be broken, and I will be able to walk normally.

Most likely this reading is speaking about falling spiritually, not physically. Paul wrote that "for all have sinned and fall short of the glory of God" (Rom. 3:23). To guard themselves from falling, older people hold tightly to the rails when they climb stairs.

We can prevent ourselves from falling spiritually when we guard the gates to our minds—the eye, ear, and mouth gates. You have probably heard the expression, "An idle mind is the devil's playground [or workshop]." We cannot afford to let our guard down, because Satan is just waiting to push through the gates of our minds so that he can set up shop and play there all day. The chances of us falling short of the glory of God will greatly be diminished when we ask the Holy Spirit to help us guard the gates to our minds. Join me this morning as I pray.

> Lord, set a guard over the gates of my mind today. Help me to see no evil, hear no evil, and speak no evil.

Evening Watch: Read Psalm 74:1–23. History repeats itself. Iran and other Muslim countries vow they will push Israel into the sea. This psalm describes the enemies of Israel. Verse 7 says, "They have set fire to Your sanctuary; They have defiled the dwelling place of Your name to the ground. They said in their hearts, 'Let us destroy them altogether.'" The psalmist asks, "O God, how long will the adversary reproach? Will the enemy blaspheme Your name forever?" (v. 10). I'm sure many in Israel today have asked that same question. This small nation is only the size of New Jersey. It is surrounded by Muslim nations that would love to see them destroyed. It is a miracle that Israel has been able to defend itself in many wars.

The psalmist asked the Lord not to forget His covenant and cried, "Arise, O God, plead Your own cause" (v. 22). The Lord will never forget His covenant with Israel.

Before you go to bed tonight, pray for the peace of Jerusalem.

> Lord, I pray for the peace of Jerusalem. Protect Your people.

OCTOBER 3

Morning Wisdom: Read Proverbs 24:17–20. Even God is displeased when we rejoice over the defeat of our enemies. We have to remember that every human being has value to God. God has the power to pit nation against nation, but I know He grieves when He sees the suffering and degradation war brings. Many people who read the Old Testament are troubled by God's command to Israel to kill those who occupied their Promised Land.

God never sends judgment upon a land without first warning a people. For example, God sent Jonah to warn the great city of Nineveh that in forty days they would be destroyed. (See Jonah 3:4.) Nineveh was a pagan nation that was extremely wicked. Nineveh heeded Jonah's message and was spared destruction.

As I write this devotional we are at war with terrorists. How should we view these worldwide terrorists and insurgents in Iraq? Jesus told us to love our enemies and do good to those who hate us and to bless those who curse us and pray for those who spitefully use us. (See Luke 6:27.) Perhaps if we did more praying for our enemies, we would see them repent as the city of Nineveh did.

Lord, thank You for Your warnings and that You desire that no one perish.

Evening Watch: Read Psalm 75:1–10. We learned this morning that God always warns a people before He sends judgment to their land. This psalm tells us that God chooses the proper time to judge a nation, and He judges with righteous judgment. (See v. 2.) God is the Judge, and He alone promotes and demotes nations. He puts down one nation and exalts another.

History tells us that those nations that have blessed and helped Israel have prospered. I praise God that so far our nation has not turned its back on Israel. I pray that our nation will be faithful to support Israel. If we withdraw our support, I fear what will happen to our nation. Pray that our leaders will understand the importance of blessing Israel. God said those who bless the descendents of Jacob will be blessed, and those who curse Israel will be cursed. (See Genesis 27:29.)

Lord, I pray the leaders of our nation will always support Israel.

Morning Wisdom: Read Proverbs 24:21–22. These verses remind us that we are at the mercy of the Lord and those who are in authority over us. We are exhorted to fear (honor and respect) the Lord and those in authority over us, because they both have the power to change our lives in a moment of time. We also are encouraged not to associate with those who are given to change, because their indecisiveness can suddenly bring calamity upon themselves and those who associate with them.

People who are given to change or who are double minded are unable to stand firm during trials. Instead of turning to the Lord instantly they sit on the fence and never make the decision to yield to God in prayer and trust in His Word. People who change their minds all the time are definitely not grounded in God's Word. We serve a God who is unchanging, stable, and trustworthy. People who always change their minds are unstable and untrustworthy. Such people do the "Hokey Pokey." They put one foot into God's kingdom and then they take it right back out again. They never plant their feet on our solid Rock, Jesus Christ. I can see why this reading from Proverbs warns against associating with such people, because they usually will make decisions that will lead to destruction.

Lord, help me to be always stable and unmoving in my trust in You.

Evening Watch: Read Psalm 76:1–12. The Proverbs and Psalms readings for yesterday addressed the issue of God's judgment. Today's reading also speaks about God's judgment. When God judges, I believe His heart is to deliver a people, not destroy them. Verse 9 of this psalm reveals that "God arose to judgment, To deliver all the oppressed of the earth." His judgment upon a nation now can spare the oppression of other nations many generations later.

Verse 10 describes how God girds Himself with wrath. That picture of God is not quite complete, because God also girds Himself with praise. God's wrath was poured out upon Jesus on the cross so that He might spare many from His wrath to come. As believers in Jesus Christ, we are not appointed to God's wrath.

We recently had a Bible study titled "The Beautiful Wrath of God." I thought this was a strange title until I studied the lesson. The lesson pointed out that Jesus was the beautiful One, sent to absorb the full wrath of God for our own sin and to deliver us from the wrath of our old nature. Because of Jesus the wrath of men on Earth is restrained. God has from the very beginning of the earth purposed to deliver us from His wrath. He purposed to send Jesus Christ, the Lamb who was slain for our sins from the foundation of the earth. God has purer eyes than to behold evil, but He now looks at us through the shed blood of Jesus. Jesus Christ earned for us the right to stand before our Most Holy God. Praise the Lord!

Lord, thank You for paying the price for my redemption.

Morning Wisdom: Read Proverbs 24:23–25. Proverbs is often called the "book of wisdom." These verses convey three ways we can act wisely. They are:

- Show no partiality in judgment.
- Never call the wicked righteous.
- Rebuke the wicked.

When I read this I had to ask myself, *When was the last time I rebuked the wicked?* Frankly, I could not remember one time in which I rebuked the wicked. Then the Holy Spirit reminded me about my morning prayers. Every morning I do warfare for my family by binding every spirit that cannot confess that Jesus Christ of Nazareth is God in the flesh and canceling out their assignments against my loved ones. I heard that still, quiet voice within me say, "You stand and rebuke the wicked every day of your life."

I realized that wicked people are motivated by wicked spirits, so whenever I do spiritual warfare I am rebuking the wicked.

When we cry out to God for wisdom, He will help us to show no partiality. He will also give us clear discernment to identify those who are evil and those who are righteous.

Lord, help me to remember to ask daily for Your wisdom.

Evening Watch: Read Psalm 77:1–20. Have you ever felt like God has forgotten you? The writer of this psalm felt like God did not know about his suffering and anguish. He was losing sleep and asked these questions in the night, "Has God forgotten to be gracious? Has He in anger shut up His tender mercies?" (v. 9). Satan was up to his old tricks. Satan loves to attack us at nighttime. He was trying to convince the writer that God simply did not care about his suffering.

The Holy Spirit, however, was on duty that sleepless night and helped this psalmist remember all the good works of the Lord. One of the assignments of the Holy Spirit is to take the things of Jesus Christ and reveal them to us. (See John 14:26.) The rest of the psalm extols the greatness of God. The psalmist wrote, "You have with Your arm redeemed Your people, The sons of Jacob and Joseph" (v. 15).

Whenever we feel like God has forsaken and forgotten us, we need to submit ourselves to the Holy Spirit and ask Him to remind us of God's faithfulness to us.

David exhorted us to remember God's faithfulness at night. (See Psalm 92:2.) Begin tonight to rehearse out loud God's faithful works in your own life. Satan will flee.

Lord, thank You for Your faithfulness.

Jeremiah 6:15–8:7; Colossians 2:8–23; Psalm 78:1–25; Proverbs 24:26

Morning Wisdom: Read Proverbs 24:26. This is an unusual verse. It says, "He who gives a right answer kisses the lips."

Have you ever seen people who throw a kiss in response when someone thanks them or gives them a compliment? I don't think the proper response would be to kiss a person on the lips to show our gratitude. However, we might feel like kissing someone who has helped us find the right answer to a problem or given us wisdom about a situation in our lives.

The sign for the phrase *thank you* in sign language is made by putting your hand to your lips. Then you release your hand just like you would to throw a kiss to someone, and you throw your hand upward. I love to make this sign when I sign during some of our worship songs. I always feel like that thrown kiss goes right into the throne room of God and lands on Jesus' cheek. Jesus is the One who always can give the right answer, and even though we cannot kiss Him on the lips, we can throw a kiss towards heaven to thank Him for His wisdom. Have you thrown Jesus a kiss today?

Lord, thank You for Your wisdom.

Evening Watch: Read Psalm 78:1–25. Hidden in the marvelous psalm that reviews God's wondrous works are valuable lessons we should pass on to our children. I was just talking to a friend at church last night about what a blessing it is to have children who love and serve the Lord. Having adult children who instruct their children in the ways of the Lord does not just happen. It is the result of training our children in the ways of the Lord.

The Jewish people passed down the stories of God's great strength and power to their children. The psalmist wrote that his generation would not hide the stories of God's greatness from their children. They would tell the generation to come the praises of the Lord.

Throughout our lives God is establishing a testimony. It would be a good idea to write down the ways God has spoken to you and what He has done in your own life so that those stories can be passed on to your children. One of the reasons I write these devotional books is to pass on my encounters with God to my own children in hopes they will pass my books on to their children. The reason for declaring the works of the Lord to our children is to give them hope and to be sure they never forget God's faithfulness.

The psalmist related what happened to the stubborn, rebellious generation who refused to obey God's instructions in spite of the marvelous miracles God did for them. That generation spoke against God, and the results were disastrous. Because they did not believe in God or trust in His salvation, they died in the wilderness. If you still have children or are privileged to have grandchildren, begin to share your own testimony with them. You will be surprised how interested they will be to find out the miracles God has performed in your own life.

Lord, thank You for the miracles in my life.

Morning Wisdom: Read Proverbs 24:27. Before a house can be built, the land has to be cleared. When we were building an addition to our church, the surveyors discovered that the quality of the soil where we wanted to build was poor. Before we could pour the foundation of this new addition, gravel had to be added to strengthen the soil. Preparing the soil before the building was built prevented us from having many problems later. Proper preparation spared us from having a cracked foundation and a sinking building.

Today's verse reads, "Prepare your outside work, Make it fit for yourself in the field; And afterward build your house." The field in this passage can be compared to the outreach we have in the field of God's kingdom. We are colaborers with Christ in this last great harvest. God wants us to begin to build houses (churches, home and fellowship groups) where He can dwell. First we have to survey the land and then prepare the field.

Evangelism is most effective when we pray for hearts to be prepared to receive the gospel.

Lord, thank You for preparing the hearts.

Evening Watch: Read Psalm 78:26–58. I believe the one sin that leads to all other sins is the sin of unbelief. Satan's fall was caused by pride, but the basis for his pride was his unbelief. He did not accept God's goodness, and he rejected God's love. He took his eyes off of God and put them on himself. Satan began to believe in himself more than he believed in God. He was deceived and thought he could become greater than God. Whenever we begin to doubt God's goodness and His love, we open ourselves to deception and ultimately to unbelief.

The psalm today reveals the basis for the failure of the children of Israel to enter the Promised Land. Even though they saw God's wondrous works in the wilderness, they turned aside from God like a "deceitful bow" (v. 57). They did not believe in God's power or His faithfulness even though they had seen it in the past. God's anger was kindled against them because of their unbelief. God had prepared a place of rest for them, but they could not enter that rest because of their unbelief.

Lord, help me to always believe.

OCTOBER 8

Morning Wisdom: Read Proverbs 24:28–29. "But he bit me, so I bit him back!" Most of us heard that exclamation from our children when they got into fights. The payback mentality of little children often carries over into our adult years. We forget that God is the Avenger. If we will allow God to defend us and refuse to seek retribution, we will remain in a state of peace and joy.

Proverbs 24:28–29 cautions us not to say, "I will do to him just as he has done to me." God is the One who renders to all according to their works.

Just this morning I discovered another name for God in my daily readings. Jeremiah 51:56 says, "For the LORD is the God of recompense, He will surely repay." Recompense occurs when we repay or compensate someone for a loss.

We can trust the Lord God of recompense to right the wrongs done to us and to repay us for any losses we have experienced in our lifetime.

Lord, thank You for being the God of recompense.

Evening Watch: Read Psalm 78:59–72. God always chooses the weak to confound the wise. Paul wrote:

> But God has chosen the foolish things of the world to put to shame the wise, and God has chosen the weak things of the world to put to shame the things which are mighty; and the base things of the world and the things which are despised God has chosen, and the things which are not, to bring to nothing the things that are, that no flesh should glory in His presence.
>
> —1 CORINTHIANS 1:27–29

Paul went on to explain that now we are in Christ who is our wisdom, righteousness, sanctification, and redemption. (See 1 Corinthians 1:30.) What a comfort it is to know that we do not have to have a high IQ or great physical strength to be used by the Lord!

The end of Psalm 78 reviews how God chose the tribe of Judah to build His sanctuary. Judah was one of the smallest tribes. He also chose a lowly shepherd boy to become king of Israel. God observed how David shepherded his father's sheep and He knew that David would be a good shepherd over the children of Israel. Verse 72 says, David "shepherded them [his sheep] according to the integrity of his heart, And guided them by the skillfulness of his hands." God looks at the heart first. God has always entrusted His work into men and women who have integrity of heart.

Lord, help me to lead others with integrity.

Jeremiah 12:1–14:10; 1 Thessalonians 1:1–2:8; Psalm 79:1–13; Proverbs 24:30–34

Morning Wisdom: Read Proverbs 24:30–34. My friend has assumed the responsibility to care for not only her farm but also her parent's farm. She is widowed and has had to hire help to keep up with the planting and harvesting. When she writes me and tells me all she has been doing, I feel so lazy. One time she asked me what I did all day, and I was embarrassed to share my days with her, because compared to her days I did very little. A person who has the responsibility for crops or vineyards has to care for the land daily in order to have a good harvest.

Proverbs 24:30–34 describes the field and vineyard of a lazy man. Thorns and nettles covered the surface and the fields were overgrown with thorns. Verse 33–34 says, "A little sleep, a little slumber, A little folding of the hands to rest; So shall your poverty come like a prowler, And your need like an armed man."

We may not be in charge of a farm or vineyard, but the Lord has placed us in charge of His fields and vineyards. Jesus said, "The harvest truly is plentiful, but the laborers are few. Therefore pray the Lord of the harvest to send out laborers into His harvest" (Matt. 9:37–38). I believe we live in the time of the last great harvest of souls. The fact that we are still alive means that God has faith that we will both pray for laborers and be laborers in this last harvest. The body of Christ cannot afford to be lazy in these last days.

The other day when I was in prayer, I heard these words within my heart: "Work, for the night is coming when man can no longer work." That morning I made a commitment to be an efficient laborer during this harvesttime.

Lord, help me to use my time wisely in these last days. I pray for more Christians to respond to the call to labor in this last harvest.

Evening Watch: Read Psalm 79:1–13. In the October 8 devotional I shared the new name for God I learned when I read Jeremiah 51:56, which says, "the LORD is the God of recompense." This means that God promises to restore and repay us for our losses. The author of this psalm reviewed the devastation left after Jerusalem was invaded. We can identify with the cry of this psalmist when he prayed, "Oh, do not remember former iniquities against us! Let Your tender mercies come speedily to meet us" (v. 8). The psalmist asked the Lord to repay sevenfold the reproach with which they reproached the Lord. (See v. 12.)

The God of recompense will not only repay or compensate for our losses, but He will also requite our enemies.

Lord, thank You for doing battle for me.

Jeremiah 14:11–16:15; 1 Thessalonians 2:9–3:13; Psalm 80:1–19; Proverbs 25:1–5

Morning Wisdom: Read Proverbs 25:1–5. Just this morning we learned that a brother in Christ discovered that his wife had been unfaithful. When we hung up the phone, I told my husband not to share that conversation with anyone without the permission of that brother in Christ. It is so important that we allow people to tell their own stories. We have to be so careful not to share someone else's story without their permission.

Proverbs 25:2 says, "It is the glory of God to conceal a matter, But the glory of kings is to search out a matter." There is one King who we can trust never to betray a confidence. His name is King Jesus. What a privilege it is to take confidential matters to King Jesus, because He is the One who will give the best counsel and wisdom about the matter. He knows the hearts of all those concerned.

Proverbs 25:5 says, "Take away the wicked from before the king, And his throne will be established in righteousness." One of the prayers I pray when I pray for those in authority in our own land is that the wicked in authority will be removed and replaced by righteous men and women.

Lord, raise up godly leaders in our nation.

Evening Watch: Read Psalm 80:1–19. "Cause Your face to shine, And we shall be saved" is the phrase repeated several times in this psalm. Throughout the Bible we have the exhortation to seek God's face.

For a period of six months many years ago I did just that. I sought God's face and I asked specifically to see a manifestation of Jesus. I claimed John 14:21, which says: "He who has My commandments and keeps them, it is he who loves Me. And he who loves Me will be loved by My Father, and I will love him and manifest Myself to him." The word *manifest* means "to reveal or show."

When I was waking from a long Sunday nap, I saw a ball of light in the distance. As that ball of light drew nearer I saw the face of Jesus in that light. His countenance was radiant and His eyes pierced through me like lazar beams. My spirit leaped within me, and I wanted to run to Him. His face relayed such peace, love, and joy that I prayed, *Lord, if the world could just see Your face, the whole world would repent and be saved.* Then I heard with my heart these words: "I have not chosen to reveal My face to the world. Instead, I have chosen to reveal My face through the faces of My faithful ones on Earth." When we lift of the Lord's countenance by shining His love, peace, and joy to others, Jesus will be able to draw those we know to Him.

Lord, cause Your face to shine through my face every day.

OCTOBER II

Jeremiah 16:16–18:23; 1 Thessalonians 4:1–5:3; Psalm 81:1–16; Proverbs 25:6–7

Morning Wisdom: Read Proverbs 25:6–7. When we were in Israel a lady prophesied over us. She said that we would stand in the place where kings stand. My quick, unspoken response was, "Sure!" Whenever I receive a prophetic word I usually put it on the shelf and ask God to perform it in His timing if it is true. Shortly after this word was given to us we had the opportunity to visit Russia. It was 1992, just after the Soviet Union had dissolved. We were touring with a college group who were invited to go to the White House where the Russian Parliament meets. Just before the interview we were given a tour of the building. I was impressed. Suddenly I realized where we were standing and I asked someone to take our picture. My husband and I were standing in front of huge portraits of Peter and Catherine the Great. I looked at my husband and exclaimed, "See, the prophecy we received in Israel has come true!" Proverbs 25:6–7 warns against exalting ourselves in the presence of kings or other great people. We should only stand before kings when they invite us to do so. Otherwise, we might be commanded to step down from that position of exaltation.

There is one King that we can stand before daily. His name is King Jesus. He invites us to come to Him, but when we approach His throne room, we should come with a humble attitude. Jesus daily invites us to come and learn from Him meekness and lowliness of heart. (See Matthew 11:29.) When we learn meekness and lowliness of heart we will never exalt ourselves in the presence of King Jesus. Instead, we will humble ourselves before Him and allow Him to instruct us and teach us His class on meekness.

Lord, thank You for teaching me meekness.

Evening Watch: Read Psalm 81:1–16. We just celebrated the Feast of Trumpets (Rosh Hashanah). (See Leviticus 23:24.)

Trumpets were blown at the time of the new moon and full moon on the solemn feast day. The trumpets are blown to herald the beginning of a new year, and the promise is that God will remove every burden from the shoulders of His people in the coming year. (See v. 6.) Verse six also states that God will free the hands of His people from the baskets (pots). I have been claiming that promise for years, since I have longed to be set free from the task of cooking three meals a day. Praise the Lord! This promise has finally been fulfilled in my life. I feel like blowing the trumpet.

Lord, thank You for all the occasions that You give us to celebrate.

Jeremiah 19:1–21:14; 1 Thessalonians 5:4–28; Psalm 82:1–8; Proverbs 25:8–10

Morning Wisdom: Read Proverbs 25:8–10. This reading from Proverbs gives good advice. It warns against going to court hastily. Instead we should debate with the person who is against us. We should seek to come to an agreement without having to go to court. We should not share those debates with others, because the situation could be exposed, and our own reputation could be ruined.

I have a divorced friend who was forced to go to court because her husband wanted full custody of their children. She wanted to have the case mediated, but her husband was unwilling to do this. My friend is still paying the legal fees, but the good news is that the courts did award her joint custody of her children.

Both parties in this divorce were Christians, and they would have saved themselves thousands of dollars if they had mediated their divorce out of court. Taking someone to court about any matter should be a last resort for a Christian.

Lord, You are the best mediator. I pray more Christians will seek Your services rather than trust in the arm of the flesh.

Evening Watch: Read Psalm 82:1–8. We talked this morning about how Jesus is our faithful Advocate. This psalm tells us that God is the Judge of the whole earth. As I read this psalm I felt like the author was blaming God for the injustice in the world. However, he soon came to the conclusion that God would judge righteously, and all those who put their trust in Him would inherit the earth.

It is so easy to blame God for the things that are occurring on Earth. Satan loves for us to accuse God of being unjust and uncaring. Satan is the accuser, and he always tries to besmirch the reputation of God. We should never cooperate with the accuser of the brethren. The moment we feel like blaming God or even another person, we need to pour out our complaint to the Lord.

The author of this psalm was pouring out his complaint as he observed the instability of this earth. Our earth right now is very unstable. Massive earthquakes are happening in many places. The tragic tsunami in the 10/40 window and the earthquake in Pakistan and India are signs that the earth is travailing like a woman in labor before the Lord comes again. Jesus told us that this instability in the earth would be one of the signs of His coming. (See Matthew 24:7.) More than ever we need to submit ourselves to God and resist the devil in these last days. Never allow the devil to tell you that God is not good.

Lord, help me to never cooperate with the accuser.

OCTOBER 13

Morning Wisdom: Read Proverbs 25:11–14. I love word pictures, and this reading is full of them. The godly deeds done are painted on the canvas of God's earth when the author compares our good deeds to the beauty of God's creation. Listed below are those comparisons:

- Speaking a fitting word is like apples of gold and settings of silver.
- Wisely rebuking those who have an obedient ear is like an ornament of gold.
- Being a faithful messenger to bring good news is like a refreshing, cold snow at harvesttime.

Today is Yom Kippur, the highest holy day on the Jewish calendar. It is the Day of Atonement, a day of fasting when Jewish people gather to repent of their sins and to ask the Lord to keep their names in the book of the righteous. The book of Jonah is read on Yom Kippur to remind the people of the importance of obeying God's instructions. Between Rosh Hashanah and Yom Kippur, Jewish people think over the last year. They confess those times they did not please the Lord. Those ten days are called "the days of awe."

It might be well for Christians to join our Jewish brothers and sisters as they fast this day. When you read this devotional, the date of Yom Kippur will be changed. Look on your calendar to discover when Yom Kippur falls in the year you read this devotional. In addition to joining our Jewish friends on this high holy day by fasting and reading the book of Jonah, you may want to review this reading from Proverbs, which challenges us to speak wise words and to be faithful messengers of God's Word to others.

Lord, I confess my sins before You.

Evening Watch: Read Psalm 83:1–18. This morning we read the beautiful word pictures that compared our good deeds to God's magnificent creation. Today's reading in Psalms also contains descriptive word pictures. However, the word pictures in this psalm are used to describe God's power to destroy His enemies. The psalmist listed his enemies and then asked God to deal with them as He dealt with the enemies He defeated in the past.

The psalmist asked God to make his enemies like whirling dust and like the chaff before the wind. He asked God to pursue his enemies like an uncontrollable fire in the mountains. He called on God to frighten his enemies with His storm. The heart of the psalmist is revealed in the last two verses of this psalm: "Let them be confounded and dismayed forever; Yes, let them be put to shame and perish, That they may know that You, whose name alone is the Lord, Are the Most High over all the earth." The psalmist did not want his enemies to be defeated just because they came against him. He wanted them to know God's power in hopes that future generations might repent and turn to God.

Lord, thank You for Your awesome power to deal with our enemies.

Jeremiah 23:21–25:38; 2 Thessalonians 2:1–17; Psalm 84:1–12; Proverbs 25:15

Morning Wisdom: Read Proverbs 25:15. It says, "By long forbearance a ruler is persuaded, And a gentle tongue breaks a bone." We forbear when we are willing to suffer long and be patient with people. The law of kindness on our tongues will always produce good fruit. You have probably heard the expression, "Sticks and stones may break my bones, but words will never hurt me." Words can hurt and cause deep wounds in our souls, but a gentle tongue can break those who are stubborn and proud. I call such people "boneheads." Make it your goal today to have the law of kindness on your tongue.

Lord, help me to speak only kind things to others.

Evening Watch: Read Psalm 84:1–12. I was just talking with my friends Isaac and Betty. Isaac was sharing with me about the three pilgrim feasts—the Feast of Tabernacles, the Feast of Weeks, and the Feast of Passover. Every man was required to make their pilgrimage to Jerusalem to celebrate these three feasts in the temple. The writer of this psalm had probably traveled miles to observe one of these pilgrim feasts. As he entered the courtyard he observed the birds as they nested on the walls of the temple. He wrote, "Even the sparrow has found a home, And the swallow a nest for herself, Where she may lay her young...'Blessed are those who dwell in Your house; They will still be praising You'" (v. 3–4). He added, "For a day in Your courts is better than a thousand. I would rather be a doorkeeper in the house of my God Than to dwell in the tents of wickedness" (v. 10). He ends the psalm with this wonderful declaration, "No good thing will He withhold From those who walk uprightly" (v. 11).

Lord, I worship You and give You praise!

OCTOBER 15

Morning Wisdom: Read Proverbs 25:16. We keep one of my devotional books in the car along with our Bible. I often read the devotional for the day to my husband as he drives the car. As I read the reading from Proverbs for today, which is my birthday, I asked my husband, "What can I say about this unusual verse from Proverbs in my third devotional book?"

Proverbs 25:16 says, "Have you found honey? Eat only as much as you need, Lest you be filled with it and vomit." This was not a pleasant scripture to read on my birthday, but my husband helped me to discover the nugget of truth in this verse. He said, "The Word of God is compared to honey." Psalm 19:10 compares the Word of God to honey and the honeycomb. I then understood that when we begin to taste the sweetness of God's Word, we should be careful how we digest it. We should not gulp it down like a starving person. On the contrary, we should meditate on God's Word. We meditate on the Word when we chew it slowly and allow the truths found in passages to digest and touch our souls. If we take too much of the Word of God in at one time, we likely will miss some of the treasures hidden in Scripture.

One year I read the Bible through four times instead of just once. At the end of the year I could not remember any revelatory truths I had discovered that year. This year as we slowly go through Proverbs together, take time to meditate on the wisdom revealed in each verse. I can already see some changes in my own life because of the wisdom I have gained through the discipline of reading only one or two verses from Proverbs daily. I hope you can say the same.

Lord, help me to apply the wisdom found in Proverbs patiently.

Evening Watch: Read Psalm 85:1–13. Most of us have memorized Psalm 23. This psalm is like a twin sister to Psalm 23. It confirms all that Psalm 23 says. This psalm declares how we shall not want, because His salvation is near to those who fear Him. (See v. 9.) Verse 10 says that mercy and truth have met together, and verse 13 declares, "Righteousness will go before Him, And shall make His footsteps our pathway." Verse 12 states that the Lord will give what is good.

David wrote, "He leads me in the paths of righteousness For His name's sake" (Ps. 23:3). "Surely goodness and mercy shall follow me All the days of my life; And I will dwell in the house of the LORD Forever" (Ps. 23:6). Both Psalm 85 and Psalm 23 are comforting psalms to mediate on before retiring. Knowing that God is good and that His mercies are new every morning gives us confidence that the Lord will go before us in all we do tomorrow.

Lord, Your mercies are new every morning. Great is Your faithfulness.

Jeremiah 28:1–29:32; 1 Timothy 1:1–20; Psalm 86:1–17; Proverbs 25:17

Morning Wisdom: Read Proverbs 25:17. This verse warns us to seldom set foot in our neighbor's house, because he might become weary of us and eventually hate us. Doesn't the Word of God tell us to love our neighbor as ourselves? How can we show love to our neighbors if we seldom see them and have no communication with them?

Over the years I have lived in several neighborhoods. The neighborhood I enjoyed most was when we lived in New Jersey. The houses were arranged in a circle around one common playground. We could see our children play when we sat on our back porch. Often I went to the playground and talked with the parents who were watching their children. We had neighborhood picnics in the park during the warm months, and in the winter we often gathered together at different homes for dessert or dinner.

Recently I invited the neighbors who live closest to our home to come for dessert. Some new neighbors had moved in, and I wanted them to meet their neighbors. Everyone had a wonderful time, and they were so grateful we made the effort to host the party. However, since that time not one of those neighbors has invited us to come visit them in their homes.

I have been careful not to visit any of my neighbors without an invitation. I would love to get to know our neighbors better, so I guess I'll have to host another get-together at my home.

I have never had a neighbor who visited me so many times that I became weary of them. However, we can learn from today's verse never to knock on our neighbor's door unless we have first called them to ask them if we could drop by.

Lord, help me to be a good neighbor.

Evening Watch: Read Psalm 86:1–17. Psalm 86 is one of my favorite psalms. It is a prayer of David that extols the greatness of God and reveals the determination of his heart to walk in God's truths.

I pray a prayer based on verses 11 and 12 of this psalm often. You may want to pray with me:

Teach me Your ways, O Lord. I want to walk in Your truths. Unite my heart to fear Your name. I will praise You, O Lord my God, with all my heart, and I will glorify Your name forevermore.

When we pray this prayer we are lifting our souls (our minds, emotions, and wills) up to the Lord. We lift our minds up to the Lord when we study God's Word. We lift our emotions up to the Lord when we trust Him to anchor our emotions in hope. We lift our wills up to the Lord when we pray:

Not my will but Your will be done.

OCTOBER 17

Morning Wisdom: Read Proverbs 25:18–19. God has called us to be faithful to Him, to our spouses, to the saints in the body of Christ, to our friends, and to our neighbors. Faithfulness is a fruit of the Spirit that can only be formed in us as we are conformed to the image of Jesus Christ. The results of unfaithfulness in a marriage or a friendship are disastrous. Betrayal can cause wounds that may take years to heal.

Proverbs 25:18 compares a man who bears false witness against his neighbor to a club, a sword, and a sharp arrow. When I received the lawsuit from the parents of the little boy who was injured when my car struck him, I felt like a sharp arrow struck me in the stomach. I was shocked, but then I held their lawsuit before the Lord. I prayed, *Lord, these neighbors have borne false witness against me, and You have commanded us not to do this. I trust you to be my Advocate to right this wrong.* The Lord defended me, and the whole matter was settled out of court. Our insurance did not even go up.

Proverbs 19 compares confidence in an unfaithful man in a time of trouble to a bad tooth or a foot out of joint. When we are in trouble we should first go to the Lord. He is always faithful, and we can put our confidence fully in Him. When we go to the Lord instead of trusting in the arm of flesh to get us out of trouble, we will not experience the pain of betrayal.

Lord, thank You for Your faithfulness.

Evening Watch: Read Psalm 87:1–7. We have had the privilege of visiting Israel eight times. Every time I go, my heart is overwhelmed with compassion for Israel and the people who dwell there. The next time I go to Israel and pass by the gates of the wall that surrounds Jerusalem, I will remember that the Lord loves the gates of Zion. Psalm 87:2–3 says, "The Lord loves the gates of Zion More than all the dwellings of Jacob. Glorious things are spoken of you, O city of God!" Throughout the psalms, glorious things are spoken in reference to Jerusalem. Jerusalem is God's hometown. His heart has been and always will be towards Israel and His chosen people.

Our precious guide's grandfather and great grandfather were all fisherman and carpenters who lived on the Sea of Galilee. I believe this guide is especially equipped to lead us because of his heritage. What a privilege it must be to be born in God's hometown. Psalm 87:6 says, "The Lord will record, When He registers the peoples: 'This one was born there.'"

Lord, thank You for Your beautiful golden city, Jerusalem! Remind me to pray for the peace of Jerusalem daily.

Jeremiah 31:27–32:44; 1 Timothy 3:1–16; Psalm 88:1–18; Proverbs 25:20–22

Morning Wisdom: Read Proverbs 25:20–22. Proverbs 25:20 warns against singing to a heavy-hearted person, because that person will not be able to receive our cheerful song with grace. Singing a cheerful song to such a person would be like adding soda to vinegar. I can remember putting a teaspoon of soda in vinegar when I was a young chemist around eight years of age. The fizz that mixture made was exciting to watch, but the excitement was short lived.

When a person is heavy hearted, the last thing they want to hear is someone singing to them. Even songs of praise to the Lord can be hard to listen to when we are in the depths of despair. However, Isaiah 61:3 says the garment of praise is for the spirit of heaviness. When we are heavy hearted, we need to ask the Holy Spirit to help us sing songs of praise. As we by faith begin to sing those songs, our downcast souls will be lifted up.

Proverbs 25:21–22 tells us how we should treat our enemies. When we show kindness to our enemies by feeding them when they are hungry and giving them water to drink to quench their thirst, the Lord will reward us, and it will be like heaping coals of fire on our enemy's head. I used to think that heaping coals of fire upon someone's head was a bad thing, but I learned recently that this is a kind thing to do. When these verses were written people warmed their homes with hot coals that they purchased from the marketplace. These coals were carried in a container on top of the heads of people. Sometimes people would have to travel a long distance before they reached their homes and their coals would begin to go out. Kind people who also were transporting coals would add a few hot coals to the container on another person's head so their coals would be rekindled. We can kindle the fire of the Holy Spirit in people who have lost their zeal for the Lord by saying kind words and doing kind things to them.

Lord, help me rekindle the fire of the Holy Spirit in others.

Evening Watch: Read Psalm 88:1–18. I can identify with this psalmist when he cried out to the Lord. He felt like God had deserted him. When we lived in Savannah, Georgia, my husband went through severe depression. I can remember crying out to the Lord, *Lord, if You are there please let me know that you are hearing my prayers.* I was folding clothes in the guest room while my husband was sprawled almost lifeless on the sofa in the den. About five minutes after I cried out to the Lord, the telephone rang. It was a former prayer partner who had moved to Florida. She asked me, "Linda, is everything all right?" I began to cry, and I could not even complete my first sentence before my friend interrupted me. She said, "Linda, I have a word the Lord gave me to give you: though our outward man is perishing, yet the inward man is being renewed day by day" (2 Cor. 4:16). I knew then that the Lord had heard my cries. You may not receive an answer on Earth to your cries as quickly as I did, but you can rest assured that the Lord hears you the instant you cry out to Him, and He will send the answer in His time.

Lord, thank You for hearing me when I cry out to You.

Jeremiah 33:1–34:22; 1 Timothy 4:1–16; Psalm 89:1–13; Proverbs 25:23–24

Morning Wisdom: Read Proverbs 25:23–24. Proverbs 25:23 says, "The north wind brings forth rain, And a backbiting tongue an angry countenance." Many things can cause an angry countenance. While I was babysitting two young girls, I noticed the angry countenance of the four-year-old. She stormed around the house with her hands folded and her face was frozen in a frown. I thought to myself, *What on earth can a four-year-old be so angry about?* Then I watched one of their favorite TV cartoons with them, and I realized that this four-year-old was imitating one of the characters in that cartoon. That character had the same angry expression that this child displayed. We have to be so careful about what children watch, because they are so impressible.

A backbiting tongue can cause an angry countenance. We backbite when we speak about others behind their backs. We should never speak something about someone unless what we say can be said to that person face-to-face. Whatever we say about another person usually comes back to them, and when it does, that person will certainly have an angry countenance.

Contention can cause an angry countenance. Proverbs 25:24 says, "It is better to dwell in a corner of a housetop, Than in a house shared with a contentious woman." Whenever I read this verse I pray, *Lord, help me not to be a contentious woman.*

The word *content* is found in the first part of the word *contentious*. A contentious woman is a discontented woman, and such women can convey their discontent by nagging, murmuring, complaining, and arguing. They often convey their discontent with an angry look. The source of all contention is pride. When we humble ourselves daily before the Lord, we will not become contentious.

Lord, may my actions and my countenance convey Your love always.

Evening Watch: Read Psalm 89:1–13. We talked this morning about an angry countenance and a contentious woman.

A good way to guard ourselves against ever displaying an angry countenance or stirring up strife with our words is to remain in praise all day long. The psalmist began this psalm with these words, "I will sing of the mercies of the LORD forever; With my mouth will I make known Your faithfulness to all generations."

When we sing songs, make melody in our hearts, and stay in an attitude of praise and thanksgiving, we will remain filled with the Spirit all day long. Paul exhorted the church at Ephesus to be filled with the Spirit by speaking to one another in psalms and hymns and spiritual songs, singing and making melody in their hearts. (See Ephesians 5:18–20.) The psalmist exhorts the assembly of saints to fear and praise the Lord. (See v. 7.) Make it your goal tomorrow to declare God's faithfulness in song and make melody in your heart while you are at your workplace. There will be no room for contention and anger in your life if you remain filled with the Spirit all day long.

Praise You!

Jeremiah 35:1–36:32; 1 Timothy 5:1–25; Psalm 89:14–37; Proverbs 25:25–27

Morning Wisdom: Read Proverbs 25:25–27. We have a little more than two more months to finish our readings from Proverbs.

The divisions of the verses of Proverbs in *The One Year Bible* sometimes are not connected, but they all have an important message. The first two verses of this reading do seem to be connected. Both speak about water. Proverbs 25:25 says, "As cold water to a weary soul, So is good news from a far country." Proverbs 25:26 says, "A righteous man who falters before the wicked Is like a murky spring and a polluted well." There is nothing more refreshing than a cold bottle of water on a hot day. Passing on a good report is like giving a cup of cold water to a hot, thirsty soul. Such a report can build the faith of a weary soul and make their day.

In addition to passing on good reports to others, we should exhort and encourage our Christian brothers and sisters daily. I am convinced that one of the main reasons Christians give in to temptation and falter is because they become discouraged and begin to doubt that anyone even cares about them. Worldly people will always try to get us to go their way. We will not falter before the wicked when we stay in fellowship with our brothers and sisters in Christ. This is why the writer of Hebrews exhorts us not to forsake the assembling of ourselves together as the day draws near to Christ's coming. (See Hebrews 10:25.) The writer knew that in the last days seducing spirits would be on the prowl to try to persuade Christians to give in to temptation.

The last verse in this reading is not connected, but it presents a worthy warning that we should all hear and obey. Proverbs 25:27 warns us not to seek our own glory. When we seek our own glory, God's glory vanishes from our lives. God shares His glory with no man. Paul wrote, "He who glories, let him glory in the LORD" (1 Cor. 1:31).

Lord, let me always glory in only You.

Evening Watch: Read Psalm 89:14–37. We talked yesterday about what causes an angry countenance. Today's psalm shares what causes a beautiful, bright countenance. Psalm 89:15–16 says "Blessed are the people who know the joyful sound! They walk, O LORD, in the light of Your countenance." If we walk daily in the light of the countenance of Jesus, we will live blessed lives. How do we do that? John told us how when he wrote: "If we say that we have fellowship with Him, and walk in darkness, we lie and do not practice the truth. But if we walk in the light as He is in the light, we have fellowship with one another, and the blood of Jesus Christ His Son cleanses us from all sin" (1 John 6–7). In this same passage from 1 John we are told to confess our sins so that we can be cleansed from all unrighteousness. When we do not walk in righteousness, our countenance will be darkened and our fellowship with Jesus, the Light of the World, will be broken. The good news is that our countenance will immediately be brightened if we confess our sins and turn away from them.

Lord, help me to daily walk in the light.

Jeremiah 37:1–38:18; 1 Timothy 6:1–21; Psalm 89:38–52; Proverbs 25:28

Morning Wisdom: Read Proverbs 25:28. Proverbs 25:28 confirms that we are three-part beings when it says, "Whoever has no rule over his own spirit Is like a city broken down, without walls." Human beings can be compared to a city. Our souls and spirits are walled in by our bodies. The gates to the wall reside in the mind part of our souls. The mind part of the soul has three gates—the ear gate, the eye gate, and the mouth gate. If we open the gates of our minds to seducing spirits when they tempt us, our souls can be influenced by Satan and his demonic spirits. When we open the gates of our minds to the enemy, the whole city of our being can be broken down. We lose control of our own spirit when we allow our souls to take ascendancy over our spirits.

Lord, help me to close the gates of my city to Satan.

Evening Watch: Read Psalm 89:38–52. The writers of various psalms often poured out their complaints to the Lord. This psalm, which is a contemplation of Ethan the Ezrahite, certainly began well with the exaltation of God. The faithfulness, long-suffering, and mercy of God are reviewed in the first thirty-seven verses of this psalm. Beginning with verse 38, there is a shift from exaltation to exasperation. I would love to know what caused this shift in the author's attitude.

Most of us can certainly identify with the emotional shift of the author. I know I have experienced those days when I am full of faith and thanksgiving in the morning, and by evening I question whether or not God was even on the scene during the day. Circumstances and relational situations occur in the period of a day, and often things do not turn out as we hoped they would. If your day was like that today, just pour out your complaint to the Lord. He will not fall off His throne. He can take it.

Lord, thank You for hearing my complaints.

October 22

Morning Wisdom: Read Proverbs 26:1–2. We should give honor where honor is due. Proverbs 26:1 says that it is not fitting to give honor to a fool. I know I have done and said some foolish things in my lifetime, and I condemn myself when I mess up. It took me a long time to recognize that whenever I condemn myself I am cooperating with Satan because he constantly accuses.

Romans 8:1 says, "There is therefore now no condemnation to those who are in Christ Jesus, who do not walk according to the flesh, but according to the Spirit." God knows that my desire is to walk always in the Spirit. However, sometimes my spirit is willing but my flesh is weak. When this happens God does not write me off, because He knows my heart. It comforts me to know that God is more interested in my heart motivation rather than my actions and words. God always honors the humble in heart.

I have heard Proverbs 26:2 quoted many times in teachings about generational curses. Proverbs 26:2 says that every curse does have a cause. The major cause for all curses is simply not hearing and obeying God's Word. If you would like to discover the curses for breaking God's laws, read Deuteronomy 28:18–68. The good news is that Jesus Christ has redeemed those who put their trust in Him from the curse of the law. Galatians 3:13 says, "Christ has redeemed us from the curse of the law, having become a curse for us (for it is written, 'Cursed is everyone who hangs on a tree')."

Lord, thank You for delivering me from condemnation and curses.

Evening Watch: Read Psalms 90:1–91:16. Psalm 90 is the only psalm written by Moses. Throughout this psalm Moses emphasized the brevity of our lives. He compared our lives to grass that grows in the morning and then is cut down in the evening. He wrote, "The days of our lives are seventy years; and if by reason of strength they are eighty years." He prayed, "So teach us to number our days, That we may gain a heart of wisdom" (v. 12). He concluded the psalm with a prayer that I have summarized and personalized. I plan to pray the prayer below daily:

Let Your work be demonstrated to me and Your glory to my children. Let Your beauty be upon me today. Let the work of my hands today be established.

Jeremiah 42:1–44:23; 2 Timothy 2:1–21; Psalms 92:1–93:5; Proverbs 26:3–5

Morning Wisdom: Read Proverbs 26:3–5. This chapter of Proverbs describes foolish people, lazy people, contentious people, hypocritical people, and people who gossip and lie. I trust that you do not fall into one of those categories, but more than likely you do know people who do. The first twelve verses of Proverbs 26 describe a foolish person. We learned in yesterday's reading from Proverbs (Prov. 26:1–2) that God is more interested in the motivation of our hearts than He is in what we say and do. There used to be a song in the late fifties, "My Foolish Heart." The song describes how a young man has foolishly fallen for a girl who treated him badly. If we have foolish hearts we can easily be deceived.

The verses in our reading today seem contradictory. Verse 4 gives the advice to "not answer a fool according to his folly," and verse 5 exhorts us to "answer a fool according to his folly." The warnings in both of these verses clarify the meaning of these two verses. Verse 4 warns us not to answer a fool, because if we do we could become like him. If our answer to a fool is one that agrees with what he has said, we do run the risk of becoming just like him. Verse 5 exhorts us to give an answer to a fool with the warning that no answer at all would cause the fool to think he is totally right. The lesson here is to never answer a fool with a statement that agrees with his folly. Instead, answer a fool with a statement filled with wisdom.

The wisest answers to anyone's questions are found in God's Word. If we counter foolish questions with wise answers from God's Word, at least we have given an answer that might change the foolish heart of a person. Only the Word of God has the power to transform a person's mind and soften his heart. I am challenged by this reading to hide God's Word in my heart so that I will be able to answer a fool wisely.

Lord, help me to be faithful to hide Your Word in my heart.

Evening Watch: Read Psalms 92:1–93:5. This morning we learned more about foolish people and how to interact with them. One of the major faults of a foolish person is that they lack understanding. Verse 6 in Psalm 92 confirms this observation. Verse 6 says, "A senseless man does not know, Nor does a fool understand this." A foolish person can never understand the works of God.

One might question, "Is there any hope for a fool?" Psalm 92:13 gives the answer to this question when it says, "Those who are planted in the house of the LORD Shall flourish in the courts of our God." The only hope for a fool is for someone to share the gospel with him or her. The ignorance and lack of understanding that a fool has can only be countered by an atmosphere where the water of God's Word is continually being poured out upon that person. If you know foolish people, begin today to pray for them and look for opportunities to invite them to places where they will hear God's Word.

Lord, help me to pray more for people who have no clue about You.

Jeremiah 44:24–47:7; 2 Timothy 2:22–3:17; Psalm 94:1–23; Proverbs 26:6–8

Morning Wisdom: Read Proverbs 26:6–8. These verses present three vivid word pictures to describe what happens if we deal with a fool. Verse 6 says that when we send a message by a fool, we cut off our own feet and drink violence. You are probably familiar with the expression, "We cut off our own nose to spite our face." Maybe the basis of that expression comes from this verse.

Another word picture is given when the author compared a proverb in the mouth of fools to legs of a lame person whose legs hang limp. A foolish person will never be able to walk in the truths given in the book of Proverbs. Truths from God's Word have no affect on the lives of fools.

The last word picture in this reading says, "Like one who binds a stone in a sling Is he who gives honor to a fool" (v. 8). We should give honor where honor is due.

A foolish person deserves no honor. However, he does deserve our prayers. Jesus Christ died for us when we were foolish. Someone was praying for us when we did and said foolish things. We should also pray for those who need to be delivered from their foolish ways. Their deliverance will come when they accept Jesus Christ as their Lord and Savior, because He is the very wisdom of God. There may be those who you should pray for this morning. Join me as I pray:

Lord, open the eyes of the understanding of those I know who are walking contrary to the truths found in Your Word.

Evening Watch: Read Psalm 94:1–23. This psalm also talks about fools. Verse 8 says, "Understand, you senseless among the people; And you fools, when will you be wise?" We answered this question in this morning's devotional. Transformation from our foolish, sinful ways can only occur when we repent and receive Jesus Christ as our Lord and Savior. Foolish people think that God does not see their actions and that He cannot hear their words. The truth, however, is that God knows the very thoughts of every man, and He alone is able to impart true knowledge to us.

We turn from our foolish ways when we turn our eyes upon Jesus. We have to recognize our total dependence upon God for instruction and correction. We will only stay on His righteous path when we daily enter the classroom of the Holy Spirit, who is able to lead and guide us into all truth. When we do slip up (and we all do), we can have confidence that the Lord will help us and hold us up. This knowledge should comfort us when we become anxious about the possibility of falling away from the Lord.

A friend had a vision of how Jesus daily helps us keep walking on His path of righteousness. She saw the Lord with His hands outstretched to her. He was coaxing her to keep walking towards Him just as a father coaxes a young child to take his first steps.

Jesus never turned His back on her, and He will never turn His back on you. He will always have His hands outstretched to catch you if you begin to fall.

Thank You, Lord.

OCTOBER 25

Jeremiah 48:1–49:22; 2 Timothy 4:1–22; Psalms 95:1–96:13; Proverbs 26:9–12

Morning Wisdom: Read Proverbs 26:9–12. Today's reading continues the discussion of foolish people and how we should relate to them. Another characteristic of a fool is that he keeps doing foolish things. Foolish people do not learn anything from their past mistakes, and they even repeat the same mistakes over and over again. Verse 11 confirms this fact about fools when it says, "As a dog returns to his own vomit, So a fool repeats his folly."

Verse 9 says, "Like a thorn that goes into the hand of a drunkard Is a proverb in the mouth of fools." Foolish people usually try to impress others with their words, but their actions do not line up with their words. They may even quote scriptures, but their hearts are still dull to the Word of God. A drunk is so anesthetized by alcohol that he cannot even feel a thorn in his hands. A foolish person has been anesthetized by Satan. This person may hear and even speak God's Word, but there is no transformation of his or her heart, because the Word is not able to prick and convict his heart.

A foolish person is wise in his own eyes. Pride is the stronghold in a foolish person. Until a foolish person admits his need for God and cries out for true wisdom, the hope of change in that person's life is nonexistent.

As we read through these verses about foolish people, we might just sigh and say, "Why even try to convince a foolish person that they need Jesus?" However, that question is like asking, "Why even try to minister to a drunken beggar on the street?" Foolish people are drunken beggars who need to be filled with the new wine of the Holy Spirit and the Bread of Life, God's Word.

Lord, help me never to give up on foolish people.

Evening Watch: Read Psalms 95:1–96:13. There is hope for foolish people, because we were once like foolish sheep that went astray and followed our own ways instead of God's way. On the cross, however, God made provision for all lost sheep. God laid upon Jesus the iniquity of us all. (See Isaiah 53:6.)

When we were in Bethlehem we observed the shepherds' fields from the balcony of our kibbutz. We noticed that when the shepherds called for their sheep, the personal flock in the care of each shepherd would gather at their shepherd's feet. However, we also noticed that a few sheep in each flock refused to come to the feet of their shepherd even though they heard his special call.

Psalm 95:6–7 says, "Let us kneel before the LORD our Maker. For He is our God, And we are the people of His pasture, And the sheep of His hand." Both Psalms 95 and 96 are psalms of praise that extol the greatness of God. Psalm 95 warns us not to harden our hearts as the children of Israel did in the wilderness. They saw God's mighty works, but they refused to walk in His ways. They were like rebellious sheep that went astray in their hearts, because they never got close enough to their Shepherd to learn His ways.

Lord, help me to learn Your ways.

Morning Wisdom: Read Proverbs 26:13–16. We leave our discussion of foolish people and go on to the description of lazy people. Hopefully none of us fall into this category of people, but I must admit sometimes I am just plain lazy. After reading these few verses in Proverbs 26, I am challenged not to be lazy. Proverbs 26:13 says that a lazy man is too lazy to warn others that there is a lion in the street. Proverbs 26:14 says that a lazy man even turns slowly in his bed like the hinge of a door. Proverbs 26:15 says that a lazy man is too lazy to feed himself. Proverbs 26:16 says that a lazy man thinks he is wiser than even seven sensible men.

At least I have never been too lazy to feed myself. However, I can remember days when I slowly turned in my bed and didn't want to get up in the morning.

Probably most of us could use a wake-up call in the morning that will get us moving and a megavitamin that will sustain us and energize us all day long. God has provided us a means by which we will always be on the alert and energized. He has given us the Holy Spirit, who loves to give us a wake-up call so that we can spend the first part of the morning in prayer. God has also supplied us with the vitamin pills that will sustain us all day long. These vitamins are labeled "The Promises of God."

I like to keep a little promise box nearby during the day so that as I do my various chores, I can draw a promise out of the box. Just reading those Scripture promises helps to feed my soul. I am energized by the Holy Spirit and sustained by the Word of God. When my focus is on the Lord and I allow Him to work through me both to will and to do His good pleasure, there is no time in the day for me to be lazy.

Lord, help me to take my daily vitamins from Your Word and to stay filled with the Holy Spirit.

Evening Watch: Read Psalms 97:1–98:9. Psalm 98:1 says, "Oh, sing to the LORD a new song!" Have you ever tried to sing a new song? I love to do this in my morning quiet times. I will sing in the Spirit for a season, and then the Holy Spirit will help me interpret what I just sang. The words are usually so edifying and most of the songs convey the Lord's love to me. If you never have tried this, I pray you will. You will be blessed.

A good way to stir up that gift within you is to read these psalms. Both Psalms 97 and 98 exalt the Lord and declare His might and power. If you don't have your prayer language, try putting these psalms to music. I know God will love the sound of your voice, and don't concern yourself if you can't carry a tune. God loves joyful noises from His saints just as much as He loves beautiful harmony. God is no respecter of persons. Ask the Holy Spirit to help you sing praises to His name tonight before you go to bed. You will have a sweet sleep.

Holy Spirit, help me to sing a new song.

Morning Wisdom: Read Proverbs 26:17. We have a friend who employs an unusual method to train his dogs not to go into the street. If he catches them going into the street, he bites their ears. When he uses this method consistently, the dogs soon learn not to go into the street. Proverbs 26:17 says, "He who passes by and meddles in a quarrel not his own Is like one who takes a dog by the ears." I imagine if you take a dog by the ears he might become enraged and bite you.

Our son is a peacemaker, and it always concerned me that he might get hurt if he tried to break up a fight. In most cases we should let people settle their own differences. Dr. Dobson, a well-known Christian psychologist, even recommends that as much as possible we should allow siblings to settle their own differences. We are called as Christians to seek peace and pursue it, but this does not mean that we should try to settle other people's quarrels.

Lord, help me to seek peace and pursue it.

Evening Watch: Read Psalm 99:1–9. We talked this morning about children's quarrels. Children usually get into fights because they think their sibling did something unfair to them. I can remember hearing the screams of my own children when they got into quarrels. I usually heard, "He did this to me, and that's not fair!"

We are human, and there are times when we cry out to God, "That's not fair!" We have a dear brother who just lost his own wife to breast cancer, and he said he cried out to God many times, "This just isn't fair!" Life is not fair. One thing we have to realize about God's character is that He also is not fair. He is just. Fairness is the world's idea of making things equal. God's idea of equity is not like our view of equity. He observes this earth, and He is just in His judgments. Our psalm today talks about God's justice when it says: "You have established equity; You have executed justice and righteousness in Jacob" (v. 4).

This psalm goes on to list those God appointed to carry out His righteous judgments. This list included Moses and Aaron and Samuel. God has always set people in positions of power to carry out His justice on Earth. Sometimes we do not get the leaders we desire. Instead, we get the leaders we deserve. We need to pray for our nation to become a righteous nation. When Christians begin to pray and turn from their own unrighteousness in repentance, we can be assured that God will appoint and anoint righteous leaders for our nation.

Lord, help me to pray more for my leaders.

OCTOBER 28

Morning Wisdom: Read Proverbs 26:18–19. We thank God that we do not have neighbors who are practical jokers. I do not know where the expression *practical jokers* came from, because any joke played on another person is neither practical nor prudent. I have never had much patience with people who tease. I think it is because I am so gullible that I usually believe what people say to me is the truth. The reading from Proverbs today compares the person who deceives his neighbor and then just says, "I was only joking!" to a madman who throws firebrands, arrows, and death.

We have to realize that we can wound and hurt others when we tease or pull practical jokes on them. We are told to love our neighbors as we love ourselves, and I don't think any of us enjoy having someone tease us. Teasing or playing a joke on someone is equivalent to lying. Our motivation is to trick and deceive the other person. We may get a laugh out of the other person's response to our teasing, but the other person feels like they have been made a fool.

The prime motivation when we communicate with anyone should be to edify the hearer. If what we are about to say does not build up or help another person, we should keep our mouths shut.

Lord, order my conversation aright.

Evening Watch: Read Psalm 100:1–5. This morning I was awakened with songs the Holy Spirit was singing to me. This happens quite often, and I much rather awake to heavenly music than a talk show on the radio. I wanted to stay in the warmth of my covers, but I felt the Holy Spirit had already started my worship of the Lord, so I got up and joined the concert. There are several songs I sing to the Lord every morning, but this morning He gave me new songs to sing.

The psalm today says, "Come before His presence with singing" (v. 2). This is the way I have always entered the Lord's throne room. Of course I have my list of requests, but somehow as I sing to the Lord those things on my list are released to Him. I sing in the Spirit, and I sing with my understanding. Many times I will have words sung back to me by the Holy Spirit after a season of singing in the Spirit. As I receive the interpretation of those songs in the Spirit, I am edified. Paul wrote, "I will pray with the spirit, and I will also pray with the understanding. I will sing with the spirit, and I will also sing with the understanding" (1 Cor. 14:15).

After the season of singing, I enter a time of thanksgiving that flows right into a time of praise. This psalm says, "Enter into His gates with thanksgiving, And into His courts with praise" (v. 4). The Lord rejoices over us with singing every day, so we also should rejoice with singing in His presence.

Lord, remind me to sing to You every morning.

Morning Wisdom: Read Proverbs 26:20. Fall is in the air. As we take our walks in the neighborhood we see smoke coming out of the smokestacks of many homes. That delightful smell of burning wood fills the atmosphere. I always look forward to the first fire in our fireplace. We thought about getting gas logs, but we decided we would miss the smell of well-aged wood burning in the fireplace.

Proverbs 26:20 says, "Where there is no wood, the fire goes out; And where there is no talebearer, strife ceases." The smell of burning wood is able to travel quite a distance. The messages a talebearer delivers also can travel a long distance. Like a radio relaying a message across the ocean, one juicy bit of gossip can be relayed from one receiver to another very quickly. Those receiving the message usually embellish it, and the small tale soon becomes a huge tale.

"Tattletale, tattletale," was the cry I often heard from my sons when they were children. After an argument one of my sons would come running and say, "He did this to me, and that's not fair!" The strife between brothers birthed the story, but the "tattletale" hoped to create even more strife when he delivered his message to one of his parents. He hoped his brother would get a good whipping.

A talebearer usually has the stronghold of pride. The talebearer hopes to receive attention, because he was the one who heard the story first. Like a reporter who gets the first scoop, he runs to pass the big story so that it can be heard by many. We should be on the alert not to pass on anything that is a bad report, even if it is true.

Lord, forgive me for the times I have passed on a bad report.

Evening Watch: Read Psalm 101:1–8. This psalm includes a prayer I often pray. David made the declaration, "I will walk within my house with a perfect heart. I will set nothing wicked before my eyes" (v. 2–3).

Throughout most of my married years I have not had to work outside the home. My husband always had a job that met our daily needs. Because I am home most of the days of the week, I try to set an atmosphere that welcomes the presence of the Lord. In order to do that, I have to daily ask the Lord to cleanse my own heart. If I let the sun go down on my anger or I am prideful during the day, the atmosphere in our home is tense, because anger and pride cause strife. If I want to walk in my house with a perfect heart, I need to confess my sins at the start or end of each day so that my heart can be cleansed. Many times I am not aware of those things I have done or said that displeased God, but I pray this prayer:

Create within me a clean heart, and renew a right spirit within me. May the perfect One, Jesus, live His life through me today.

Lamentations 2:22–3:66; Hebrews 1:1–14; Psalm 102:1–28; Proverbs 26:21–22

Morning Wisdom: Read Proverbs 26:21–22. James compared the tongue to the rudder of a ship and a roaring fire. He wrote:

> Look also at ships: although they are so large and are driven by fierce winds, they are turned by a very small rudder wherever the pilot desires. Even so the tongue is a little member and boasts great things. See how great a forest a little fire kindles! And the tongue is a fire, a world of iniquity. The tongue is so set among our members that it defiles the whole body, and sets on fire the course of nature; and it is set on fire by hell.
>
> —JAMES 3:4–6

Proverbs 26:21 compares a man who stirs up strife to charcoal or wood that kindles a fire. Pride is the root of all contention, and a contentious man seeks to win every argument, because he is confident that he is always right. A contentious man keeps adding fuel to the fire of an argument every time he opens his mouth. I have discovered the best way to deal with a contentious person is to agree with them. You can simply say, "I believe you may have a point. Let me think about what you have said, and I'll get back with you later." That response will put the fire out quickly, and it is a scriptural response.

Jesus told us to agree with our adversary quickly while we are on the way with him. (See Matthew 5:25.)

Proverbs 26:22 describes the words of a talebearer as tasty trifles that go down into the inmost body. Whenever we pass on a negative story, we are gossiping. What we share with someone will usually get back to the person we were talking about. A good prayer to pray daily is:

> *Set a guard over my lips, and stop me if I am about to speak something I should not.*

Evening Watch: Read Psalm 102:1–28. Whenever David was overwhelmed, he poured out his complaint to the Lord. David poured out his complaints in the first half of this psalm, but the rest of the psalm extols the greatness, faithfulness, and mercies of the Lord. David learned that he had to be honest with God. He knew God was aware of his every thought, so he just said it like he felt it. He expressed his distress and anguish to God. Once he expressed his feelings to God, he was able to receive a refreshing from the Lord, and the anguish of his soul was lifted. When we are overwhelmed, we need to do as David did. If we pour out our complaint to others, we are then guilty of murmuring, which God hates. God's complaint department is always open.

> *Lord, may I always just complain to only You.*

Lamentations 4:1–5:22; Hebrews 2:1–18; Psalm 103:1–22; Proverbs 26:23

Morning Wisdom: Read Proverbs 26:23. Proverbs has many descriptive passages about the power of words. One verse says, "Death and life are in the power of the tongue" (Prov. 18:21). Today's verse warns against saying loving words to cover up how we really feel on the inside. Proverbs 26:23 says, "Fervent lips with a wicked heart Are like earthenware covered with silver dross."

We may fool others with our words, but we will never fool God. He knows what is in our hearts. He knows what our motivation is when we speak. You may say, "But I never have a wicked heart." However, whenever we speak words to manipulate others or to flatter to get our own way, the motivation of our hearts is wicked. We may lay it on thick with kind, loving words when we are really boiling inside with anger against the one with whom we are speaking.

Our words may appear to be silver words on the outside, but they are like hollow earthenware to God. Our only hope to be sincere when we speak is to have Jesus cleanse our hearts daily. A good prayer to pray this morning and every morning is:

> Let the words of my mouth and the meditations of my heart be acceptable in Your sight. Create within me a clean heart, and renew a right spirit within me so that I will speak the words from a heart filled with the Holy Spirit.

Evening Watch: Read Psalm 103:1–22. We talked this morning about how our words can be used to harm or to edify. We can edify ourselves by our own words when we remain in praise all day long. David wrote, "Bless the LORD, O my soul; And all that is within me, bless His holy name!" (v. 1).

Praising the Lord is one way we can lift our souls up to the Lord so the meditations and motivations of our hearts become pure. David listed the many benefits of the Lord that will cause us to bless Him throughout the day. We can bless and praise the Lord because He forgives, heals, redeems, satisfies, provides, strengthens, justifies, and cleanses us. His mercies are new every morning, and He is able to remove our transgressions far from us.

Tomorrow morning and every morning begin to declare what the Lord has done for you. When you start every day with praise, the Lord will set the rudder of your tongue to go in the right direction, and you will sail through the day on the wind of the Holy Spirit. Happy sailing!

> Lord, I praise You for all of Your benefits. Help me to remain in praise all day long.

NOVEMBER 1

Ezekiel 1:1–3:15; Hebrews 31:19; Psalm 104:1–24; Proverbs 26:24–26

Morning Wisdom: Read Proverbs 26:24–26. Satan is a liar and the father of lies. These verses share the futility of trying to cover hatred with lying lips. If there is hatred in our hearts toward anyone, that hatred will eventually be uncovered, even though we try to deceive others by what we say. God hears our hearts before He hears our words. We cannot hide the sin of hatred.

A person with hatred in his heart can speak so kindly to the person they hate, but within they are boiling. When we share with another person a wrong that has been done to us, we can cause that person to take up our offense, and they too can become angry.

Chances are you may instantly forgive a person who wrongs you, but the one who hears the story may be in a state of turmoil for days after you told the story. I try very hard not to pass on anything negative about anyone or share how others have hurt me.

Lord, help me to not spread any evil report, and help me to pray and not say anything that would put another person in a negative light.

Evening Watch: Read Psalm 104:1–24. What a joyful way to conclude a day! These verses in Psalm 104 extol the Lord for His manifold works. The description of God clothed with honor and majesty, dressed in a garment of light, creates a sense of awe for God in my heart. Verse 3 says that God makes the clouds His chariot. He walks on the wings of the wind. Verses 5–13 review how God sets a boundary over the waters of the earth and causes the springs to flow among the hills to give drink to the beasts of the field. All of creation is dependent upon God to provide and sustain life.

The creativity of God is evident as I enjoy the fall season in Atlanta. The trees are dressed in a glorious array of colors, and there is a quietness that settles over this season. The sounds of summer have ceased. The crickets and katydids no longer make their choral sounds. All of creation seems to be rehearsing for the dormant season of winter. Take time to enjoy God's beauty and worship Him while you walk tomorrow. He truly is an awesome God.

Lord, thank You for the display of Your beauty on Earth.

Ezekiel 3:16–6:14; Hebrews 4:1–16; Psalm 104:25–35; Proverbs 26:27

Morning Wisdom: Read Proverbs 26:17. You have probably heard the expression, "He dug his own hole and fell in it!" That expression I am sure came from Proverbs 26:27, which says, "Whoever digs a pit will fall into it, And he who rolls a stone will have it roll back on him."

We do not have to use a shovel to dig our own pit. Nor do we have to use our hands to roll a stone that will roll back on us. The instrument used to accomplish both of these tasks is the tongue. Whenever we use our tongues to speak negative, judgmental, and critical words, those words will come back to us. Jesus said, "Judge not, that you be not judged. For with what judgment you judge, you will be judged" (Matt. 7:1–2).

There is a teaching about bitter-root judgments based on these words of Jesus. The principal of this teaching is that if we are judgmental, we have a root of bitterness in our hearts that needs to be removed.

One only has to review the murmuring and complaining of the children of Israel in the wilderness to discover that they were bitter against Moses and against God. They felt like both God and Moses had brought them to the desert to die. They dug their own pit with their judgmental, murmuring tongues, and their generation did die in the wilderness.

Hebrews 12:14–15 says, "Pursue peace with all people, and holiness, without which no one will see the Lord: looking diligently lest anyone fall short of the grace of God; lest any root of bitterness springing up cause trouble, and by this many become defiled." I am challenged by this devotional to ask the Lord to examine my own heart and remove every vestige of bitterness that might be there.

Lord, search my heart and reveal any bitter roots of judgment I may have.

Evening Watch: Read Psalm 104:25–35. More wondrous works of God are described in this psalm. The last verses in this psalm talk about the powerful ability God demonstrates when He provides for the living and takes away the breath of the dying. Verse 27 describes how God gives all creation their food in due season. Verse 29 says, "You take away their breath, they die and return to their dust." Verses 33–34 say, "I will sing to the LORD as long as I live; I will sing praise to my God while I have my being. May my meditation be sweet to Him; I will be glad in the LORD." Years ago our church put those verses to music. I can still hear the beautiful chorus. Tomorrow when you wake up, begin to praise the Lord and sing to Him. Make it your goal to remain in praise all day long.

Praise You!

Morning Wisdom: Read Proverbs 26:28. We talked yesterday about how we can dig our own holes with our tongues. Proverbs 26:28 continues the theme of the power of the tongue when it says, "A lying tongue hates those who are crushed by it, And a flattering mouth works ruin."

We lie for many reasons, but one of the major reasons we lie about other people is to hurt and crush them. If someone has hurt us, we can easily embellish the story of how they hurt us with facts that simply are not true. Our motive is to create an evil image of the person who hurt us. When we are wounded by another person's words, the words we speak about them are usually based on misperceptions about them. Satan loves to feed those misperceptions to our minds, because he knows those false images will fester into the poison of resentment and unforgiveness in our own hearts.

Just as lying lips can destroy another person, flattering lips can also work ruin. The motivation of flattery is to manipulate the person we flatter. If that person falls into the snare we lay for them through flattery, that person can become a slave who accomplishes all we want them to do. Ruin will come to such a person because he or she no longer submits to the will of God. Instead that person submits to our will for them, and God's voice is silenced by the flattering words that tickle his ears.

Lord, help me to be truthful in all of my ways.

Evening Watch: Read Psalm 105:1–15. The theme of the wondrous works of God continues in this psalm. One only has to look at the nation of Israel to understand that God is a covenant-keeping God. In spite of the many times Israel has broken her covenant with God, God has remained faithful to her. If you ever doubt that God is faithful to perform His Word, just read some of the prophecies that God has already fulfilled concerning the nation of Israel.

Isaiah prophesied that roses would bloom in the deserts of Israel. (See Isaiah 35:1.) He also prophesied that one day the fruit of Israel would fill the earth. (See Isaiah 27:6.) Jeremiah prophesied that the exodus from the north of Israel would be greater than the exodus of Israel from Egypt. Jeremiah 16:14 says, "'Therefore behold, the days are coming,' says the LORD, 'that it shall no more be said, "The LORD lives who brought up the children of Israel from the land of Egypt," but, "The LORD lives who brought up the children of Israel from the land of the north and from all the lands where He had driven them." For I will bring them back into their land which I gave to their fathers.'" Over one million Jewish people have immigrated to Israel, and most of them have come from Russia, the land of the north.

Psalm 105:8 says "He remembers His covenant forever, The word which He commanded, for a thousand generations." What an awesome God we serve!

Lord, thank You for Your faithfulness to keep Your Word.

Ezekiel 10:1–11:25; Hebrews 6:1–20; Psalm 105:16–38; Proverbs 27:1–2

Morning Wisdom: Read Proverbs 27:1–2. Both of today's verses warn against boasting. We should not boast about what we will do tomorrow, and we should not boast about ourselves. Proverbs 27:1 warns us not to boast about tomorrow, because we do not know what a day may bring. "I'll be there if the creek don't rise!" is a southern expression I have used often in response when someone invites me to go somewhere. We do not know what tomorrow will bring, so none of us can guarantee that we will be present at future events.

Proverbs 27:2 advises us not to boast about ourselves. Have you ever met people who verbally give their resumé to you before you even have a chance to introduce yourself to them. I have concluded that people who boast about themselves are usually insecure. They have not discovered their true identity in Christ Jesus. Instead their identity is wrapped up in what they do instead of who they are. We should let others praise us, and when they do we should receive their praises with a simple thank you.

We do not have to say, "I give all the glory to the Lord." Somehow that response does not seem to be quite sincere. God wants us to receive praise, and He does not have to get credit for anything in our lives simply because He is our life.

> *Lord, thank You for working in me both to will and to do of Your good pleasure.*

Evening Watch: Read Psalm 105:16–38. These verses in Psalm 105 review the mighty works God did for His children when He delivered them out of the hand of the Egyptians. God's plan to deliver Israel from the cruel bondage of the Egyptians was in motion, and there was no stopping Him.

God even told Abraham years earlier that Israel would be in bondage for four hundred years. (See Genesis 15:13.) We talked this morning about how man may make his plans, but God directs his steps. (See Proverbs 16:9.) We will wake up tomorrow with our to-do list, but God may have other plans for us. We can be assured that God's plans will never be thwarted. Every morning I pray:

> *Lord, I commit my plans to You. Alter my plans according to Your will.*

Morning Wisdom: Read Proverbs 27:3. The subjects of wrath and anger are discussed in Proverbs 27:3–4. God's wrath is always purpose driven. His wrath is shone to avenge the enemies of His people or to judge His own to bring them to repentance. The purpose of God's wrath is never to destroy for the sake of destroying. God is not a God of destruction. We know that the purpose of Satan's wrath is always to destroy. The good news is that Jesus came to destroy the works of the devil.

Proverbs 27:3 says, "A stone is heavy and sand is weighty, But a fool's wrath is heavier than both of them." A fool's wrath has only one purpose—to smash and destroy. You may have heard this expression, "I could just cream that guy!" When I read this verse I pictured pounds of bundled sand weighted down by stones attached to a cable over the fool's victim. The stones represent the unresolved anger and unforgiveness the fool has towards his victim. The sand represents the times the fool felt offended by his victim. Every time an offense was not cleared in the fool's life, more sand and stones were added to the bundle he planned to one day release against the one who offended him. The day of wrath comes when the fool cuts the cable and releases the bundle to smash his victim.

This vivid picture in my mind challenges me to always clear offenses and to never allow the sun to go down on my anger. Paul exhorted us to always forgive, lest Satan should take advantage of us. (See 2 Corinthians 2:10–11.) He also wrote, "'Be angry, and do not sin': do not let the sun go down on your wrath, nor give place to the devil" (Eph. 4:26–27). A fool is unforgiving, never clears offenses, and allows the sun to go down on his anger.

Lord, help me to never be foolish, but always forgiving.

Evening Watch: Read Psalm 105:39–45. Just as God's wrath always has a purpose, His deliverance also always has a purpose. This psalm describes all the mighty ways God delivered His chosen people from their enemies. "He brought out His people with joy, His chosen ones with gladness" (v. 43). Verse 45 reveals the reason God delivered His chosen. It reads, "That they might observe His statutes And keep His laws" (v. 45). Sadly, God's chosen did not fulfill the purpose of His deliverance. They went their own way and forgot the works of the Lord. They saw God's works, but they were ungrateful. They never learned His ways or walked in them.

Lord, help me to always be grateful for Your deliverance.

Ezekiel 14:12–16:42; Hebrews 7:18–28; Psalm 106:1–12; Proverbs 27:4–6

Morning Wisdom: Read Proverbs 27:4–6. Proverbs 27:4 continues the discussion of anger and wrath. Verse 4 reads, "Wrath is cruel and anger a torrent, But who is able to stand before jealousy?" In past devotionals we learned that pride is the root of all contention. There is another wicked root of contention that can even lead to murder. That root is jealousy. The first murder in the history of mankind happened when a jealous man murdered his own brother. (See Genesis 4:3–11.) The question God asked Cain just before he murdered his brother was, "Why are you angry? And why has your countenance fallen?" (v. 6). Cain killed Abel because God accepted Abel's offering and rejected his offering. A vicious cycle is revealed in the story of Cain and Abel. Jealousy began the cycle that led to a torrent of anger, cruel wrath, and finally murder. If Cain had confessed his anger when God asked him why he was angry, the murder of Abel could have been prevented. Abel could not stand before Cain's jealousy.

Proverbs 27:5–6 conveys a message that should alert every Christian to the importance of dealing honestly with our brothers and sisters in Christ. The message is that we should confront, warn, and rebuke our fellow Christians when they deliberately sin and continue in sin. We cannot just speak into every Christian's life if they are in continuous, willful sin. We only earn the right to speak if we are friends of theirs.

Proverbs 27:6 says, "Faithful are the wounds of a friend, But the kisses of an enemy are deceitful." Even though a rebuke may temporarily wound our friend who is in open sin, he may repent and ask for deliverance. Open rebuke is something most Christians shy away from, but if it will cause our Christian brothers and sisters to be delivered from bondage, the rebuke is a loving act.

Lord, help me to be honest with my Christian friends.

Evening Watch: Read Psalm 106:1–12. There are many names for God, and it seems like each year I go through the Bible I see more names for God. In October we talked about the "the Lord God of recompense." As I was reading Psalm 106, I remembered another name I like to call God. Of course, this is not an official name, but it is a name that fully describes the merciful, long-suffering character of God. The name I love to give God is "the Lord God of the nevertheless." Throughout Scripture we see the rebellion of those He loved, but nevertheless God showed mercy and forgave them.

The author asks the questions, "Who can utter the mighty acts of the LORD? Who can declare all His praise?" (v. 2). Confession is made for Israel's sin of rebellion at the Red Sea. Then the author says, "Nevertheless He saved them for His name's sake, That He might make His mighty power known" (v. 8). After the Red Sea, Israel believed God's Word and sang songs of praise. Their praise was short lived, however. They soon began to murmur and complain again. The Lord God of the nevertheless never gave up on Israel. He has not given up on them today.

Lord, thank You for not giving up.

Morning Wisdom: Read Proverbs 27:7–9. All three of these verses relate to the condition of a man's soul. Proverbs 27:7 says, "A satisfied soul loathes the honeycomb, But to a hungry soul every bitter thing is sweet." We experience many bitter things in our lives, but if our souls hunger for God, He is able to make the bitter sweet.

Proverbs 27:8 says, "Like a bird that wanders from its nest Is a man who wanders from his place." In recent years we have seen so many people in this world displaced by storms, floods, famine, and earthquakes. The little nests we make for our families can be swept away in a moment in time. However, when we experience sudden loss, we will be able to find a resting place if we daily dwell in the presence of the Lord.

Proverbs 27:9 days, "Ointment and perfume delight the heart, And the sweetness of a man's friend gives delight by hearty counsel." Yesterday our pastor read a list of children's definitions for *love*. One definition read, "Love is when a man puts on shaving lotion and a woman puts on perfume, and they go out and smell each other." Two of the sweetest smells that express love to our souls are the presence of the Lord and the company of a friend who gives wise counsel.

Lord, help me to be such a friend.

Evening Watch: Read Psalm 106:13–31. We talked yesterday about "the Lord God of the nevertheless." God's patience and mercy was extended to Israel continually, but the time came when even the Lord God of the nevertheless was ready to destroy Israel. Moses interceded for his people, and God's wrath was turned away. Israel continued in their idolatry, but God was faithful to raise up someone to stand in the gap for the people. Phinehas stood up and intervened when Israel joined themselves to Baal of Peor. God is always looking for an intercessor who will stand in the gap for His people. This challenges me to intercede more for Israel and our own nation.

Lord, forgive me for the times I have failed to pray for Israel and our nation.

Ezekiel 18:1–19:14; Hebrews 9:1–12; Psalm 106:32–48; Proverbs 27:10

Morning Wisdom: Read Proverbs 27:10. This reading from Proverbs exhorts us not to forsake our own friends or our father's friends. It also advises us to not go to a brother who lives far away when calamity strikes us. Instead we should call upon our nearby neighbors for help. We never know when a disaster might strike, and that is why we need a great company of friends and relatives who we can call upon in times of need.

No matter what calamity may come our way, we can take comfort in the fact that we have a friend who sticks closer to us than a brother. That friend is Jesus. We sing a song in our church called "I Am a Friend of God." What a privilege it is to be a friend of God and to know that He is in the business of redemption and restoration.

> *Lord, help me to reach out more to my neighbors when they go through hard times.*

Evening Watch: Read Psalm 106:32–48. Once again we see the word *nevertheless* in verse 44 of this psalm. The review of Israel's rebellion against God in verses 32–44 is shocking. Psalm 106:39 says, "Thus they were defiled by their own works, And played the harlot by their own deeds." Verses 44–45 say, "Nevertheless He regarded their affliction, When He heard their cry; And for their sake He remembered His covenant, And relented according to the multitude of His mercies." God's mercy far outweighs His wrath. We serve a merciful God who sees our rebellion, but who continues to reach out to us in His mercy. Aren't you thankful for the many times God's mercy has been poured out upon you?

Before you go to bed tonight, review the times in your life when God's mercy was extended to you in spite of your disobedience. One incident in my own life comes quickly to my mind. I read a book called *Healing Hands.* I so wanted to be used of God to pass His healing power to others. At the time I read this book, I knew very little about the occult. I was almost ready to delve more into the occult when I heard the Holy Spirit within me ask, "Where is the name of Jesus Christ in this book?" I realized then that the god described in this book was the "god of this world," not the God I knew. God in His mercy spoke to my heart through the Holy Spirit and kept me from veering off the righteous path He had prepared for me to follow the rest of my life.

> *Praise the Lord!*

Morning Wisdom: Read Proverbs 27:11. One of the joys we experience as parents is hearing wisdom flow out of the mouths of our three adult sons. We recall the days when they thought they knew everything and no one could tell them anything. Now we know they are smarter than we are. We often ask ourselves, *How did our sons become so wise?* Proverbs 27:11 says, "My son, be wise, and make my heart glad, That I may answer him who reproaches me." A son who is not wise is a reproach to his parents.

The book of Proverbs was written by Solomon to give young men knowledge, discretion, and instruction in wisdom. We have almost completed our study of Proverbs, and we all need to ask ourselves this question, *Has the study of Proverbs made me any wiser?* I trust your answer is yes. I know I personally have gained many insights into how to relate and respond to others. I have also learned much about what is really important in life and where my priorities should be in this coming year. The study of Proverbs, however, does not guarantee that we will be all the wiser.

Wisdom is applied knowledge. All the wise sayings in the book of Proverbs will avail nothing if we do not apply the knowledge we have gained. One way parents can attempt to impart wisdom to their children is to read one chapter of Proverbs daily to them. We know a family who did this and none of their children strayed from God's righteous path.

Today is November 9, so it might be beneficial for you to read Proverbs 9 before you retire. Hopefully you will walk tomorrow in the knowledge you glean from this chapter.

Thank You for Your Word that will help me to live wisely.

Evening Watch: Read Psalm 107:1–43. Today's psalm reveals the secret to living a wise life. The psalm ends with this statement, "Whoever is wise will observe these things, And they will understand the lovingkindness of the LORD" (v. 43). What are the things we need to observe to cause wisdom to flow like a river throughout our lives? As I reread this psalm I discovered seven things that will release the flow of wisdom in our lives:

1. Give thanks to the Lord (v. 1).
2. Remember His mercy (v. 1).
3. Share with others the redeeming power of the Lord (v. 2).
4. Cry out to the Lord when trouble comes (v. 6).
5. Follow the leading of the Lord (v. 7).
6. Declare God's works of deliverance, healing, and salvation with rejoicing (v. 22).
7. Exalt the Lord in the assembly (v. 32).

Lord, help me to daily observe these actions that will allow the flow of wisdom in our lives.

NOVEMBER 10

Morning Wisdom: Read Proverbs 27:12. Prudence is a virtue that accompanies wisdom. Proverbs 27:12 says, "A prudent man foresees evil and hides himself; The simple pass on and are punished." Sometimes comfort and materialism will prevent us from seeing or believing the evil that is ahead.

An example of how comfort can blind us is what happened just before the holocaust. Hitler was in power in Germany, and the persecution of Jewish people began. Those who were willing to leave all and flee were spared the holocaust.

Wealth and comfort have a way of lulling us into the belief that all will remain well. What happened in Germany should give us a wake-up call in America. Our religious freedoms are slowly being removed by judicial decisions. It is not time for Christians to hide, but it is time for Christians to hide themselves daily in the Rock, Jesus Christ. More troubled waters are coming to America, and only those who put their trust in God, not the world system or material wealth, will be safe in the flood of evil that is coming upon our land.

Lord, help me to daily dwell in Your presence, which is my hiding place.

Evening Watch: Read Psalm 108:1–13. This morning we learned in our reading that prudent men can foresee the evil to come. We were warned in this morning's devotional not to put our trust in this world's system. Instead we should trust in the Lord and hide ourselves in the safety of His presence. Psalm 108:12 clearly tells us how futile it is to put our trust in anything but the Lord. This verse reads, "Give us help from trouble, For the help of man is useless."

Dark clouds are on the horizon for America, but we always have to remember who rides on the clouds. Psalm 108:4 says, "For Your mercy is great above the heavens, And Your truth reaches to the clouds."

Even when the storm clouds gather, we can be confident that our Lord God is completely in control. He knows what is ahead. One can discover more about the future from reading the prophecies in God's Word than reading the daily newspaper.

The last verse of this psalm gives us this hope: "Through God we will do valiantly, For it is He who shall tread down our enemies." There is no need for those who trust in the Lord to fear the future, because the future ends in complete victory. The Word of God says that we are more than conquerors through Jesus Christ. (See Romans 8:37.)

Lord, help me never to trust in the arm of flesh.

Morning Wisdom: Read Proverbs 27:13. When I read this verse I remembered the story of Judah recorded in Genesis 38. Proverbs 27:13 advises, "Take the garment of him who is surety for a stranger, And hold it in pledge when he is surety for a seductress." The only garment we can wear that will make us sure that we will not give in to Satan's seductive temptations is the garment of praise. When we put on the garment of praise daily, nothing the devil has planned for us will succeed.

Lord, help me to put on the garment of praise daily.

Evening Watch: Read Psalm 109:1–31. David shared in this psalm how he was persecuted and accused, but he was able to stand fast because he gave himself to prayer. (See v. 4.) In his prayer David declared many curses that he wanted God to bring upon his enemies. He even prayed that the very prayer of his enemies would become sin. David prayed, "As he [his enemy] loved cursing, so let it come to him; As he did not delight in blessing, so let it be far from him" (v. 17). David's prayer for his enemies certainly was not a prayer of forgiveness and blessing. This prayer was David's vehicle to release his anger against his enemies by declaring just how he felt about those who had wronged and hurt him. God wants us to pour out our anger and hurt to Him instead of hurting others by our angry words.

If there is someone you have had a hard time forgiving, talk to the Lord and release your anger and bitterness to Him. Tell the Lord exactly how you feel about the person who has wronged and hurt you, and then release that person into God's hands. God is the avenger, not us. Empty yourself of all bitterness in prayer, and then ask God to fill you with His supernatural love.

Lord, remove all bitterness from my heart.

Morning Wisdom: Read Proverbs 27:14. Have you ever met people who are oozing with cheer even before they have their first cup of coffee in the morning. Proverbs 27:14 talks about such a person when it says:

> He who blesses his friend with a loud voice, rising early in the morning,
> It will be counted a curse to him.

Early morning risers do need to be sensitive to those around them. I am an early riser, and I usually have lived at least one-third of my day before my husband wakes up. When my husband and I go on trips where we are confined to a motel room, I creep quietly into the bathroom to read my Bible and pray. Some of my greatest quiet times have been in the "throne room."

We had a Russian young man live with us for seven years. He became like a son to us. He was a bodybuilder, and I learned early on to stay out of his way until he had downed his first cup of coffee.

Some people are not equipped to receive a cheerful greeting first thing in the morning. There is one, however, who loves for us to greet Him at any hour. His name is Jesus. He longs for us to spend time in His presence, no matter what time that might be. He also sings over us with joy when we wake up with praise and thanksgiving to Him on our lips. Quite often I hear the Lord's songs to me before I even fully open my eyes in the morning.

Jesus said, "In the world you will have tribulation; but be of good cheer, I have overcome the world" (John 16:33). Jesus can give us His unspeakable joy every morning. However, we might want to pour out our cheer to Jesus first during our quiet times with Him and give the rest of our household a chance to drink their first cup of coffee before we greet them.

Lord, thank You for Your unspeakable joy.

Evening Watch: Read Psalm 110:1–7. Even though Jesus had not yet been born, David prophetically spoke about Jesus throughout the book of Psalms. Psalm 110 is a classic example of how the Holy Spirit revealed to David many facts about his coming Messiah.

The first verse in this psalm was quoted by Jesus when He was attempting to prove His divine identity to the Jewish leaders of His day. Psalm 110:1 says, "The LORD said to my Lord, 'Sit at My right hand, Till I make Your enemies Your footstool.'" When David referred to "the LORD," I believe he was speaking of God, our heavenly Father. When David said, "my Lord," he was referring to Jesus Christ. The remainder of this psalm supports that belief.

David prophesied that God would send Jesus to rule out of Zion and that Jesus would be a priest forever according to the order of Melchizedek. (See vv. 2, 4.)

Melchizedek was a forerunner to Christ. (See Hebrews 7.) This psalm presents clear evidence that Jesus is the Messiah.

Lord, thank You for the witness of Your Word.

NOVEMBER 13

Ezekiel 27:1–28; Hebrews 11:17–31; Psalm 111:1–10; Proverbs 27:15–16

Morning Wisdom: Read Proverbs 27:15–16. This morning's reading from Proverbs is very convicting. Every time I read it I ask myself, *Am I a continual drip?* Proverbs 27:15–16 says, "A continual dripping on a very rainy day And a contentious woman are alike; Whoever restrains her restrains the wind, And grasps oil with his right hand."

Proverbs has a lot to say about contentious people, but this one hits too close to home. I have to admit that on occasion I have been a contentious woman, but those occasions occur only when my husband disagrees with me. When he disagrees with me, I just keep talking until I wear him down. I am sure my constant chatter is like a continual dripping to him.

A contentious woman is compared to the wind and oil in a person's right hand, because we cannot control either. A forceful wind can blow everything down in its path and so can a contentious woman. She uses her flapping tongue to stir up a breeze of words that will blow away everyone who disagrees with her. It is also impossible to grab hold of oil with the right hand. Just as oil is hard to contain, a contentious woman is uncontainable. The root of all contention is pride. Whenever we think we know more than the person with whom we are discussing a matter, we can easily become contentious. I am challenged to pray this prayer before the day begins:

> *Lord, search my heart, and if there is any pride, remove it far from me. I humble myself before You and ask You to convict me if ever I become contentious.*

Evening Watch: Read Psalm 111:1–10. The assignment of the Holy Spirit is to conform us to the image of Christ. This process will not be completed in this life, but we can take comfort from the promise that when we see Him we will be like Him.

Jesus is God in the flesh, and the character qualities of God described in this psalm give us some idea of the work the Holy Spirit has to do in our lives. As you read the following character qualities of God, ask the Holy Spirit to develop them in you. God is righteous (v. 3), gracious (v. 4), compassionate (v. 4), giving (v. 5), faithful (v. 5), powerful (v. 6), and truthful (v. 8).

This psalm also describes God's works, which are honorable (v. 3), glorious (v. 3), wonderful (v. 4), just (v. 7), and everlasting (v. 8). Our only hope to become more like Jesus and to accomplish His work on Earth is to yield daily to the Holy Spirit. We do this when when we pray, receive God's Word, and humble ourselves by casting every care upon Jesus. We have the promise that God will perfect those things that concern us, and my greatest concern is that I become more like Jesus today.

Holy Spirit, help me to love like Jesus and do His will on Earth.

Morning Wisdom: Read Proverbs 27:17. This is one of my favorite verses in Proverbs. It says, "As iron sharpens iron, So a man sharpens the countenance of his friend." As I write this devotional I am on a trip with friends my husband and I have had for over fifty years. This couple has introduced us to friends of theirs who have become friends of ours, and we are all the richer for these relationships.

The common goal of these friendships has been to help one another in the various activities of life. Through these friendships my husband and I have gained a tour guide, event planner, personal shopper, culinary expert, stock adviser, sports authority, and many other experts who have given us good information and advice that has helped us along life's way. None of these experts require any payment for their services. They only ask for lots of fun and fellowship.

True friendship offers more than just fellowship. Good friends can sharpen not only our countenance but also every area of our lives. I thank God for the many friends we have had in our life's journey.

Lord, thank You for good friends.

Evening Watch: Read Psalm 112:1–10. This psalm talks about the blessings that will come to those who walk in the fear of the Lord and who greatly delight in His commandments. I can honestly say that my husband and I have already experienced most of these blessings in our lives. Psalm 112:3 promises that wealth and riches will be in the homes of those who delight greatly in God's commandments.

The riches we have experienced in our home have not been material wealth. Our home has often been filled with jewels, gold, silver, and other rich treasures. The jewels have been the many laborers in the kingdom of God who have visited us in our home. The golden vessels we have collected are filled with golden times of fellowship around our table with many in the body of Christ. The silver artifacts we have gathered over the years are the foreign students who grew in their walk with the Lord during their stay with us. All of the treasures in our home are priceless. We will enjoy these treasures not only on this earth but also in heaven.

Lord, thank You for using our home as Your treasure house.

Morning Wisdom: Read Proverbs 27:18–20. We do not have the ability to read minds or to unveil the hearts of men, but God has provided other ways we can discern much about people. He has given us eyes to look into the eyes of others and ears to hear not only people's words, but also their hearts. If we submit these senses to the Holy Spirit, He can sharpen our discernment of others.

The eyes are the windows of the soul. When I talk to people, I love to have eye contact with them, because I can survey the condition of their soul. People who refuse to have eye contact with others are usually suffering from rejection, fear, shame, or guilt.

The very countenance of a person often reveals the condition of his or her soul. Proverbs 27:19 says, "As in water face reflects face, So a man's heart reveals the man." As we look into the eyes of others we can also determine if that person has lustful thoughts. Proverbs 27:20 says, "The eyes of man are never satisfied." This statement describes the eyes of a lustful man, because he always wants to see more. He has greedy, covetous longings in his mind that drive him to keep looking.

The Bible says God has purer eyes than to behold evil. (See Habakkuk 1:13.) My prayer is that God will give me pure eyes to see others as He sees them. No matter how evil a person is, God always sees that one with eyes of compassion. God longs to redeem and restore even those who rebel against Him.

Lord, help me to see others as You see them.

Evening Watch: Read Psalms 113:1–114:8. This psalm reveals that whatever circumstance we experience in life or whatever condition we experience in our souls, God can deliver and lift us to a better place. If we are poor, He can raise us out of the dust and ash heap and even cause us to become one of His children. God did this for Esther, Gideon, Abraham, and Moses, and He can do it for you.

If we are spiritually or physically barren, He can cause us to birth both spiritual and physical children. Psalm 113:9 says, "He grants the barren woman a home, Like a joyful mother of children."

Psalm 114 declares the might and power of the Lord to do the impossible. Psalm 114 says God is able to turn a rock into a pool of water and flint into a fountain of water.

Do you find yourself between a rock and a hard place today? God is able to turn that rock into a pool of water. Are there people whose faces are like flint against you? For some reason, they just do not accept or like you. God is able to melt the hearts of those people who reject you. There is nothing impossible with God.

Lord, thank You for Your saving and delivering power.

NOVEMBER 16

Morning Wisdom: Read Proverbs 27:21–22. *Were they whispering about me?* Have you ever asked yourself that question when you enter a room and see two people whispering? No matter how much we would like to deny it, the fact is we all do care what other people think of us. We want them to think the best of us, and we all want to have a good reputation. Proverbs 27:21 says, "The refining pot is for silver and the furnace for gold, And a man is valued by what others say of him." We need to be so careful about what we say about people to others. Before we say anything about anyone, we need to ask ourselves the following questions: *Is what I am about to say going to put this person in a good light? Will what I say cause others to think well of them? Will my words edify this person or will they tear them down? Am I passing on a negative report or a positive report?* If we will be faithful to ask ourselves these questions before we speak anything about anyone, we will avoid the snare of gossip.

Solomon did not single out people and call them foolish, but he spoke often about foolish people. He described in many verses what a foolish person does and says.

Proverbs 27:22 contains one of these descriptions when it says, "Though you grind a fool in a mortar with a pestle along with crushed grain, Yet his foolishness will not depart from him." I have never ground anything with a mortar and pestle, but I know the purpose of this instrument is to crush something into fine powder. God has a way of sending us all through what I call His "humbling machine." He allows trials in our lives to cause us to become like gold dust that can bring brightness and beauty to all we influence in this life. The Holy Spirit uses the pestle of pressure to conform us to the image of Jesus Christ. However, no matter what the pressures in this life are, the foolish person will continue in his foolish ways unless he cries out to the Lord for salvation.

> *Lord, help me to cooperate with Your Spirit by daily speaking and doing only what He desires.*

Evening Watch: Read Psalm 115:1–18. We talked this morning about how we all want others to speak well of us. This chapter in psalms talks about God's reputation. God's reputation will always be pure and wonderful, despite those who would try to besmirch His reputation on Earth.

When things do not go well with us we may have unbelievers who question, "So, where is your God?" We can respond to this question with the same response given in this psalm. We can say, "Our God is in heaven, and He does whatever He pleases. He is our help and our shield, and we put our trust in Him." We can add these statements to our response, "God is mindful of us and blesses us, and we choose to continually bless the Lord." Such a response will silence those who ask, "So, where is your God?"

> *Lord, thank You for all the opportunities You give me to declare Your greatness to those who doubt You.*

NOVEMBER 17

Morning Wisdom: Read Proverbs 27:23–27. Today's reading begins with this warning, "Be diligent to know the state of your flocks, And attend to your herds; For riches are not forever, Nor does a crown endure to all generations" (vv. 23–24). The remainder of today's reading gives the promise that if a person is diligent in taking care of his flocks and herds, he will never lack food for his household or nourishment for his maidservants. I try not to spiritualize verses in the Bible, but this reading certainly could apply to pastors of spiritual flocks.

Some people are called to pastor, and others are called to preach and evangelize. There is a great difference between a preacher and a pastor. Paul listed the various gifts Jesus gives to believers when he wrote to the church at Ephesus. He said, "And He Himself gave some to be apostles, some prophets, some evangelists, and some pastors and teachers, for the equipping of the saints for the work of ministry, for the edifying of the body of Christ" (Eph. 4:11–12). It is interesting that "preaching" is not mentioned as one of the gifts given to edify the body of Christ. I believe Paul did not mention preaching because we are all given that gift. Whether you like it or not, every day of your life you preach a sermon to those around you by both your actions and your words.

A pastor is called not only to preach, but also to care for his flock. He is the under shepherd who listens carefully to the Good Shepherd and relays His message to the flock. A pastor is called to do more than just edify the flock he has been given. He is called to feed them well and bind up and comfort the sick in his flock. He is called to keep thieves from coming in to steal his flock, and he keeps his flock from the dangers of false doctrine. The call to pastor is a high calling that can only be filled well by those who humble themselves daily to the power of the Holy Spirit to conform them to the image of Christ.

Lord, help me to preach good sermons to others daily.

Evening Watch: Read Psalm 116:1–19. I love to converse with people who are good listeners. They make me feel like they are hanging on my every word. Good listeners are not just waiting to chime in with their own opinion about what is being discussed. They do not interrupt you in the middle of a sentence and somehow make you feel like what you are saying is extremely important. God is the best listener in the whole universe. Psalm 116 begins with these words, "I love the LORD, because He has heard My voice and my supplications. Because He has inclined His ear to me, Therefore I will call upon Him as long as I live" (vv. 1–2).

The psalm goes on to describe God's faithfulness to hear our cries when we are in trouble and to be merciful and preserve us even when we do not fully obey Him. The psalmist continued to declare how God delivers his soul from death, his eyes from tears, and his feet from falling. To demonstrate his gratefulness to the Lord for His faithfulness to him in every situation of life, the psalmist declared, "I will take up the cup of salvation, And call upon the name of the LORD" (v. 13).

Lord, help me to call upon Your name continually.

Morning Wisdom: Read Proverbs 28:1. Throughout Proverbs Solomon compares the wicked to the just. Proverbs 28:1 presents this comparison, "The wicked flee when no one pursues, But the righteous are bold as a lion." The wicked flee, because they are afraid they will be caught in the middle of one of their wicked deeds. The wicked are always looking behind their backs to see who might be watching. They cloak their wicked deeds in the darkness of night. Their ears are always listening out for the siren of a police car or the knock on the door of a person who will discover what they are doing. The wicked have no understanding that God sees all and knows all. One day they will receive just recompense for all their wicked deeds.

The righteous, however, are not afraid, because they fear the Lord. The righteous do not fear what men can do to them, because they know what God will do to those who come against them.

Lord, help me always to walk uprightly.

Evening Watch: Read Psalm 117:1–2. This is a short psalm of praise and a good way to end the day. The psalmist exhorted all nations to praise the Lord. We know that one day every knee will bow and every tongue will confess that Jesus Christ is Lord. Every nation and tongue will praise the Lord. Until that day we have the great privilege of declaring the merciful kindness of the Lord to all we see each day. We can daily share how God has revealed His greatness to us through the various situations of our lives. We can also share the truths of His Word with those we speak to daily. Every conversation that declares God's truths is a conversation that is eternally fruitful. Praising God and sharing His truth with others are two of the ways we can magnify the Lord and give Him glory.

Before you retire think about some of the times God has revealed His truth to you and that truth sustained you through a difficult trial. Then end your meditation by reviewing the many times God has revealed His greatness and kindness to you.

Great is the Lord and worthy are You to be praised!

NOVEMBER 19

Morning Wisdom: Read Proverbs 28:2. This verse challenges me to pray more for my president and more for future elections of state and national leaders. Proverbs 28:2 says, "Because of the transgression of a land, many are its princes; But by a man of understanding and knowledge Right will be prolonged." You have probably heard the expression, "There are too many chiefs."

When a leader does not walk in a righteous way, he becomes dependent on the voices of too many people. He can easily become confused by these many voices. Righteousness exalts a nation. When a righteous person is in leadership, the voices of unwise counselors will be silenced by the voice of the Lord. I pray this morning for God to surround our president with wise counselors who daily seek Him for guidance.

> *Lord, give us righteous leaders in this nation who seek Your face and who hear Your voice.*

Evening Watch: Read Psalm 118:1–18. The psalmist who wrote this psalm must have faced much persecution. He declared, "I called upon the LORD in distress; The LORD answered me and set me in a broad place. The LORD is on my side; I will not fear. What can man do to me?" (vv. 5–6). The psalmist knew that God would one day avenge him of his enemies. He knew it was better to put his trust and confidence in God rather than in men. The psalmist knew the power of the name of the Lord. He wrote, "All nations surrounded me, But in the name of the LORD I will destroy them" (v. 10). The psalmist had seen the Lord do valiantly for him in the past, and he was confident that the Lord would always have the victory.

Have you seen God's victory in the various situations of your life? Close your eyes and begin to review some of the victories God has won in your own life. Counting victories is much better than counting sheep to go to sleep. You will wake up with great confidence that no matter what you face in the coming day, the Lord will ultimately win the victory. I often say, "The battle is the Lord's, and the victory is ours."

> *Lord, thank You for all the times You have given me the victory through Jesus Christ, who always causes me to triumph.*

Morning Wisdom: Read Proverbs 28:3–5. Oppression can take many forms. We can be oppressed by governments, trials, persecution, emotional torment, terrorism, and many other situations in life. God has promised to deliver us from oppression. One of my favorite scriptures in the Bible is Isaiah 54:14, which says, "You shall be far from oppression, for you shall not fear; And from terror, for it shall not come near you." God uses the body of Christ on Earth now as instruments to deliver people from oppression.

God does not look kindly upon those who oppress others. Proverbs 28:3 compares the poor man who oppresses the poor to a driving rain that leaves no food. When people are starving they will fight or even kill to get a morsel of food. My nephew was assigned to a war-torn country in Africa. He gave a candy bar to a young child. When he returned he found the child shot in the head and the candy was gone. Proverbs 28:5 says that evil men do not understand justice. Whoever oppressed and murdered this child will ultimately receive God's justice. God is always the defender of the poor.

It is unimaginable that people will actually praise the wicked actions of others.

Proverbs 28:4 says, "Those who forsake the law praise the wicked, But such as keep the law contend with them." Disobedient, rebellious people will continually break God's laws. When we see wicked people oppress others, we need to take action against them. One of the horrors of the Holocaust was that so many Christians in Germany remained silent when their Jewish neighbors were being shuffled off to concentration camps. Holocaust survivors today are still asking why others did not come to their aid. I believe those who truly seek the Lord will stand up for what is right when they see the wicked oppress others, because they understand the compassion of Jesus Christ. Proverbs 28:4 says, "Evil men do not understand justice, But those who seek the Lord understand all."

Lord, help me always to stand up for what is right.

Evening Watch: Read Psalm 118:19–29. I recently heard someone say that we needed to know what tribe we are in so that when we get to heaven we will know what gate to enter. I could not believe that someone actually believed this. There is only one gate we need to know about when we go to heaven. That gate is mentioned in verses 19–20. It says, "Open to me the gates of righteousness; I will go through them, And I will praise the Lord. This is the gate of the Lord, Through which the righteous shall enter." On the cross, Jesus opened the gate for all those who believe in Him to enter the gate of righteousness. On that fateful day, Jesus provided the way for us to become the very righteousness of God through Him. (See 2 Corinthians 5:21.) We will go through the gate of righteousness, and our tribe will be Judah, because we are one with Christ. He was in the tribe of Judah.

Lord, thank You for making me righteous in the Father's sight.

Morning Wisdom: Read Proverbs 28:6–7. Both of these verses reveal two characteristics God wants us always to display to the world. These two characteristics are integrity and discernment. Proverbs 28:6 says, "Better is the poor who walks in his integrity Than one perverse in his ways, though he be rich." A person who has integrity will be preserved and guided and blessed by God. Psalm 25:21 says, "Let integrity and uprightness preserve me, For I wait for You." Proverbs 11:3 says, "The integrity of the upright will guide them, But the perversity of the unfaithful will destroy them." Proverbs 20:7 says, "The righteous man walks in his integrity; His children are blessed after him."

When we walk in integrity we will also have clear discernment about people and situations we encounter in life. Proverbs 28:7 says, "Whoever keeps the law is a discerning son, But a companion of gluttons shames his father." A man of integrity will seek to obey God's laws, and he will be able to choose the right friends. If we are rebellious, we will surround ourselves with rebellious friends. When two of our sons went through a period of rebellion in their teen years, they got involved with the wrong friends, who pulled them even further into rebellion. God promised me at the time my boys were not following the Lord that the day would come when they would consider His Word more important than their necessary food. God kept that promise, and both of these sons love God's Word and seek to walk in God's truths. The friends they have now encourage them in the things of the Lord. When we walk in integrity we will have friends who also are people of integrity.

Lord, help me always to walk in integrity.

Evening Watch: Read Psalm 119:1–16. David was a man of integrity who knew the value of God's truths in his life. Throughout this psalm David described how important God's Word was in his life.

These first sixteen verses list some of the reasons reading and heeding God's Word should be the top priority in our lives. When we walk in the law of the Lord we will be:

- blessed (vv. 1–2);
- kept from sinning (vv. 3, 11);
- cleansed (v. 9).

As you read Psalm 119 make your own list of the fruits that come from walking in and obeying God's Word. That list will encourage you to be faithful to both read and heed God's Word daily.

Lord, thank You for Your Word.

Morning Wisdom: Read Proverbs 28:8–10. We talked yesterday about walking in integrity. We will walk in integrity when we read and heed God's Word. Proverbs 28:8–9 describes what will happen to the person who refuses to walk in integrity. Proverbs 28:8 says, "One who increases his possessions by usury and extortion Gathers it for him who will pity the poor." Proverbs 10:2 says, "Treasures of wickedness profit nothing, But righteousness delivers from death." People who use wicked means to gain wealth in the end will see their wealth go to the poor. Goodwill and the Salvation Army daily distribute valuable treasures that once belonged to rich people to the poor.

Proverbs 28:9 shares how even the prayer of someone who is rebellious against God's law is an abomination. Proverbs 28:10 describes what will happened to the man who persuades others to go astray in an evil way. That man will fall into a pit.

We learn from all three of these verses that the eternal profit gained by walking in God's truths far outweigh any gain of earthly wealth. That eternal profit includes answered prayer, God's provision, and His protection.

Lord, help me always to seek to gain eternal profit.

Evening Watch: Read Psalm 119:17–35. This reading from Psalm 119 contains a prayer that I often pray before I read God's Word. David prayed, "Open my eyes, that I may see Wondrous things from Your law" (v. 18). God's Word is filled with many wondrous things, but it takes the inspiration and instruction of the Holy Spirit to convey those things to us. The assignment of the Holy Spirit is to take the things of Jesus Christ and show them to us. Jesus said the following about the Holy Spirit: "However, when He, the Spirit of truth, has come, He will guide you into all truth; for He will not speak on His own authority, but whatever He hears He will speak; and He will tell you things to come. He will glorify Me, for He will take of what is Mine and declare [show] it to you" (John 16:13).

The Holy Spirit is able to give us insight and understanding of God's Word, and He also transmits the power to us to obey God's Word. The Holy Spirit is able to transform the daily duty of reading God's Word into a delightful privilege. Tomorrow when you open God's Word pray this prayer:

Teach me, Holy Spirit, and open the eyes of my understanding to see all the wondrous things in God's Word.

Morning Wisdom: Read Proverbs 28:11. Riches have a way of blinding us. The only way to keep us from being blinded by the glitter and gold this world offers is to walk daily in the glory of the light of God.

When we walk in God's light, He will be able to give us the wisdom from above. James described this wisdom when he wrote, "But the wisdom that is from above is first pure, then peaceable, gentle, willing to yield, full of mercy and good fruits, without partiality and without hypocrisy" (James 3:17). Proverbs 28:11 says, "The rich man is wise in his own eyes, But the poor who has understanding searches him out."

True wisdom and understanding come from the Holy Spirit, who is able to give us clear discernment of others. The Holy Spirit not only opens the eyes of our understanding to the truths in God's Word, but He also opens our eyes to see into the hidden motives of others. If we will listen carefully to that still, quiet voice within who says, "This is the way. Walk in it," we will be spared many disastrous consequences of wrong decisions and relationships.

Lord, thank You for sending the Holy Spirit to open my eyes and ears.

Evening Watch: Read Psalm 119:36–52. The Holy Spirit is able to open our spiritual ears and eyes so that we can apply God's Word to our hearts. David prayed, "Incline my heart to Your testimonies, And not to covetousness" (v. 36). If there is any covetousness in our hearts, the understanding of God's Word can cleanse and deliver us from it. Suddenly the things of this world that we thought were of such great value become worthless in our sight. David prayed, "Turn away my eyes from looking at worthless things" (v. 37). One of the most worthless things we view daily is TV. When our boys were in their formative years we made the choice not to have a TV. They thank us today for that decision we made because their grades improved, and we had much more family time together.

It is so easy to give in to the temptation to just "veg out" in front of the TV. We have to remember that Satan is the prince and power of the air and that he is the master of imagery. One of the major ways Satan can influence us is through what we watch on TV. The images we receive from the TV screen can impact our lives for good or evil. We need to ask the Holy Spirit to guide us as we use our remotes to change channels on the TV.

Holy Spirit, help me to not watch anything that is not edifying.

Ezekiel 47:1–48:35; 1 Peter 2:11–3:9; Psalm 119:53–70; Proverbs 28:12–13

Morning Wisdom: Read Proverbs 28:12–13. We all want to obtain God's mercy. His mercies are new every morning, but in order to tap in to His mercy, we have to cooperate with the Holy Spirit. One of the major ways to obtain mercy is to show mercy to others. If we listen carefully to the Holy Spirit's guidance, He will reveal specific ways we can show God's mercy to families, friends, and neighbors.

Another way we can cooperate with the Holy Spirit to receive God's mercy is to ask Him to reveal any sins we may have hidden in our hearts. Proverbs 28:13 says, "He who covers his sins will not prosper, But whoever confesses and forsakes them will have mercy." We cannot confess our sins if we refuse to face them. It is so easy to be in self-denial when we sin. We often are blind to those things that we say and do daily that do not glorify God. Sin is simply falling short of the glory of God.

I am challenged to daily pray the following prayer:

> *Lord, search my heart today and reveal to me those things I need to confess that I have done or said that displease You. Forgive me for the times I have excused my sins rather than confess them to You.*

Evening Watch: Read Psalm 119:53–70. The list of what God's Word can do for us continues as we look at this psalm David wrote. David credited God's Word for giving him both life and hope. He said God's Word comforted him and even gave him new songs.

We talked this morning about obtaining mercy. When we know God's Word we can appeal to His mercy on the grounds of what He has promised in His Word. David wrote, "I entreated Your favor with my whole heart; Be merciful to me according to Your Word" (v. 58). This portion of our Psalm 119 reading ends with these words, "The earth, O LORD, is full of Your mercy; Teach me Your statutes" (v. 64). God has enough mercy to be shared with the whole world. The sad news is that so many in this world have no idea of how to tap into God's mercy. Pray for those you know who have not yet discovered how to receive and give God's mercy.

> *Lord, thank You for revealing everything about Your mercy in Your Word.*

Daniel 1:1–2:23; 1 Peter 3:10–4:6; Psalm 119:71–80; Proverbs 28:14

Morning Wisdom: Read Proverbs 28:14. Our verse today says, "Happy is the man who is always reverent, But he who hardens his heart will fall into calamity." Reverence is taught not caught. Unfortunately many parents are not taking the time needed to train and teach their children to show the proper reverence toward God and the things that are holy. Many TV programs today display great disrespect for God and anything holy. In fact, fun is poked at anything that is religious. I'll never forget the experience I had when my husband and I had guests from India stay in our home.

We were hosting a family from India and had taken them to Stone Mountain for a picnic. We took our Bibles with us to have a time of study. In the bustle of setting the picnic table I placed my Bible on the grass under the bench. Immediately the little six-year-old in the family ran and picked up the Bible and kissed it. She said, "This is precious." A similar experience happened recently when I gave one of my devotional books to an Egyptian who was a Coptic Christian. He kissed the book and said he would put a cover on it to protect it. He said he covered all of his religious books so they would not be torn or soiled.

The root of the word *reverence* is "revere." The definition of *revere* in *Webster's New World Dictionary* is: "To regard with deep respect, love and awe or to venerate."[3] When we revere something, we lift it to a higher position. Jesus said, "And I, if I am lifted up from the earth, will draw all peoples to Myself" (John 12:32). When we show reverence to God and the things that are holy, we demonstrate to others how precious our faith is to us, and others will be drawn to Jesus. I heard that a congregation in Caracas, Venezuela, enters their sanctuary with singing. The worship begins even in the parking lot before the congregants enter the door. We need more reverence for God in America. Let's pray to that end.

Lord, help the body of Christ in America to teach others to reverence the things of God.

Evening Watch: Read Psalm 119:71–80. David wrote, "It is good for me that I have been afflicted, That I may learn Your statutes" (v. 71). Just recently we heard a great message on the reasons God allows affliction in our lives. One of the reasons given was so that we would run to His Word to find strength and wisdom during trials. If we do go to God's Word in the midst of affliction, He will give us revelations that we could not have gained otherwise.

No one likes affliction, and God does not like to see His children suffer. We suffer for many reasons. We suffer persecution for our faith. We suffer illness and disease because we live in a fallen world where everything is in a state of progressive corruption. We suffer because of the fruits of our own sins. God can use every suffering time in your life as a stepping stone to come up higher in your spiritual walk.

Lord, help me always to go to Your Word in times of suffering.

Morning Wisdom: Read Proverbs 28:15–16. As I read today's reading from Proverbs, my mind raced back to various tyrannical leaders of nations in the past. Today's reading compares wicked rulers to roaring lions and charging bears. Proverbs 28:16 says, "A ruler who lacks understanding is a great oppressor, But he who hates covetousness will prolong his days."

The major strongholds in the lives of wicked rulers are greed and covetousness. They oppress the poor to make themselves rich. One only has to read history books to discover the tyrants like Hitler and Stalin who oppressed the poor and killed millions in order to establish their rule. Such leaders were greedy for power. Leaders like Castro disguised his covetousness by becoming the peasant ruler who said he would set the oppressed free. We have friends who have visited Cuba, and their country is still poverty stricken.

God does not look kindly upon those who oppress the poor. Proverbs 28:15 says, "Like a roaring lion and a charging bear Is a wicked ruler over poor people." One of the major reasons God destroyed Sodom and Gomorrah was because they did not reach out to the poor. Ezekiel wrote, "Look, this was the iniquity of your sister Sodom: She and her daughter had pride, fullness of food, and abundance of idleness; neither did she strengthen the hand of the poor and needy" (Ezek. 16:49).

As we approach this next year, you might think of ways that you can reach out to the poor. I know the Holy Spirit will give you some creative ideas, and God's blessings will be upon you as you meet the needs of the needy.

Lord, help me to give to the poor.

Evening Watch: Read Psalm 119:81–95. Have you ever cried out, "Lord, help me!" David knew exactly where to go for help. In these verses David reviews the suffering he experienced at the hands of the proud. He said they almost made an end of him. Then he cried out, "Help me!" He prayed, "Revive me according to Your lovingkindness, So that I may keep the testimony of Your mouth" (v. 88). David knew God's Word was forever settled in heaven. He knew that God's Word would give him hope and faith for whatever trials he faced in life.

David said, "Unless Your law had been my delight, I would then have perished in my affliction" (v. 92). Sometimes when I experience trials during a one-day period, I call those days help-me-Jesus days. Whenever I cry out, "Help me, Jesus!" He always leads me to His Word. His Word throws a light on what seems to be a dark day, and faith and hope begin to arise in my soul.

Lord, thank You for Your Word!

Daniel 4:1–37; 2 Peter 1:1–21; Psalm 119:96–112; Proverbs 28:17–18

Morning Wisdom: Read Proverbs 28:17–18. These two verses give two good reasons why we should keep walking on the righteous path our Lord has prepared for us. Verse 17 says "A man burdened with bloodshed will flee into a pit; Let no one help him." A pit awaits those who demonstrate violence on Earth. You might say to yourself, *Well, I have never been violent.* Whenever we neglect God's Word and withdraw ourselves from fellowship, we are violent toward our Lord. Unfaithfulness to God and others are violent acts. We may not strike others in anger or speak damaging, hurtful words out loud, but God knows what is in our hearts. Whenever I mutter under my breath, *I could just kill that person,* I have committed a violent act in my heart. God hears my heart. We all need to remember that.

Proverbs 28:18 says, "Whoever walks blamelessly will be saved, But he who is perverse in his ways will suddenly fall." We will fall when we become perverse in our thoughts. Pornography presents a perverted view of sex. When anyone becomes entrapped by pornography, he or she can expect a fall. Until that one repents of this sin, he may fall many times. God wants us to walk blamelessly, because He knows we will be saved much misery in this life if we do.

Lord, help me to keep on Your path of righteousness.

Evening Watch: Read Psalm 119:96–112. David continued to declare his love for God's law in these verses of Psalm 119. He said, "I have seen the consummation of all perfection, But Your commandment is exceedingly broad. Oh, how I love Your law! It is my meditation all the day" (vv. 96–97). He said God's Word was able to make him wiser than his enemies and that his understanding was increased because he meditated on the Word all day long. God's Word restrained him from doing evil and guided him like a light. He considered God's Word as his own heritage.

When the body of Christ in America thinks of God's Word in the same way that David did, we will see revival in our nation.

Lord, help me to meditate on Your Word all day long.

November 28

Daniel 5:1–31; 1 Peter 2:1–22; Psalm 119:113–131; Proverbs 28:19–20

Morning Wisdom: Read Proverbs 28:19–20. Faithfulness is one of the fruits of the Spirit. Galatians 5:22–23 says, "But the fruit of the Spirit is love, joy, peace, longsuffering, kindness, goodness, faithfulness, gentleness, self-control. Against such there is no law." The reading today describes the fruits of frivolity and faithfulness. Proverbs 28:19 says, "He who tills his land will have plenty of bread, But he who follows frivolity will have poverty enough!" You may not be a farmer, but I am sure you have passed by fields along the highway that have not been tended. Thorn bushes, trash, and weeds are the unfruitful crop of an unattended field.

Farmers have to clear their land faithfully and till their soil if they expect their fields to be productive. The opposite of faithfulness is frivolity. This person produces little in life and is only interested in partying and having a good time. Sometimes after a hard week of work, I tell my husband, "I am ready for a play day." All of us need play days, but if every day of the week is a play day, we will not have any fruitfulness in our lives.

Proverbs 28:20 says, "A faithful man will abound with blessings, But he who hastens to be rich will not go unpunished." Blessings upon blessings will come to us if we will be faithful first to the Lord.

Some people are very faithful on their jobs and even become workaholics. The fruit such people will produce is not eternal. God is a relational God who wants us first to have an intimate relationship with Him, next an intimate relationship with our mate and family, and finally a good relationship with our employer.

Lord, help me with my priorities.

Evening Watch: Read Psalm 119:113–131. We talked this morning about faithfulness. To discover how we can be faithful to God every day, we need to take a closer look at the word *faithful*. We could say that in order to be faithful, we have to be full of faith. Faith comes by hearing and hearing by the Word of God. (See Romans 10:17.) Jesus said, "If you abide in My word, you are My disciples indeed. And you shall know the truth, and the truth shall make you free" (John 8:31–32). We abide in God's Word when we continue reading it daily. David was a faithful servant of the Lord because he abided in God's Word. Almost every verse in Psalm 119 declares the importance of reading and heeding God's Word.

Our reading today begins with these words, "I hate the double-minded, But I love Your law. You are my hiding place and my shield; I hope in Your word" (vv. 113–114).

David said he would observe God's statutes continually and that he loved His testimonies. He declared that he loved God's commandments more than fine gold. The entrance of God's Word gave David light and understanding. Do you love God's Word as much as David did? If you love God's Word and obey God's Word, you will be a faithful servant, and Jesus will call you His disciple.

Lord, help me to abide in Your Word.

Daniel 6:1–28; 2 Peter 3:1–18; Psalm 119:132–155; Proverbs 28:21–22

Morning Wisdom: Read Proverbs 28:21–22. "For what will it profit a man if he gains the whole world, and loses his own soul?" (Mark 8:36). Jesus asked this question to the people who were with His disciples. Peter had just rebuked Jesus, because Jesus said He would be rejected by the chief priests and elders and finally be killed. Jesus then rebuked Peter and said, "Get behind Me, Satan! For you are not mindful of the things of God, but the things of men" (Mark 8:33). Jesus added, "Whoever desires to come after Me, let him deny himself, and take up his cross, and follow Me" (v. 34).

Recently we had a lesson on what it means to be a disciple. Several questions were asked to determine if we were disciples of Jesus. Sadly everyone present could not pass all the questions. As human beings we do often mind the things of this world rather than the things of God. The two verses today tell us what will happen to those who are absorbed with this world rather than the kingdom of God.

Proverbs 28:21 says, "To show partiality is not good, Because for a piece of bread a man will transgress." It is a great temptation to pay more attention and show partiality to those who have wealth instead of reaching out to the poor. A rich man has many friends, but those friends are superficial. Those who befriend the rich to gain favor and money will quickly end that friendship if they meet another rich person who will show them more favor.

Proverbs 28:22 says, "A man with an evil eye hastens after riches, And does not consider that poverty will come upon him." When seeking wealth is the top priority in a person's life, that person will have a poverty-stricken soul. Greed and covetousness will absorb his mind and he will have no lasting joy or peace. "The kingdom of God is not eating and drinking, but righteousness and peace and joy in the Holy Spirit" (Rom. 14:17). It is a foolish man who seeks to gain the world, because he will be robbed of the inheritance of lasting peace that Jesus can give him. Such a person exchanges the temporary joy of wealth for the eternal joy of the Holy Spirit. Eternal poverty will come upon such a person.

Lord, help me to seek first the kingdom of God.

Evening Watch: Read Psalm 119:132–155. We learned this morning that a man who hastens after riches does not realize that poverty will come upon him. When we leave this world, we will all be poor in material things. I have never seen a hearse pulling a U-Haul trailer. The second book in the trilogy of devotions I have written is called *You Can Take It With You*. At the end of every devotional, I share a deposit that we can add to our heavenly bank accounts. David probably had many material riches, but he considered God's Word more precious to him than fine gold. In this passage David declared that the testimonies, judgments, and statutes of the Lord were all righteous. When we enter the gates of righteousness, we will be able to take the Word with us. Are you making deposits in your heavenly bank account daily?

Lord, help me to make daily deposits of Your Word in my heart.

Daniel 7:1–28; 1 John 1:1–20; Psalm 119:156–176; Proverbs 28:23–24

Morning Wisdom: Read Proverbs 28:23–24. Throughout our study of Proverbs I have tried to find some connection between the verses presented for each day in *The One Year Bible*. However, I could not find the connection in today's reading. Both verses stand alone. Proverbs 28:23 says, "He who rebukes a man will find more favor afterward Than he who flatters with the tongue."

To understand this verse we must look at other verses that cover the subject of rebuke. Proverbs 9:8 says, "Do not correct a scoffer, lest he hate you; Rebuke a wise man, and he will love you." Proverbs 13:1 says, "A wise son heeds his father's instruction, But a scoffer does not listen to rebuke." Proverbs 13:8 says, "The ransom of a man's life is his riches, But the poor does not hear rebuke." Proverbs 24:25 says, "But those who rebuke the wicked will have delight, And a good blessing will come upon them." Finally, Proverbs 27:5 says, "Open rebuke is better Than love carefully concealed."

Have you ever heard a sermon titled "The Art of Rebuking"? It seems that the subject has not been taught in many churches. However, our responsibility as believers is to rebuke our brothers and sisters in Christ who are disobedient to God's Word and to rebuke and warn the wicked. No one wakes up in the morning and says, "Today I am going to spend the day rebuking others." Not one of us enjoys rebuking others, but we learned in Proverbs 24:25 that those who rebuke the wicked will have delight. It may not be delightful when we give a rebuke to a wicked person, but later if that person hears the rebuke and repents, we will have delight.

The lesson learned from this study about rebuke is that rebuking is just as important in the body of Christ as exhortation. We should not concern ourselves about whether or not a person will hear our rebuke. However, we should truly seek the guidance of the Holy Spirit before we give a rebuke. Wise men will receive a rebuke, but often the poor and the wicked will not. The purpose of a rebuke is not to criticize or judge another person. The purpose of a rebuke is to lovingly warn another person to turn away from sin and to turn to God. Perhaps we all need to ask the Holy Spirit to help us know when and how to rebuke others.

Lord, help me not to fear what others may think of me if I am led to rebuke another person.

Evening Watch: Read Psalm 119:156–176. Many intercessors are praying for revival in the United States. In the November 27 devotional we talked about the need for Christians in America to return to God's Word. David had such a love for God's Word, and he knew that meditating upon God's Word would stir revival in his own heart. He prayed, "Revive me according to Your judgments" (v. 156). He declared, "Consider how I love Your precepts; Revive me, O LORD, according to Your lovingkindness" (v. 159). David declared that even in affliction he would not turn from God's precepts. Pray that the body of Christ in America will be renewed in their love for God's Word.

Lord, may I never take Your Word for granted.

Daniel 8:1–27; 1 John 2:1–17; Psalm 120:1–7; Proverbs 28:25–26

Morning Wisdom: Read Proverbs 28:25–26. Proverbs 28:25 says, "He who is of a proud heart stirs up strife, But he who trusts in the LORD will be prospered." Whenever we get into strife with another person we are usually trying to win an argument or prove our own opinion in a discussion. What we think about a matter is not really that important. However, what God thinks about it is extremely important. We never have to win an argument or have to prove our own point when we trust in the Lord to be our advocate and avenger. If someone starts to argue with you, you can simply say, "I'll have to get back with you about what you are saying, because I think you may have a valid point."

Jesus advised us to agree with our adversary quickly while we are on the way with him. (See Matthew 5:25.) If the argumentative person thinks you are really going to consider his point, he will cease his argument. Then we can submit whatever point that person had to the Lord in private and give our response later. The trap Satan wants us to fall into is to react to people rather than respond to them. There is a waiting period for a response, but a reaction is always the operation of our own flesh. We do not take the time to pray about matters.

If we are the one who starts an argument, we need to recognize the pride in our own hearts. Proverbs 28:26 says, "He who trusts in his own heart is a fool, But whoever walks wisely will be delivered." We can never trust our own hearts, because only God knows our hearts. Whenever we have an argument and make a statement like, "My heart tells me I am right and you are wrong," we are just blowing hot air. We can only trust God and His Word to have the correct instruction and counsel about every matter. We are foolish if we think our hearts can tell us anything. Only the Holy Spirit can give us wise counsel, and we need to lift our hearts daily to Him for Him to instruct us through God's Word and counsel us according to His wisdom.

> *God, forgive me for thinking I am right about anything. You are the only One who is right about everything.*

Evening Watch: Read Psalm 120:1–7. The psalms we are looking at now are called the "Songs of Ascents." These psalms were sung as the pilgrims made their journey three times a year to the temple in Jerusalem to celebrate Sukkot, the Feast of Tabernacles; Shavuot, the Feast of Pentecost; and Pesach, the Feast of Passover. These psalms describe the protection and provision God grants to those who trust Him.

Today's psalm is a psalm of distress. The psalmist wrote, "Deliver my soul, O LORD, from lying lips And from a deceitful tongue" (v. 2). The psalmist declared his desire for peace, but he seemed to be surrounded by those who hated him and who were on a mission to destroy him. This psalm would be appropriate for everyone in Israel to sing in this hour, when the plan to destroy all of Israel and push her into the sea is uppermost in the minds of the enemies who surround them.

> *Lord, I pray for the peace of Jerusalem.*

Morning Wisdom: Read Proverbs 28:27–28. When I watch the news on TV sometimes I am tempted never to go out of my home again. Robberies, rapes, kidnappings, and murders are the usual menu of the local news. Proverbs 28:28 says, "When the wicked arise, men hide themselves; But when they perish, the righteous increase." The Bible tells us that the day will come when men's hearts will fail because of fear. (See Luke 21:26.) Wickedness in our nation is on the increase. Should we run and hide? I believe the only place we should hide during these end times is in the Rock, Jesus Christ. He is the One who will give us the power to overcome. He said, "In the world you will have tribulation; but be of good cheer, I have overcome the world" (John 16:33).

Proverbs 28:27 warns us not to hide our eyes from the poor, because if we do many curses will come upon us. Just the other night I was guilty of hiding my eyes from the poor. I saw many street people and beggars on the street as we walked to see a football game. I must admit that I walked briskly by these people and looked down at my feet rather than looking into their eyes as we walked.

Lord, forgive me for hiding sometimes from the needs of others.

Evening Watch: Read Psalm 121:1–8. We talked this morning about not hiding our eyes from the poor. We will not be guilty of doing this if we will daily lift up our eyes to heaven. My grammar-school class memorized this beautiful psalm in school, and I can still say it from memory.

The major promise in this psalm is that the Lord is our keeper. At this age I am getting very forgetful, but I cannot use age as an excuse since even in my younger days I always left something in the home I just visited. I can remember going to teas with my twin sister and both of us would leave our purses in the host home. The hostess did not have to guess who left the purses since they were identical. Today my twin sister lives in the apartment next door to our home. We go on shopping trips together, and we still forget where we parked the car or leave our keys in the store. I always laugh and say, "We both need a keeper." It is good to know that angels do keep charge over us, and the Lord always watches over us, because He never slumbers or sleeps.

Lord, thank You for being my keeper and setting angels over me.

Daniel 11:1–34; 1 John 3:7–24; Psalm 122:1–9; Proverbs 29:1

Morning Wisdom: Read Proverbs 29:1. We learned a little about the art of rebuking in our November 30 devotional. We discovered that it is pointless to rebuke a foolish person because he or she will not listen. Today's verse conveys a similar message when it says, "He who is often rebuked, and hardens his neck, Will suddenly be destroyed, and that without remedy." There are many stiff-necked people in the world who refuse to receive correction or rebuke. The neck brace around every stiff-necked person is pride. Pride always comes before destruction. (See Proverbs 16:18.)

If a believer displays pride, God in His mercy will put him through His "humbling machine." Have you ever gone through His humbling machine? I know I have many times. I will share with you just two incidents in my life when I went through this unique machine.

I was practicing a duet with my mother in preparation for a women's meeting. We sang "Fill My Cup, Lord" several times when our accompanist said, "I believe this song would be better if it was a solo rather than a duet." I replied, "I'll be glad to do the solo." The accompanist said, "I had your mother in mind to do the solo rather than you."

A similar occasion happened when I was at a retreat. We were gathered in circles to pray, and I knew I needed to break out in song during our prayer circle. I said, "Now, everyone close your eyes while I sing 'To God be the Glory.'" Everyone closed their eyes while I sang, and I heard tittering and quiet laughter that accompanied my song. While I was singing I opened one eye to behold several people whispering and pointing my way during my magnificent delivery of this majestic song.

The Lord truly has a way of humbling us. He humbled the Israelites for forty years in the wilderness, and He is the same yesterday, today, and forever. God knows that if we are stiff-necked and proud, we will never receive the grace He wants to pour out to us daily. James wrote, "God resists the proud, But gives grace to the humble" (James 4:6).

Lord, help me to humble myself before You daily.

Evening Watch: Read Psalm 122:1–9. We are exhorted in this Song of Ascents to pray for the peace of Jerusalem, and it gives the promise to prosper all those who love her. (See v. 6.) When we pray for the peace of Jerusalem we can declare the words written in verses 7 and 8:

"Peace be within your walls, Prosperity within your palaces." For the sake of my brethren and companions, I will now say, "Peace be within you."

Lord, strengthen the saints in Israel and let Your peace reign in their hearts.

DECEMBER 4

Morning Wisdom: Read Proverbs 29:2–4. All three of these verses challenge us to pray continually for wise, righteous, just leaders in our land and in other countries. Proverbs 29:2 reads, "When the righteous are in authority, the people rejoice; But when a wicked man rules, the people groan." Our youngest son served in Hungary to reach out to Jewish people and to try to pull down walls of anti-Semitism in this country. He saw firsthand how so many Hungarians still have broken hearts because of the suffering they experienced during the rule of Germany and Russia over their country.

Wise leaders will not waste their time or wealth to satisfy their own flesh. Proverbs 29:3 says, "Whoever loves wisdom makes his father rejoice, But a companion of harlots wastes his wealth." Our heavenly Father rejoices when we are wise and use what wealth we have to further His kingdom on Earth. He also rejoices when He sees leaders who meet the needs of the poor rather than establishing wealth for themselves.

Most wicked rulers willingly receive bribes from those who want to protect themselves from unjust policies. Proverbs 29:4 reads, "The king establishes the land by justice, But he who receives bribes overthrows it."

Lord, establish wise, just, and righteous leaders in our land.

Evening Watch: Read Psalm 123:1–4. We talked this morning about unjust, wicked leaders who cause those they rule over to suffer. This Song of Ascents cries out for the mercy of the Lord, because the proud troubled the souls of many. The pride of life and the lust of the flesh are the strongholds in those who war for gain. James questioned:

> Where do wars and fights come from among you? Do they not come from your desires for pleasure that war in your members? You lust and do not have. You murder and covet and cannot obtain. You fight and war. Yet you do not have because you do not ask. You ask and do not receive, because you ask amiss, that you may spend it on your pleasures.
>
> —JAMES 4:1–3

In this Song of Ascents we see the comparison between the proud and the humble. The humble look up to see God and seek to obey Him just as a servant or a maid looks to the hand of his or her master and mistress. We are humble servants of the Lord who should daily lift our eyes to the Lord with a heart to obey whatever He desires for us to do and say daily. The proud, however, look to satisfy their own flesh, and their eyes are only on themselves and their own needs. The proud will never receive the mercy of the Lord, because they show no mercy toward others. The humble will daily receive both the grace and mercy of the Lord.

Lord, may I daily be Your humble servant.

Morning Wisdom: Read Proverbs 29:5–8. These four verses continue the comparison between the wicked and the righteous. The wicked lay their own trap by their greed and covetousness. We discussed yesterday how the wicked walk according to their lusts rather than walk the righteous path. When we seek to fulfill our own lusts rather than to fulfill God's will, we will never experience the liberty God has promised us. When we walk in the Spirit we will not fulfill the lusts of the flesh, and we will always have liberty.

Those who seek to fulfill their own lusts gain favor through flattery. Proverbs 29:5 says, "A man who flatters his neighbor Spreads a net for his feet." Flattery may temporarily cause us to gain favor with others, but eventually those who we have manipulated through flattery will turn against us.

Proverbs 29:6 says, "By transgression an evil man is snared, But the righteous sings and rejoices." You have probably heard the expression, "Be sure your sins will find you out." (See Numbers 32:23.) Our sins will always find us out, and we will be bound by many strongholds if we do not confess our sins and repent of them. Only a clear conscience experiences liberty.

Proverbs 29:7 says, "The righteous considers the cause of the poor, But the wicked does not understand such knowledge." Selfish people do not realize that it is more blessed to give than to receive. We reap what we sow, and when we refuse to reach out to the poor we will be ensnared by our own greed and covetousness. I have never seen a joyful selfish person. The slogan, "He who has the most toys wins," is simply not true. The truth is he who gives the most toys wins.

Proverbs 29:8 says, "Scoffers set a city aflame, But wise men turn away wrath."

There are many scoffers in these end times. Scoffers stir up strife and can even cause riots in a city. Those who are wise do not scoff and refuse to be ensnared by strife.

When we look at the fruits produced by selfishness discussed in these four verses, we see the need to humble ourselves daily by walking in the Spirit instead of fulfilling our own lusts.

Lord, reveal any selfishness in my own life, and help me to daily walk in the Spirit.

Evening Watch: Read Psalm 124:1–8. We discussed this morning how the wicked are ensnared by their selfish transgressions. This Song of Ascents praises the Lord for His power to deliver Israel out of every snare of the enemy. The psalmist wrote, "Blessed be the LORD, Who has not given us as prey to their teeth. Our soul has escaped as a bird from the snare of the fowlers; The snare is broken, and we have escaped" (vv. 6–7). The very fact that Israel still exists and has not been destroyed by the enemies who surround her is evidence that the Lord is on her side. May our nation always be on the side of Israel.

Lord, give our leaders the wisdom to always support Israel.

DECEMBER 6

Morning Wisdom: Read Proverbs 29:9–11. Throughout Proverbs we see the comparison between the righteous and unrighteous, the godly and ungodly, and the wise and the foolish. A man who lacks godly wisdom will be contentious and will always stir up strife. Proverbs 29:9 warns that it is useless to get into an argument with a fool. This verse says, "If a wise man contends with a foolish man, Whether the fool rages or laughs, there is no peace." We can never win an argument with a foolish person. This is why we should avoid being drawn into arguments with ungodly people. Foolish people also vent all of their feelings. Proverbs 29:11 says, "A fool vents all his feelings, But a wise man holds them back."

When we converse with a foolish person the conversation will often end up in a heated argument. A foolish person will always try to prove his point and will usually become quite angry if we do not agree with him.

Proverbs 29:10 compares the righteous person to the unrighteous one. It says, "The bloodthirsty hate the blameless, But the upright seek his well-being." When we seek the kingdom of God first and His righteousness, we will not be foolish, and we will always seek the well-being of others.

Lord, help me to walk in Your righteousness today.

Evening Watch: Read Psalm 125:1–5. This morning we shared how wicked and foolish people hate those who walk in righteousness. We never have to worry about wicked men. God is big enough to take care of them. Psalm 125:5 says, "As for such as turn aside to their crooked ways, The LORD shall lead them away With the workers of iniquity." We only have to concern ourselves with doing good. If we seek peace and desire to do and speak good things, the Lord will be good to us. (See v. 4.)

I was with a lady this morning who said she had lived such a blessed life. She said she couldn't think of a thing she needed, because God had been so good to her. I know this lady well, and even though she has gone through a divorce and some hard times, she refuses to be bitter about the past. She said, "We have to seize the moment, because that may be all we have." I think she gained that great attitude when she was operated on for a melanoma in her brain. She received the strength of the Lord then, and ever since her surgery, she considers each day a gift. What will you do tomorrow with the day God gives you?

Lord, help me to do Your will tomorrow and help me to be always grateful for each day You give me.

DECEMBER 7

Morning Wisdom: Read Proverbs 29:12–14. These verses all talk about the ability to have our eyes opened to see the truth. One of the ways I pray for the leaders of our nation is that their eyes would be open to discern the truth and that their ears would be closed to the lies. Every leader is surrounded by many counselors. Some of these counselors will deliver unwise counsel and even lies in order to manipulate their leader into making decisions that will benefit them. Proverbs 29:12 says, "If a ruler pays attention to lies, All his servants become wicked." Satan's major weapon is deception, and Jesus called him the father of lies.

To make wise daily decisions we need to abide in God's Word by reading and heeding it daily. Only the truth of God's Word will give us the ability to discern all lies.

Proverbs 29:13 says, "The poor man and the oppressor have this in common: The LORD gives light to the eyes of both." Jesus said, "He makes His sun rise on the evil and on the good, and sends rain on the just and on the unjust" (Matt. 5:45). Both the wicked and the just can be bathed daily in the warmth of God's sunshine. However, the wicked usually like to cloak their wicked deeds in the darkness of the night. God's truths are available to both, and God has the ability to even open the eyes of the wicked so that they will see the light of His truth. A prayer I pray for those who I know who are not walking in the light of God's truth is, *Holy Spirit, open the eyes of their understanding, and give them the gift of repentance so that they might be changed by God's truth.*

Proverbs 29:14 continues the theme of the light of God's truth. This verse says, "The king who judges the poor with truth, His throne will be established forever." History records multitudes of evil rulers who oppressed the poor to gain riches for themselves. The leader who judges the poor according to God's Word will experience the kingdom of God, which has no end.

Lord, help me always to walk in the light of Your truths.

Evening Watch: Read Psalm 126:1–6. This Song of Ascents contains one of my favorite scriptures. Verses 5 and 6 give a wonderful promise to those who are experiencing a sorrowful time in their lives. These verses read, "Those who sow in tears Shall reap in joy. He who continually goes forth weeping, Bearing seed for sowing, Shall doubtless come again with rejoicing, Bringing his sheaves with him." Whenever I read these verses I picture an intercessor who has cried out to God for the lost. Many tears were shed in this intercessor's prayers, and only God knows the souls that were saved because of these faithful prayers. When this person reaches heaven, he will see the souls that were touched through faithful prayers. The sheaves at this harvesttime are souls. The seed is the Word of God. I am challenged by these verses to pray more for the lost and to share God's Word with many. How about you?

Lord, help me to be a faithful intercessor.

DECEMBER 8

Morning Wisdom: Read Proverbs 29:15–17. Why do the wicked prosper? David wrote that the ungodly seem to be always at ease, and they even increase in riches. (See Psalm 73:12.) However, Proverbs 29:16 declares that the righteous will see the fall of the wicked. Proverbs 29:16 says, "When the wicked are multiplied, transgression increases; But the righteous will see their fall."

The wicked only have worldly wisdom. James described the wisdom of this world when he wrote, "But if you have bitter envy and self-seeking in your hearts, do not boast and lie against the truth. This wisdom does not descend from above, but is earthly, sensual, demonic" (James 3:14).

In earlier readings from Proverbs we learned that people who lack wisdom will not receive a rebuke. Proverbs 29:15 says, "The rod and rebuke give wisdom, But a child left to himself brings shame to his mother." Proverbs 29:17 says, "Correct your son, and he will give you rest; Yes, he will give delight to your soul." The son who receives correction and rebuke is a wise son who operates in the wisdom that comes from above. James shared these facts about the wisdom that is from above when he wrote, "But the wisdom that is from above is first pure, then peaceable, gentle, willing to yield, full of mercy and good fruits, without partiality and without hypocrisy" (James 3:17).

The question we must ask ourselves daily is, *Am I operating in the wisdom from above, which is heavenly, or the wisdom from below, which is earthly?* The way we respond to correction and rebuke will reveal the answer to this question. Do we receive rebuke and correction with a humble heart that is willing not only to listen but also to change?

Lord, help me to walk in Your wisdom today.

Evening Watch: Read Psalm 127:1–5. I never have understood Psalm 127:2, which reads, "It is vain for you to rise up early, To sit up late, To eat the bread of sorrows; For so He gives His beloved sleep." I usually stay up until 11:00 p.m. and awaken at 5:00 a.m. I love those early morning hours when the house is quiet and I can be alone with the Lord without any interruptions.

David wrote that he sought the Lord early in the morning. We learn in the Gospels that Jesus spent all night in prayer. I guess it would be vain to stay up all night if you were doing something that was evil. Wicked men usually choose the night to do their dastardly deeds, because they think no one will see them in the dark of night.

During those early morning hours I pray for my husband, three sons, and our nine grandchildren.

Verse 3 says, "Behold, children are a heritage from the LORD, The fruit of the womb is a reward." I know those grandchildren will be sharp arrows in the hands of the Lord, because they will do warfare against Satan. Even though you may not have physical children, you do have a heritage of spiritual children you have mentored.

Lord, I pray for You to bless both my spiritual and physical children.

Morning Wisdom: Read Proverbs 29:18. This verse reads, "Where there is no vision, the people perish: but he that keepeth the law, happy is he" (KJV). The New King James Version reads, "Where there is no revelation, the people cast off restraint; But happy is he who keeps the law."

After 9/11 many repented and turned back to God, because they knew God was their only hope to maintain sanity during this age of terrorism. However, others began to cast off restraints and did whatever their lusts dictated, because they believed in Solomon's exhortation, "Eat, drink, and be merry" (Eccles. 8:15). The people who cast off restraint had no vision or revelation about the soon coming of Jesus Christ, who will be the Judge of our actions and words on Earth.

There was no fear of the Lord in those who became lawless. Even after the tragedy of 9/11 we see a rise of lawlessness in our nation. This thought challenges me to pray more for revival to be birthed in our nation. The first step to revival is to recognize our lawlessness and then to repent of it.

> *Lord, I pray that revival will come to America, and let it begin with me.*
> *I pray for the conviction of the Holy Spirit to create godly sorrow that will*
> *usher repentance and revival throughout the church and the nation.*

Evening Watch: Read Psalm 128:1–6. Last night we shared how blessed we are to have both spiritual and physical children as our heritage. The psalmist prayed that he would be able to see his children's children. (See v. 6.) My husband and I are blessed, because we have been able to see our children's children. One of the ladies in our Bible study now has thirteen great-grandchildren. What a blessing! If we walk in the fear of the Lord, we can look forward to having many spiritual children, grandchildren, and great-grandchildren. The person we witness to today may lead millions to the Lord.

God has blessed my husband and me with three natural sons and many spiritual sons and daughters. We had the opportunity to parent a Russian boy for seven years.

While he was in our care, he came to know the Lord personally. We also were blessed to have a Chinese daughter live with us for five years. We know God will use both of these young people in a mighty way in their own countries.

Verse 3 compares children to olive plants around our tables. My husband and I may never be able to visit other countries, but our Russian son and Chinese daughter can be planted and produce good fruit in their own countries. Two of our natural sons were planted in foreign lands as short-term missionaries. The fruit produced by our middle son in China and our youngest son in Hungary will remain. Even a single person can add to the plantings of the Lord when they share the gospel with others.

> *Lord, help us to add olive plants to Your table.*

Morning Wisdom: Read Proverbs 29:19–20. Words fill containers that hold rich treasures of unwanted trash. I remember when my husband Tom was in the army we lived in a small trailer near the post for a few months while he had special training. One day I had the opportunity to go into the trailer that was owned by the people who rented to us. Every container in their house was overflowing with rotting garbage and trash. I wondered why these people never emptied their garbage. I concluded that the odor and the clutter did not bother this couple at all.

Both of today's verses talk about words and how they affect our own lives and the lives of others. Proverbs 29:19 says, "A servant will not be corrected by mere words; For though he understands, he will not respond." Have you ever given instructions to your children only to see blank stares and no action as a response to what you said? No doubt your children have understood what you said. They are just not motivated to follow the instructions. The content of our words will have little effect if we stuff them into the wrong container (the mode of delivery). The container is more important than the content of the words spoken. With the help of the Holy Spirit we can speak words that will influence and motivate people to have a deeper walk with the Lord. Nagging others will never produce good fruit. Exhorting and praising others will cause others not only to listen to the words we speak but also to obey those words. People were drawn to Jesus, because He had a way of saying things that pierced their hearts and caused them to want to change.

Proverbs 29:20 says, "Do you see a man hasty in his words? There is more hope for a fool than for him." Sometimes when we are irritated and frustrated we dump words on others that are hurtful and burdensome. We are exhorted in the Bible to bear one another's burdens, but we are never to burden another with the gory details of our personal lives. What we say and how we say it will affect others for good if we follow the example of Jesus, who only said what He heard the Father saying to Him. Every day the Holy Spirit is speaking to us, but we must be honest and admit that quite often we do not hear what He is saying. The Holy Spirit can empower you to speak words of life to those you meet today. Will you listen to Him and then will you boldly repeat the words He gives you to say? Your heart may be filled with bitterness or resentment. God wants you to pour that garbage out to Him and allow Him to scrub your heart clean with His blood. When you confess your own sins and receive cleansing, your words will produce good fruit.

Lord, help me to speak Your words.

Evening Watch: Read Psalm 129:1–8. We can rest assured that our enemies will never prevail against us. Psalm 34:19 says, "Many are the afflictions of the righteous, But the LORD delivers him out of them all." Psalm 129:2 says, "Many a time they have afflicted me from my youth; Yet they have not prevailed against me." When we have the assurance that we win in the end, we can have a sweet sleep.

Lord, thank You for Your prevailing power.

Morning Wisdom: Read Proverbs 29:21–22. In our culture today only the rich have servants. However, in Israel whole families served their masters. It is important to note that God does not condone slavery.

However, when Israel defeated a pagan nation they were allowed to use the survivors as bond slaves. It was common in the culture of ancient Israel to allow Hebrew men to work off their debt by becoming servants to those who could pay them. When his debt was paid or forgiven in the year of Jubilee, the servant had the option to remain under his master or to leave. If he chose to remain with his family, he then became a love slave. His ear was pierced to signify that he had chosen to remain with his master forever.

Proverbs 29:21 says, "He who pampers his servant from childhood Will have him as a son in the end." The children in the family of servants were usually treated like they belonged to their master's household. They played with their master's children and often even received special gifts from their master. If a servant chose to stay with his master until he died, his sons then would have the choice to remain or continue to live with their father's master. If the son had been treated well, he would continue to serve his master forever.

We are love servants to our Master Jesus Christ, because we have chosen to serve Him forever. However, Jesus considers us to be not just His servants but also His friends and even His brothers and sisters. When we accept Jesus Christ we become joint heirs with Him, and our heavenly Father does much more than just pamper us. He graces us with His glory. It is a joy to be a colaborer and joint heir with Jesus. The wages God pays us when we become His love servants are all the riches of His glory through Jesus Christ and the privilege of being in His family forever.

Proverbs 29:22 says, "An angry man stirs up strife, And a furious man abounds in transgression." Both an angry man and a furious man are prideful men who are determined to have their own way. Pride is the root of all contention. We need to pull down any stronghold of pride in our own lives by daily humbling ourselves before the Lord. A good prayer to pray is:

> *Lord, I offer myself as Your willing servant. Use me to do Your will today. I offer my body as a living sacrifice—my voice to speak Your words, my mind to think Your thoughts, my hands to serve others, and my feet to go Your way, not my way.*

Evening Watch: Read Psalm 130:1–8. I believe forgiveness is a supernatural occurrence that originates with the love of Jesus in our hearts. No man can truly forgive another unless Jesus gives him the power to forgive. Psalm 130:3 says, "If You, LORD, should mark iniquities, O Lord, who could stand? But there is forgiveness with You." This psalm closes with this statement, "For with the LORD there is mercy, And with Him is abundant redemption" (v. 7).

> *Lord, thank You for redeeming me so I can forgive others.*

DECEMBER 12

Morning Wisdom: Read Proverbs 29:23. In the economy of God's kingdom the way up is the way down. In the world's economy the way up is to pull others down. When we travel through the Bible each year we clearly see that the lives God used to further His kingdom on Earth first had to be servants or esteemed others higher than themselves. Abraham gave Lot first choice over the land God had promised. Jacob served Laban. Joseph served his brothers, Potiphar, the governor of the prison, and Pharaoh. Moses served his father-in-law. It might be a good exercise for you to make your own list of humble servants. Of course, Jesus was the greatest of all servants.

Proverbs 29:23 says, "A man's pride will bring him low, But the humble in spirit will retain honor." Whenever we are prideful we have two enemies—God and the devil.

The devil tempts us to remain in pride, and God resists us. James wrote, "God resists the proud, But gives grace to the humble" (James 4:5). God honors those who are willing to honor others above themselves. He promotes those who rejoice at the promotion of others.

In these last days God is searching for those who will be colaborers with Him in this last great harvest. He is schooling those laborers to be servant leaders. It will take all the grace of God, the supernatural ability to do His will, to be a colaborer with Him.

God's sufficient grace will empower those who are willing to lay down their own plans and desires to do His will. Do you feel like you are in the "school of hard knocks" right now? God is training you to be a servant leader.

> *Lord, give me a servant spirit.*

Evening Watch: Read Psalm 131:1–3. David was a man after God's own heart because he had a humble heart. If anyone ever went through the school of hard knocks, David did. His whole life was one of fight or flight. Those closest to him betrayed him. In this psalm David reminded God that throughout his life he had resisted pride and desired to always be humble. David wrote in verses 1–2:

> LORD, my heart is not haughty, Nor my eyes lofty. Neither do I concern myself with great matters, Nor with things too profound for me. Surely I have calmed and quieted my soul, Like a weaned child with his mother; Like a weaned child is my soul within me.

A weaned child does not continually cry to receive food. A weaned child finally comes to the place of calmness, because he knows and trusts that his mother will feed him. The child does not have to cry uncontrollably in fear that his mother will not hear and answer. David had his moments when he complained to the Lord and did cry out to Him, but he was able to keep his sanity, because he cast every care upon the Lord and remained in His presence.

> *Lord, help me to cast every care upon You.*

Morning Wisdom: Read Proverbs 29:24–25. When I first married, I was so bound by the fear of what others thought of me. I wondered if my mother thought I was a good mother. Did my husband think I was a good wife? Did my neighbors think I was a good neighbor? I remember my next-door neighbor coming to my home and telling me how she cleaned her oven and range every day. From that day forward I made sure my oven and range were spotless just in case "Mrs. Clean" dropped by uninvited. Before I was delivered from the fear of man, I never really listened to what people were saying. I was too busy thinking about what I would say to them when they finished talking.

One day I was listening to a teaching tape on my back patio. The subject was the fear of man. As I listened and discovered how the fear of man is a snare, I asked God to deliver me from that fear. That day I was delivered, and now I can honestly say I fear God more than I fear man. I desire to please God first in all of my ways and honor Him instead of trying to please man.

Since that significant prayer of deliverance from the fear of man, I have been free to esteem others higher than myself and to think of others rather than myself, and I don't seek to impress people. Instead, I now want to make a spiritual impact for God upon people. I seek now to put His best foot forward instead of my own. What a blessing to be free from the tension and pressure of trying to please others. Now I just want to please God. Has the fear of man been a snare in your life? If it has, maybe you would like to get set free of that wicked snare today. If you do, you can pray with me the following:

> *In the name of Jesus Christ, I bind the spirit of fear of man in my life and command it to leave me this moment and never return. I refuse to ever receive the fear of man again. I will no longer be concerned with what people will think of me. Instead, I will only be concerned with what You think about me.*

Evening Watch: Read Psalm 132:1–18. David longed to build a temple for the Lord. He said he could not sleep until he found a place for the Lord to dwell. (See v. 4–5.) We do not have to lose sleep to find a place for God to dwell. We are the temple of the living God. When we recognize that the King of glory dwells within us, we should humble ourselves before Him and ask Him to rule our tomorrows and every day.

It is overwhelming to think that God would allow us to contain His precious Holy Spirit. May we always be worthy of His trust. I am reminded of 2 Corinthians 4:6–7, which reads, "For it is God who commanded light to shine out of darkness, who has shone in our hearts to give the light of the knowledge of the glory of God in the face of Jesus Christ. But we have this treasure in earthen vessels, that the excellence of the power may be of God and not of us."

Lord, help me to shine for You.

DECEMBER 14

Morning Wisdom: Read Proverbs 29:26–27. In this last decade certain circuit courts have made decisions that restrict freedom of speech and religion in their districts. Many Christians are praying that our citizens will elect just judges who will uphold our constitution.

Proverbs 29:26–27 gives every Christian a strategy for prayer that will not fail. Proverbs 29:26 says, "Many seek the ruler's favor, But justice for man comes from the LORD." God is a just judge who grants favor to the righteous. Second Chronicles 7:14 says, "If My people who are called by My name will humble themselves, and pray and seek My face, and turn from their wicked ways, then I will hear from heaven, and will forgive their sin and heal their land." If every Christian would seek the Lord first and pray for those in authority, the Lord's justice will reign in our land.

Proverbs 29:27 says, "An unjust man is an abomination to the righteous, And he who is upright in the way is an abomination to the wicked." Maybe a good prayer to pray is that Christians will become so upright in their daily walk with the Lord that we will be an abomination to the wicked and a real threat to the devil. Light always dispels the darkness, and if Christians in this nation will commit themselves to walk in the light, the darkness in this nation will have to flee.

Lord, help me daily to walk in the light.

Evening Watch: Read Psalm 133:1–3. "Every…house divided against itself will not stand" (Matt. 12:25). One of the tactics of the enemy is to divide and conquer. If he can divide brothers and sisters in Christ, Satan can then destroy a whole church. We are members of a church that has had only one split, but that split did not destroy us because the offenses that occurred were forgiven. Some of the people who left over certain issues in the church are still friends. We all had the same goal, and that goal was to do the will of the Lord.

Psalm 133:1 describes how good and how pleasant it is for brethren to dwell together in unity. It was not a pleasant thing to go through when we saw some of our close friends leave the church, but in the end Satan won no victory. Many of those who left were planted in other bodies of Christ, where they became even more fruitful than they were as members of our congregation.

Nothing can divide us if we allow the love of Jesus to be shed abroad in our hearts. We can never let the roots of bitterness and unforgiveness grow in our hearts and hinder Jesus' love from freely flowing from our hearts to others. Forgiveness paves the way to unity, and we are exhorted in God's Word to forgive as Jesus forgave.

Lord, fill my heart to overflow with Your love.

Morning Wisdom: Read Proverbs 30:1–4. We are nearing our last readings in Proverbs. Most of Proverbs was written by Solomon. Chapter 30, however, was declared by Agur, the son of Jakeh. Ithiel and Ucal recorded Agur's proverbs.

Agur certainly did not consider himself wise. He declared, "Surely I am more stupid than any man, And do not have the understanding of a man" (v. 2). I do not think Agur was stupid, because the verses that flowed from his lips belong to a man who has both wisdom and understanding. He had the wisdom to know that God had a Son. He asked the question, "Who has established all the ends of the earth? What is His name, and what is His Son's name…?" (v. 4). Those questions reveal that Agur was a man of great spiritual insight. He believed in intelligent design and without a doubt understood the triune nature of God.

If Agur was alive today, we could easily answer his questions. God the Father is God's name and His Son's name is Jesus Christ. This passage can provide evidence to the Jewish mind-set that questions the sonship of Jesus Christ.

> *Lord, You made the heavens and the earth and named the stars. Thank You for becoming Immanuel (God with us) to make it possible for us to actually know our heavenly Father in a personal way.*

Evening Watch: Read Psalm 134:1–3. This morning we read the questions Agur asked about God. He asked, "Who has ascended into heaven, or descended? Who has gathered the wind in His fists? Who has bound the waters in a garment? Who has established all the ends of the earth? What is His name, and what is His Son's name, If you know?" (Prov. 30:4). God created all things by His Word, and that Word became flesh and dwelled among us. His name is Jesus. For by Jesus were all things created, and for Jesus all things were created that are created. (See John 1:3, 14.) Colossians 1:16 says, "For by Him all things were created that are in heaven and that are on earth, visible and invisible, whether thrones or dominions or principalities or powers. All things were created through Him and for Him."

When we begin to understand the majestic power of God manifested in the creative power of His Son, we cannot help but bless the Lord by raising our hands in the sanctuary. Every time we raise our hands to worship the Lord, He is blessed. I am so glad that I belong to a church where people freely raise their hands to worship Jesus. Raised hands in worship symbolize both surrender and trust. We have nine grandchildren under seven years of age, and when they see their dads, they lift both hands up to them in full expectation that they will lift them into their arms. When we lift both of our hands up to God we are saying, "Daddy, I surrender my life to You and trust You to take care of me. Come and bless the Lord with me now."

> *Lord, I raise my hands to worship You.*

DECEMBER 16

Morning Wisdom: Read Proverbs 30:5–6. We continue with the verses declared by Agur. He definitely was not stupid. He knew the source of all wisdom when he wrote, "Every word of God is pure: he is a shield unto them that put their trust in him. Add thou not unto his words, lest he reprove thee, and thou be found a liar" (vs. 5–6, KJV). The shield of faith is raised whenever we declare the Word of God out loud. Faith both speaks and acts. When Jesus was tempted by the devil for forty days and forty nights in the wilderness, He resisted the devil by declaring God's pure Word. Every Word Jesus quoted was like a sword that pierced the devil. If you want to keep the devil on the run, the way to do it is to declare God's Word out loud.

The Word is like a two-edged sword that jabs Satan, but the Word of God also forms an invisible shield that keeps the devil's fiery darts from penetrating us. (See Ephesians 6.)

Jesus was sorely tempted in the wilderness. He had been fasting for forty days, and I know Satan was able to provide even the smell of fresh baked bread to tempt Jesus to turn the stone into bread. However, the moment Jesus said, "It is written, 'Man shall not live by bread alone, but by every word of God'" (Luke 4:4), the invisible shield of faith went up and the devil could not penetrate Jesus' desire for food.

Lord, help me to be faithful to memorize Your Word.

Evening Watch: Read Psalm 135:1–21. Many actors, writers, presidents, and philanthropists have their claim to fame, but no one can compare to the fame of God almighty. Psalm 135:13 says, "Your name, O LORD, endures forever, Your fame, O LORD, throughout all generations." This psalm extols the greatness of our God. As I read this psalm, I can picture throngs of people standing in the courts of the temple in Jerusalem. They had finished their ascent to Jerusalem to celebrate one of the feasts of the Lord. One side of the crowd yelled, "Praise the Lord!" The other side responded, "Praise the name of the Lord." The psalm continues with the exhortation to stand in the courts of the Lord and sing praises to His name.

The reasons to praise the Lord are simple. We praise the Lord because the Lord is good and He is great. (See vv. 3, 5.) My mind flashes back to the blessing I used to pronounce over my food when I was a child. I prayed, *God is great. God is good. Let us thank Him for our food.* This psalm of praise thanks God for making the heavens and Earth and for destroying the enemies of Israel and the idols of other nations.

I heard a friend once say, "If you can't think of anything to praise the Lord about, you can praise and thank Him for giving you fluid in your eyeballs." I always can think of something to praise the Lord about. How about you? If you have a hard time entering into praise, I suggest you read this psalm out loud. Before you know it, you will be singing the praises of the Lord.

Praise the Lord for all You have done in my life.

DECEMBER 17

Morning Wisdom: Read Proverbs 30:7–9. Perhaps the term *convenience foods* originated from these verses. I love convenience foods, because such foods make hosting dinners so easy. Proverbs 30:8 says, "Remove far from me vanity and lies: give me neither poverty nor riches; feed me with food convenient for me: Lest I be full, and deny thee, and say, Who is the LORD? or lest I be poor, and steal, and take the name of my God in vain" (KJV).

The author of this verse told the Lord that he did not want to be tempted by pride, covetousness, or gluttony. He was afraid that if he became too rich he would forget God, and if he was too poor he would become a thief. He knew if he became full he might deny the Lord and forget who He was. The author wanted the Lord to give him only what he needed and nothing more.

God is full of grace, and He longs to bless us with the abundance of His kingdom.

Paul described the abundance of God's kingdom when he wrote, "For the kingdom of God is not meat and drink; but righteousness, and peace, and joy in the Holy Ghost" (Rom. 14:17, KJV). We can all use the abundance of God's kingdom in our lives, and we are guaranteed to receive all we need when we seek first the kingdom of God and His righteousness. (See Matthew 6:33.) God is not a God of convenience. He is a covenant God who delights in blessing His children.

Lord, thank You for providing Your kingdom for me to enjoy on this earth now.

Evening Watch: Read Psalm 136:1–26. Years ago when I was in a denominational church, we always participated in responsive readings before the sermon was delivered. The pastor read a few verses from Psalms and the congregation responded by reading the next verses. I believe we read this psalm quite often as a responsive reading. Those gathered in the courts of the Lord centuries ago also participated in responsive declarations. One of the priests shouted, "Oh, give thanks to the Lord, for He is good!" Those pilgrims gathered in the courts of the Lord responded, "For His mercy endures forever."

This psalm will have a great impact on you if you read it responsively. Maybe you have no one in the bed with you tonight, but the Holy Spirit is always present with you. Read this psalm out loud, and let the Holy Spirit make the declarations about God. Then lift up your own voice and respond with, "His mercy endures forever." The Holy Spirit does not have an audible voice, but He can always have a heart-to-heart conversation with you. As I declared, "His mercy endures forever," I pictured myself standing in the courts of the Lord in heaven. Many of my loved ones who are now in heaven were standing with me. The angels and the twenty-four elders joined us as we declared, "His mercy endures forever." Whenever we praise the Lord there the distance between heaven and Earth dissolves.

Praise the Lord for His mercy endures forever!

Morning Wisdom: Read Proverbs 30:10. Throughout Proverbs we are warned not to be "tattletales." Proverbs 30:10 gives this warning, "Accuse not a servant unto his master, lest he curse thee, and thou be found guilty" (KJV). It is not our job to accuse anyone. There is one who already has that full-time job, and his name is Satan. The word *Satan* means "accuser and slanderer." Even if we feel we have proof that someone is guilty of a certain sin, we should not accuse to others. Instead, we are to pray for that brother or sister who has committed sin, and if the Lord leads we should go to that brother and rebuke him. When we rebuke a brother or sister in the Lord, our words should be rooted in love, and our motivation should be to restore that brother or sister.

Whenever we accuse someone we become a hit man for Satan. His words of accusation fly from the barrel of our mouths like bullets that can destroy another person's testimony and even his life. John wrote exactly what to do when we see a brother or sister commit a sin that is not unto death. He wrote, "If any man see his brother sin a sin which is not unto death, he shall ask, and he shall give him life for them that sin not unto death. There is a sin unto death: I do not say that he shall pray for it" (1 John 5:16, KJV). The only sin that a man could sin that would lead to death is the sin of rejecting Jesus Christ as Lord and Savior. If the body of Christ prayed for one another instead of accusing one another, we would see revival in the church.

Lord, never let me be a hit man for Satan.

Evening Watch: Read Psalm 137:1–9. This psalm would be a depressing way to end the day if we did not find a ray of hope hidden in one verse. The children of Israel were bemoaning their captivity in Babylon. They were asked by their captors to sing a song of joy in the midst of their despair. The verse that challenges us all to pray daily for the peace of Jerusalem is verse 5, which says, "If I forget thee, O Jerusalem, let my right hand forget her cunning" (KJV).

In the midst of their tragic captivity, Israel remembered Jerusalem. We can learn a lesson from this verse. No matter how tough things may get in these last days, we need to remember that one day Jerusalem will be where Jesus will set up His throne, and we will reign with Him for one thousand years. The rest of the story gets even better. One day there will be a new heaven and a new Earth, and we will live in the joy of the presence of the Lord there forever and eternity. As you close your eyes, meditate on the rest of the story. What occurs during the story of each of our lives cannot compare with the glory that will be revealed to us when the rest of the story unfolds.

Lord, help me to sing a song of joy no matter what my circumstances are.

DECEMBER 19

Morning Wisdom: Read Proverbs 30:11–14. As my husband and I grow nearer to the time when we will depart from this earth, we think often about the inheritance we will leave our children. My boys joke with me when they see me with a measuring tape in the house. They say, "There goes our inheritance!" We have updated the home we have lived in for over thirty-three years, and over the years we have added a sunroom and an apartment to our home. We have also finished our basement and added a bathroom. I've been measuring the dining room lately in hopes of a possible expansion project, but I do have to keep in mind that we want to leave our three sons some money. However, there is an inheritance we can leave them that is much more precious than money. We can leave them the prayers we have prayed for them and their children. The prayers we pray now for our children and grandchildren can affect generations to come. If you are single, your prayers for this generation and those to follow it will also be able to affect many lives now and later.

Proverbs 30:11–14 is a dismal description of the wicked generation the author observed. However, the same wickedness exists in the current generation we observe. The author of this chapter paints a vivid picture of a lawless generation that is disrespectful, prideful, and selfish. We will be dismayed if we only look at the wicked in this generation. However, I was filled with hope today as I heard our six-year-old grandson, Tyler, name all sixty-six books of the Bible from memory. I was filled with hope when I saw our five-year-old granddaughter draw pictures of angels and the manger scene when I asked her to draw some things that related to Christmas. We recently took Christmas to our middle son, who has five children, and the oldest in the family ran to find gifts in her room that she could quickly put in sacks to give us. She knew the spirit of Christmas is giving.

The inspiration we receive from our nine grandchildren, who are all still very young, encourages us to pray more for them and for their children and their children's children if the Lord tarries. Why don't you add to your inheritance on Earth today by praying for this generation and those to follow? Prayers prayed today can touch lives tomorrow.

Lord, help me to pray for Your glory to be revealed in this generation and those to follow.

Evening Watch: Read Psalm 138:1–8. David never had a problem praising the Lord, because he gave his heart to the Lord daily. When we give our hearts to the Lord, suddenly the Holy Spirit within us rises above our fleshly worries and cares about the tomorrows we face and our hearts begin to sing. When we have a heart-to-heart connection with God, the Word of God that we read daily becomes personal. David praised the Lord for His loving-kindness and His truth, and he declared that God had magnified His Word above all His names. (See v. 2.)

Lord, praise You for Your truth and Your loving-kindness.

Haggai 1:1–2:23; Revelation 11:1–19; Psalm 139:1–24; Proverbs 30:15–16

Morning Wisdom: Read Proverbs 30:15–16. Lasting satisfaction only comes from the Lord, but there are four things that are never satisfied on Earth. Proverbs 30:15–16 describes those things: "the grave, The barren womb, The earth that is not satisfied with water—And the fire never says, Enough" (v. 16). The grave is never satisfied, because death will continue until the Lord comes again. The barren womb is never satisfied, because the barren woman always longs for a child. The earth never has enough water, even when there are massive floods like the ones we observed when Hurricane Katrina hit New Orleans and Mississippi. I am sure that other parts of the world were experiencing drought when our Gulf Coast was flooded.

Fire never says there is enough, because it seeks more land to devour. If a fire is left uncontained it has the power to burn the whole earth.

I am so thankful that I can enjoy complete satisfaction in the presence of the Lord. That satisfaction, however, does cause me to long for more of Him. The more we know Him, the more we love Him, and the more we want to spend every waking hour with Him.

Are you hungry for more of Him? He longs to enjoy every minute of every day with You.

Lord, thank You for filling me full of joy when I am in Your presence.

Evening Watch: Read Psalm 139:1–24. Before daylight this morning, I went down to my dark basement to get a bottle of juice from the pantry. I'm not a "scaredy-cat," but I just couldn't wait to turn on the light so I could experience some assurance that nothing was lurking in the dark to jump out to get me. I wish I had read this psalm before I made my descent down the basement stairs. The words in the psalm are very comforting. We learn that we are never alone, even in the darkest hours of our lives.

Listen to David's words, "If I say, 'Surely the darkness shall fall on me,' Even the night shall be light about me; Indeed, the darkness shall not hide from You, But the night shines as the day; The darkness and the light are both alike to You" (vv. 11–12).

David continued his discussion of darkness in verses 13 and 16 of the psalm. In these verses he described the darkest hours we have ever experienced. Those hours were spent before we saw the light of day when we were in our mother's womb. David began to praise the Lord, because he was fearfully and wonderfully made. (See vv. 13–16.)

People who have never been born again are still in the dark womb of worldliness where there is no light at all. They long to see the daylight, but they must have someone to help them be delivered into the light. God wants to use you to be a midwife to help deliver babies from darkness into the light of God's love.

Lord, give me opportunities tomorrow to share Your gospel.

December 21

Morning Wisdom: Read Proverbs 30:17. This verse should send chills up the spine of every rebellious teenager. The promises given in this verse are not ones any person would want to claim. The promise given to children who mock their fathers and who despise and disobey their mothers is that they will have their eyes plucked out by ravens and eaten by young eagles.

I wish I had known about this verse when two of our sons went through various stages of rebellion. I can imagine how the conversation with these sons would unfold. It would go something like this, "Sons, if you do not obey your parents your eyes will be plucked out by ravens and eaten by eagles!" I can almost envision their puzzled looks in response to such a declaration. Even though two of our sons got into some worldly activities, they always showed respect for us. They never mocked us, and they did not despise us. Disrespect was something my husband and I never put up with, and our sons knew it.

Peer pressure drew these two sons into a season of worldliness, but the love of God drew them back. I used to bind the seducing spirits that were operating to entice our sons to go the way of the world. Then I asked the Holy Spirit to put a hedge of protection around them. I knew the persuasive power of the Holy Spirit was much more powerful than all seducing spirits. Maybe you have rebellious children. A good prayer to pray is the one my husband and I prayed daily in agreement over our sons. The prayer is based on Psalm 35. I'll share it with you:

> *Father, in the name of Jesus Christ of Nazareth, I bind every demonic spirit that has an assignment to seduce my children and cause them to go the way of the world. I command those demonic forces to be confounded and turned back away from my children. My children are children of the light, and they are God's property. The Word of God says the seed of the righteous will be blessed and will be a blessing. I declare the seed of the Word of God will not depart from our children. I silence the whispers of seducing spirits, and I cover the ears, eyes, noses, and mouths of my children with the blood of Jesus. I loose to my children the excellent Spirit of the Lord.*

Evening Watch: Read Psalm 140:1–13. This morning I shared a powerful prayer we prayed when two of our sons were going through stages of rebellion. We could add to that prayer some of the words David wrote in this psalm. He prayed in verse 4:

> *Keep me, O Lord, from the hands of the wicked; Preserve me from violent men, Who have purposed to make my steps stumble.*

Morning Wisdom: Read Proverbs 30:18–20. This passage in Proverbs has always fascinated me. The author lists four things that are too wonderful for him. He listed the following: the way of an eagle, the way of a serpent on a rock, the way of a ship in the midst of the sea, and the way of a man with a woman. This passage ends with the description of the way of an adulterous woman.

Recently I heard a magnificent teaching on the ways of an eagle. After hearing the way eagles teach their young to fly, I understood why the Lord wants us to rise up with wings like an eagle. Eagles glide with motionless wings with the wind currents and soar to great heights. I too stand in wonder of the way of an eagle, but I am even more astounded when I observe Christians who glide through severe trials, because they have learned to ride on the wind of the Holy Spirit.

I have never watched a serpent on a rock, but I do know that they slither up rocks to take a sunbath. They lay motionless while they soak up the rays of the sun. God does not want us to go the way of that wicked serpent, the devil, but we can learn something from the way a serpent rests on a rock. God wants us to rest daily on the Rock, Jesus, and allow the light of His love to soak into our souls to give us rest from every care.

I have observed the way of a ship in the midst of the sea. The author was probably speaking of a sailing ship that trusts the wind currents to take it to its desired destination. What is even more wondrous is to observe dying Christians who so completely trust the Lord to carry them safely into the arms of Jesus that their last breaths are breathed with peaceful smiles.

The sexual union between a married couple is so beautiful. Even more wondrous than that is to observe a committed elderly couple who can no longer participate in the sexual part of marriage. Their eyes dance with love for one another and just being close to one another fulfills them.

Over the years I have seen many marriages break up because of adulterous affairs. It truly is a wonder how an adulterous woman seems to be ignorant of her own sin. Proverbs 30:20 reads, "This is the way of an adulterous woman: She eats and wipes her mouth, And says, 'I have done no wickedness.'" What is a wonder to you? The most wondrous way I have observed is the way God gave His only begotten Son to deliver me from sin.

Father, thank You for Your wondrous gift.

Evening Watch: Read Psalm 141:1–10. When I read this psalm, I was convicted. I have never raised my hands to praise the Lord before I go to sleep. David said, "Let my prayer be set before You as incense, The lifting up of my hands as the evening sacrifice" (v. 2). David praised the Lord seven times a day. One of those times was just before he laid his head on his pillow to go to sleep. I usually fall asleep watching the eleven o'clock news. Then I drag myself from the lounge chair to bed.

Lord, forgive me. I lift my hands to praise You now!

December 23

Morning Wisdom: Read Proverbs 30:21–23. The author continues his list of things that he has observed during his life. Yesterday we read his list of wondrous things. Today's reading includes his list of perturbing things in the earth. His list certainly is not what perturbs me in this life. He listed: a servant who reigns, a fool who is filled with food, a hateful woman when she is married, and a maidservant who succeeds her mistress. Most husbands would agree that an angry wife is very perturbing. Employers who have employees who usurp their position and become their employer would certainly be grieved and perturbed over such an occurrence.

I would have to agree that people who see food as their only source of enjoyment in life are perturbed emotionally. Few people in the body of Christ want to admit that gluttony is a sin. Most of us in this culture do not have maids, but it would be perturbing to see someone who had cleaned your toilets inherit your home and become the manager of your home.

My list of perturbing things are: Christians who are not willing to open their Bibles daily to receive God's Word; Christians who are not committed to their church and leave because they have been offended; people who refuse to believe and repent when the gospel is shared with them; and Christians who simply want to be receivers rather than givers. One of the most magnificent characteristics of God is that He is a loving giver. When we fail to give His love and ours to others, we perturb God.

Lord, help me to be a loving giver.

Evening Watch: Read Psalm 142:1–7. We talked this morning about perturbing things. David was desperately perturbed when he wrote this psalm. He was hiding from Saul in a cave probably located at Engedi. His companions were depressed and distressed men who feared Saul. We have been to Engedi and observed signs over the caves located in this oasis near the Dead Sea that read, "Beware of leopards." Leopards were also the companions of David and his men.

David poured out his list of perturbing things to the Lord, and it would be prudent for us all to follow his example. He wrote, "I pour out my complaint before Him; I declare before Him my trouble" (v. 2). David knew that only God had the power to deliver him in the midst of his trials. David felt like no one cared for his soul, but he was confident that God cared for his soul. Otherwise, he would not have poured out his complaints to the Lord. David knew that God was His refuge in times of trouble. He wrote, "I cried out to You, O LORD: I said, 'You are my refuge, My portion in the land of the living'" (v. 5). David ended this psalm with a true statement about God that should comfort all those who are going through difficult times. He wrote, "For You shall deal bountifully with me" (v. 7). By faith we must see as David saw that God will deal bountifully with us and deliver us through every trial.

Lord, thank You for hearing our complaints!

December 24

Morning Wisdom: Read Proverbs 30:24–28. Agur, the author of this chapter in Proverbs, was a list maker just like my middle son. I am still finding lists in our home that he wrote out on index cards. He also wrote out his exercise program and schedule for each day. In these verses Agur lists four of God's creatures that are wise. I have only observed one of these wise creatures—the ant.

Ants are fascinating insects. I had the opportunity to observe ants when I was doing a science project in high school. In the late fifties ant farms were all the rage.

Someone was extremely inventive and decided to capture ants, put them in some sand, and enclose them in glass. The proud owner of the ant farm could watch the activity of the ants, who were especially active after crumbs of food were dropped on the scene.

Ants are wise enough to prepare their food in the summer.

Jesus told us to take no thought for tomorrow. "Therefore I say to you, do not worry about your life, what you will eat or what you will drink; nor about your body, what you will put on. Is not life more than food and the body more than clothing?" (Matt. 6:25). He promised that if we seek Him and His kingdom first, God would take care of these things for us.

Does this mean that we are to go through life without making lists or planning? Jesus in the Sermon on the Mount exhorted us not to be absorbed with worry about the things of this world. Instead, we should have our minds centered upon Him each day and trust Him to take care of our daily needs. His kingdom has nothing to do with meat or drink. It has everything to do with our walking daily in righteousness, peace, and joy. (See Romans 14:17.)

We can be as wise as the aunts if we prepare for the future by trusting God to fulfill all of our needs according to His riches in glory by Christ Jesus. (See Philippians 4:19.) Don't worry about what you will do today. Make your to-do list, grocery list, shopping list, and appointment list. Then release those lists to the Lord. Also join me in praying the following:

> *Lord, I have so much to do today, but I refuse to worry about this to-do list. Put me in the right place at the right time, and do not let me miss any divine appointments.*

Evening Watch: Read Psalm 143:1–12. David wrote, "I spread out my hands to You; My soul longs for You like a thirsty land" (v. 6). This morning we talked about centering our minds on Jesus and walking in His kingdom, which is righteousness, peace, and joy. Tomorrow when you have your quiet time, spread out your hands and lift them up to the Lord. Let your left hand represent trust and your right hand represent surrender, and then pray:

> *I surrender myself to You, and I give You all my cares.*

December 25

Zechariah 8:1–23; Revelation 16:1–21; Psalm 144:1–15; Proverbs 30:29–31

Morning Wisdom: Read Proverbs 30:29–31. Just recently the secretary of our church mentioned that my husband walks with a military walk. Others commented on my husband's military walk. I guess he began walking that way when he was an officer in the U.S. Army. People do walk differently, and even God's creatures have unique ways of walking. Agur, the author of this chapter in Proverbs, observed four of God's creatures and described the way they walk. He said that the lion, the greyhound, the male goat, and a king all walk with great confidence. They do not turn away from the path. I believe these creatures have their eyes focused on two things—the prize and prey that await them.

We also can walk daily with great confidence without fear of getting off the righteous path God has chosen for us when we have our eyes on the prize and the prey. Daily we need to focus our eyes on the prize—Jesus Christ. Paul wrote, "I press toward the goal for the prize of the upward call of God in Christ Jesus" (Phil. 3:14). As we press toward that prize, we need to also keep our eyes on the prey. We need to stand ready like a lion to pounce daily on three enemies that try to woo us off God's righteous path. Those enemies are the world, the flesh, and the devil. How do we pounce on the world, the flesh, and the devil? We can do the following:

The world

When our minds become absorbed with the things of this world, we need to set our affections on the things that are above.

The flesh

When our minds begin to be overwhelmed with worry thoughts, we can release our cares to Jesus. When our emotions begin to be stirred with strife, we can refuse to allow pride to reign by esteeming others higher than ourselves. When our wills are determined to do our own thing instead of God's thing, we can surrender our wills afresh to God.

The devil

When the devil gives us his thoughts, we can take those thoughts captive and give them to Jesus.

Today keep your mind stayed upon the Lord, and be ready to use your weapons of warfare against these three enemies.

Lord, thank You for overcoming the world, the flesh, and the devil so that I can overcome these enemies today. These are Your Christmas gifts.

Evening Watch: Read Psalm 144:1–15. Just as the Lord, the Rock, trained David to war, Jesus trains us to win the battles of life. He has already won every battle, but we need to receive His victory and apply it.

Lord, give me the faith to believe and receive Your victories.

Zechariah 9:1–17; Revelation 17:1–18; Psalm 145:1–21; Proverbs 30:32

Morning Wisdom: Read Proverbs 30:32. Have you ever been about to say something when you heard that still, quiet voice within you say, "Don't say that!" Proverbs 30:32 says, "If you have been foolish in exalting yourself, Or if you have devised evil, put your hand on your mouth." Sometimes we turn on the motor of our mouths before we put our minds in gear. We say things that we wish we could take back. Jesus made it clear to us that we speak those things that are in our hearts when He said, "For out of the abundance of the heart the mouth speaks" (Matt. 12:34).

There is a major difference between having an evil thought and having an evil heart. Satan has the power to send us all kinds of evil thoughts. However, we have the power to take those thoughts captive and to pull down any strongholds in our lives where those thoughts could build a fortress in our hearts.

Today my husband and I are celebrating forty-seven years of married life. Through the years Satan has whispered many negative thoughts that he wanted me to voice against my husband. I can remember soaking in a steamy bath at the end of an exhausting day of caring for my children and husband. Satan took advantage of my tired mind and body and began to shoot all kinds of fiery darts into my mind about my husband. The devil wanted me to repeat those negative words against my husband, but I told the devil, "If you think I am going to repeat what you just said you are crazy." I tell people my husband and I would not be married today if I had repeated all the negative thoughts I have had over the years.

I have learned the hard way that when I repeat any negative thoughts about anyone, I become a hit man for the devil. He wants me to pull the trigger of my tongue to release harmful, hurtful words from the double barrel of my lips. Pray that the Holy Spirit will set a guard over your tongue today and also help you to recognize the fiery darts of negative thoughts Satan wants you to receive and pass on to others.

Lord, set a guard over my mouth, and reveal any strongholds in my mind.

Evening Watch: Read Psalm 145:1–21. Have you ever meditated on the glorious splendor of God's majesty and on His wondrous works? (See v. 5.) I believe before David went to sleep, he meditated on the ways God had revealed His works to him during the day. I have always wanted to write down five ways the Lord blessed my day before I go to sleep every night. I think I'll start doing this tonight. Every year I make a New Year's resolution to keep my journal by my bedside so I can write those five things down in my journal. We are about to enter a New Year, so you might want to join me in this New Year's prayer.

Lord, help me to write down five things I am thankful for every night in this new year.

DECEMBER 27

Morning Wisdom: Read Proverbs 30:33. This verse presents two vivid pictures that describe how strife can begin. It reads, "For as the churning of milk produces butter, And wringing the nose produces blood, So the forcing of wrath produces strife." Most people do not get into strife unless they are churning on the inside about something or someone. The acids in their stomachs are churning, and they often will even feel a pain on their left side, because they are so upset. How do I know this? I have felt these symptoms just before I have blown it and gotten myself into strife.

When I was a child I had many nose bleeds, and my mother always warned, "Linda, don't wring your nose, because it will cause your nose to bleed even more. Simply hold your nose tightly between your two fingers until the bleeding stops!" That was good advice, and we can apply it to avoid strife. However, instead of holding our nose we need to tightly close our lips and refuse to speak anything that will cause strife in a relationship.

Satan loves to dance to the tune of voices raised in strife. He loves it when we turn up the volume, because he then has a chance to violently dance on the red carpets of our tongues. He uses our tongues as a springboard for his words to fly out of our mouths and wound the hearer.

The next time your digestive juices begin to churn because you are angry, hold your tongue and count to ten. Chances are you will prevent Satan from doing his dastardly dance of strife.

Lord, help me to hold my tongue when I am angry. Help me to pour out my complaint to You instead of getting into strife with another person.

Evening Watch: Read Psalm 146:1–10. This morning we talked about how strife can affect our digestion. We were told as children never to argue at the dinner table. My mother knew the dinner she had labored over would just cause us indigestion if we devoured it while we were in strife. My mother also was careful to praise my dad before she gave him a delicious dinner. Her praises soothed my dad after he returned from a hard day's work. Strife always causes hard days and can lead to indigestion at night.

This psalm gives us some good suggestions about how we can all avoid strife-filled days. The first suggestions are given in verses 1 and 2. David said, "Praise the LORD! Praise the LORD, O my soul! While I live I will praise the LORD; I will sing praises to my God while I have my being." If we all lived a life of continual praise, there would be no time for us to get into strife. The second suggestion is given in verse 5, which says, "Happy is he who has the God of Jacob for his help, Whose hope is in the LORD his God."

When we put all of our hope and trust in the Lord, we will have peace even when others strive against us.

Lord, I trust You with my day tomorrow. Thank You for Your peace.

Morning Wisdom: Read Proverbs 31:1–7. The verses in this chapter were written by King Lemuel. He recorded the words declared to him by his mother. The desire of most parents is to speak into the lives of their children words of wisdom that will help them throughout their lifetime. Some of the most precious treasures I found after my mother died were the writings she did for a high-school English class. The essays were in her handwriting, and the content revealed her philosophy of life. She loved life and considered every day as a gift to her to use for God's glory. One of the reasons I have written a trilogy of devotionals that are companion books to *The One Year Bible* is to share my thoughts on God's Word with my children and their children. I encourage everyone over the age of fifty to begin to record some of the words of wisdom they want to pass on to their children.

King Lemuel's mother warned her son not to drink excessively. I can still hear my mother's instructions to me and my two sisters: "Now girls, do everything in moderation." Drinking to the point of intoxication is dangerous because we become very vulnerable to the devil's temptations.

King Lemuel's mother advised her son to give strong drink only to those who are poor or perishing to help them forget their misery. A better suggestion would be to give the new wine of the Holy Spirit to those who are poor or perishing, because the wine of the Holy Spirit will impart joy, peace, and hope instead of more heaviness to the receiver.

Lord, help me to pass Your words of wisdom on to my children.

Evening Watch: Read Psalm 147:1–20. Recently a mother in our church asked me to search out verses in the Bible that describe the greatness of God. Her son was asking her what God was like, and she wanted to tell him what the Bible says instead of using her own words. I plan to give Psalm 147 as a scripture reading that describes God's greatness.

The psalmist declared that God builds up Jerusalem and gathers the outcasts of Israel. (See v. 2.) We see this aspect of God's greatness today. In little more than a decade over one million Jewish immigrants have settled in Israel. One of the greatest things God does is heal the brokenhearted. (See v. 3.) We experienced the mighty hand of God healing many of the hearts of women who experienced abuse and abandonment in Peru. In all of God's greatness, He takes time to humble Himself to see the hearts of men. He lifts up the humble-hearted and casts down the wicked. (See vv. 5–6.) God demonstrates His greatness to us through His provision and protection of us. (See vv. 12–14.) God reveals His majesty and power in and over all of nature. God is able to send frost and snow and instantly melt both with the power of His Word. (See vv. 15–18.) God has infinite understanding.

Great is the Lord and greatly to be praised!

DECEMBER 29

Zechariah 14:1–21; Revelation 20:1–15; Psalm 148:1–14; Proverbs 31:8–9

Morning Wisdom: Read Proverbs 31:8–9. I would love to meet King Lemuel's mother. The words she passed on to her son that are recorded in Proverbs 31 are both wise and prudent. As I read her words I recognized that she shared with me this common goal—to train and teach our children to love God, love people, and meet their needs. She declared, "Open your mouth for the speechless, In the cause of all who are appointed to die. Open your mouth, judge righteously, And plead the cause of the poor and needy" (v. 8).

So many of the verses we have studied this year discuss the power of the tongue. Death and life truly are in the power of the tongue, and the authors of Proverbs often exhorted us to use our tongues wisely. The overriding theme of the book of Proverbs is to instruct us in wisdom and to reveal how we can apply that wisdom daily to our lives. The words a person speaks will quickly reveal whether or not that person operates in the wisdom that is from above. James described the wisdom from above when he wrote, "But the wisdom that is from above is first pure, then peaceable, gentle, willing to yield, full of mercy and good fruits, without partiality and without hypocrisy" (James 3:17).

King Lemuel's mother exhorted her son to judge righteously and to defend the cause of the poor and needy. She wanted him to use his authority wisely to overthrow the wrong judgments. We need leaders who will implement the words of King Lemuel's mother. Make it your goal today to pray for the leaders in your nation and in the body of Christ. Ask the Lord to help you instill the fear of the Lord in your children and grandchildren. We fear the Lord when we have an awesome respect for His power and authority and a willing heart to obey what He commands. A prayer I used to pray for my children daily was:

> *Father, in Jesus' name, give my sons the same excellent spirit as Daniel and his companions had.*

Evening Watch: Read Psalm 148:1–14. We once visited a church in North Carolina. As we entered the church, the keyboard player was going wild on the keyboard. He was shouting, "Praise Him! Praise Him! Praise Him!" The audience was really getting worked up and almost reached the level of a wild frenzy as the worship leaders sang, "Praise Him!" at least one hundred times. Frankly, I was getting pooped out. Then I thought about David, and I wondered if he ever got pooped out praising God. I doubt it. He praised God seven times a day and each time he praised him, he was strengthened. This psalm declares the phrase, "Praise Him," eight times in the first few verses. The psalm ends with the praise, "Praise the Lord!" The psalm presents many reasons why we should praise the Lord. Read it carefully and then begin to praise the Lord with your whole heart. That was David's secret. He always praised the Lord with his whole heart. I got pooped out praising the Lord in the church we visited, because my whole heart was not given over to the Lord.

> *Lord, help me to always praise You with my whole heart.*

Morning Wisdom: Read Proverbs 31:10–24. Most of my friends wish Proverbs 31 was not in the Bible. The wisdom and works of this mother and wife seem too lofty for any woman to obtain. The woman described must have taken megavitamins every day to fuel her for her many tasks.

As I read this passage I noticed the many times she used her hands to serve and create. She willingly worked with her hands to provide food for her family, purchase fields, plant vineyards, weave material to clothe her family, and make tapestry and clothing for herself and others. She also extended her hands to help the poor and needy. In order to accomplish all of these tasks she had to get up before dawn, and she often did not go to bed early. Do you feel a little self-condemnation as I do after reading about this superwoman? I am always so glad when daylight savings time comes, because at least I am able to say, "Like the proverbial woman, I get up before dawn."

How on earth did she do it? I found her secret in verse 17 of this passage, which says, "She girds herself with strength, And strengthens her arms." When I read this verse I immediately had a mental picture of this woman with her hands raised in praise to the Lord. I believe she girded herself with strength by praising the Lord at least seven times a day just like King David did. When I went through the trial of severely injuring a little boy with my car, I was given the instructions by the Lord to praise Him seven times a day. The boy almost died, but I got through that trial because I remained in praise. Later when my car hydroplaned and I was in a wheelchair and experienced great pain, I received the same instructions—"Praise Me seven times a day."

As I write this devotional my family just learned that our beloved nephew, Chris Van Der Horn, was killed in Iraq. The first words my older sister, Nancy, received from the Lord after she heard the news was, "The joy of the Lord is your strength." I exhorted her to praise the Lord seven times, and the last time I spoke with her she sounded so strong. God dwells in the midst of our praise, and He is able to impart His joy to us when we remain in praise all day long. Instead of grumbling when you are stuck in traffic today, try praising the Lord. Most of us experience twelve waking hours a day. Try praising the Lord every hour on the hour today, and you will be amazed at what you will accomplish during the day.

Praise the Lord!

Evening Watch: Read Psalm 149:1–9. This chapter exhorts us to sing new songs of praise and to be joyful as we praise Him with the dance and play various instruments. When we remain in praise we please the Lord, and He is able to beautify us. Day and night we should praise the Lord. Praise is the devil's death knell, and when we praise the Lord we are able to bind the enemy. Declarations, praise, and God's Word, the two-edged sword, will defeat the enemy.

Lord, praise You for giving me victory over every enemy!

Malachi 3:1–4:6; Revelation 22:1–21; Psalm 150:1–6; Proverbs 31:25–31

Morning Wisdom: Read Proverbs 31:25–31. We talked yesterday about how the proverbial woman strengthened herself by praising the Lord daily. Proverbs 31:25 says, "Strength and honor are her clothing; She shall rejoice in time to come." She girded herself with praise, and the joy of the Lord became her strength. This woman experienced the fruit of her hands, and her children and husband rose up to call her blessed. Her husband praised her, and the Lord Himself praised her.

How was this lovely lady able to keep moving forward to accomplish her two main goals in life, which were to daily operate in the fear of the Lord and to watch over the needs of her family? She was careful about what she spoke and did. When she opened her mouth she declared words of wisdom, and she used her tongue to speak the law of kindness. She refused to be lazy. She refused to fall into the snare of idle words and idle hands. This lady was not a busybody, because she was too busy ministering to the Lord and her family. Gossip and critical words never proceeded out of her mouth because she used her mouth to continually praise the Lord.

God was gracious to allow this woman to experience the fruit of her hands and her lips. As she entered the gates of heaven I believe Jesus and all the saints and angels gave her a standing ovation. May we all live lives that glorify the Lord the way this precious lady did while she was on Earth.

I believe King Lemuel's mother was giving her own character sketch at the end of this reading. You might think she was not very humble, but true humility is seeing yourself as God sees you. She had no problem with low self-esteem, because she saw herself as one of the Lord's many excellent daughters. I hope you see yourself that way.

Lord, thank You for seeing me with eyes of compassion and acceptance.

Evening Watch: Read Psalm 150:1–6. This psalm is an appropriate way to end our yearly reading of the Bible. This chapter describes the many ways we can praise the Lord. It also tells us the many reasons we should praise the Lord. We can praise Him in the sanctuary and in the earth. We can praise Him for His mighty acts and His excellent greatness. We can praise Him with the dance and with all kinds of instruments.

This psalm ends with these words, "Let everything that has breath praise the LORD" (v. 6). As long as you have breath spend your days praising the Lord, receive the daily portion of God's Word, which is the Bread of Life, and let your tongue and works glorify God. Most of the chapters in Proverbs were written by King Solomon, and most of the psalms were written by his father King David. King Solomon had great understanding and wisdom, but the glitter of the things of this world caused the glory of God to dim in the sunset years of his life. He finally learned that the chief end of man is to fear the Lord. He wrote, "Fear God and keep His commandments, For this is man's all" (Eccles. 12:13).

Lord, help me to glorify You from sunrise to sunset.

TO CONTACT THE AUTHOR

Linda Sommer
6716 Wright Road
Atlanta, GA 30328
(404) 252-3187

trsommer@aol.com